NIGHT SYMBOLS
11,000 Dreams and Interpretations

R. M. Soccolich

Copyright © 1998 by RM Soccolich & Seaburn Publishing
All Rights Reserved including the right of
reproduction in whole or in part.

For information about this dream book write to Seaburn Publishing,
PO Box 2085, Long Island City, NY 11102

Library of Congress Cat. Num. in Pub. data

Night Symbols, 11,000 Dreams and interpretations
    1. Dreams. 2. Dream interpretations. 3. References. 4. Tarot
    I - Title.
    pm5 / Auth   BK   Soccolich   98-813.

Collection and interpretations by RM Soccolich.

ISBN 1-885778-36-8 (trade paperback)

Also by the author and published by Seaburn:
100 Steps Necessary for Survival on the Earth
100 Steps Necessary for Survival In the Global Village
Mischievious Acts & Repercussions, co author with Sam Chekwas.

Printed in the United States of America

Introduction

Long before Sigmund Freud wrote that dreams were mental windows opening wide before the landscapes of our psyche enigmatically called 'The Unconscious', tribal Shaman, Orichas, Medicine-Men and Temple Priests the world over guided their people by symbols found in the DIVINE IMAGES of their sleeping mind.

Far from being a fruitless practice, these magic-men translated the instructions of the gods who spoke through the INCARNATE (and thus, visible) FORMS of their specific creations. For instance, in the Celtic tradition, the 'Oak Tree', became a holy vortex (or spiritual power point) in the ceremonial circular dances around its formidable and age-old trunk. When this mighty Oak appeared in the dreams of the northern Shaman, it was clear that the 'Supreme One' had miraculously spoken to them and would expect the full and undivided attention of the entire community (about whatever matter was at hand.) Correspondingly, in the Old Testament, Moses (in a dream-vision) is summoned and overcome by a burning bush, in other words, a flaming TREE! And, further back into the biblical tradition, we witness the imagery of Adam and Eve's TREE OF KNOWLEDGE, which we all know, brought forth an apple of REASON, EQUIPPED WITH OUR ORIGINAL VISION OF MORTAL SHAME.

Carl Gustav Jung, originally a student of Freud's, branched off from the elder mentor's teaching and founded a new school of psychological thought based upon the foundation of ancient Dream Analysis and mystical dream Interpretation. This later led him to theorize his own unique viewpoint of a sound, unchanging and universal 'Collective Unconscious' found in all mankind.

To Carl Jung, the Oak Tree of the Celtic Shaman, Moses' burning bush and the wisdom of the 'Tree of Life' (followed by the ancient Kabbalists,) were all collective 'Archetypes' which meant 'eternal' symbols etched in the mind of ALL human beings. In other words, in the mind of man, the 'Tree' had persisted as a symbol of human transfiguration and spiritual uprightness. At the same time, the tree remained deeply rooted in our earth (or flesh) experience. Jung's thought process informs us that this SYMBOL is not merely a man-made creation, but a transcendent message RECALLED within the very matrix of our own human DNA, a kind of built-in LIVING MEMORY, as old as our primordial gene-pool.

In accordance with this line of thought we travel back in time away from modern thinking (and with Jung's full permission to do so,) to primitive cultures who naturally and fluidly traveled the vital landscapes of their sleeping mind's eye. We travel from the pre-cultures of Great Asia in the Far-East to furthest points south to the wind-swept interiors of Sacred Africa and Aboriginal Australia. We venture to return west to the Earth Natives of the South and North Americas and completing the compass circle, we land upon the frozen northern mounts where prehistoric Celtic freemen walked steadily in the ice-age trances of divine illumination, the vision of heaven and earth gods etched upon their furrowed brows.

In Asia sat Siddharta, the Silent One, who dreamt under the Bodhisattva Tree the dream of the Buddha who was dreaming the far reaches of the universe itself, an illusionary test-ground for mortal men. Men like Chang Tsu who dreamt of a butterfly and then understood that it was he the butterfly, who dreamt of a man dreaming about himself, the unknown and the unknowable.

Similarly, the unknowable men who built the Great Pyramid alters to the firmament of heaven in Ancient Egypt, along with their not altogether distant neighbors the Assyrians, took to writing the tale of their dreams in elaborate 'Dream Texts' which mapped out the meaning of their divine-inspired existence. Further south, existence was pure and idyllic in the so-called 'Dream-Time' of the Australian Aborigines, a Garden of Eden whereupon the 'Extraterrestrial Ancestors' had descended upon a barren planet and transformed themselves into the lush species of plants and animals encircling the far-reaching horizon lines.

Following suit to the majesty of the dream vision, Ancient Greeks erected Incubation Temples where the sick and suffering ingested herbal sleep-inducing extracts which invoked and conjured dreams. In these temples, the temple priests would await to interpret the dream's message. It was understood that the dream imagery would reveal the medicine necessary for the poor patient, twisted in the unyielding arms of a dark illness.

Just north, and years earlier in Jerusalem, Jacob dreamt of a ladder to heaven where angels and saints ascended and descended lightly and without effort as the Hebrews became further aware that Yahweh was communicating to them by way of dreams. At this juncture, the voice of the 'One True God' became persistent in their perception both day and night. Returning across the globe, the highest and most holy God of the ancient and illuminated Aztec chieftains was called the 'Maker of Dreams', and HE too, led men with the guidance of HIS own dream creations. These dreams outlined a rich and unparalleled thousand year culture.

Which brings us back to the Celts, who carved niches in their mighty Oaks where young warriors could sleep and dream of GODS who existed in a timeless place within the tree, solely to greet the anxious souls of these brave men. Here, secured within the ancient and eternal SYMBOL, man, begins his world of dreams...

As the reader reads the pages of this book he or she should keep in mind the pure vision of his or her primordial ancestors, remembering that the language of dreams are not mere pictures provided by a sleeping brain, but the intense personal images that complete the psyche of self. As we travel through the interpretations of universal dream symbols found in this book and make the connections which link the meaning to our personal lives of experience, we should be comforted in the realization that dreams have guided our human kind for as long as we can remember, and that same memory, brings us closer to ourselves, and our deepest elusive purpose in life, the dream within the dream, within the dream...

Dream Interpretation

As human beings we possess a brain and physiological system which slowly developed an increased potential over the course of countless millennia and successive generations. From the earliest forms of man's predecessors, a steady evolutionary learning and adaptation transformed the extraordinary ability of neural consciousness into the worldly perception we enjoy today. However, the story doesn't end there. Researchers have found the human brain's long evolutionary process of development has traveled an unfolding and labyrinth-like course. The implications of such a miraculous progression involves the singular retention of each and every successive stage of neural completion. Hence, within our brain's activity, (or consciousness,) resides an innate comprehension of ALL stages of human development and a subsequent RACIAL MEMORY of an entire living history.

Herein, we begin the examination of the very crucial reality of dreams. The mysterious component of consciousness which retains the aforementioned collection of memory, Jung referred to the as the Unconsciousness. In the course of his life, Jung pointed out how this unconscious is not at all LIMITED to the temporal or spatial conceptualization of waking consciousness. He further expounded how this vast information storehouse does not communicate via a normal language, which is grounded inexorably in a linear and scientific understanding of reality. Instead, the complex and ancient unconscious translates feelings and psychological states through an elaborate and boundless series of dynamic visual memories. Consequently, the dream, which is the projection screen of this limitless unconscious, presents images appropriate to their symbolic meaning. For example, in the language of the dream, fire is not just flame, but also burning passion, anger or heated confrontation. Hence, a man's head may be on fire all night and not sustain any injury, whatsoever. Simply put, physical reality takes a back seat to symbolic reality. Accordingly, in dreams, people can fly, cry and even die, with equal ease. At the same time, monsters, serpents and mermaids can play a very crucial role in a serious individual's (night by night) dream excursions.

In this sense, we examine in the context of this dictionary, the symbolic language of the unconscious revealed to us in dreams and nightmares. Moreover, we follow the guidance of an age-old mental framework which elucidates its wisdom to us each and every night; with sharp precision, fierce passion and the profound insight of humanity's grandiloquent and immense history.

How To Use This Dream Book

1) Upon waking, write down every aspect of the dream including colors, backgrounds, characters and objects.

2) List these separate components in the order of their significance within the dream.

3) Refer to this guide book for specific and possible meanings for each of these entries. It is recommended the dreamer adds his own personal feelings about each item, since all of us in one form or another, has experienced a unique history of intimate memories and associations regarding life's perception.

4) The combined symbolic references will begin to unravel and reveal a psychological portrait of the dreamer's overall concerns, desires and perhaps, inner-most aspirations.

5) This complete procedure should be conducted over an extended series of nights to illustrate prominant intellectual and emotional concerns, therefore disclosing the heading of their real waking-life influences.

• • • • • • • •

This book was written to clarify the LANGUAGE of our dreaming mind. This vernacular, presented in lucid images while we sleep, communicates our internal variables of personality. In the course of this work, we will explore how these tenets of self, (including and especially our personal fears, desires and hopes,) are REVEALED to us in the FORMAT of our dream landscapes. That is to say, the VISUAL FIELD of our dream IMPRESSION. Moreover, we will separate the METAPHORIC DREAM down to its individual SYMBOLIC ELEMENTS. Doing so, the reader may explore each separate component of the dream as it pertains to his or her personal concerns in daily life. The reader is then asked to cross-correlate each dream reference and find the overall connective theme as it relates to the picture of their larger waking experience. There is an assumption made that our unconscious mind brings together these disparate dream images (or, references) in a similar fashion to words combined to form sentences and finally, a defined language. We will uncover EXACTLY how the LANGUAGE communicated from the deepest part of our human memory illuminates our understanding about who we are AND why we behave the way we do. In this sense, we are taught about our mind, body and soul by the greatest teacher of all.
Ourselves...
R.M.S.

A

ABANDON A feeling of desperate isolation. This isolation stems from the childhood 'feeling' of parental separation felt from infancy when the guardian parent left the room or immediate field of vision. In adult life, Abandonment translates into the fear of an unknown which must be faced entirely alone, for instance, embarking on a business proposition on one's own that is risky or otherwise perilous. This isolation or abandonment can also express sexual or emotional transitions in life, which tends to make one unsure of his or her footing in a new or changing relationship. The fear of abandonment is an unconscious metaphor that the dreamer may need to make an entirely 'individual' decision in his or her life.

ABBEY Hopes and schemes will fall under religious scrutiny of a 'higher' order. An individual is faithful in the merit of a decision made, however he or she may harbor feelings of guilt or spiritual repercussion for the particular act chosen. If the dreamer is female the Abbey may represent spiritual or emotional cleansing. The abbey therefore, is a double-edged sword which may represent purity, or conversely, repressed guilt, dependent upon the psychological make-up of the dreamer.

ABBESS A feeling of spiritual leadership and comradeship is applied to this dream form. Responsibility and social vision usually accompanies this figure. A woman, upon placing herself unconsciously as a spiritual leader, may be experiencing the wisdom of her matriarchal character as it pertains to the context of her community. This incorporates various formulations of selfless love including the acceptance of worldly suffering, analogous to child-birth and unconditional caring of the innocent and vulnerable. If she is simply an outsider addressing the abbess, the dream vision may imply devout or religious trust in some 'outside' female figure in her own life; including, but not necessarily, her own mother. (see Angel)

ABBOT To dream that you are an Abbot, may signify a suspicion that others are misjudging you, or conversely, that others are jealous of your position of social power. In essence, you have a platform and a pulpit in community and OTHERS (in your immediate social sphere,) may not enjoy your real influence over ALL peers. However, the dream vision of oneself in the clergy may also indicate hiding something immoral about oneself. These repressed thoughts may be masked behind the hard stone walls and thick robes of organized religion and its accepted standards of morality. To further understand the significance of the abbot, the dreamer must note the exact appearance and manner of the religious figure and determine the nature of that figure's ethical platform. Moreover, the dreamer needs to clarify the EXACT message given by the abbot himself in the dream layout. The unconscious finds various and dynamic ways to translate its advice into our waking consciousness. For many, an abbot reflects real wisdom and spiritual meditations upon the worldly plane. Gestalt therapy may absolutely be advised if this dream is a recurring one.

ABDOMEN All dreams relating to the stomach or stomach regions can be observed metaphorically as a physical center of anxiety, or unnatural pain. If the dreamer is a woman, a natural fear or anxiety about childbirth, (which itself may not signify birth, but sexual consequences,) should be examined thoroughly. Another series of dream interpretations reveal that dreams of abnormal abdomen conditions infer an 'unattainable' hunger or longing. However, therapists agree that since the Unconscious is revealing something about the exact nature of the goal of the dreamer, that THAT particular goal may indeed be VERY attainable. We also find references to 'gut' feelings, which defy our logical determination, yet seem to ring true on another level of our awareness. The dreaming consciousness may be well aware of these instinctual urges and their viable involvement in our waking experience.

ABHOR A person dreaming that they are Abhorred demonstrates a feeling of self-disgust or chastisement. It is a conscious reflex and reaction to feelings of guilt or interpersonal wrong doing. It may also signify a deeply repressed social fear. A young child thrives on the POSITIVE attention and acknowledgement of his or her parents. When this attention is not forthcoming, or the child receives NEGATIVE attention, the child associates that it has done something absolutely wrong and is now being punished. Therefore, simply put, to be 'abhorred' represents a refraction, or social castigation, which may need to be examined. In order to function as a well adapted individual in culture, we need to adopt a feeling of belonging from our social peers. In this sense, we may need to confront our feelings of alienation, simply to erase any forms of self-guilt, or a general lack of personal self-worth. In order to build loving relationships, we must first determine ourselves fully deserving of this love.

ABJECT To dream that one is Abject refers to a feeling of loss or a loss of ones resources. This human symbolism, or archetype, refers to weaknesses or a general inability to defend oneself against the 'natural' hardships in life. The implications of this dream involve a complex series of repressed emotions which signal the 'giving up' of mature responsibilities. As such, the dreamer may (irrationally) feel unworthy in specific social situations. This is especially true in new sexual relationships. This seems to be the case because the feeling of wretchedness exists as a comparative assessment to certain individuals around us. On the other hand, if the dreamer is abject, in the sense of feeling personal humility, it may be an Unconscious signal of 'soul cleansing' and a release of his or her 'earthly shackles'. (see Tarot)

ABODE To dream that you can't find your Abode, may signify a loss of personal belief and may signify a huge transition in your life. The abode is symbolically understood as a place of comfort, familiarity and sanctity in one's own state of mind. Therefore, to erase one's abode implies a nervous 'plunge' into the future, (which is of course,) the unknown. We must take this one step further. When examining the absolute loss of one's abode, we may categorize fundamental changes in the 'look', 'familiarity', and overall functionalism found within the normal parameters of an individuals lifestyle. The dreamer may feel as though his actions are becoming suppressed or violated by some outside force. We may need to question ANY new and unsettling influences in our life. As an archetype, the abode can vary in meaning from a unified family to a satiated sexual experience. Therefore, we need to interpret ALL symbols found within the abode itself, especially personal items. All persons (and animals) found in the abode represent psychological determinations of our own character. Our own personality is deeply reflected in our dream's vivid cast of characters.

ABORIGINAL Many researchers note that the Aboriginal figure represents the Unconscious itself: a kind of primal look into the human heart, brain and soul. In more practical terms, the aboriginal represents a dual quality within ourselves. The first quality is the untamed, natural self that exists hand in hand with 'the wild' world or landscape. He or she has no restrictions and no parameters other than pure and fluid existence. This figure may represent an extremely clear vision of the dreamer choked by the responsibilities of accountability posed by the 'civilized' world. The second quality of the aboriginal dream figure is an innocent return to divine faith with child-like, yet immensely powerful, conviction. Conversely, to fear the Aboriginal demonstrates the Unconscious warning us against an overabundance of emotionalism. The dreamer may be harming him or herself with an unrestrained style of exuberance. All in all, the Aboriginal represents the measure of our own primal nature. We need to determine whether this 'native' feeling empowers us, or leads us into peril.

ABORTION The complexity of the Abortion dream relates to the exact nature of what is being 'aborted' in the psyche of the individual dreamer. An original idea (of one's own making) which is abruptly 'cut-off' or even challenged by some over-powering force is Unconsciously felt as the pain of a 'loss of life'. In reality, the life lost is fundamentally the stunted 'life-force' of the dreamer. The abortion signifies a very personal loss which cannot be wholly understood, felt or even appreciated by others. Naturally, because of the intense individuality of the abortion image, every other aspect of this dream should be honestly approached and systematically interpreted in order to best understand the source of the dreamers anxiety.

ABOVE When something is hanging over your head and about to fall, the obvious implication is that something, or some force, is out of reach. As such, it can cause immense and irreparable psychological harm. The dreamer may need to remember that the laws of physics do not apply in dreams and therefore the Unconscious may be stating that what is above is simply above, and can easily be reached, overcome and absorbed. Our feelings of helplessness in dreams is equally combated by the knowledge that our dreams are 'given' to us by our minds to better understand (and eventually master) our own human obstacles. Therefore, we should not only look at the 'motivation' of the dream, but also the 'implication' and 'conclusion' of the dream. In dreamland, what goes up will not necessarily come down, including our own human bodies!

ABROAD To be Abroad is a concept which refers to, or symbolizes, a unique and separate country or land. It may symbolize one's past or 'homeland' which a person longs for (or more commonly) needs to escape to, in order to regain psychological freedom and sanctity (see ABODE). It may also represent travel or a form of travelling toward some foreseeable goal which is strange and unique, yet entirely pleasurable. Conversely, the concept of abroad may simply mean that contact with old friends is desired and that preparations for this reuniting need to be made, as soon as possible!

ABSENCE To dream about the absolute Absence of a particular individual in your dreams may signify that this individual has been upset or set apart from you by some 'wrongful' behavior done to him (or her) by you. In most cases the wrong doing occurred unintentionally. Unconsciously, you need to 'find' this individual again and perhaps seek atonement for your abnormal behavior.

ABSORB When one is Absorbed in the context of the dream it is once again necessary to know what being or force is doing the absorbing. The symbolism of absorption is personal defeat or personal surrender to some anxiety-provoking power or nemesis. Another aspect of the dream is the implied 'disappearance' of self which indicates that some important aspect of yourself is changing. Furthermore, the disappearance of self usually denotes a change in the perception of 'others' in society who may be perceiving you differently or perhaps can no longer 'see' you at all, due to your new emotions or psychological changes.

ABUNDANCE To dream that you are possessed with an Abundance of goods represents one of two possible meanings dependent on the psychological feeling placed upon the goods themselves. For instance, if an individual is comfortable and entirely at ease in the midst of his or her abundance, the notable significance of the opulence is satisfaction or personal achievement, the pride of the fruits of labor. In other words, your abundance represents your own hard-earned rewards. If however, the dreamer is stressful and anxiety-ridden in the midst of their own abundance, it usually signifies that the dreamer has not 'earned' the abundance and therefore feels it can be taken away just as easily as it came. Alongside this latter definition, we also find guilt in the dreamer because of his or her fragile self perception, which is falsely inflated to grandiose proportions which compensate for a repressed and extraordinarily low level of self-esteem. Many heads of corporation seem to experience this latter dream. Their 'guilt of wealth' seems to drive them toward various means of self debasement, torture and finally, destruction.

ABUSE To dream that you are Abusing an innocent person represents an uncanny way for the Unconscious to illustrate that you are harming or psychologically mutilating different aspects of yourself and consequently, injuring others by the sheer imbalance of your personality. On the other hand, if you are the abused, or victim in the dream, the symbolism is unjust punishment and a cry for help. Moreover, elements of helplessness (versus defensive behavior) should be analyzed against real life similarities concerning our own victimization. Accordingly, it is crucial to understand the 'conclusion' of the dream vision, as well as the initial 'motivation'. In the case of a recurring abuse dream, professional therapy is strongly suggested to aid in the understanding of its source and to develop a means to find its end. We cannot allow our fear to interfere with our determining psychological development.

ABYSS Strange as it may seem, the Abyss may represent a complete loss of control in one's waking life. The notion of 'falling' into a place of no fixed reference can be devastating to the conscious mind which needs something, (some REASON to grasp,) to align itself with a perception of reality. The reason why the abyss appears so often in dreams is because dreams are the reflection of the Unconscious which is boundless, a natural terrain for the expression of the Infinite Self. However, we cannot dive too deeply into this Unconscious unless we are fully prepared for its eternal spiritual communication. (see Tarot) Like pearl divers, we need to delve far enough into this realm to find the immediate answers which we seek. Accordingly, positive associations of the abyss reflect our most complete individual freedom and a tearing away of ALL limiting parameters. We are experiencing a fearless step into the exhilarating unknown.

ACADEMY To attend an Academy in your dreams has diverse meanings dependent on your age and associations with education and possibly discipline on the whole. An older individual may be experiencing feelings of regret about the opportunities that passed them by through sheer indifference or possibly difficult economic times. A young person, on the other hand, may feel locked-up in an institution and unable to 'free' him or herself out of its complicated maze. It is interesting to note, in both cases, the academy appears as an 'obstacle' which needs to be overcome by the mental processes of the dreamer.

ACCEPTED For a lover to dream he or she has been Accepted by a desirable counterpart, may signify something lacking in the way of personal self-worth. This overcompensation may be projected toward an individual's loved ones or potential lovers. This dream-inspired acceptance can be looked at as ego-guarding 'wish fulfillment'. This of course, is not a hard rule and 'acceptance' can signify (in certain cases) a comfortable feeling of well-being within an unfamiliar, yet altruistic, social group. Perhaps we are becoming acclamated to our current peers and in the specific sense, perhaps we are gaining sublime comfort within the bounds of a new relationship.

ACCIDENT   In general, Accidents are understood as aggressive events which occur suddenly and are completely uncontrollable. It is the uncontrollable aspect of the accident dream which symbolizes an abnormal anxiety or fear of 'things getting out of hand' in a very short time. Accident dreams, by and large, express an internal struggle based on new and sudden events occurring in the otherwise organized and consistent life of the dreamer. Conversely, if the dreamer is NOT personally involved in the accident itself, but merely (or casually) observing it, the implication may be one of hidden and very turbulent feelings of aggression. Individuals who are unable to express their hostility in everyday life often require violent dreams as a necessary outlet for their overload of physical tension. There is some controversy over the nature of prophetic, (or visionary,) accident dreams. To better understand these arguments, we ask to reader to study the sections on Clairvoyance, The Collective Unconscious and Lucid Dreaming. (see Crash)

ACCORDION   The playing of music or a musical instrument suggests the invocation of intense emotions. Strangely enough, there is a subtle connection between the shape and sound of the instrument itself and the emotion it most often reflects in test cases. For instance, the acoustic guitar, with its feminine shape and lush sweeping tones suggests sensuality and eroticism, while the bugle with its short, stout, piercing shrill seems to suggest an almost adolescent fear involving human contact. Accordingly, the Accordion is a rather large instrument involving the continuous physical movement of squeezing and pulling, roughly synonymous with ones own breathing. Taken together, the symbolism of the accordion is one of intense 'physical' emotion demonstrating a kind of bodily weariness involved in sustaining a certain powerful emotion. Since the accordion 'breathes' it is only natural to assume that the dreamer 'becomes' the instrument of music, dance and merriment. Moreover, if the dreamer dances while he or she plays the accordion the instrument itself may be an illustration of an emotion which the dreamer is 'juggling in uncertainty' to the point of exhaustive delirium.

ACCOUNTANT   To 'count-up' ones belongings is roughly akin to weighing or accessing oneself. In dreams, we express concepts like 'value' and 'worth' or conversely, 'greed' and 'misfortune' with human-like figures who visually represent these thought constructs. One such figure, known as the accountant, may be perceived as a negative force who projects our deepest fears of worthlessness or social shame, or conversely, a virtuous presence who reminds us to 'surrender our greed' etc. If the dream of the accountant is recurring, it may be necessary to confront the figure and determine his (and your?) complete intentions.

ACE OF SPADES   In a deck of cards the Ace of Spades is the card given the highest value, dominating even the vainglorious king of diamonds. Spontaneous, mischievous and heartless, the powerful ace comes crashing down on all 'games' with an all-seeking and all-possessing authority. Consequently, the ace card is a very peculiar dream symbol representing extreme competitiveness complicated by an equal fear of loss and ultimate submission. Many analysts have argued that this kind of submission is actually sought after by the dreamer. (see Sigmund Freud)

ACHAEMENEDS The Zoroastrians in the period of Acheameneds followed the theory of Sifat-i-Sirozah who posed that dreams could only be interpreted in accordance to the day of the year in which that dream occurred. Each day of the year coincided with a prophetic and/or religious event, which significantly colored and shaped the overall meaning of the dream. Moreover, the connection (or joining) of symbolic meaning further focused exactly upon the dream's message to the dreamer within that active society.

ACHILLES HEEL In Greek mythology, Achilles represented a turning point in dream symbolism when the man himself broke the Homeric tradition of receiving dreams solely from Gods. Instead, Achilles dreams of Patroclus who demands a decent burial for his deceased body. This sensitive mortality of Achilles is echoed in his infamous wound which could never heal. When WE ourselves dream of a wounded Achilles heal, which prevents us from escaping an enemy, we are implying that our own HUMANITY may be allowing others to take advantage of us. This is a rich and complex example of the langauge of the Unconscious psyche.

ACID In dreams, Acid represents simmering feelings of revenge or long-standing rage or hatred. An alternate viewing of an acidic substance refers to introversion and insecurity. These dream appearances require immediate analysis. It is our unconscious' way of demonstrating the harm done by the prolonged stress of hatred and conversely, fear. Naturally, their exist recorded cases where analysts find a combination of hatred AND a paralyzing fear of retaliation in acidic dreams. These dreams illustrate a complicated emotional immobility, which (as previously stated) may require some form of general counciling.

ACORN The Acorn is the archetype of potential as it is a seed which grows into the formidable adulthood of a mighty tree. Potential is also a representation of a brand new beginning in one's life. Human nature detests change because new environments are fearful, alienating and disorientating. The Acorn dream is the psyche's way of providing hope in order to build up the courage necessary to create changes which may be needed in life.

ACROBAT There is a duality in the Acrobat dream figure based on the skill of the acrobat. If the acrobat is bungling and falters in her performance risking harm to either herself, her fellow performers, or the audience itself, a deep distrust in ones own abilities is being expressed rather colorfully. The indication of this illustrious symbol is an apparent lack of discipline in ones own life. This unfocused behavior may be causing a psychological or emotional imbalance which the dreamer is struggling (perhaps in public) to change. Conversely we find the alternate side of the dualistic Acrobat which is poised, talented and innately coordinated. She represents a balance in ones life in dealing with psychological and emotional obstacles with apparent ease.

ACTIVE IMAGINATION A technique developed by Carl Jung where a dreamer is encouraged to spontaneously play with and otherwise fantasize upon a remembered dream. This technique often involves 're-creating' characters within the dream and establishing a 'conversation' with them. The power in this technique lies in the agreement of the dreamer that all thoughts should come naturally into the mind and not be 'forced' or 'concentrated' upon. This way, the elaborate and explanatory images perceived are considered to emerge directly from the Unconscious.

ACTOR Primarily, an Actor in ones dream refers to feelings of personal deception, in other words, not expressing ones true self. Implied in this symbol is a deep concern about the repercussions of ones own recent 'actions'. In this sense the audience represents our peers, the people who we care about. An interpretation of the actor or actresses dialogue in the performance and the audience reaction to it is crucial in the understanding of the dream itself. One solid archetype of the actor figure is a compensatory need for public acclaim in ones waking life.

ADAM AND EVE This biblical figure may represent moral guilt and a metaphoric fall from grace. However, the complexity of the dualistic nature of male and female is also explored in this dynamic archetype. Crucial in the understanding of this dream is the tempoal element involved in its re-enactment. Are we observing, the paradise before the fall, or the sudden awareness of the harsh reality of life, after the ingestion of the fruit of knowledge? In any case, our innocence is thrown into question and we may need to determine the spiritual implications of our own waking behavior. (see Apple) (see Tarot Major Arcana) (see Paradise)

ADDICT The dream of an addiction demonstrates anxiety about something unshakable in ones life. There are many powerful intrusive forces in a persons life, therefore, the addiction symbol is not necessarily drug or alcohol related. Rather, the dreamers Unconscious is clearly warning against escapism in the face of seemingly unstoppable obstacles or (extremely seductive) influences. To dream of an addict is to dream of a person in trouble who may need to defiantly face and finally overcome his or her personal demons. In this sense, it is a very powerful and uplifting dream symbol. It is an Unconscious attempt to instill hope within an otherwise personal darkness.

ADVENTURE When there is an Adventure in a dream landscape it is an example of compensation in a persons waking life which may be uneventful or even dull. The adventure dream is a call for danger, peril and uncertainty. Conversely, if a person is already living a dangerous life; and DANGER (as we all know) is a very relative term, then his or her adventure dream may be a warning to slow down the pace. Our daredevil behavior may have become too perilous and may cause irreparable harm. The subtle environment and its physical and psychological impact upon the dreamer, need to be analyzed with great detail to aid the dreamer in the understanding of this personal and perhaps prophetic message.

AESCULAPIUS In ancient Greek mythology Aesculapius was a mortal doctor who was trained in the art of healing by the centaur Chiron. His healing ability became so great that soon Aesculapius was bringing the dead back to life. This of course angered Hades, who in turn petitioned Zeus, who 'dealt' with the problem by striking Aesculapius dead with a bolt of lightning. Subsequently, INCUBATION temples were erected in Greece in the name of Aesculapius where sick and dying Greek citizens were encouraged to sleep and dream (sometimes for weeks and months.) This was done so that temple priests could later analyze and interpret the dreams and find within their context suitable medical treatments for the disease. The whole process was empowered by Aesculapius himself. Sometimes, one of his two daughters Panacea and Hygeia, were summoned by the dream priests for further assistance.

AFRICA In our Unconscious we think of Africa as the birthplace of mankind. In this context we are expressing feelings of our inner 'free' and 'natural' being unconstrained by the stressful and dehumanizing modern world. In this sense, we are being set free into a vast primordial earth. Additionally, there is an illustration of submission and love for this immense and life-giving landscape which symbolizes the mother of our race. Mother earth is an archetypal symbol which spans virtually every culture known to man and therefore cradles our people's entire psyche. (see Aboriginal) (see Black) (see White)

AGE A major concern in the dreams of aged men and women entail a loss of resources. For example, numerous studies have shown that elderly women often dream of running out of food which could otherwise be served to their relations. In this largely researched statistic we find a complex feeling of loss regarding the nurturing abilities built into the fabric of women: the gender blessed with the gift of bringing life into this world. Therefore, a main archetype of old age in dreams involves the loss of one's vitalness and usefulness. The Unconscious is demonstrating for us an image of regret and remorse which has (for whatever dynamic reason) thrown us into feelings of insecurity and worthlessness in our waking life. We are feeling situationally obsolete. However, an alternative symbol of age, involves the very real and crucial knowledge which guides us through life with the 'Eyes of Experience.' Hence, taken together in our dreamscape, we interpret one main wisdom. It involves obtaining the courage and patience to learn the lessons of experience in order to fully internalize them. This way the feeling of regret (for a life not lived to its potential) will be avoided, avoided perhaps, forever. Since the truth is: we can never lose a WISDOM which has become an essential part of ourselves.

ALBATROSS The Albatross flies high above the horizon line with the widest wingspan of all birds and therefore represents freedom hampered by an almost extreme vulnerability. In ancient times, it was believed that a dying or dead albatross signified harsh and immediate bad luck for the dreamer. This makes sense when one determines that the dreamer is feeling exposed and vulnerable in his extremely visible, slow glide through the heavens. We find in this figure, the exact opposite of the notion of 'a cloud with a silver lining'. As such, we witness a peaceful tranquility, which may be threatened, or susceptible, to a negative outside force.

ALBINO In dreams, the Albino represents the 'Spirit Being' who allows transcendence through the purity of his or her appearance and demeanor. This He/She figure, symbolizes the walk past death into eternal life. This archetype is perhaps as old as mankind itself and should be taken very seriously. If the albino figure is feared, there may be an implication of irrational worry concerning a loved ones well being. However, in a more dramatic sense, the dream may involve reluctant acceptance of a loved ones passing. The albino symbol may need to be embraced and followed via Active Imagination in the dream landscape. We cannot fear the natural course of life's reality. We need to recall that our mortality is sometimes our most miraculous gift. It is what makes us human beings. We are not Gods, but fragile mortals who nevertheless possess compassionate souls and joyous spirits. Accept the authenticity of Self, and we accept an infinite creation. (see White) (see Aboriginal)

ALCHEMIST Dreams themselves are representations of Alchemy, in that they are separate elements which combine to bring together greater meaning and comprehension of a coherent psychological whole. What are the parts we wish to bring together? Dreams of alchemy usually refer to (both psychologically and archetypically) a significant change in ones life. This may occur when a certain situation is considered far better than it was before. The change may be material (turning stone to gold) or spiritual, which is (believe it or not) far more often the case. This form of 'Spiritual Enlightenment' may be rationally considered in this context simply because alchemy is profoundly tied to magic and the ancient art of hierophantry. The Hierophant is the archaic figure which brings SOUL into man. It is no small irony that this soul is exactly what it takes to make a man, a man. (see Tarot for a detailed explanation of the Hierophant and the Spiritual Journey in general) (see also: Magic)

ALLEY A normal Alleyway has only two means of escape: an entrance and/or an exit. Therefore, to dream of an alley refers to a difficult emotional situation where a person is forced to make an important decision. In this decision there are very few options to choose from. Moreover, since an alley is symbolic of a dangerous isolated space, difficult choices are viewed as potentially harmful to the dreamer and his or her immediate associates. The dreamer is advised to take a stand and choose ONE way out of the alley and begin the therapeutic process of dealing with whatever the real consequences are in a life with difficult decisions.

ALLIGATOR The image of the Alligator involves an emotional threat which lurks just below the surface of our perception. Nevertheless, the Unconscious illustrates our subtle awareness of the potential jeopardy. As such, we may need to interpret surrounding signs in the overall dream landscape. This expanding interpretation must be adhered to solely to determine the specifics of this personal (and conceivably difficult) emotional predicament in our waking day to day experience. We have to lure the gator out of the water and onto to dry land of reason. (see Reptile) (see Water) (see Jaws)

ALPHA WAVES Brain wave patterns are measured on a sophisticated piece of equipment known as an electroencephalograph or EEG. These EEGs measure electrical energy released by the brain in terms of amplitude and frequency. These recorded brain waves assist researchers in understanding patterns of sleep (NREM Stages 1-4) and (REM stage 1) and wakefulness (A1-A2). Alpha waves appear when a person is awake yet falls into a very relaxed and meditative state (A2). Furthermore, Alpha waves are characterized by a frequency of 8-12 cycles per second as compared to Delta waves (occurring in deep sleep) which demonstrate high amplitude but very slow frequency, in the range of 1-2 cycles per second.

AMAZON The image of a large and powerful female warrior is complex and certainly dependent on the gender of the dreamer. If the dreamer happens to be an elderly woman, the vision of the Amazon symbolizes inner strength still felt and perhaps requiring a sympathetic audience of peers. If on the other hand, the dreamer is a very young girl, the vision symbolizes an archetype of wish-fulfillment in terms of body growth and health and/or power. In the case of a man dreaming about an amazon warrior, there is an indication of insecurity and unsure feeling towards a particular woman, or women in general. In these latter cases the symbol is usually a recurring one, finding itself in many different dream landscapes. There is an added dimension of free-spirited or aggressive sexual symbolism present in this archetype, an archetype which expresses itself fully and equally for both genders.

AMPUTATE Dreams of Amputation, which are quite common, refer to a very serious and perhaps permanent loss. In general, the 'body' is
symbolic of the 'true' person or 'inner' self. On the body, ones legs refer to movement and travel; hands represent possessions, or motivations; and sex organs illustrate sex-drives or unspoken desires. The removal by amputation of these body parts represents the loss of their symbolic psychological status.

ANALYST To dream about an Analyst is to observe oneself in a symbolic third person. It is an attempt to record and REVEAL a self-expression upon ones own submerged and otherwise repressed feelings. Accordingly, all other aspects of the dream landscape containing the analyst, as well as a detailed account of every opinion brought forth by the analyst figure, is necessary to interpret the dreamers' graphic Unconscious message.

ANCIENT ARCHITECTURE The archetype of Ancient structures involves the very real arena of human transcendence, replete with the struggle of beauty, mortality and physical sacrifice. The building of the Great Pyramid, the arrangement of Stonehenge and the eloquent horizon line of the Parthenon (in Athens) all reflect the need for earth-bound man to align his soul with an eternal beyond. In dreams, these ancient edifices become symbolic of the dreamers longing for an eternal spiritual existence. In short, this architecture represent a rallying cry against the absolute silence associated with worldly parting. From another stand-point, we may feel empowered in life, but at the same time we irrationally fear death and the gradual dissolution of Self. We need to come to terms with our own mortality and accept death when its eventual time ensues. And of course, no time sooner! (see Tarot Major Arcana: Judgement (20) and The World (21))

ANGEL The Angel is a symbol for moral decision making, as opposed to the 'little devil', or Demon, which represents an immoral choice. If the angel symbol is angry or annoyed, feelings of personal guilt are apparent in the dreamer. The winged angel is also symbolic of ones 'Holy' or 'Guardian' Spirit. The angel may also represent feelings of personal elation and subtle euphoria. These may involve simple passionate idealizations or far deeper transfigurative depictions of purity and truth. In most test cases, the angel is entirely illuminated in light and remains faceless. However, if the angel is recognized as someone known, (either living or dead,) we need to determine the dreamer's relation to, or feelings about, EXACT that person. All of these interrogations are entirely necessary to properly elaborate upon the 'Dream Angel's' concurrent meaning. (see Tarot) (see Bird) (see Fly) (see Float)

ANIMA/ANIMUS Carl Jung developed an ideology which uncovers why men and women continually observe dream figures of their opposite sex appearing as themselves! He did this in order to elaborate on their converse feminine and masculine natures. In other words, MEN possess recurring 'dream-women' or Anima, to act out their own internal, stereotypical, and perhaps repressed, feminine natures. A few superficial examples would include: moodiness, sensitivity and emotionalism. While WOMEN externalize their same repressed masculine natures such as: stubbornness, aggression and fierce competitiveness. Women too use this replete, yet (gender) opposite, 'male figure', or Animus. It is the Unconscious way to balance a being. Little wonder hermaphrodites were worshipped in many aboriginal societies.

ANT The image of the Ant denotes hard work and a practical focus toward a difficult goal. However, if the poor, little ant confronts insurmountable obstacles, for example, a mighty river or deep canyon in its path, we may be witnessing a symbolic fear. This fear may involve ones tangible ability to provide for oneself, or moreover, ones family. The extent of this phobia may be vividly implied within the harsh landscape of the dream vision itself. We may need to note any conditions in the environment which assist the ant (ex: wind, raft etc.) or hinder the ant (ex:

giant stomping feet!) These variables each have their own vital significance, crucial to the dreamer's personal acknowledgement and overall awareness. Naturally, a solid raft may represent (for example) a raise in ones salary, while a giant foot may represent a mindless corporate take over which leaves him out on the street. Can the ant see if the feet are wearing designer shoes?

ANTARCTICA The archetype of a world of ice is deeply rooted in our Unconscious and genetic memory. The idea of extreme cold and all its obvious obstacles against our own survival is relevant in our understanding of a battered and paralyzed emotional state. As such, all elements in the antarctica dream which Ease Our Suffering and Provide Movement are extremely crucial in interpreting the Unconscious' answer (or psychological course of action) regarding the cessation or elimination of this fearful and isolated emotional state of being. (see White)

APE The symbol of erratic, mischievous behavior which is intelligent yet 'over the top' illustrates the Ape archetype. The meaning of this dream implies 'compensation' on the part of the dreamer who may feel too stiff, or rigid, in his day to day behavior. In another sense, many REM tests report male dreamers being chased by the ape and then somehow begin sexually competing with the ape or 'unmanageable, hairy man'. Therefore, the ape refers to a wild 'inner' nature, especially sexual, which has been repressed and now seeks expression in the dreamers outward life. Each symbol which the ape touches, caresses or destroys are ALL demonstrative of the dreamers libidinous desires, fear and overall sexual development. (see Africa)

APPLE In Greek mythology the image of the apple is symbolic of sexual awareness or sexual pleasure. In the Judea-Christian world, the apple continues to be the representation of human sin based upon the biblical story of Adam and Eve. Both of these interpretations are valid. Other focused elements in the dream landscape containing the 'apple' will readily reveal the significance of the 'forbidden fruit'. Incidently, this fruit is taken from the tree of 'wisdom', which the apple also represents. We see this in the Hemetic expression of 'Opening ones eyes, and suddenly seeing the whole world around oneself.' (see Adam and Eve)

ARCHETYPE Archetypes, in the sense that Carl Jung incorporated them into his theory of the human Unconscious refers to instinctual and genetic memories held by man. Archetypes are 'visual symbols' which portray deeply embedded human concerns such as 'life after death'; 'sexual awakening at puberty'; 'the conceptual madonna or mother image'; 'relations to our environment'; 'elaborate fears of animals'; and countless other subtleties of the human experience. Archetypes have existed as long as recorded and unrecorded human history and are well documented from cave drawings to computer animation. Archetypes represent the modern understanding of the soul's travel into the infinite pool of the potential primal consciousness.

ARROW While Arrows are in fact weapons, as dream symbols, they take on far more 'romantic' notions of love (aka Cupid,) and skill (aka Robin Hood.) There is an overriding view of the arrow as phallus which 'finds' the target of sexual union based not only upon its shape, but also its launcher. This would be 'The Bow', which creates (sexual) tension and then releases it.

ARTEMIDORUS (A.D.150) A Roman, Artemidorus wrote the first 'comprehensive' and 'modern' book on the interpretations of dreams. In his enormous five volume work entitled the Oneirocritica, Artemidorus demonstrated how dreams were dependent upon the uniqueness of the dreamer. He explained how the concerns of the dreamer, such as his status, health and family figured greatly into the working fabric of the dream figures and overall dream landscape.

ARTIST The dream figure of the artist usually refers to untapped creative potential (in any of the arts) which has remained untested or unfulfilled. The painting created by the artist should be analyzed thoroughly because it may hold some indication as to why the dreamer has repressed his creativity. Moreover, the rendition may reveal what the dreamer needs to fulfill within his or her own experience, before tapping into his or her deepest artistic pool. On another level, the artist may serve as a reckless, destroyer of self. The 20th century has brought about many complex images of the artist and his relation to both society and himself. As such, we need to be sure if the artist is destroying himself to create a better society, or conversely, is he destroying the social order around himself solely in order to preserve the egocentric uniqueness of his own name and (perhaps insecure) character? In a dream, we are both the artist and his world, we draw no line between the creator and his creation. We are more concerned with motivation and apparent consequences.

ASHES Although there is an allusion to death in its symbolism, the predominant meaning of Ashes seems to be change. We are witnessing thoughts which are scattered into new worlds and transfigurations without any regret. Ashes symbolize a spiritual 'letting go' of the fire of suffering, found in an all too real human mortality. In the words 'Ashes to ashes, dust to dust' an implication is made wherein the earth accepts worldly flesh back into its own sacred folds. Therefore, Ashes represent a hopeful return to ones environment and one's 'true' self. (see Phoenix)

ASTROLOGY Primarily, dreams focusing on Astrologers refer to a concern about the future, a sort of sought after, dream horoscope. Should the astrologer in the dream give advice or a prediction, the message given should be thoroughly analyzed. This is primarily because the zodiac involves within its parameters the four seasons, the four elements (fire, air, water, earth), and the characteristic birth sign of the dreamer. Each of these carry very significant references to the dreamer. In the case of the astrologer dream, every symbolic facet of the dream needs to be deeply considered for a proper interpretation. We are in fact, interpreting interpretation, (which is not as strange as it sounds.) This layered representationalism naturally includes the date on which the dream occurred. This simple astrological meter, may itself, be the single motivating psychological factor, involved in this specific dreams personal meaning. Since the zodiac involves balanced personality, the dreamer may be implying a general lack thereof. (see each specific archetype of the zodiac chart: lion, scale, scorpion etc.)

ASYLUM The idea of a 'crazy house' is symbolic for disorder and 'apparent' chaos in ones emotional life. Actual mental illness is rarely a factor. Instead, the image of mental anguish illustrates a powerful emotional distress signal. The dream tells us this deviation of our normal behavior has caused an 'overload' in our comprehension and acceptance. We need to entirely dismantle any chaotic situation in our life piece by piece. We do this in order to achieve a firm grasp upon its apparent complexity. The asylum in this regard, is a mirror of our own desperation. We arrive in the asylum a sick patient. We must allow ourselves to fully recover, in other words, regain our normal equilibrium, before any return home can be expected. In this imagery there is also an indication of emotional sacrifice which must be undertaken to regain absolute faith in oneself.

ATHLETIC Dreaming about Athletics primarily involves a symbolic contest and competition in general. This competition is rarely pitted against another person. Instead, the event is representative of overcoming our own obstacles. In a very real sense, success in sports seems to come to individuals who are able to surmount inner dissension. When this is achieved (and only when this is achieved,) can the athlete function at his or her maximum level. The Unconscious utilizes these doctrines of athletics and illustrates their metaphoric analogy to the percussions of our own inner conflicts found in every day life. As such, we need to interpret the colors worn in the game, intention and ethics of opponents and our own strengths and weaknesses in the contest as a whole. What does winning mean to us? Are our motivations pure? What are the consequences of our losing? (see Acrobat)

ATTACK The Attack dream is very common and reflective of the stressful society in which we live. This is primarily because the attack dream demonstrates an assault upon our 'waking' selves, that is, our character, personality and outward social behavior. In most cases, our own feelings of guilt may generate this self-chastisement. This is why, in a large majority of dreams, attackers' faces and intentions cannot be identified. In other cases, attackers may be people known to us, in which case, a need to understand feelings held about those individuals is essential in overall interpretation. If the attacker is an animal, it should be noted what species it belongs to, and that species' appropriate symbolism. (We have a large variety of animals in this text, perhaps it is listed.) When common associations of certain animals are understood, their psychological intrusion can be immediately recognized by the dreamer. In all cases, learn who the assailant is by bravely facing up to him, her or IT! Revelation always brings relief.

ATTORNEY The ideas of 'law', 'guilt' and 'punishment' rely heavily on this dream figure. There is also a notion of frustration involved in having ones affairs handled by a stranger in this dream archetype. This symbolism involves an intellectual impotence to defend ones own actions and moral integrity. The court of law represents an authority figure which we must yield before. (see Father) (see Police)

AURA In the dream sense of the word, Aura depicts a viewpoint about an individual or object which is multi-layered and multi-dimensional. For example, a man in a dream who is simultaneously happily married, father of five children, avant-garde artist, visionary, hockey player, world class bicyclist AND an all-around nice guy, must possess an aura. This is because of the superimposition of all these separate 'attributes' which the dreamer has placed upon this person. All these attributes must convert into emotional 'sensations' about the dream subject. It does not necessarily mean that the subject is a 'holy' man in the mind's eye (although this sometimes is the case), but rather a 'complicated' and 'out of reach' force which must be dealt with carefully and emphatically. It is crucial to notate the color of the aura and its relative intensity. (see Color) (see Tarot)

AUTHORITY FIGURE Our childhood life is by and large dominated by Authority Figures who instruct our behavior by either sheer force or good sound reason. We are taught how to behave socially, first, by our parents, then by our teachers, and finally by our financial leaders, otherwise known as 'Our Bosses'. In dreams, authority figures are representations of what we may have learned (OR NOT LEARNED) from the original authoritative influence in our life. It is our Unconscious' way of targeting a lapse in our responsibility and\or direction. Conversely, the dream may be demonstrating our own tyranny, in taking on the role of Authority Figure in our waking daily lives and wrongfully harming certain people around us. Whether they be employees, friends or family members. The message communicated by the authority figure in the dream, will aid in the understanding of its own archetypal symbolism. This revelation must be combined with an analysis of ones feelings toward the commanding figure acting in the dream itself.

AWAKE To dream oneself sleeping and then in the dream suddenly awakening may be an allusion to the mind's awareness of its own dream state. In other words, the conscious and unconscious overlap and bridge respective functions and concerns. The conscious mind is immediate and rational, 'organizing' as it does our day to day activities in a linear schedule (based on available time.) On the other hand, the Unconsciousness is not grounded in time and soars over and around the entirety of our human perception. Together, the separate levels of consciousness found in our dreams may reveal a deep counsel about enigmatic situations and conceptually confusing dilemmas. However, on the other side of the coin, we may need to determine in the 'dream within the dream' if some FUNDAMENTAL aspects of our life are unrealistic and hence, illusional. While it is true that a dream acts as a guide, it should not be taken as a physical reality. In the end, we always live in the real world.

AXIS The Axis is the center of the sphere which allows balance, rotation and overall equilibrium. Therefore, to be interacting fluidly with the axis found in the dreamscape may signify psychological and emotional balance in both ones personal and professional life. Moreover, the axis always involves whatever is at the core, or heart, of a matter. In this sense, the axis may not be seen, but rather felt. It is in this same way that the human soul is fully understood. It is the unseen catalyst of our essential being. Lastly, when considering the axis, we find a hub which points in no direction at all, and yet, can enable the absolute pointing of 360 compass extents of direction. Conceptually, the axis allows all philosophical wheels to turn without ever touching the ground (reality.) We need to ask ourselves: what aspect of our waking life seems to be guided by a force uneffected by its own power or ruling; is it possible, we are somehow, at the core of ALL these problems? The question needs to be carefully considered in the axis dream. (see Tarot, The Wheel of Fortune.)

B

BABY The vulnerable infant found in our dream suckling or crying, perhaps hungry, is a clear description of our own fragile inner selves. Some deficiency in our life now requires immediate gratification in the form of care and especially attention. This Unconscious dramatization was referred to as 'The ID' by Sigmund Freud. When situations in our waking life become overbearing and overly complicated we have a tendency and outright desire to revert back to our child-like self; sometimes, in the form of a baby. This is primarily because a baby's needs are meticulously taken care of by an outside force, namely the mother. This shift from responsibility to dependence, occurs quite often in the human psyche as a defence mechanism against difficult decision-making and stressful environments. This regression is especially subject to individuals who fear for the well being of their own loved ones. Instead of rising to the threat of a fearsome external world, the dreamer regresses into himself in an effort to avoid realistic consequences. The dreamer must gain confidence in his ability and durability in the waking world. The baby can be viewed as ones own innocence. In that scenario the baby is tranquil and content. In his simple way, he or she seems to possess faith in life itself.

BACKGROUND It is essential in the understanding of dreams to be fully aware of every element found within the dream itself. The background of a dream is in no way incidental. The environments chosen as 'landscapes' for dreams reflect subtle psychological states of mind and are not necessarily consistent with 'waking' life. In dreams, skies may be green, turtles may be purple and trees may be rainbow-colored (and even able to walk, talk and laugh hysterically.) Therefore, it is necessary to isolate and then analyze each element of a dream in its own context and on its own terms. When the separate psychological facets are understood individually, then and only then, can they be pieced together to form a symbolic 'storyline' which reveals something about the dreamer. This revelation may be pinpointing several aspects of the waking conscious itself.

BACON The symbolism of Bacon is wealth and excess as remarked in the quote, 'The head of the family brings home the bacon.' The image of thick, fatty meats frying on the stove and filling the house with certain sumptuous aromas is not lost on the Unconscious. This concentrated symbol reminds us that material life is plentiful, nevertheless, no grandiose physical reality should overshadow our spiritual grounding. In many cases, men and women dream of burnt bacon which falls to the floor and is immediately swallowed up by hungry dogs. The implication here is a loss of wealth due to unnecessary greed, (symbolized in the over-cooking,) and distrust of our peers and associates (hungry dogs).

BAG/BAGGAGE The symbolism of a Bag lies in what one carries. A person may carry the responsibility of faith, trust or even love. Therefore, if the bag is too heavy or tears apart, a reflection is given of a burden too difficult to 'carry out'. A person may need to examine his or her waking life to determine which of their obligations is tearing away at the fabric of their psyche.

BALD The image of Baldness is entirely different from the image of losing ones hair. Hair is a symbol of sexuality, virility and strength. Therefore losing ones hair, or having ones hair cut off against ones will, is a representation of anxiety felt about ones sexuality or overall good health. On the other hand, 'normal' or intentional baldness (which is what we are now addressing,) signifies humility, purity and personal sacrifice. Moreover, baldness suggests a surrendering of ones ACCEPTABLE cloak of deception. We must consider why we are AT THIS MOMENT confident in fully exposing ourselves. What are our motivations for this unmasking of ourselves?

BALANCE The dream of maintaining ones balance is central to erect-standing human beings who must sustain balance in order to stand, walk and perform daily functions. Our equilibrium has therefore become a symbol for proper, upright behavior. Since we fear 'falling down' in our tasks and responsibilities we go to great lengths to create fluid equilibrium in every aspect of our lives. We court love, money, friendship, skill and security. As such, we hope to acquire an equal and healthy 'share' of each gift of life. However, if one of our 'gifts' is absent we experience stress about the possibility of 'falling down' into the darkness of human failure. In most cases the dream character maintaining balance indicates which psychological limitation of oneself is threatening the whole process. (see Tarot Major Arcana: Justice (11)) (see Acrobat)

BALLERINA Lyrical beauty, innocence and subtle coordination are all features present in the archetype of the Ballerina. In the dream landscape, a ballerina is the representation of a smooth, flowing musical life with no obstacles and no restrictions. The ballerina is thought to be so light and agile that she can leap up into the night sky and land again weightlessly into the waiting arms of her many admirers. Therefore, in a dream, the ballerina represents fluid order in ones own life which (depending on the other elements of the dream landscape) may be threatened by a new and unforeseen force. As such she possess arather frail aspect of vulnerability. In some cases, the Ballerina is simply representational of unreachable and divine beauty which weighs heavily on a dreamer's waking life. (see Albatross) (see Acrobat) (see Balance) (see Fly)

BALLOON The balloon is a double-archetype of childhood innocence and total freedom. Therefore, there can be negative associations with the balloon symbolizing children who are so 'free' that they are left alone and placed into jeopardy. Supporting this approach is the fragile nature of the balloon which can 'burst' or become 'lost' at any time. However, notwithstanding its apparent and perhaps misleading vulnerability, the balloon primarily illustrates merriment, mirth and brightly colored emotional jubilation. (see Baby)

BAMBOO The Bamboo plant is known for its strength and resiliency. In the dream, it signifies a strong bond or agreement with ones associates. The bamboo plant is also symbolic of native, (and therefore, trustworthy) behavior. Therefore, in a dream, goods wrapped in Bamboo may be representational of sound and fair business transactions. In this figure, we find an allusion to upright and spiritual behavior. Since the bamboo plant is found in tropical climates we may also be referring to a need to escape from our everyday reality. (see Tree) (see Abroad)

BAPTISM The archetypal symbol here is the fourth element (not fire, air, or earth...but Water.) It is the clear and unpolluted purifier, the cleansing away of sins and the attainment of spiritual rebirth. Psychologically, we need to purify (or renew) ourselves after, (or prior to,) periods of intense emotional difficulty. The dreamer may be experiencing guilt for wrong behavior which has left them feeling 'unclean' in the moral sense. The image of Baptism is one of these intense 'character transfigurations' replete with a new lease on life. It is a second chance to provide atonement. This archetype may contain elements of regression in its return to childhood innocence and absolute purity. But this seldom is the case in dream analysis. Baptism is extremely entrenched in the ritual of its own cleansing purpose. We may consider the erasing of 'original sin'. Are we referring to guilt about our sexuality? If not, what do we perceive as our original sin? (see Water) (see Basin)

BAR The dream image of the Bar is a common one, in that it contains within its well-structured landscape, an array of deeply seated human rituals. A primary example of this is the 'right of passage' critical in the development of young men moving into 'adulthood'. A young man is encouraged to 'drink' himself into a state of 'mental disorder', an entirely preconceived yet 'irrational' step into the beyond. This is akin to young native warriors who are cast into the 'wild' to prepare their souls and bodies for the responsibilities of age and/or tribal leadership. This formal ritual of intoxication sometimes leads to alcoholism (in the young men in the bars, not the warriors.) This alcoholism is a genuine anxiety reflected in the dream exile of the pub and ale house itself. As it concerns sexuality, the bar is a 'stage' or 'forum' for both men and women to reveal and perform their social poise and sensual posture to an audience of their peers. Taking all this into account, the bar archetype provides an ideal landscape to demonstrate a characterization of ones 'inner' self and personal desires, dependant upon ones actions or 'performance' within its well-defined parameters. In other words, to succeed, fail or remain anonymous in a particular bar ritual represents a psychological message about a dreamers deepest fears and concerns in everyday life. Will he emerge from the bar old and cool, or young and foolish? The bartender who serves up the elixer knows best.

BARREN   The clear symbolism of the Barren field is a lack of fertility or the lost harvest. However, this dream landscape indicates not only infertility and its masculine counterpart impotency. Sometimes the symbolism of a barren state of being rather dramatically reflects desperate isolationism, loss of relationship, or hanging on to changing (and perhaps outdated) methods. The dream may also represent a simple overview of the personal anxiety involved in enduring a plain and otherwise flat lifestyle. We may need to seek the lifeblood waters of emotional challenges, combined with the 'seeds' of new and wondrous experiences. In other words, this may be a call to go out and brave existence, once and for all. (see Aboriginal)

BASEMENT   The Basement archetype often refers to our Unconscious, which 'stores' within its unknown depths, the long file of our living memories, some of which may be unpleasant and entirely repressed. In our dreams we may experience unspeakable horrors which seem to be hiding in our Unconscious basement. These forces are impatiently waiting to return to our surface lives and they seem to seek dreadful revenge. In dreams, we sometimes experience a turning point in our repressed emotions. We are confronting our own hidden fears which suddenly need to re-emerge into our conscious psyche. The basement represents consternation tinged with acknowledgement and most importantly, an engagement of our own demons. In the therapeutic sense, the dreamer is expressing a need to free his Shadow figure in the basement, this to undo its presumed fearful and vengeful harm. When our darkest secrets are brought into the light of day they often lose their real impact. This is because their impact was predominantly based on their internal suppression anyway. We may need to consider what event in our waking life is causing us to confront our own demons at this point of time. Is it a positive force, or a negative one? (see Chase) (see Monster)

BASIN   The symbol of the Basin depends heavily on the fullness and contents of the vessel itself. For example, a wash basin filled with dirty water which cannot be drained out, is a clear indication of an emotional predicament which is stagnating and refuses to go away. Some examples of this may include: illness, tragedy, or a bad relationship. In another sense, we may be expressing a concern about a pregnancy, or the related difficulty of child-rearing. On the other hand, when the basin is empty and drains everything poured into it, the dreamer may be experiencing an extreme fear of loss. In the psychological sense, he or she may be fearing the loss of a sane, yet fragile perception, or 'hold', upon life. In this state of a perceived draining existence, the dreamer runs the risk of 'throwing away' good and valuable human contact. The empty tub in this sense, is symbolic of emotional isolation and a sinking feeling of an absolute withdrawn nature. We cannot seem to hold on to the things (and persons) we need most. The dreamer must drain the sink of ALL its dirty contents and then bravely fill it once more with clean, purifying waters. (see Leak) (see Baptism) (see Water) (see Active Imagination)

BAT The bat as winged creature, refers to ones erratic state of mind and the distinct danger associated with that kind of unsteady 'focus' in ones everyday consciousness. The Bat (as baseball stick) symbolizes hitting for glory, and otherwise, attempting to 'score' or 'win' some critical game. The 'game' itself is symbolic of life. Therefore, naturally, the hit or miss of the bat, singular in the game process, is significantly expressing a determining event in ones own life. Some crucial event which may effect our social standing has already transpired, or will take place in the very near future. In this sense, the bat is the archetype of promise, potency and potential. Moreover, as phallus, the bat can 'score' (sexual fulfillment), be broken (castration or impotence), or strike out (a general lack of self-confidence). As such, we need to wholly understand the significance of whatever occurs while we are 'up at bat'. (see Bar) (see Vampire)

BATHROOM The symbolic reference of the Bathroom landscape, entirely familiar in the modern world, concerns the absolution of the 'sins' of every day life. We remove our uncleanliness and 'recreate' ourselves through cleaning, grooming and the application of makeup. In dreams, we are expressing transition and renewal in the bathroom landscape. We find ourselves in a place where we may 'ward off' the reality of mortality which weighs us down and brings us closer to our 'uncivilized' selves. We may be expressing a need to forgive someone who has treated us in an uncivilized manner or, conversely, we may be communicating a desire to return to 'society' with a new (and better) face. In another sense (but not entirely unrelated,) we may fear the finality of death itself and the normal changes that come with age. (see Baptism) (see Water) (see Age) (see Mirror) (see Image)

BEACH The Beach represents a borderline between two states of mind, one solid and well thought out, and the other unsteady, emotional and perhaps wrought with danger, or adventure. The interpretation is dependent on whether we are in the ocean, or on the sand, and in which direction we respectively face. If we face the ocean, we may be preparing ourselves for the unknown and vast changes in our life which may effect us, (or our families,) in an unalterable way. It must be noted whether the ocean is calm, pleasant and inviting, or stormy, dark and forbidding.

If there is a hurricane brewing, we certainly need to heed the intense fear of change which is expressed in the dream. On the other hand, if we are returning to land, we may be expressing a return to what is familiar to us. Perhaps an unusual (and unsettling) event has recently occurred in our lives and we are finally adapting to it and accepting its parameters. (see Water) (see Ocean) (see Bikini)

BEAM   If the Beam is sturdy in the dream and supports our home, (which is symbolically a reflection of our own body,) it is a clear indication of a solid psychological framework. We are expressing a general satisfaction with our choices in life. If the beam is new, we are reflecting a recent decision which seems to give us security and a general sense of well-being. On the other hand, if the beam is cracked and shaky, we may be expressing anxiety about the health and welfare of our families or other persons close to us. If the beam is crumbling and the house is falling down all around us, we may be expressing a fear of sickness or a tremendous personal loss. Two examples: losing ones job, or preparing for a divorce. (see House) (see Wood)

BEARD   The Beard is symbolic of virility, strength and vigor. However, the beard can also represent a mask, or something to hide behind. Therefore, it is crucial to understand why the person in the dream wears the beard. If the man is a stranger and the dreamer is attracted to him, it may represent a desire to return to a natural, unhampered way of life reminiscent of the 'mountain man'. On the other hand, if the dreamer himself suddenly has a beard, he may be expressing guilt and a need to get away from himself for a specific reason. Conversely, the dreamer may feel out of place in a certain situation and therefore, places himself 'undercover' in order to rationalize for the perceived intrusion incurred on his associates. If a woman dreams of wearing a beard, she may be expressing hostility about being treated 'like a woman' rather than being treated as an equal. In so doing, she becomes both sexes and can conquer all who would attempt to belittle her. In dreams, the bearded lady is more than a side show freak, but a real and formidable archetype worshipped in ancient times. She becomes the symbolic hermaphrodite. (see Anima/ Animus)

BED   The Bed is symbolic of ones most intimate self. It represents the discovery of ones sexuality in puberty , the sublime union of marriage, the recovery center in times of sickness and the place of sleep. Moreover, (you guessed it,) it is the land of dreams! Therefore, when we refer to a bed in our dreams, we are revealing a piece of our deepest selves. As such, we may be offering a fundamental and honest part of ourselves to another. Needless to say, this could be a very difficult proposition in our life. We may need to examine the condition of the bed, the color of the sheets, and our feelings about the bed in general. If the bed seems uninviting and dangerous, we could be experiencing deep emotional fear and difficulties which may in fact require professional counciling. If (on the lighter side) we have a big, brass bed, we may be hoping our poetry stirs up some real romantic interest in our mate.

BEGGAR The Beggar is symbolic of life out of balance, a failure of society, and the surrender of an individual against the harsh pressure of that society. He or she is the embodiment of poverty and the reality of mortality and its needs. To dream of oneself as a beggar indicates a drifting away from others. A dreamer may be experiencing difficulty within his or her immediate social environment. The Unconscious therefore, is calling out for help, not in the form of spare change, but rather, acceptance and honest guidance. It is a dream search for the generosity of soul. (see Image)

BELL A Bell usually signifies a call to order, command or warning. In a dream, a ringing bell illustrates a signal by the Unconscious to be 'prepared' for whatever will happen next, either in the dream or in real life itself. If there is a significant occurrence in the dream after the ringing of the bell, analyze its meaning thoroughly, because it may hold the key to a pending situation in waking life. If the bell rings relentlessly in the dream and never stops, we may be certain a warning has already been issued to the dreamer who may be experiencing extreme anxiety about the situation and needs to face up to its reality. Can we be saved by the bell? (see Noise)

BETWEEN There are moments in dreams where we find ourselves crushed Between two opposing forces. This dream situation is clearly indicative of outside forces pushing us in different directions. Each outside force desires us to join their side and not the others. In life, we realize the reality of opposing viewpoints and the pressure placed upon us to make a decision and 'choose a side'. The Unconscious is illustrating our frustration in this predicament and reflecting the absurdity of non-movement which occurs from resistant and close-minded points of view. (see Alley)

BIKINI The Bikini dream is indicative of superficial desire and an almost prepubescent eroticism as opposed to nakedness which may indicate more than a primal sexuality. The bikini symbolizes a return to youth and innocence, desire and connection made without consequence. It is an image of sexual and voyeuristic freedom coupled with a playful, yet nonthreatening, eroticism. The bikini dream may be expressing a desire to 'lighten up' current psychological or emotional states of mind in order to re-establish a relationship with another, or even with oneself. (see Beach) (see Abroad)

BIRDS Primarily, birds represent the spiritual longing of mind because of their ability to fly and their melodious song which may move our human spirit. However, there are also images of nesting in the bird archetype which may have references to our own family and homelife. In this case, it is important to observe the condition of the nest and the young within the nest. Is the nest safe? Are the chicks crying or chirping happily? Is the nest being built? All these answers are symbolic to the state of well-being in the home for the dreamer. Certain birds carry their own unique archetypical meanings. (see Crow, Eagle, Chicken, Owl) (see Flying) (see Phoenix) (see Tarot, The Star 17)

BINOCULARS In dreams, Binoculars generally refer to searching, perhaps searching for hope in the symbolic form of land. However, binoculars may conversely signify, seeing what should not be seen. In this case, binoculars represent guilt about knowledge which should not be known. Perhaps this knowledge was gained by spying or some form of eavesdropping. What are the motivations for our extended vision? (see Spy) (see Police)

BISEXUAL If a person is not Bisexual and dreams him or herself as bisexual, there may be an indication of sexual repression or wish fulfillment. The dreamer may be compensating for his or her lack of sexuality with a 'heightened' sense of all-encompassing eroticism. In some cases, the bisexual dream may simply represent sexual confusion in ones own life, not even necessarily cross-gender, but rather general confusion. What will sexually fulfill me, is it kissing, touching, perhaps playing the violin? (see Anima/Animus) (see Hermaphrodite) (see Wish-fulfillment)

BITE In a dream, to Bite someone is a complicated expression of aggression which implies 'devouring' another person's attributes or 'lifeforce' (see Cannibalism). However, biting some object or ones own lip may simply imply attempting to control ones own aggression. If the dreamer is bit by a wild animal, he or she may be experiencing fear or anxiety about their own natural or sexual feelings which may be repressed in waking existence. In another sense, the soul of man is often symbolized as the mouth, (or in the mouth,) providing the circular breath of life. In this sense, the biting motion of teeth may imply a resistance of spiritual faith. Moreover, since we ourselves perform the action of biting, we may be questioning our very own moral strength and fiber. (see Tarot Major Arcana: Judgement (20))

BITTER In life, many situations leave the idiomatic 'bad taste' in ones mouth. A dream utilizes Bitterness to exaggerate this harsh anxiety. It is absolutely necessary to analyze the characters and landscape surrounding the moment or 'phase' of bitterness experienced in the dream to better understand the source from which comes the reality too difficult to swallow. If, as in a nightmare, the bitterness is prolonged or persistent in its agonizing, the dreamer may be experiencing guilt about betrayal or the allowance of continual abusive behavior inflicted by a loved one. We may also be experiencing a taste of our own medicine. In all cases, honest revelation can be extremely bitter. (see Bite)

BLACK The color Black in the dream sense is almost always indicative of the mysterious and unknown. If a figure wears a long black robe, black cape, or black hood in a dream landscape we fear a power and knowledge which is entirely unknown to us. Often, as is the case with Carl Jung's interpretation of the Shadow figure, the man in black is a reflection of our hidden or repressed desires. In this manner, all objects which are encased in shadows, or darkness, are representations of our deepest Unconscious, the darkest pool of reason. Moreover, since the color black is the result of all colors occurring simultaneously, so to is our Unconscious the accumulation of all collective human experience. Sadly, wherever there is infinite potential, fear and ignorance always follow close behind, waiting to dismantle and destroy. As such, we need to come to terms with our feelings about the Shadow Figure. (see Collective Unconscious) (see Aboriginal) (see Jung) (see Color)

BLANKET The Blanket is primarily a symbol of protection and warmth. If in a dream, we wrap a cold or wet loved one in a blanket, we are expressing a need (or desire) to care for that person. In the visual sense, the blanket is the antithesis of the bikini, the former representing 'love' and the latter 'lust'. A blanket may also symbolize our fear of the outside world. We choose to remain hidden and protected under our blanket because the world is cold, revealing and threatening. Our blanket, in this sense, represents the shelter we find in our own imaginations. Little wonder, lovers wrap up in a blanket next to a roaring fire. Both symbols are hallucinatory and escapist. This type of retreat into oneself, (if short-lived,) can be extremely therapeutic in an otherwise chaotic environment. (see Fire) (see bed)

BLAZE The concept of the Blaze refers to passionate anger and a sudden emotional release. Moreover, the symbolism of fire is synonymous with both creation as well as, destruction. As such, we need to determine the nature of the blaze. For example, is the roaring flame in the fireplace representing hearth and family, or conversely, is it burning through the woods and therefore, demonstrating the devastation of our natural and creative instincts. In both cases, like passion itself, the dream indicates the symbolic reference of blaze in our waking life, may need to be harnessed toward our real desires and aspirations. As such, the rising flame should never be allowed to rage out of our complete control. In this, a dream may ask us to heat up our passions to a feverish pitch, and yet, warns us not to cross that HOT line into a raging and potentially murderous obsession. (see Ablaze) (see Fire) (see Hearth) (see Wood) (see Kindling) (see Water)

BLEED In dreams, a loss of Blood implies a loss of vitality and faith in oneself. In ancient times, blood was symbolic of life itself. Therefore, to spill an enemies blood in battle was the equivalent of draining the life out of not only the soldier, but also his people. Worldwide, there have been accounts of tribes, (throughout the years,) who believed in drinking the blood of their enemies in order to absorb their respective and respected powers. As a symbol of sacrifice, blood is the physical embodiment of our own spirit, or life-force. This would explain why people regularly mutilate themselves to show allegiance to their social organizations and sometimes far more brutally, to demonstrate their love for a potential consort. In order to interpret the blood dream properly, we must analyze both the person who bleeds and the person who has caused them to bleed. Lastly, we must determine where the person bleeds and decode the symbolism of that body part. Taken together, these three components may aid in understanding the message of the (bloody?) Unconscious. (see Impale) (see Vampire)

BLIND The Blindness dream implies closing ones eyes to a given truth which cannot be seen (coped with) for some unknown reason. It is the symbolic equivalent of wishing for the DISAPPEARANCE of ones enemies. There is a strong rationale for this behavior, in that our enemies, represent a failure or limitation in ourselves. There is a psychological implication made therein, that our enemies seek to destroy us because they 'feel' we are somehow inappropriate or inferior as human beings. In dreaming of blindness, we close our eyes to what is horrendous and not at all viewable. In many cases, the hideous object of repulsion may be ourselves, and the grotesque manifestations of our own actions.

BLUE The color Blue contains two distinct emotions revealed in subtle differences in shade. Light blue represents the sky and the morning sea, bright, limitless and eternal. All light blue objects in a dream fit well within the spectrum of birth and the infinite. On the other hand, the application of dark blue or navy blue represents deep and slow depression, a cessation of forward movement and innocent hope. A dark blue sky illuminates the beginning of night and physical uncertainty. In dreams therefore, a deep blue depression can be encoded on clothing, skin tone and the entire landscape. We must ask: which blue are you? (see Water) (see Sky)

BOAT The symbolism of a Boat is dependent on the movement and type of craft positioned in the dream landscape. Should the boat be sailing along effortlessly on a smooth turquoise sea, the dreamer is feeling vital, energetic, free and potent (with full blown sails which echo health and the expectant flowering of pregnancy). If instead, our dream reflects a row boat which is moored and sways unsteadily in a stormy sea, our Unconscious may be illustrating fear, and uncertainty in our emotional affairs. There are social aspects to the boat archetype which 'carries' upon its deck handfuls of different individuals. In many respects, this small social arrangement upon the boat is reminiscent of family. Therefore, a boat sinking may represent a fear of losing ones children, due for instance, to a difficult and insurmountable emotional circumstance. (Ex: Divorce) (see Ocean) (see Water) (see Wind)

BONE The Bone is not necessarily a symbol of death. The skeletal frame of the human body represents its infrastructure and basic form. Therefore, bones can represent life and body intact. Since the immune system is based upon chemicals secreted from glands found within bone marrow, the Unconscious may (in fact) be reflecting sound and stalwart physiological and psychological health. However, in dreams, cracked bones may symbolize the reverse symptoms, those being: poor health and a shaky psychological grounding. A need to analyze which bone on the body is broken and what that particular part of the body may represent to us may be absolutely necessary. (see Body) (see Bleed) (see White) (see Tarot, Death (13)

BOOK In dreams, Books represent old wisdom, memory and a collection of personal experiences. In many ways, ALL books represent the single book, or story, of our life. However, if a particular book is singled out in a dream, the dreamer needs to understand his or her feelings about that particular work. Perhaps the book angered the reader by illustrating a CHARACTER DEVELOPMENT similar to a repressed trait or 'characteristic' within him or herself. On the other hand, the book might represent a significant calling, such as religious leadership, or an invitation into the field of education, as teacher, or perhaps, student. (see University) (see Academy)

BOTTLE A Bottle is symbolic of sensual celebration. It is the representation of the 'pouring' of life in all its spirited animation. As such, a bottle is broken on a ship to 'christen' its first (release) journey into 'wondrous' travels. Along these same sacred lines, the bottle is thought to be symbolic of the vagina and moreso, the womb itself. Because of its shape and the free pouring of its emotional and intoxicating liquids, the bottle has in many ways become symbolic of femininity and eternal womanhood. (see bar) (see Glass)

BOX A Box is a solid structure with eight (which is the symbol of both strength and infinity) corners. It provides shelter for both ourselves and our belongings. Naturally, it has become the symbol of our psychological and spiritual building. Out of this 'Pandora's Box' comes all human invention and unique creation. In dreams, a box may be a gift from our Unconscious to our conscious, in other words, a representational transition point from internal idea, to external worldly realization. (Ex: Engagement ring which is revealed and displayed from a tiny box with emerges suddenly and unexpectedly) What is OUR relationship to the box? Are we inside it? Is it a gift we bring? What mystery does the box contain? The box may be representational of God, or alternatively, the entire basis of our perceived universal comprehension. Never forget the allusion of the television set, which is itself a box! (see Tarot, Strength (8)) (see Ring) (see Gift) (see Prize) (see Television) (see Image)

BRAINWAVES Our brain produces pulses of varying wavelengths. These pulses are dependent upon separate states of mind. For a detailed analysis, review both sections concerning Alpha and Delta waves. (see Alpha & Delta Waves)

BREAD In dreams, Bread may be symbolic of any knowledge or physical reality which is crucial or basic to our very existence. Bread is a basic nourishment and the complement to meats, cheeses and most other food sources. Therefore, in the representational sense, bread is the symbol for the 'essential' physical Self. (Compare blood as the symbol for 'spirit.') In this way, we understand that bread, or 'the body', is both the foundation and the completion of the (animation) of life. In other words, bread is what the blood animates. Accordingly, when we dream of bread, we are dreaming of our own physiological reality and how it may be currently effected by situations in direct contact with us. In the religious sense, we may be referring to some form of sacrifice which must be made; since Jesus in the New Testeament uses bread and wine to signify his own body and blood. In religious study, this was a body about to be sacrificed to 'Save the sins of the World.' In this sense, are we punishing ourselves for the wrong-doings of others? Lastly, shared bread refers to social acceptance and altruistic tolerance. In short, what are we doing with this bread, the very essense of our own worldly being? (see Abundance) (see table) (see Eating) (see Dinner)

BREATH How we Breathe in a dream is symbolic of how we may be experiencing variable states of our waking reality. If we find ourselves breathing rapidly, we may be expressing anxiety, tension or outright fear concerning a new situation in our waking lives. On the other hand, if we stop breathing as though submerged under water, we may be experiencing womb-like memories replete with biological or psychological dependence upon another. (Ex: Mother Figure.) In this context, we may be communicating a temporary inadequacy to care for ourselves. In this sense, we may find an inability to fulfill our own needs and therefore, we surrender, or 'sink' into a sort of 'prebirth' helplessness. Another Unconscious illustration, (that of holding of ones breath,) indicates a stubborn state of mind and an almost childish reflection of our own single-minded willfulness to demonstrate this same resolve. On yet another level, the nightmarish sensation of experiencing a shortness of breath (and an outright difficulty in normal breathing,) may be a more direct Unconscious message to examine our own physical health, or the delicate health of certain members of our own family.

BRICK The image of a Brick, may represent psychological or emotonal obstacles which pile up and create internal barriers or walls. Alternatively, bricks may represent hard labor and the mental pain of conviction. As such, we need to determine the goal and relative accomplishments associated with the bricks themselves. The final, or proposed, construction of the bricks is perhaps more symbolically conclusive, than the individual bricks. (see Wall) (see House) (see Rocks)

BRIDGE In dreams, Bridges represent transitions in ones emotional life. Changes which may effect our delicate emotional balance are approached slowly and with great caution. We may even be asked to pay a symbolic 'toll' to enable our emotional passage. When we end a relationship, we talk about 'burning the bridge behind us' which implies enacting a clean cutaway from the person with which we were involved. The purpose of this is to remove all 'problematic' emotional ties which prevent both individuals to complete their emotional transitions intact. This enables them to begin their own specific means of healing, on their own. Every individual should be given the opportunity to learn the lessons of life in their own way. Until the lesson is internalized within oneself, it may linger on and cause deeply repressed heartache. When we build a bridge, we give ourselves enough distance to reflect on the truth and turbulence of emotional break-ups. At the same time, this bridge provides a way of return if that is what is desired by both parties. (see Water) (see fire)

BROKEN In a dream, any shattered ideal state, whether it be physical, psychological or emotional is represented to the psyche as a Broken symbol. In order to analyze the dream message we first need to understand the importance of the object which is broken in our dream vision. For example, if a wine glass is broken, we may be expressing superior emotional vigor; on the other hand, if a child's doll is broken, we may be depicting a deep deficiency in our most basic emotional cravings which need to be fulfilled. The perception of broken objects may also indicate the release of tension. When certain realities are broken they can be sicerely examined and pieced together again. Nothing is absolute. Our emotions and sensitivities allow much space for mending, repair and sometimes, even improvement. (se Mirror) (see Image)

BROTHER In a dream, a person's Brother may represent a mirror image of the person dreaming, regardless of the dreamers gender. Because of the normal psychology in sibling rivalry, our brother may represent qualities which we may or may not possess. We may be experiencing an Unconscious desire to express these traits in a more forceful manner. On the other hand, we may be experiencing guilt for recently behaving in a childish manner reminiscent of our early years of rivalry; where, competing for the favor of our parents, sometimes overshadowed the human consequences of our actions. This may include the harmful and pointed physical or psychological attacks on our own brother or sister. We may be trying to impress an authority figure. (see father)

BUDDHA The Buddha represents a worldly calm which he creates for himself in a dream state. Should he awake, all of reality, which is his own manifest illusion, would vanish. Therefore, when we dream of the buddha, we are dreaming of the frailty and insubstantiality of our own existence. The implication of this dream may involve the mechanics of the dream process itself. We may be observing the landscape of our living experience in order to shape and become a better figure within that reality. In essence, we are asking the dream (the Unconscious) to show our place within the dream (reality). If our waking life is filled with pressure, confusion, depression and anger, the Buddha may be the Unconscious way of demonstrating how to turn our 'nightmare' back into a calm, purposeful and transcendent dream life.

BUG With the exception of the ant (see Ant), Bugs generally refer to psychological irritations or fears. If we are annoyed by a single bug in our dream, we simply need to face our symbolic tormentor and calmly brush it away. If on the other hand, our dream pests consist of a handful of black widows, scorpions or a swarm of locust, we need to analyze what psychological fear in our life is causing this degree of anxiety. The indication of the insect/bug symbolism refers to a large number of small grievances which may have accumulated and now surrounded us, or conceivably our family. We need to seriously assess what exactly is pestering us. (see Locust) (see Scorpion) (see Insect)

BULL   In dreams, Bulls represent blind aggression and rage. However, unlike a tiger, which is also an aggressive powerful animal, the bull has no poise and lacks grace. Therefore in the dream, we may be referring to recent impulsive actions which may have left others with the impression of us as a 'bull in a china shop'. Conversely, because of its blind rage, the Unconscious may use the bull archetype to illustrate a deeply repressed sexuality which is in need to 'charge out' and face its opponent. The extensive mythological use of a minotaur inside the labyrinth is further and undoubtably suggestive of our repressed sexual and so-called 'evil' natures. However, the reverse definition may also hold true. In this manner, the minotaur of the labyrinth blocks the final entrance into spiritual enlightenment with its sexual and stubborn physical nature. Appropriately, we need to determine the relative physicality of the bull and how it applies to our own peculiar situation. When we confront the bull we confront ourselves. Are we worthy of heaven? The bull represents our self-examination and our deepest confessions. (see Horn) (must see Tarot, Judgement (20))

BUTTER   In dreams, if our bread is thick and covered with butter, we are experiencing a rich, healthy life. However, if we choke on that butter or find it spread too thick upon the bread, our unconscious may be expressing excess in our life which must be curtailed in order for us to maintain our physical, psychological and emotional balance. Conversely, if our bread lacks butter and tastes bland, we may be expressing a need to add quality (Ex: art, leisure, travel, new environment) and fullness (Ex: friends, family) into the context of our day to day lives.

BUTTERFLY   In dreams, a Butterfly is significant of fragile and beautiful, yet elusive hope. In many traditions, it is the single metaphor of the human soul. Analogous to the world dream of the Buddha, the butterfly is so delicate it nearly defies existence. It is a gift, rather than a right. To dream of capturing a butterfly may be symbolic of a child-like desire to 'capture' beauty. In adulthood, we learn to cherish and respect beauty, to hold it in our hands and watch it fly free: without remorse for the joy which it has given us. We have learned to return the gift of love back into the maternal arms of nature who dreams silently on the long and translucent wing of the sole butterfly. It is she who travels faithfully on her timeless and sacred journey into night, and eternal memory.

C

CABIN   In a dream, a Cabin may be symbolic of protection from 'elements' in our life which may be closing in on us. There are factors in our day to day waking life which we cannot escape in the confines of our own home (Ex: bills, marriage, poverty). Consequently, we seek to escape these realities by changing our location, which is our symbolic psychological landscape. Keeping this in mind, we return to a natural setting and a simpler way of life. Dream reality does not concern itself with the waking realities of cabin cost, available vacation time, or the availability of an ax to chop fire wood. The dream instead, reveals a message to the dreamer to keep things simple and approach life's difficulties one at a time. Approach life in a straight forward manner not entirely unlike a mountain man or female pioneer. (see Wood) (see Aboriginal)

CACTUS A Cactus is known for its ability to survive in harsh elements with its long, hard thorns and water saving physiology. However, human beings are not cactus, and this dream may imply the raising of ones own defence mechanisms. If the cactus defies the dreamer's need to hold it, or drink its water, the Unconscious might be telling us to leave someone or something alone which we may be harming with our own selfish actions. Conversely, if we picture ourselves as the cactus, we may be expressing a difficulty in allowing people into our lives. Naturally, this causes us loneliness and desperate isolation. Sometimes, we must remove our thorns and offer the sweetness which is inside us. (see Desert)

CADET The image of a young soldier carries with it a complex range of emotions. This factor is primarily centered around the opposite concept of youth and innocence versus the murderous, adult reality of war. Within the nucleus of these polar opposites we find transitional roads of psychological and spiritual learning and transcendence in both directions. As such, we see a young adult step into the responsibility of full adulthood, just as we see the potential older and hardened soldier, jeopardizing his or her life for youth and freedom. Moreover, the rites of passage involved in adulthood are drastically illustrated in this dormant war-like figure. In another sense, we witness a call to duty, or a hunger for valor and/or honor, all in the name of our peers and social influences. Accordingly, the cadet dream illustrates harsh, yet productive, transformations into maturity which are often experienced in the context of our waking encounters. (see Bar) (see Warrior)

CAGE When we are held back from expression, movement and especially, freedom, we inevitably illustrate the dream symbol of the Cage. In waking life, there are numerous laws, rules, codes, regulations and limitations which in theory provide structure and organization in society. When a dreamer feels trapped by these binding knots in the fabric of society and civilization, he or she visualizes him or herself as dislocated from choice. Therefore, he or she may feel removed from the independence of individuality. On the other hand, if the dreamer feels that they 'belong' behind bars, it may be a clear representation of feelings of guilt over ones wild, uncontrolled and perhaps violent behavior.

CAKE In a dream, a Cake may symbolize social or family unity. It is a food source intended for many people to celebrate with (and of course, honor) a particular individual and his or her achievement. The dreamer needs to examine whether he is the honorary member in the dream, or simply, one of the well-wishers. In the latter example, if the celebration cake is sliced and the dreamer receives a wedge of cake which is in some way spoiled or inferior to slices received by other members of the celebration, the implication may be jealousy on the part of the dreamer toward ones family or peer group. Conversely, if ones slice is bigger than everyone else's, guilt about ones greed or excess should be examined. If, as originally stated, the cake in the dream is intact and whole and the dreamer is sitting at the head of the table, this individual may be expectant of an important emotional celebration, including marriage, a better job, or perhaps, the birth of a child. The cake represents plentiful existence. (see Abundance)

CALENDAR   In dreams, a Calendar may represent the passage of time, which may carry with it a concern about ones age. A calendar may also illustrate ones apprehension, anxiety or fear concerning an approaching date. If there is a date displayed in the dream, a need to analyze its specific significance may be ENTIRELY necessary. If the date means nothing to the dreamer, he or she may be alerted that they themselves need to make something happen on that date. This may be the Unconscious's way of revealing an unexpected window of opportunity. (see Clairvoyance) (see Prophesy)

CAMEL   The Camel is symbolic of healthy, stalwart life. Because of this, and the shape of its hump, it may also indicate pregnancy or birth. Moreover, since the camel is an obedient, trustworthy animal which can carry a human being through the harshest of elements, its dream appearance indicates deep trust or spiritual transcendence in that dreamers life. We need to analyze our behavior with and acceptance of the camel in order to better understand the dream's message. For example, if the camel is dying, we may be witnessing a change in our own trustworthiness or altruistic behavior. On the other hand, if we watch the camel drink for a long period of time, we may be referring to our own patience in receiving spiritual transfiguration, or at very least, a certain level of emotional maturity. (see Water)

CANDLE   In a dream, lighting or carrying a single Candle may represent a ray of hope where there is nothing but darkness. In this, a candle is akin to a prayer for knowledge and guidance. In many cultures a candle is lit for a loved one who has passed away. The candlelight is symbolic of the loved ones soul which burns bright and flickers its warmth and light through the worldly haze. If, in our dream, a candle is blown out, we may be experiencing the surrender of an important part of ourselves. If many candles are lit in a dream, we may be surrounding ourselves with a certain faith in ourselves, our loved ones, our society, or a spiritual calling in general. It must be remembered, in all cases, that a candle is a delicate and soon parting moment of love and hope. In this, we need to fill ourselves with the candles precious warmth and hope. The Unconscious may be warning us not to overlook some small miracle of promise which may have recently appeared in our present waking life. (see Fire) (see Wax) (see Butterfly)

CANNIBAL   Cannibalism implies the giving of oneself completely when a dreamer views him or herself as the human sacrifice which will be 'carved' and 'devoured' by the tribe. In this coerced offering of ones own flesh, their may be a deep repressed sexuality which is revealed at the root of this particualr dream landscape. We may be referring to our own sexual submissiveness, or a need to be 'taken' sexually by an overpowering and aggressive force. In another sense, we must examine the connection with Mouth, which is symbolic of SOUL and an entry into heaven. In this, we see how the dreamer may be demonstrating a desire to surrender his or her own life-force for the prolonged existence of another in the most extreme form of altruism, (which is a form of selfless love,) imaginable. In the Christian religion, Jesus is said to have offered and given his body and blood for the redemption of the sins of man. In yet another context, if the dreamer happens to be the cannibal who eats or desires to eat human flesh, he or she may be seeking to absorb the vitality, moral consciousness, or perhaps, the open sexuality of another. The complexity of devouring human flesh, therefore, must be examined in great detail and with unbiased self-reflection. What are our feelings about release and the 'giving' of Self. Are we confirming our own morality, or sacrificing it. (see Bull) (see Mouth) (see Tarot, Judgement (20)) (see Eating) (see Table)

CANYON A Canyon is a huge natural phenomenon which dwarfs the size of a single individual. Therefore, its vastness can be approached with wonder, joy and enlightenment of being a part of it all. On the other hand, it can be approached with fear, apprehension and a loss of self-importance and significance. Notwithstanding an overriding fear of heights, which will erase the dream's symbolism in turn of a clear apprehension of personal misgivings and trepidations about height itself. The dreamer overlooking the overwhelming canyon has the option of feeling in tune with 'everything', or conversely, feeling him or herself as the embodiment of 'nothingness' and hopelessness. The canyon represents coming face to face with a seemingly infinite reality. How we view ourselves in the dream and how we feel about the canyon may reveal something crucial about our respective personality. Are we moved by reality, or mortified by it? In any case, it is important to realize that the canyon only SEEMS infinite. This implies that all difficult and seemingly insurmountable realities can eventually be overcome and put behind us. With patience and faith we can travel into the heart of the canyon and drink from its ancient stream of water. Is it perhaps, reflective of our own stream of consciousness? (see Mountain) (see Water) (see Hole)

CAR The automobile has become a major component of the American psyche. Advertisers, almost universally, have anthropomorphized the sexuality, status and dire familial necessity of the mechanical beast. It has become almost unthinkable to approach adulthood in today's society without a driver's license and accompanying shiny new, (or slightly used) vehicle of choice. This fact remains consistent even in our major cities, where driving is unnecessary and at times, environmentally crippling. Conversely, the rebuilding of America, and the world proper, to accommodate for these automobiles, via highways, byways, roads, streets, cul-de-sacs, parking zones, traffic helicopters, scooters, gas stations riddled across the landscape, and motor maintenance, exotic and classic car clubs nationwide, have ALL unceremoniously changed the country's panorama in a very real and permanent fashion. In this psychological terrain, the automobile takes center stage and is reflected appropriately in our dream consciousness. Accordingly, the movement, freedom, sexuality and status offered by our car is examined and thrown into symbolic light by our ever-useful Unconscious. In this complex symmetry of society and understanding, our vehicle becomes the single embodiment of ourself, in both its glory and limitation. Hence, we ordinarily use ordinary metaphors like, 'She's a hot, 68 Caddy with pink tails, soft cushions and plenty of bite and throttle for the long, hard open road.' or 'He's a 38 Desoto, from his short block, crop top, to his pudgy old fenders, without any hint of style, flash or imagination, whatsoever.' All this would lead us to believe that a car's appearance in a dream landscape may reveal a deeply held truth about the totality of our waking experience. (see Image)

CARAVAN The dream symbolism of a caravan may well be an expression of social union in order to withstand the harsher elements of life. The archetype of a 'journey' refers to physical and/or spiritual transcendence. The caravan unifies and guides the human journey, becoming a world unto itself and therefore, it absorbs the difficult journey of transcendence back into its own folds. In a dream, the caravan may be an implication to organize or join others, perhaps a family, to achieve the greater good of the whole. We need to consider the direction which the caravan travels. Does it head north, into more favorable weather conditions, or does it burrow deeper into the heart of the desert. The latter example often refers to harsh individual or social determination. Moreover, we must take note of ALL the persons, animals and objects which we come across in the caravan itself. Each of these is highly reflective of the journey itself. We also need to determine if we are we out of place in the caravan, or if we fit snugly into its entourage. (see Desert)

CASTLE A Castle represents the myth and archetype of power, both good and bad. To be a part of the castle reflects nobility, comfort, and protection, as well as 'romantic' desire and adventurous passion. A castle is also reminiscent of the mystery of its many rooms, which may represent the complexity of the human mind or human heart. In a dream, we must analyze our 'place' in the castle and our behavior in this capacity. We may be experiencing guilt about our royal, yet pompous behavior, or, we may be expressing a form of wish-fulfillment in being 'saved' from the high tower of our own morals by some young, willful knight or some large, lustful dragon! (see Knight) (see Dragon) (see King) (see Queen) (see Ring)

CASTRATION Castration may imply ones anxiety about impotence or a perceived loss of masculinity. If a person is intimidated or brought into submission by a man or woman's strong aggressive nature, that person may dream of being severely mutilated. Conversely, if the dreamer dreams of mutilating another person, he or she may be illustrating a need to strike out against the unfeeling, aggressive and otherwise tactless behavior of another individual. Since sexuality can often be aggressive by nature, mutilation may simply involve an Unconscious surrender of oneself. This is a form of sacrifice offered up to ones mate. On the other hand, to willfully cut off ones own phallus in a dream implies a severe repression of ones own sexuality and the inability to interact (or perform with) individuals of the opposite sex. (see Sacrifice) (see Impale) (see Blood) (see Cut)

CAT The cat is the symbol of mystery, independence and sex. Because of these qualities, the cat has often been compared to mysterious, independent and sexual women. The author would argue that the cat is closer aligned to the Unconscious, which is mysterious, dark, silent and contains all the wildness of our natural selves, including our lustful sexuality and violent aggression. Accordingly, we need to follow the cat who stalks in our dreams in order to 'see' where it leads. If the cat kills, we must examine what exactly it has killed, and where has it 'placed' its kill? Is this place significant of our own guilt in some way? We must understand that the cat combines elements of our 'wild' self and our 'calculating' self. Are we planning an act of aggression, or some form of sexual seduction? If the cat fights other cats, we must determine what color they are, and, who the other cats remind us of? Are these figures our enemies, or more appropriately, our sexual competitors? The three most important questions about this dream figure concern gender and qualitative emotion. Is the cat male or female, and what are our feelings about this male or female cat itself. What is the cat illustrating about ourselves in its curious, yet coordinated, behavior? (see Balance) (see Wolf) (see teeth) (see Eyes)

CAVE In many ways a Cave is symbolic of the womb because of its shape and protection. In dreams we may need to run back into our cave, (infantile dependence,) to escape the larger, fierce reality of every day life. On the other hand, if we fear the cave and its darkness, we may be expressing a lack of self-confidence about our ability to cope with the unknown. We need to analyze our behavior in and around the respective cave, to better determine the message related to us by our Unconscious. A simple assessment of the cave's psychological implications can be determined in the climate of the cave itself. Is it warm and inviting, or cold, wet and mortifying? (see Womb) (see Hole) (see Regression) (see Baby)

CELEBRATION A Celebration in our dream primarily reflects an awakening found in our psychological experience. Naturally, the ritual of celebration involves sacred rites of passage, including birthdays, weddings and sometimes even funerals. As such, the awakening may involve a personal or social transfiguration into another plane of perceptive reality. Moreover, the emotional aspect of the dream imagery is centered around the support of our loved ones and encouraging admirers. Are they there for us, or against us? In this, we find an Unconscious allusion to the mechanism of our own well being. This involves, the understanding circle of human beings who comprise the day to day interpersonal relationships which make or break our waking life's full, and fertile, experience. (see Cake) (see Ritual) (see Candle)

CENOTAPH A number of dream reports indicate individuals witnessing their own name on the marble plaque of a Cenotaph. The implication of this recurring dream image may demonstrate that a dreamer no longer recognizing him or herself; that gradually in the course of their life, all hopes and aspirations were forced into the background by the real pressures of every day life. The Unconscious now illustrates the grim search for a displaced body and soul. Moreover, the cenotaph reflects ones real accomplishments in life, or lack thereof. In this sense, the Unconscious may be instructing the dreamer to create something personal in the world, something which demonstrates the spirit of humanity, and which just may live on, in the minds of future generations and kin. This concerns leaving behind a memory, other than ones own tall and fancy tombstone. Naturally, we need to determine any writing which is carved into the cenotaph itself. What is the message to ourself? (see death) (see Stone)

CENTAUR In dreams, the mythological Centaur represents music, powerful magic and lustful abandon. As is the case in most archetypical examples of Zoomorphism, (half-man/half-animal figures,) man is responding to his primal and 'animalistic' nature. He deems to project this nature onto a third party in the fully realized synthesis of his own animal characteristics. Unlike the minotaur (which is half bull,) the centaur (being half horse,) portrays graceful, nearly musical powers of persuasion. In another sense, the centaur dream may reveal a resistance to ones own personal and powerful feelings of love or passionate desires. In other words, we do not want to be 'broken', or 'tamed'. Conversely, if we ride the centaur, our Unconscious may be signifying that we are being 'carried away' by our own sexual needs and galloping desires. (see Zoomorphism) (see Horse) (see Goat)

CENTER The image of the Center of an object, as seen in a dream, may refer to that object's essential meaning and core purpose. As such, our Unconscious may be implying that we get to the 'heart of the matter' in one particular situation. As such, the object may allude, in the sense of an archetype, to the exact nature of whatever circumstances are involved. Moreover, the center of any physical article in space usually provides balance and support for its overall structure and relative function. Accordingly, we may witness a symbolic reference to the human soul. In this, we find a religious or spiritual allusion equated to the physical parameter of our dream impression of 'center'. (see Axis) (see Balance) (see Tarot, Wheel of Fortune)

CEREMONY As opposed to a celebration, which involves elation and merriment, the Ceremony is a very serious event of human transfiguration and is usually met with somber dedication and commitment. The Unconscious therefore, may be alluding to thoughtfulness and the deliberate meditation involved in some crucial event in waking life. The concept of 'Open-Eyed' preparation is inherent in this dream image. Accordingly, we may need to take a long look at ourselves and determine if we are ready for the sacrifice and devotion required to successfully move into a higher plane of existence. The ceremony therefore, is the proving ground of our merit and the vortex of our self sacrifice, made entirely real. (see Ritual) (see Path) (see Tribe) (see Sacrifice)

CHALICE In dreams, any holy vessel, and most especially, the Chalice, refers to ones own emotional sacrifice. The Unconscious may be rhetorically asking us if we have been offering enough from the 'cup' of our spirit and good will to the people who surround us in our life. In the infamous legends of King Arthur, all the knights of the round table were sent out to find the Holy Grail (chalice) in order to restore England to her former glory. The symbolic implication was that England's spiritual cup had been emptied and only the 'highest' of all spiritual vessels (upon being found and refilled) could restore the spirit of England herself. In dreams, when we drink from a chalice, we may be illustrating a preparation to take on a major emotional and spiritual responsibility, for instance, the adoption of a child. On the other hand, to spill blood from a golden chalice may imply an emotional sacrifice which has terribly wounded us and left us feeling drained, empty and desolate. However, as the Arthurian eventually learned, ones spiritual cup will always be drained, refilled and poured faithfully once again, when and only when, it is in the cause of helping those less fortunate than ourselves. (see Bowl)

CHARGE To seize a moment with ardent passion and wild instincts is a figurative illustration of our primal self. In this, we witness the release of our once repressed, pre-ancestral nature. As such, we act on our inner most drive of attacking an opponent before he or she may attack us. In the primal sense, the opponent may have been our quarry and as such, the living being needed to be killed in order to provide our very own valid sustenance for survival. This instinct validates the notion of 'kill or be killed'. Alternatively, when a charge is organized in a dream, as in the case of an army, we may be referring to the social aspects of our primal self. In this, we may be witnessing a rebellion from our entire social group. If this is ture, is our community threatened in some way? We need to determine exactly why are we on this battlefield. In a humanistic sense, we must understand why we are charging toward our enemy. Does it imply, that we ahave refused to reason with that enemy? What aspect of our psychological makeup has put us on the offensive? Why are we acting upon a bull-like rage. The bull charges a red sheet because it feels threatened by its violent color (fire, blood, etc.) Hence, are we threatened by some outside force? For all these reasons, it is crucial to understand who is doing the charging, and who, or what, the target of the charge may be. (see Bull) (see Horn) (see Tarot, Judgement 20)

CHASED The Chase dream implies running from ones own fear. Therapists recommend turning around and facing ones tormentor, in order to obtain the FULL knowledge of exactly who or what it is which brings us such unreasonable trepidation. Accordingly, since knowledge is power, understanding the source of our misgivings may aid in the eventual vanquishing of its authority over our psychological mind. The act of running symbolizes continuous movement and energy expenditure which yields little results. In most chase dreams, the dreamer loses more and more ground, yet never gets caught. Why are our efforts in waking life failing? Why are we threatened by stopping these actions? Is the threat real? We need to face the force which chases us in order to confront its real meaning in our life. Are we running away from ourselves? What will happen when we catch up to ourselves? Why is the truth, fearful? These questions must be faced, before we can truly end the chase scene. (see Attack)

CHERUB   In dreams, a Cherub symbolizes child-like innocence and a slight mischievousness. The cherub may be a clear symbol that we need to take life a little less seriously. Conversely, it may serve as a gentle reminder that we have been recently dishonest, or manipulative in our actions, and now we feel some form of guilt. Perhaps we acted hastily in our impish and mischievous behavior and harmed someone close to us. Accordingly, the child's face and adult mind of this unique being, serves as a kind of reverse reflection of our adult face, and childish behavior. The cherub balances our immature self. In fact, in many art forms, this figure has become an archetype for our own conscience. However, on a deeper level, as we witness the cherub as 'little angel' or 'little devil', we are really seeing the so-called demonic figures of the medieval world. These demons, or daimons, represented supernatural forces which entered the souls of the weak-willed, or 'immoral of heart'. In this sense, the cherub represented ones own fragile and exposed psychological state of mind. Little wonder, it was the baby cupid who shot arrows of love into unsuspecting mortals. In all this clear symbolism, we see the danger of naivete and innocence. We should have faith, but NEVER in the wrong things. We must be strong in our mind, as well as our heart. The cherub figure reminds us to stop and think. He seems to be questioning us, "I have gained deepest wisdom in MY purity and innocence, have you done the same?" (see Flying)

CHEST   In many ways a Chest symbolizes our hidden truths and our ignored history. Furthermore, as it may contain dark, secret mysteries about ourselves and our past, the chest or trunk may represent endless movement and a fugitive outlook upon life. If then, in our dream, we find ourselves searching through the trunk, we may be looking to recapture something from our past. In this sense, we may be expressing an Unconscious desire to stop ALL this business of running and trying to hide from others, especially ourselves. Accordingly, the Unconscious may be preparing the dreamer to reveal something (about ourselves) with the full realization of the possible harsh and intolerant judgement of our respective peers. On the other hand, if we are filling the chest, we may be expressing a feeling or warmth, love and hearth. We may be experiencing feelings of deep-rootedness in our new environment. Perhaps, we have come to terms with a partner in a long-standing relationship. The chest signifies our sense of place and personal grounding, it holds our past, assures our present and attempts to gauruntee our future. In this sense, if their are clothes in the chest, we must determine whether they are clean, or dirty. Naturally, clean clothes represent security and dirty clothes signify an absense of self-worth. In all cases, the dream chest must be pried open to reveal the current nature of our real 'grounding' in the waking world. (see Box) (see Gift)

CHILD   To dream of a Child may involve a personal regression into ones past, back when the little dream boy or girl 'assumed' almost no responsibility whatsoever. This was simply because all needs were fundamentally fulfilled. The dreamer may be expressing the anxiety of a 'high-pressure' adulthood, where he or she must answer for their actions, create and reinforce their own support systems and yes, reach old age. In an entirely different sense, the dream child may be symbolic of the renewal of life found in spiritual conversion or any profound worldly awakening. For interpretation, the dreamer needs to analyze the activity, facial expressions and dress of the child to better understand its allegorical presence alongside the other components found within the dream. Is the child's innocence refreshing and pure, or, does it lead the child into danger? Moreover, is the child existing in his or her own world of fantasy? As the child represents ourself, WE must determine whether the child is enacting a form of wish-fulfillment, or, if his or her behavior is real, vituous and immaculate. (see Baby) (see Cherub)

CHILDBIRTH There are numerous recorded cases where men dream of giving birth to a child. In this context, a dreamer may be expressing a complicated message concerning the fear of his own paradoxical emotional needs. For example, in a new marriage, a man may feel the need for a caring mother figure in his new wife, which may clash with his OTHER need for an alluring, seductive and desirable woman. This is known as the mother/whore complex. It is primarily experienced by women, but it has been known to appear in men experiencing emotional confusion. The birth of a child from a man may represent his need to internalyze the mothering aspect within himself. He is expressing his own paralyzing fear of child-rearing, coupled with his duty to endure the sacrifice as well as he can. If, however, the dream image of the birth of a child is experienced as a painful sacrificing of the man's own life, professional guidance may be necessary to work him through this very difficult period of his life. On the other hand, a FEMALE dreamer may be experiencing the symbolic miracle of birth as an illustration from the Unconscious 'announcing' a new hope, including a newly acquired and completely unexpected, relationship. Men do not take the psychological aspect of childbirth as naturally and fluidly as women. For this, we should all be thankful. (see Baby) (see Cherub) (see Child) (see Blood) (see Womb) (see Sacrifice) (see Mother)

CHIMNEY In a dream, a Chimney represents warmth, family life and the removal of harmful spirits. When the chimney outside is discharging heavy plumes of smoke, the family inside the home is warm, healthy and presumably content. Furthermore, because of its connection with the fireplace and the warming of bones and flesh, the chimney is intimately linked with the union and celebration of love, including the affectionate memory of loved ones. However, if we spot old Santa Claus on the chimney, we may be expressing a longing for the innocence and faithful belief of childhood. Moreover, we may yearn for a charitable gift from an outside force. This could range from a simple raise of salary in our paycheck, to spiritual inspiration which could change the course of our lives. We need to assertain which way the smoke blows. Does it blow straight up into the heavens and Is it crisp, white and fluffy, like a postcard? Perhaps it streams down in threatening plumes of dark gray and blue which signal strong winds and perhaps impending hardships. Is the chimey tall and firm, or it is crumbling and ready to snuff out the flame of our emotional life? Why does Santa Claus emerge from the place of the flames. Is he family? If so, why does he appear to be a cherub? Is he up to mischief? Does the fireplace signify hearth, or escapism. In the dream, call in the chimney sweep and ask him to reveal the subtle workings of this particulary complex dream imagery. (see Cherub) (see Fire) (see Smoke) (see Gift)

CHORUS In a dream, when we sing in a Chorus, it may well be a representation of our 'performance' within the society of our friends, family and co-workers. Naturally, if our dream voice is boisterous and entirely out of key with the rest of the singers, we may be expressing enthusiasm for the group's ideology, but a lack of faith in our own intimacy within the group. We may be experiencing feelings of self-doubt which can certainly lead to a deep anxiety about our personal acceptance within the sphere of all our peer's activities. On the other hand, if our voice is majestic, clear and overpowering, we may be expressing a need to stand out as an individual. Perhaps we feel we have (in some way) 'surpassed' our own group. Like so many others, we may want to make that first SOLO album. The Unconscious often utilyzes group settings to reveal important individual discoveries of Self. The Unconscious is not above irony, the Unconscious is ITSELF irony. (see Mouth) (see Singing)

CHRIST The Christ archetype is very complex and conveys multi-dimensional psychological and emotional parameters depending primarily on our feelings about the Jesus figure or super-real image itself. A religious person who views the dream Christ, may be experiencing moral confusion and/or guilt about recent behavior. In this context, the actions or admonishments portrayed by the Christ image should be fully analyzed. On the contrary, a non-religious person may be expressing biblical Christian symbolism, for instance, the deep pain and worldly alienation of personal sacrifice. Yet another biblical symbol of the Christ figure, is personal temptation, replete with anxiety about falling under the influence of a 'less than desirable' individual (devil) or equally demonic organization. In all cases, the movements, direction and facial mannerisms of the Christ figure need to be fully interpreted within the entirety of this conscientious dream landscape. Above all, we must view the Christ figure as a powerful embodiment of tranquility and goodness. Therefore, we ABSOLUTELY must determine the nature of our own character when we are confronted with this Spiritual personage. Have we placed final judgement upon ourselves, or, is there time for personal redemption? In this biblical figure, we embody a multitude of archetypal symbols which play a direct part on our psychological, emotional and spiritual outlook on the world. Which lesson of Jesus should we remember. Conversely, which parable do we choose to forget? (see Cross) (see Sacrifice) (see Blood) (see Chalice) (see Table) (see Child) (see Tarot, Judgement 20) (see Angel) (see Cherub) (see Bread) (see Wine) (see Church)

CHURCH The house of worship, or Church, involves two direct representational figures. The first is a house, which reflects our psychological perception of self and the second is a ceremonial place, which involves the devotion necessary for spiritual transition. As such, we must examine the direct psychological effects of our own ethical beliefs and moral integrity. We may harbor doubts about our worthiness to step foot into this sanctified place. Conversely, we may view the church as an organizational evil which forcefully and figuratively (hard stone and high steeples) impedes upon our tangible freedom. Moreover, the social aspect of religious unity, whether it is perceived as good or bad, by the individual dreamer, carries great strength and enormous influence. In full realization of this consideration, our Unconscious may provide visual clues, in and around the church which clarify our relative aspirations and/or trepidations. For example, if we repaint, refurbish and bring in many and varied new members, we may be displaying an increase of our internal belief system, which may have become stagnant. Conversely, if the church looms high and dark over our horizon and seems to be full of fervent zealots who are angry with our behavior, we may be signalling oppression against our perhaps naturalistic style of life. (see Abbey) (see Ceremony) (see Christ) (see Tarot, The Hierophant 5)

CIGARETTE In a dream, a Cigarette may represent a relaxed state of mind concerning ones social environment. Conversely, the act of smoking may indicate a necessity for stress release. Naturally, our feelings concerning cigarettes need to be placed firmly into the interpretation of their symbolic presence. For example, if the dreamer finds cigarettes distasteful and obnoxious in waking life, the dream image of interacting with a co-worker who happens to be deeply inhaling (on) his cigarette and then blowing out plumes of thick smoke (especially if the co-worker is NOT a smoker in waking life), may be a lucid indication of our real (and perhaps repressed) hostility toward that person. In another incarnation, smoking refers to a 'rite of passage' communal ritual and a relaxed state of 'open' sexuality. The oral act of acceptance and release seems to indicate the control of owns emotions and animal passions. In other words, we are able to symbolically master the flame of our own deepest being. Accordingly, to obtain our Unconscious message, we must combine three feelings about cigarettes: our feelings about WHO smokes the cigarettes, what conditions may be causing that person to smoke, and lastly, how that individual physically displays the action of smoking. Is it casual, (social ease,) sexual, (emotional control,) or frantic, (entirely self-destrctive?) The cancer stick's addiction runs very deep into the heart of our archetypal psyche. (see Fire) (see Smoke) (see Breath) (see Choke)

CIRCLE In dreams, a Circle primarily represents the infinity of our perception. The archetypical image of the Mandela, which is a square inside a circle, represents the transcendence of man inside his cosmos. It illustrates a moment in time when physical man completes himself into the infinity of being. In so doing, man and his universe become one 'happening' greater than the sum of both parts. Accordingly, a circle in the dream sense, may indicate the deepest truths of ones own Unconscious, which is itself infinite (both perceptually and conceptually speaking). The circle is infinite potential; it has no points, walls or corners. Out of its center trajectories are born which must return someday upon some indeterminate curve. In all this, we see why it is crucial to determine ALL symbols which the circle may encompass in the dreams ultimate panorama and the personal potential of these objects to the dreamer's experience. (see Mandela) (see Round Table)

CLAIRVOYANCE In dream life, as well as waking life, there are concerns we all share about the safety and good health of our loved ones. In this sense, we sometimes visualize in dreams, futuristic occurrences, both negative and positive, involving the people we love. These dreams may seem Clairvoyant to the reality of the waking world, but (most) dream researchers agree, this is not necessarily the case. On the other hand, since our Unconscious may be keyed into an infinite source of mind (see Collective Unconscious), which may not be bound by individual human restrictions, including and especially the singular understanding of linear time (past-present-future), their may in fact be a legitimate argument concerning the ability of 'seeing' into the future, on a plane not yet understood or conceptualized by theorists and their awake (and still learning,) conscious mind. Throughout history, and in many diverse cultures, seerers, or visionaries, have predicted future events with an amazing amount of clarity and accuracy. Nostrodamus is the most famous visionary, but there were many others: Jules Verne, Galileo, Einstein, Ezekial, John the Baptist, Pythogoras, Plato...the list is as long and illustrious as the concept itself. (see Telepathy)

CLAW In waking life, we witness animals (and sometimes humans) using Claws as an instrument of aggression, primarily for hunting and\or self-defence. In this sense, we may visualize the claw in our dreams as hazardous to our well-being, especially our skin, eyes and flesh in general. Since our flesh represents how we 'sense' the world around us, the attack of our flesh by claws, (which scratch or puncture the skin,) may well refer to a violent attack upon our normal worldly perception and sensibility. We may be experiencing the forced 'bleeding' of emotional or spiritual suffering which accompanies a radical change in our private or professional life. To this end, we need to examine the symbolism associated with the animal which strikes out against us and determine how this dream figure parallels our own waking reality. Perhaps we ourselves are delving, or stabbing, at something with 'inhuman' determination.

CLAY Clay can be compared to the 'shaping' creativity of our quite extraordinary data bank of perceptions. We can 'shape' and 'mold' the decisions we make in life. As living creatures, possessing mind, we are far from being static. We are fluid, flexible and entirely transient. Therefore, in the dream sense, we must examine the clay form which we deem to lay our hands upon in order to fine-tune, or ultimately mutilate. In this context we must ask ourselves, does the form of clay project our own self, or our personal characteristics? If so, who do we wish to be? Do we wish to create, or destroy our perceived self-image? Ultimately, the interpretation of the clay dream may involve an internal concern about the power we possess over others and our willingness (or unwillingness) to use that authority.

We are playing with our outright psychological force and/or influence. The manipulation of soft clay may also involve sexual experimentation and on another level, an attempt to control our own emotions.

CLEANING In dreams, Cleaning generally refers to the wiping away of negative feelings. In the material sense, we are attempting to make ourselves lighter and therefore more spiritual. We may be symbolically removing the weight of mortal existence which seeks to bring us down into the reality of worldly difficulties. For instance, and in the contrary sense, the dream of a bloody hand, (one which cannot be wiped clean regardless of how many times we scrub it,) may well refer to a guilty conscious which the psyche refuses to simply wash away. We may need to 'come clean' before we can erase the stain of this, the 'blood on our hands'.

CLOCK In the dream sense, a clock refers to a concern about time. This could involve a deadline or a more broad and abstract worry about growing old. To properly analyze the clock symbol, one must analyze the time 'shown' on the clock itself, the age and make of clock and any and all dream character's visible reactions to the clock. Moreover, we need to determine personal feelings about time in general. Do we live 'hurried' lives, or are we usually bored. Primarily, changes in ones physical schedule in life will bring about the clock reference within a new dream landscape; but there can be many other complicated, time-related variations on this symbols' conclusive meaning. We may need to explore associations with numerology, as well as, personal health. Is our 'time' running out? (see Time) (see Calender)

CLOWN A Clown represents a complex figure including the archetypes of mask, fool and performer. As such, its dream appearance may denote a psychological revelation about a dreamer who pretends to be happy in waking life, while actually experiencing deep melancholy. We may be 'crying out' for professional guidance. On the other hand, the clown figure may simply represent mockery (the fool), and its respective buffoonery. The dreamer may be acting out a form of personal hostility toward the behavior of another, or conversely, a chastisement of our very own actions. The clown, like the fool, seems to conceal great wisdoma and truth behind his make-up and big, red nose. He is an illustration of our own potential. He can push the envelope to its very edge. In exposing our own absurdity, do we reveal something CRUCIAL about our own truest self? (see Fool)

COCK The image of the rooster, or Cock, represents a strong will and persistent determination. Unlike a tiger for example, who's power is obvious, the cock is resilient, quick and single-minded. In this he can achieve far greater results than a mightier animal who lacks focus, boldness and above all, conviction. In the chinese zodiac, the cock stands for fierce individuality and a deep understanding of the self. In this, the 'cock' personality hates to fail and rarely does. Therefore, taken together in the dream sense, we may be implying a steadfastness in our goals, desires and/or specific plans about the future.

COFFIN In a dream, a Coffin may well represent preparation for a profound change, a kind of 'emotional' rebirth. In this sense, the coffin symbolizes a dip into the Unconscious, and otherwise unknown. Naturally, there is an assumption that a coffin symbolizes death, however, it must be recalled that parting itself is symbolic of change. Given the predominant spiritual beliefs on the afterlife, its otherworldly expectations can either be very enjoyable, very discomforting, or somewhere in between. Regardless, the dream indicates a significant change, and that change is sure to bring a major modification in ones active life. The Unconscious may well be telling us to ALWAYS be prepared for the transitions found in the journey through life. In this sense, the coffin represents a shelter to guide and protect us through many of these transitional periods of our lives. (see Box)

COLLECTIVE UNCONSCIOUS Carl Jung postulated that human consciousness is linked into a great symbiotic pool that each human being (since the first human being) is intimately connected. The implications of this doctrine are extremely far-reaching and have been the center of much debate since its very onset. Jung's theory of the Collective Unconscious explains why human beings throughout history and diverse cultures, possess familiar understandings aboaut the world and reality in general. Moreover, the extraordinarily similar archetypical images found in our mind's eye indicates the connectedness of our entire species. Cave paintings, ancient carvings and modern textbooks all reveal the continuity of ALL our major human 'themes'. The theory of the Collective Unconscious postulates that humanity is communicating via a primordial language which refuses be limited by time or space. Therefore, realities may emerge into our mind's eye, realities which have yet to be born into our actual material existence. Hence, the Collective Unconscious is as limitless and enigmatic as imagination itself. (see Clairvoyance) (see Prophesy)

COLOR Different Colors have disparate symbiology. (see Green, Red, Blue, White, Black, Yellow and Purple)

CONTRACT In a dream, a Contract may refer to anxiety about keeping ones word, or, if the contract is torn, guilt about having already broken a promise involving 'sensitive' secrets. A contract may also refer to real financial concerns. In order to interpret the dream properly, the dreamer must consider three indications: the writing on the contract, who the individual who delivers (or signs) the contract is, and what agreements may the contract be binding us (or our loved ones) into. We may need to examine the worth of our own WORD (verbal aggreements) to our peers, friends and family.

CORN In a dream sense, fields of Corn (stalks) can be remarkably intimidating because of their lofty height and sheer number. In a dream landscape, we may find ourselves lost in a corn field which drastically reduces our normal human 'overview' on things and people in general. We may be experiencing feelings of inadequacy in life, or a real sense of confusion in our own personal direction. On the other hand, a clean and delicious looking kernel of corn, which is very bright in its yellow color, may be symbolic of hopeful events yet to come. The staple food may represent a 'good' feeling about recently occurring (and perhaps creative) decisions made in our waking life.

COSTUME In dreams, Costumes represent the identity of oneself. Therefore, our Unconscious may be illustrating how we appear to others. If we 'desire' to show people a simple (or elaborate) portrayal of ourselves, we may need to analyze why this is in fact the case. The dream landscape itself may yield some unique and enlightening answers to this type of self-questioning. If we find that the costume we wear, is concealing our true nature, we may be expressing a fear about 'revealing' ourselves to the outside world. This self-doubt may be extremely counter-productive in our social and professional relationships. If our costume is distasteful, strange and unfamiliar, even to our own sensibility, we may be experiencing alienation from the norms of the group with whom we surround ourselves. As such, we must determine whether the mask reflects ourself, or the society of our peers? (see mask) (see Clown)

COUNCIL In dreams, a representation of an authoritative society of our peers, generally refers to our feelings about how waking associates will 'accept' our recent actions, including job decisions and job performance, (as well as our overall behavior.) In the dream sense, we are being tested and appraised by a force greater than ourselves. Because a council is made up of many individuals, we may be expressing a 'popular' opinion about ourselves, either positive or negative. Does an agreement of many diverse individuals concerning an opinion, give that opinion validity? We need to determine who (if anybody) we need to 'answer to' in our own waking life.

COW In a dream, a Cow may represent fecundity, stability and an overall maternal state of being. The cow gives milk freely and abundantly and she is content with fresh grass and clean water. In this sense, she is nearly, even in the western mind, a spiritual being. Therefore, in a dream, the cow may symbolize spiritual or emotional events, such as the birth of a child, reunion of old friends or a brand new, love-filled relationship formed in ones recent waking life.

CRASH In the dream sense, a Crash is symbolic of the impact of two separate forces colliding together. We may be experiencing anxiety about keeping separate influences in our life apart from each other. This is often the case with an unfaithful husband or a teenager who must show one face to his friends and quite another face to his family. Alternatively, the crash dream may wholly illustrate the terrible outcome of a high-speed and otherwise stressful life. Therefore, the dreamer needs to analyze his own life decisions and resolve what revelation is found in the crash image itself. Must we finally make a mature choice in our life? (see Accident)

CROSS To a religious person, the Cross or crucifix may refer to moral guilt. To a non-religious person, it may refer to intolerable sacrifices which have already been made, or need to be taken immediately. In this, we find a reference to the crossroads in ones life. We often need to choose a path in life. The course we take not only effects ourselves, but also the whole society of man, which we are very much a reflective part. As such, the archetype of the cross transcends even Christianity and represents the struggle between the physical and spiritual world. In order to be Christ-like, we must superimpose spirituality into the material world and as such, bridge the seeming infinite gap between spirit and matter. (see Christ) (see Tarot)

CROW In a dream, the Crow archetype may symbolize an angry or restless spirit. Since it is a scavenger, the crow symbolizes the soul which stays on the earth, mingling with mortals preoccupied with the secrets of death and immortality. In the dream sense, visualizing the crow may be a revelation of our own distraught and hungry soul in search of greater knowledge and greater experience. When must the crow become the butterfly? (see Black) (see Tarot, The Star)

CRYSTAL The Crystal is a complex dream image in that it simultaneously represents clarity, balance and a reflection of light (or meaning). As such, while it may not be precognitive, the crystal dream may in fact demonstrate an accurate understanding (on our part) regarding a person or situation in our waking life. Following this line of thinking, the Unconscious may be raising this question. Are we able to accept the truth of our own insight? (see Window) (see Glass)

CUT In a dream, Cutting may represent disconnecting and dividing something which is whole, thereby releasing its inner potency. Moreover, this efficacious liberation may symbolically effect the ritualistic transfiguration of the emancipator, (in other words, the person or persons who cut.) The liberation of blood from a wound has deep archetypal connections in cultures worldwide. However, the entity (or organism) itself, which is gashed or severed in the dream landscape, may provide more clues to the dream interpretation, than merely the relative vitality which is lost from its division. The victim, either animate or inanimate, may possess an overwhelming knowledge of reality which may be painful to the dreamer in an emotional and/or psychological sense. This is why the dreamer often finds him or herself, the victim of the cutting, at times even self-inflicted. In this, we find a release of overbearing suffering (or distress) in ones daily waking experience. As such, the agony of the wound seems to expel, via disengagement, the agony of being. We are cutting to free ourselves from intolerable pain. (see Bleed) (see Sacrifice) (see Ritual) (see Bridge)

D

DAISY In the dream sense, freshly cut daisies involve purity, innocence and the new and fragile beauty of youth. This is why a person dead and buried is said to be 'pushing up the daisies'. The implication is that a person's passing on, allows for a fresh new beginning in the afterlife. In this context, when we dream of walking through fields of daisies, or if we confront unknown children carrying daisies, we may be referring to a new Spiritual beginning in our life. Redemption and renewed hope highlight this archetype in our overall dreaming experience. (see White) (see Heaven)

DANCING Our 'working' union with another person is symbolically expressed as a Dance. Are we in step or out of step with this individual? Since there is a rhythm of life, we need to analyze the full spectrum of our wide and quite unique dances with the separate people who surround us in waking life. For example, If in our dream, we are stepping on the toes of a particular partner and causing his or her feet to bleed, we may need to analyze why we are interfering with the progress of that individual and why we feel the need to draw blood (symbolic of deep emotions) from this person. The waltz-like connection found in a relationship, where partners successively 'shift weight' and responsibility for one another, may also be explored. Dancing alone, may be indicative of unique expression and a valiant exposure of self-confidence. In all cases, in order to best understand the motivation of the dance, we must determine the emotional mood of the musical accompaniment. (see Accordion) (see Blood) (see Ballerina)

DEATH In a dream, to witness the image of ones own corpse, may be a very extreme, yet entirely effective, Unconscious illustration of deep and personal loss. However, this termination, or loss, is not necessarily negative. In life, a person may 'lose' a dependency, such as drug addiction. Similarly, a person may 'lose' a narcissistic point of view, or a person may 'lose' prejudice. The point being, many characteristics which define a person, quite frankly, can afford to be lost. Hence, a vision of personal death simply portrays the decisive end of one state of mind, either psychological or emotional, which may allow for the emergence of a new and perhaps wiser understanding of oneself. On the other hand, witnessing the corpse of a loved one who is still alive, may reflect a complicated feeling of 'loss' in the understanding, familiarity and connection shared with that person. Ancient wisdom compares symbolic death with deep and reverant change. We cannot raise to a higher consciousness without permanently altering a lower consciousness. (see Coffin) (see Tarot Major Arcana, Death)

DECEPTION In a dream, a 'performance' of Deception, may well illustrate our own mastery for misleading members of the inner circle of our own life. We may be experiencing the inherent guilt involved in deceiving our own friends and family, naturally more burdensome than doing the same to our co-workers or acquaintances. On the other hand, we may be experiencing the pain of our own folly, with a full realization that we have been 'fooling ourselves all along' concerning the integrity of our own words and actions. Conversely, our Unconscious may be warning us about the deceptive actions of someone new in our life, perhaps a recently acquired boyfriend, girlfriend or spouse. In all cases, we MUST explore the method used for deception AND what we ultimately GAIN from the deception itself. In this sense, we may expressing a fear of confronting our own desires. (see Image) (see Mirror) (see Magic) (see Hoax)

DEEP The symbolism of Deep generally refers to the infinite depths of our own Unconscious. Emotions or concepts which are difficult to accept are generally repressed into this dark region. Accordingly, when we experience confusion in decision making, due to arduous situations in our life, we may feel a desire to repress all the emotions involved. In so doing, we 'sink' ourselves into the secret depth of our own psyche. Like ancient divers, we overcome the fear of our personal unknown and 'drop off' yet another unbearable 'treasure' of Self. However, the deep wisdom of the Unconscious refuses to vanquish this enigmatic memory (which is) deposited within its folds. When the proper time emerges, so too does the full revelation of the memory. The human mind inherently comprehends the absolute need to confront ALL realities; sooner, or later. (see Water) (see Sky) (see Blue) (see Ocean) (see Sink) (see Drown)

DEER In a dream, a lone Deer depicts innocence, frailty and natural beauty. In the symbolic sense, the Unconscious may be illustrating a dire need to protect a precious quality in ourselves or someone close to us. If however, the deer is a large stag with great pointed horns, the representation is one of freedom, independence and virility. In all cases the dreamer must analyze his or her interaction with the deer, if any, and the dream landscape surrounding the animal.

DELICATE If we find a recurring object in our dreams, which is exceedingly Delicate, we must analyze what that object represents
to us. Accordingly, we need to interpret why this symbol seems so fragile, exquisite or downright breakable. Often in dreams, an inanimate object is symbolic of a psychological state, therefore, the 'delicate' illustration of some object, may be a warning about a specific psychological vulnerability. We are expressing a fear of our own destructive powers. (see Broken) (see Glass)

DELTA WAVES Brain waves are measured on a sophisticated piece of equipment known as an electroencephalograph or EEG. These EEGs measure electrical energy released by the brain in terms of Amplitude (or width) and Frequency (or speed). As opposed to Alpha waves, Delta waves occur during deep sleep and are characterized by high amplitude and very slow frequency, in the range of 1-2 cycles per second. One could conceivably view Delta waves as large sweeping electrical scans of our entire neural region. Alpha waves, on the other hand, occur when a person is awake (A-1) or meditating (A-2) and expose lower amplitude and much higher frequencies, in the range of 8-12 cycles per second. As such,

Alpha waves may be compared to sharp and focused neural activity, which bring the wide neural view into extreme close-up, where in fact, accuracy may be needed. For example, hunting for food, or a high-powered job interview, are two activities accomplished much more effectively, while wide awake. There are those who would argue that corporate executives have convincingly demonstrated how alpha waves are no longer really necessary, once their job slot is filled. (see Alpha Waves)

DEMAGOGUE Hitler was a Demagogue. If we view ourselves as a Demagogue, leading great masses of people by stirring up their prejudices, we may be experiencing deep, unconsoled feelings of personal hatred, which need to be addressed. We may feel cornered by our fears and emotions of anger and seek help (in the form of dream characters) to aid us in our own personal struggle. In the strict psychological sense, a person will fear society less when he gains an outright control over that society. As such, our need for power, aptly illustrates, a deep fear of social judgement. We must prove ourselves to be 'high and mighty' to avoid the form of personal humiliation (which we feel we will otherwise, receive.) On the other hand, if the demagogue is a person known, a dreamer may be expressing anxiety concerning ignorance or prejudice found in his or her social sphere, especially intolerance directed by an individual against the dreamer's own nationality, race or creed.

DEMON In dreams, Demons may represent the seemingly paradoxical embodiment of our fears and desires. As such, demons are voices from deep inside ourselves, which appear in our consciousness when we are faced with moral decisions. These decisions usually involve the consequences of personal ethics. The struggle between a person's symbolic demons and angels is a normal part of the checks and balances found within that person's psyche. Moreover, theorists have put forth the hypothesis which claims, to be 'wholly' influenced by either good intentions (religious fanatic), or evil intentions (demagogue), may imply an unbalanced and abnormal psychological grounding. (see Devil) (see Angel) (see Incubus)

DEN In a dream, The Den image may refer to a hideout. On the surface, the dream seems to be an indication of personal fear for oneself or ones family. However, the idea of hiding out in the earth itself may be symbolic of a regression into the safety of infancy and the womb. To this end, we may require an analysis of the need to 'wrap' our own skin (which senses the outside world), within the protective body and sanctuary of the mother figure. The regression into pre-birth itself, may imply a paralyzing social or personal fear which has reached its absolute zenith in our own daily waking life. Why is the highest level of our maturity under attack? An examination of the symbolism of the animal (if any) which chases us into our dream den, may be necessary to elaborate further on the complex meaning of this dream imagery. (see dirt) (see Cave) (see Hole) (see Chase)

DEPOT The symbolism of a Depot carries within its parameters all three archetypes of poverty, isolation and the reconstruction of life. If in the dream, we find ourselves sitting motionless in a bus depot, we may be experiencing a total loss of direction in waking life. A desire to change major aspects in our life is certainly apparent. However, the anxiety centered around the 'confusion' of choosing this new destination in our life is equally displayed. On the other hand, if we find ourselves arriving in a bus depot, we may be experiencing a mild fear pertaining to a new situation 'approaching' our waking life. In all cases, we need to interpret the color of the depot and any and all characters within the entire dream landscape. (see Highway) (see Landscape)

DEVIL The Devil in our dreams may refer to decision making which directly involves our moral basis of reality. We must ask ourselves whether we are seduced by this demon (representative of some form of worldly gain,) or terrified by its intentions. Based on this, we may be able to determine in which direction our own Unconscious seems to lean. Do we need to open up to our dangerous, frivolous and desirous self, or do we find purity in our denial of all temptation? In either case, a moral quandary in our life is clearly illustrated which needs to be resolved immediately. (see Demon) (see Temptation) (see Tarot Major Arcana: Devil (15)) (see Aboriginal)

DESERT In a dream, the Desert landscape may symbolize a cessation of psychological or emotional growth. The difficulty of desert travel, replete with intense heat, uneven terrain and lack of water are key signs of emotional stagnation. We may feel dry and incomplete in a one-sided relationship where our sentiments of love (heat) are not reciprocated. In the psychological sense, we may feel lost in the vastness of the desert plain which fails to reveal the best path to the 'better world' outside its limits. Yet, in another sense, the desert may imply ardent spiritual sacrifice experienced upon the entry into a new and moral way of life. What is our aim in the desert? Do we seek an oasis which may not exist? (see Caravan)

DIARRHEA The symbolism of Diarrhea is roughly comparable to vomiting, which is yet another form of sickness associated with ones internal system. In this sense, our stomach is entirely representative of our feelings and attitudes about ingested or 'accepted' realities. As such, our diarrhea may represent the immobilization involved with a peculiar, or set of meticulous, realities. We feel a need to immediately rid ourselves of these difficult, even painful, truths, which we were at one time forced to accept. These may include relationships or complex situations which caused us anxiety in the clearest and most articulate of metaphorical fashions. (see Feces) (see Regurgitation) (see Stomach) (see Abdomen)

DIG In a dream, the action of Digging may symbolize yet another search into ones own Unconscious. The removal of layer after layer of earth (representing our psychological consciousness and physical body) moves us closer to the 'depth' of our true and perhaps 'primal' selves. In this sense, we may be searching for the 'treasure' of our collective human wisdom. Conversely, there remains a conjecture which asserts our own personal knowledge was buried not too long ago in the ferocious storm of our upbringing or systematic socialization. Taken together, the digging dream may imply the psychological preparation necessary for a new and radical 'understanding' of our own waking lives. (see Dirt) (see Hole) (see Coffin) (see Deep) (see Chest)

DINNER A Dinner in ones dream landscape may symbolize a personal taste and/ or hunger for life and how this characteristic may effect ones interpersonal relationships. In waking life, a dinner usually consists of a group of people, perhaps a family, who 'share' a meal. In so doing, the entire group absorbs the shared human experiences of soulful gathering, healthy sustenance and social equality. Accordingly, if in a dream scenario, any of these 'illustrations' is missing in the dinner itself, the same qualities may be void in waking life. For example, if a dreamer views him or herself hoarding as much food as possible at a dinner table, personal greed or suspicion of ones business associates, perhaps in a recent transaction, may be illustrated. (see Table) (see Mouth) (see Food) (see Abundnce)

DIRT In dreams, a Dirty face may symbolize angry social defiance or conversely, repugnant emotions which need to be 'washed away'. However, finding in hand, dirt or soil which provides the rich 'environment' necessary to nourish a seedling to full growth, may be symbolic of ones cultivating or parenting skills. This dirt, or earth, is symbolic of our own human nurturing. We are placing our protective arms and skin around a more vulnerable being. Therefore, where we view the dirt, plays a significant part on its ultimate dream interpretation. (see Water) (see Cleaning) (see Dig) (see Earth)

DISAPPEAR When we fear losing someone or something, their absolute form may vanish in our dream. If we find our own body disappearing, we may be experiencing a feeling of personal insignificance in our own waking relationships. In both cases, it is naturally crucial to examine all characters and symbols to determine the source of these negative motivations. We must determine whether or not, WE, have caused these persons to leave us? If certain body parts are vanishing, we must analyze the symbolic significance of these separate appendages. (see Body) (see Image) (see Corpse)

DISTANCE Although a Distant city may suggest hope, the overall perception of distance implies a separation from ones goals. The interpretation of a dream landscape involving distance may be dependent on the speed and direction we travel toward or away from that distant location. If we move rapidly toward some welcoming object (home, oasis etc.), we may be expressing desire and emotional anticipation involving an upcoming event (marriage, birth of a child etc.). However, if we slowly move away from some beckoning object or person, we may be experiencing guilt and remorse concerning a past episode (or relationship) in our life. Consequently, in order to best understand this dream imagery, the dreamer needs to determine his or her 'feeling' about the distant 'object' and compare this awareness with the direction and speed away or toward that same article, or place. (see Landscape) (see Desert) (see Caravan)

DIVA The recurring dream symbol of a Diva may demonstrate deep wish-fulfillment on the part of the dreamer to be loved and cherished by all. The diva symbol further presupposes 'perfection' in performance. Consequently, a dreamer may be expressing anxiety over his or her lack of self-discipline or natural ability, which is 'compensated' in this captivating and irresistible dream of effortlessly reaching out to the world in song and natural beauty.

DIVER The Diver dream may be a visual representation of the link between the Unconscious and conscious mind. A diver retains air by holding his or her breath, or by utilizing the proper scuba equipment, or other breathing apparatus. The air in this sense embodies the surface, or conscious world, which 'remains' with us, even though submerged in the dark, mysterious and enigmatic Unconscious. As such, the diver dream may illustrate a dreamer searching for a 'rational' solution to a riddle which is out of his day to day experience, or understanding. Moreover, if in the dream, the diver faces difficulties or danger, all the threatening factors and forces therein, (shark, whale, whirlpool etc.,) should be analyzed for their full waking ramifications. If the diver is in control of his dive, the dreamer may be experiencing control over his or her emotions. In this sense, the dreamer is balancing his psychological and emotional foundation. (see Drown) (see Ocean) (see Deep) (see pearl)

DOCK A Dock is primarily symbolic of transitional states of emotion. A dreamer might be experiencing a welcome return from the stormy sea of a recent and perplexing relationship. On the other hand, the dock may represent the psychological preparation necessary for an emotional 'outing'. In both cases, the condition of ones boat, all characters surrounding the dock, and the dock itself, should be analyzed for peculiar representational significance. Is our boat sturdy? Do we tie her up in preparation for stormy weather? What will our emotions bring? (see Boat) (see Beach) (see Ocean)

DOG In a dream, a Dog may represent a number of complex emotions, including fear, friendship, loyalty and obedience. A dreamer needs to completely determine the color, demeanor and intentions of the dog and compare these characteristics with the landscape encircling the animal. For example, if a big, yellow dog seems friendly and leads us away from a particular location or situation, we may need to analyze the 'hidden shadows' and/or deceptions involved in the place or circumstance itself. In this example, a dog may reveal our own apprehensions, which we have foolishly, chosen to ignore. On the other hand, if the dog is fierce, foams at the mouth and chases us through our own home, we may be experiencing distrust in an individual very close to us. In yet another symbolic association, that being the chinese zodiac; the dog represents honesty and generosity, in this representative case, a dog is a straight forward companion with no ulterior motives except unification and bonding trust. (see Wolf) (see Teeth) (see Mouth) (see Bite)

DOLL   A Doll may represent wish-fulfillment on the part of the dreamer who wishes to gain a doll-like (flawless) appearance, and lifestyle (doll house). A variation of this symbolism, finds the image of a disfigured doll, which represents the psychological and emotional body of the dreamer. The doll reflects the 'pure' body which is 'torn' by life's struggles. In this context, we need to analyze the dream doll's symbolic deformities (missing arms, scratched face etc.) and how they might relate to the dreamers current outlook on life. (see Image) (see Body) (see Disappear)

DOLPHIN   The Dolphin represents emotional trust combined with psychological freedom. This marriage of ideal states borderlines a spiritual 'feeling' of love and 'highest' human 'being'. Therefore, to ride a dolphin in a dream may represent 'floating' on ones own crystalline optimism, personal faith and social altruism. Furthermore, leaping and playing in the separate consciousness of mind, body and spirit indicates a well-balanced outlook on life in general. We are aware of our own powers, yet we refuse to take them too seriously. Hence, our individual joy is shared with the world around us. (see Ocean) (see Diver) (see Drown) (see Shark)

DOOR   Since a Door is both an exit and an entrance, and can deny passage as well as welcome a person through its threshold, its symbolism is entirely dependent on its working status. Is the dreamer locked out, and refused (therefore,) passage into potential change; or are doors opening automatically, simply because of the fervor and zeal of the dreamer's self-confidence? Accordingly, we need to analyze our relative position to the door and any and all characters (or objects) which appear on either side of the door, for the legitimate meaning of our (perhaps shifting) state of mind. (see Window) (see Glass)

DOUBLE   Seeing Double refers to personal confusion and/or paradoxical viewpoints upon a certain individual or situation. If we behold ourselves in this split mirror of consciousness, we may be experiencing self-doubt, guilt, or personal wavering involving our private or professional 'roles'. Is the attitude about what our personal behavior should be, split in half? Are we sitting atop a fence, unsure of where we must stand. Double-vision in a dream implies getting hold of oneself by making a choice, (and following that choice, as best as we can.) (see Fence) (see Image) (see Mirror)

DOUBLE-JOINTED   The conceptualization of the Double-Jointed individual, illuminates potential and possibility, far beyond ANY 'naturalistic' norm. The dream may be alluding to the length and strength of our own being, (which may not be immediately apparent,) yet burns with full intensity in the underlying course of our honest expressions and vital actions. In other words, if we can bend our reality beyond its typical or standard perception, we may find that our own 'truth' can be every bit as 'infinite' as our own imaginative potential. We reach points in our life where we leap forward in our abilities. At times, we surpass even our own highest expectations. In this, we learn the limitless possibility which life has too offer, IF, we are willing to strive hard and long enough to achieve our desired realities. Is this then, the catalyst for the miraculous? Perhaps, the dream reveals to us ALL a rather surprising answer! (see Magic)

DRAGON In the Eastern (and especially Chinese) tradition, a Dragon symbolized hope, love and energetic spiritual flight. While on the other hand, (and rather quite conversely,) in the Western tradition, the Dragon represented lust, aggression and a haphazard ruin of sensible order. Taken together, it is easy to see why today the overall archetypical dragon represents the extreme coordinates of an infinite Unconscious. In the modern world, our giant, fire-breathing lizard may easily step in and out of these diverse 'worlds' of expression. Moreover, because of its snake-like movements, flying ability and mouth of fire, the dragon is predominantly associated with the specifics of flagrant and passionate love. This symbolism comes replete with all of love's sublime consequences, which of course, run the gauntlet from divine euphoria to bitter and demonic hatred. The dragon is the uncontrollable element within us all. The knight in slaughtering the dragon is representationally coming to terms with his own hot desire and finding a reconciliation for these feelings within the bounds of a sacred and selfless union. (see Knight) (see King) (see Queen) (see Tarot, The Lovers)

DRAIN In a dream, a Drain essentially represents a funneling and depletion of emotion, especially those associated with loss and heartache. However, this drain may also remind us of a cleansing and purification, which has taken away harsh impurities. Since these impurities may seem intent to cling to us in every day life, the two previous examples may be connected. We need to purge ourselves of ANY unwanted realities which may hamper our growth and overall development. (see Basin) (see Unclean)

DRAPES The image of dark colored, material-rich Drapes symbolize a multi-layered emotional state which shuts out the light of day (conscious awareness, rational thought.) For example, in a dream, red and black velvet and lace drapes, may represent a painful conflict (red vs. black) in ones relationship. This conflict may be resolved if the dreamer allows in the light of day, (reason,) which may reveal the means wherein strife can once again return to unity. In this, we see how the drapes are representational of how our emotions may cloud our better judgement. (see Red) (see Window) (see Black) (see Lace)

DRIP In the dream sense, a Drip may represent a slow, yet relentless loss of ones spiritual will. The Unconscious may be illustrating a 'gradual' deprivation in a specific area of ones waking life. For instance, if we fear losing a job, or if a loved one, sustains prolonged illness. The effect of these disturbing conditions may be slowly devitalizing our life force and real, tangible aspirations. We must explore why the disabilitating process occurs so slowly, chipping away at our sanity in

DRY   61

such a torturous manner. Is this 'torture' suggestive of some hidden truth which must be revealed to the outside world. Are we avioding making crucial changes in our life which must occur and which are already deeply effecting us? How do we tighten our emotions and return to the stability of a well-adjusted self? (see Water) (see Basin) (see Baptism) (see Ritual) (see Blood)

DROWN When we sink into the deep waters of our heightened emotions, we may experience a desperate feeling of Drowning. In the symbolic sense, we need to avoid fear (panic) and swim calmly to the surface and dry land of reason. In an ideal sense, we may need to bond our psychological and emotional consciousness, in order to float safely on the periphery of both plains. This figure represents the antithesis of the Dolphin. Its control anf fluid play act as a sharp contrast with our sinking emotional fear and paralysis. Will we sink or swim? (see Dolphin) (see Breath) (see Water)

DRUM Perhaps the most ancient human archetype is the visual and auditory beating of drums, reflective of our own heart beat and emotional rhythm of life. As such, the dream beat may represent the scope of the complete human experience, entailing love and sex (birth), life and its difficult moral standards (faith), and the final death struggle (war, afterlife.) A need to analyze the 'associative connection' of the beat (to the dreamer,) may be necessary to understand its vital position in the visionary landscape. The fact that a drum is primarily a piece of 'stretched' skin figures deeply into its overall meaning as well. We note that skin represents our sensitivity, or how we sense the world. Hence, the drum beat indicates our 'gut feelings' about the what we see around us and how it effects us. Are we excited, agitated, aroused? Do we want to march forward in the cause of a new found reality, or, are we loudly beating the drum of our awareness solely to drown out the 'finer' message of our more subtle intuitions? (see Accordion) (see Skin)

DRUG The need for a 'quick fix' promised by both legal and illegal Drugs may be revealed to us by our Unconscious. We may desire a potentially harmful, wish-fulfillment in the form of an 'instant' escape from our problems. It is crucial to analyze the escapist dream landscape for evidence pointing to what may motivate our demand to escape reality. Conversely, how must we liberate ourselves from the consolation of this personal deception? What new parameter or experience of life are we searching for? Are we unable to reach the infinite potential within ourselves? In other words, why is an outside catalyst necessary? Does the lure of anti-social behavior add to the thrill found in the dream experience? Why are we PERSONALLY upset, or angry, with society (or some aspect of society?) All these questions may be examined in the overall drug dream imagery. (see Escape) (see Wish-fulfillment) (see Addict)

DRY As opposed to water, which symbolizes deep emotion, Dryness may refer to an exhaustion of feelings and moreover, an alienation from human sensitivity. At times, this removal from interaction may serve as a necessary component for psychological readjustment to complex situations in our waking life. However, if the dream is a recurring one, we may be displaying feelings of isolation and perhaps a general and gradual fracturing of self. This imagery may involve our consciousness reminding us to return, to the rain and torrents of an unpredictable, yet life enhancing, world of emotions. We must 'feel' in order to be 'alive', for better, or for worse. (see Desert) (see Caravan) (see Water) (see Basin) (see Drip) (see Dolphin) (see Drown)

DUMB In the dream sense, Deaf and Dumbness may refer to a lack of communication in ones private or professional life. We may 'feel' our worth is ignored, or perhaps our knowledge is silenced by our own self-doubt. On the other hand, if we find a loved one or associate to be dumb in a dream, we may need to consider our own failure in 'listening' to this person. This is an individual who may just be crying out for help. Many forms of 'growing alienation' may be expressed in the simplicity of this dream figure.

DWARF The archetype of tiny magical people appears in virtually all cultures to a greater or lesser degree. The child-like adult combines the lure of innocence, with the spirit of cleverness. Therefore, in the dream sense, the dwarf, or child-spirit represents the heart's inner being, the head's inner being, and the soul's innermost being. We need to listen to these tiny magical voices which together pattern the complex fusion of Self. This figure is roughly parallel to the Cherub. (see Child) (see Cherub)

DYBBUK This figure involves being drained of our vital resources by some outside force. Does our own success depend on the sacrifice and despair of others? (see Vampire) (see Blood) (see Drain) (see Ritual) (see Mouth)

E

EAGLE The ancient Eagle archetype embodies flying alone in ones spiritual awareness of strength, freedom and purity. Consequently, the symbol is, and has been, used to motivate great warriors, tribes and nations (including the USA). In a dream image, we may be expressing a need to fly above our temptations and worldly aspirations, to enter instead, into the transfiguration of being. To this end, we need to observe the eagle and the path of its eternal and effortless flight. The flight of the eagle is the flight into paradise. In ancient times, eagles were released when very famous men died (ex. Augustus Ceaser.) This represented their entry into heaven and immortality. (see Albatross) (see Butterfly) (see Claw) (see White) (see Phoenix) (see Tarot, The Star)

EARTH The soil of our birth and the clay of our formal existence, only partially reveal the symbol of mother Earth. The earth beneath our feet and towering above us in mountain ranges represents the entire cradle, running field and closing haven of humanity. In the dream sense we must constantly analyze the earth and our position relative to its living landscape. To this end, we must continually decide whether the earth accepts or rejects our behavior. Does the earth offer a cave's shelter, or a rich field to harvest? Does she rumble in quakes and burn our flesh on her barren fields and uneven rocks? In the image of the planet earth, we find a formidable imagery of our own humanity. The globe is immense, yet fragile, covered in blue (emotional) waters, yet round and centered, like mind and soul. The earth is life suspended in space, vulnerable, and yet prepared for EVERYTHING reality has to offer. (see Landscape) (see Desert) (see Dirt) (see Tarot, The Empress) (see Tarot, The World)

EAT What we Eat (and/or desire to eat) is intimately linked to our choices in life and our general perception of reality. As such, the amount of food, color of the food and how we go about consuming the food (fast, slow, sexually, methodically, reluctantly etc.) reveal certain aspects about our acceptance and tolerance of the world around us. To say that one has a hearty appetite for life, implies that this same individual relishes the flavor and taking in of life. Naturally, WHO we happen to be dining with, is as crucial as how we happen to be dining. The internalization of a social situation, whether pleasant or unpleasant, may be illustrated in this rather heavy handed metaphorical montage of consumption. Moreover, since the mouth is symbolically related to the passage into the human soul, we may need to consider the moral or spiritual value of realities we readily accept! (see Diarrhea) (see Cannibalism) (see Dinner) (see Stomach) (see Regurgitate) (see Table) (see Abundance)

ECLIPSE The meeting of two levels of awareness, one negating the other, may be symbolically expressed in the Eclipse image. The Unconscious may be warning us that we have shut out some person or situation in favor of another, without thinking about the repercussion of our selective behavior. For instance, in the symbolism of the moon covering the sun, we may have blocked reason in the name of passion and exposed ourselves for emotional regret and anguish. We must remember that the sun has not disappeared, it merely lies behind the moon. We must find an agreement and balance of our separate states of awareness and expression. Moreover, we must remember the eclipse is neither the sun, nor the moon. It is instead the union of both, which creates a reality far grander than either one standing alone. Every reality has its opposite nature, and this opposition gives each reality its truest life. In other words, things are understood best in the measure of what they are not. (see Balance) (see Light) (see Tarot, The Moon, The Sun)

ECZEMA Since skin is representative of how we sense the world, experiencing Eczema in a dream, may symbolically reveal a complication in how we sense our emotional or psychological world. Conversely, we may be externally expressing an internal anxiety, concerning how we ourselves are perceived by others. In either case, we may need to look beyond our superficial beliefs and the shallow assumption of others, in order to find the 'sensitive' truth in life, about ourselves, and the society of individuals around us. (see Broken) (see Skin) (see Dry) (see Mask) (see Image)

EDEN   The image of Eden has a dual symbolism of natural beauty and the unnatural 'temptation' to own or consume that beauty. In the dream sense, the Unconscious may be warning us to allow certain objects, places or people, their privacy and individual sanctity. If we seek to 'physically' possess an 'abstract' emotion, such as love, we may be hurting others in ways we can scarcely imagine. Conversely, we may be expressing a personal loss of paradise due to our own foolish, unthinking or greedy behavior. (see Apple) (see Snake) (see Dragon) (see Butterfly) (see Tree)

EGG   The Egg can be symbolic of birth, creative potential or fragile perfection. As such, the egg is an extremely complex dream figure. Accordingly, we need to analyze the size, shape and color of the egg, as well as its position relative to ourselves or other dream characters. Moreover, we need to decide if the egg is in danger of breaking, or if a hatchling is emerging from its glowing shell? For instance, if at the beach, the tide washes in a sole egg and we decide to pick it up and carefully allow it to dry (incubate) in the warm sun, it may just be the expression of an 'idea', which is 'delivered' from our Unconscious, and now needs to be clearly analyzed and brought into life by our own 'dry' reason. (see Seed) (see Ring) (see Circle) (see Womb) (see Nest)

EGO   According to Sigmund Freud, the Ego represents our moral consciousness or 'highest' Self. It is the component of the psyche which keeps social order via personal restraint. As such, the ego is the opposite of the Id, which desires immediate gratification without considering any consequences of its actions. However, in another sense, we may simply be referring to egomaniacal behavior as it appears in our dream landscape. Naturally, this involves self-love taken to a (perhaps) socially unacceptable level, dependent that is, on the relative pretentiousness of the social group in question. In any case, when this behavior is demonstrated in our dream and is not natural in terms of our normal day to day deportment, our Unconscious may be illustrating either one of two things. First, we may be grossly overcompensating for a general lack of self-esteem in our waking experience, or conversely, we may be illustrating a call to be heard and recognized for our unique talent and/or abilities. As such, the dreamer may need to make an honest assessment of their own personal accomplishments and how they relate to his or her own peer group. Our Unconscious may be indicating an imbalance in the inner Self, versus the projected physical reality of our external Self. (see Image) (see Self) (see Mirror) (see Double) (see Demagogue) (see Freud)

EIGHT   Since a box consists of Eight corners, and an octave in western music returns to a 'home' note, we consider eight to represent the completeness of oneself. Moreover, since an octagon is the closest straight-line geometrical equivalent to a circle, in the visual sense, we must consider its representational strength and rotary grace. Appropriately then, in a dream, the number eight refers to psychological balance and a sound foundation in new enterprises and/or vocations. Because of its balance and perfection it is still today, (as in ancient times,) considered to be the strongest of numerical sequences. We observe this in atoms, where the atomic number always 'rests' at an ideal number eight. (see Tarot, Strength) (see Box)

ELECTRIC The force of an Electric current can create or destroy, depending on how it is utilized. In Greek mythology, the supreme god called Zeus used bolts of lightning to vanquish his enemies, or anybody who basically angered him. In Victorian fiction, Mary Shelly placed the power of electricity into the hands of Victor Von Frankenstein, to bring a conglomeration of corpses back to life in the form of one man (if only for a short time). Naturally, in today's world, we have grown quite dependent on the energy of electricity, yet even so, we still fear its potential violence. In this sense, electricity is the modern man's living fire. Taking all this into account, we need to examine the context in which electricity is placed within the dream landscape. Does the electricity merge with the energy of our own central nervous system, aiding our living processes of breathing, sensing and autonomous healing, or does it act as an agent of destruction? If the force is creative, we need to interpret the electric symbolism as potential vitality introduced into our life. If the force is destructive, we may need to be cautious in our waking outlook on certain 'volatile' situations in our own life. Electricity also refers to sudden flashes of insight which change our entire outlook on life, or a subject in particular. (see Tarot, The Tower) (see Lightning)

ELEMENT The Elements refer to the structure and materiality of nature. In this order we find grand diversity blended in an inspired symmetry which defies all human comprehension. Naturally, this unavoidable submission of man to the elements and mother nature which cradles his existence, is paramount in his ongoing perception of reality. He must learn to respect and work with his environment otherwise, the natural elements may cause his swift an unceremonious demise. Accordingly, in the dream sense, when we refer to elements, we may be alluding to a creation of balanced harmony with our outside world of experience, especially in the material sense of a physical planet. In the ancient world, the four elements which ruled temporal existence were respectively: Fire, Air, Earth and Water. Every aspect of each of these four elements were meant to be honored and even worshipped equally and with great humility. For it was understood, then as now, that man is subservient to nature (and/or God) and subsequently must thank HIM (HER) each and every day for HIS (HER) extraordinary gifts which comprise the totality of life. In short, we see in this dream image the 'spirituality' of our 'physical' existence. (see Tarot Major Arcana) (see Magic)

ELEPHANT The Elephant is symbolic of power, single-minded determination and exaggerated memory. As such, yet in an extreme sense, the elephant may represent the blind rage of vengeance, enacted as retaliation for some 'past' insult or injury. However, in a dream, an elephant primarily epitomizes will-power and fierce tenacity. The elephant, despite its size, is rarely a threatening force. The animal is grand in both its stature and its character. Moreover, in their archetypal imagery, the long ivory tusks of the magnificent elephant are symbolic of long-life and sexual vitality. Unfortunately, this latter symbolism has caused man to dwindle their species by destroying thousands of males for their splendid tusks. Man needs to understand that symbols are meant for the heart, mind and soul, not the mantle piece. (see Eden) (see Ivory) (see Horn)

ELEVATOR In the dream sense, an Elevator may represent emotional instability. In an elevator, we are carried up or down to a particular destination. Accordingly, an elevator which descends us deeper and deeper into the bowels of the earth represents being 'locked' in an emotional depression. On the other hand, if an elevator carries us to a 'higher' level, and then opens its doors welcoming us to that level, we may be expressing the exhilaration of a new found relationship, faith or personal transcendence. Taken together, the elevator which travels up and down repeatedly, symbolizes very dramatically, an emotional unsteadiness.

EMACIATE The archetype of an Emaciated person or animal centers around the fear of lacking life's nourishment. However, this 'nourishment' does not merely symbolize food, but the entire spectrum of human needs. In this sense, it is crucial to understand the symbolism of the individual or animal which is emaciated and the nature of the landscape which fails to 'nourish' them. For example, if we spot our children looking frail and sleeping curled up in the chair of our work desk, we may be ignoring their other 'real' needs in our single-minded obsession to earn money for their future.

EMBROIDERY The symbolism of Embroidery involves balance, creativity and social union. We weave together the disparate emotions and beliefs of others in this complex illustration of cohesive humanity. In the dream sense, we may be preparing ourselves for an upcoming event or union where our creativity and community skill may be called upon.

EMPTY The symbol of Emptiness represents a loss of potential. In the dream sense, a person may be expressing a lack of vital 'feelings' in the absence of fluid (emotional or spiritual realities,) in a vessel indicative of a body. However, the feeling of emptiness may be very complex in the psychological sense of its understanding. The human brain is designed to absorb information. It is the job of our awareness and our perception to assimilate the world, piece by piece, until we have a working understanding of what is (and what is not) necessary to survive best in life's arena. As we grow older, these perceptions, or wisdoms, give us a full comprehension of our relative purpose in life. We learn to love, laugh, grow, forgive, forget and cherish, in short, we find and instill the necessary ingredients of our own humanity. This is why we must carefully examine the dream imagery of emptiness to ascertain if this emptiness we feel is short-term (due to some temporal disappointment,) or long term and hence, involved with a slow implosion of our better sensibilities. To this end, we absolutely must determine the exact catalyst of our long term emptiness. What standard aspect of our normal human development was robbed from us, or at least, was perceived as being removed from our experience? Did we take part in this incident. In most cases, we must analyze the memories of our childhood and how we were parented, or raised. Chances are, if our own development is arrested, our parents suffered from a simmilar developmental obstacle. The emptiness dreamscape may give some clue toward the damaging behaviors roots. Society gives very little leeway for ANY abnormal behavior, hence an individual and his or her child is further chastised into a desperate corner. This judgemental attitude hastens the domino effect of destructive behavior. We must allow a certain measure of self-forgiveness, before we can accept the worthiness of our own fulfillment. We must accept our grand purpose in life and our unconditional merit. The Unconscious warns against our feelings of emptiness and instructs us to begin accepting and experiencing life once more. We will always do better. (see Disappear) (see Basin)

ENGRAVE The symbol of Engraving represents permanence. In the dream sense, we may be communicating a desire to make our 'mark' upon the world. This need to 'exist' forever, may stem from a fragile perception of self, a self which seems to fade into the context of a day to day reality. To further understand the engraving symbiology in our dream landscape, we must analyze exactly who's name is carved, or what illustration is chiseled. What are our true feelings abour permanence? Are we fearful of our own position in society? Are we concerned about leaving precious little impact upon the people who surround us in every day life? Is our plan to 'move' and 'effect' people, healthy, for both us AND them? (see Cenotaph) (see Stone)

EPILEPSY The symbolism of the epileptic fit refers to a loss of control. In the dream sense, this physiological limitation primarily indicates psychological confusion in the 'method' of our actions. We may be expressing paralysis in our decision making and/or anxiety in our ability to perform both personally and professionally. We may need to evaluate the energy involved in our debilitating indecisiveness. Our Unconscious may be signalling that our energy level and enthusiasm is too high to swing in alternate and opposite directions. In this, our dream may be illustrating that we aim our potential at one dynamic, yet fixed, goal. We cannot waver in our specific choices. When we fluctuate in our decision making, we allow too much room for self-doubt and hence, create an ever expanding sense of personal chaos and confusion.

EQUATION In a dream sense, an equation may represent the parameters of a waking riddle in life. Primarily, we may be searching for new connections in our interpersonal relationships. On the other hand, we may seek innovative plans geared toward making our life more productive. In any case, the nature of an equation is twofold, either you have a question which searches for an answer OR, you have an answer in search of a question. Accordingly, in a dream interpretation of an Equation symbol, we need to determine, what questions, or puzzles, we have in waking life which need to be answered, or conversely, what answers do we possess which need to be questioned. Do we give the impression of knowing more than we actually do in fact know? A question often posed to psychologists is phased as such, "Is there a clear and underlying reason for my own peculiar behavior?" The dream consciousness primarily answers in the affirmative.

EQUESTRIAN A running and leaping thoroughbred may represent grace, sexuality and natural beauty. As such, how we ride a horse in a dream may be indicative of our own personal self-confidence. For instance, if we fear falling off a horse who gracefully and skillfully leaps from obstacle to obstacle, we may be expressing sexual anxiety and/or difficulty in our relationships. Conversely, a smooth, eloquent ride epitomizes physical assurance in our undivided connection of mind, body and spirit. We need to question why we are on a 'course' at all. Do we have something to prove concerning our own expressions of passion? Exactly who, or what, are we competing with in this particular stage of self-development. (see Centaur)

ERECT The framework of our psychological self is dramatically illustrated in the architecture of an upright structure. The sexual implications of this erected monument cannot be ignored, however, the entire perception of the dreaming persona unquestionably dominates the interpretation of the dream figure itself. For example, in the solid edifice we may find the very qualities, or flaws, which define our personality structure. Another example: if our own personal 'dream' building appears forbidding, shaky and extremely unsafe, we may be illustrating our incapacity to welcome people into our life. In yet another sense, if our building appears to display sharp edges, we may unknowingly in the waking world, appear harsh and tumultuous to the people around us. We are the figure which stands tall and immovable in our dream. We need to determine the specifics of our peculiar 'stance' in the world. Have we closed our ears and eyes to the fluid changes of the worlds real experiences. Why have we stopped movement at all? Has our cessation of movement caused us to slowly crumble, both internally and externally? (see Tarot, The Tower) (see Cenotaph) (see Wall) (see Brick) (see House)

ERUPTION In the dream sense, an Eruption may stand for a harsh revelation of oneself. Moreover, the symbolism of skin or land erupting substrata involves rapid and/or drastic changes in the dreamer's immediate life. The 'rumbling' or 'irritation' of the surface plane may represent a psychological outlook and personal sensitivity scanning the outside world. The burning substance below the surface which 'bursts' through, may represent the hidden and repressed components of our own anger, fear and anxiety. In the dream sense, we may be expressing the sudden discharge of one of these emotions, involving a dire change in our life. This sudden change may have built up gradually over a long period of time. This dream landscape refers to the 'boiling point' of our tolerance and its message may need to be addressed by a professional therapist. (see Eczema) (see Ablaze) (see Drown) (see Epilepsy) (see Dirt) (see Earth)

ESCAPE To Escape in ones dream implies anxiety about a waking situation which refuses to go away. In turn, the dreamer elects to run away from the circumstance. However, problems in waking life, cannot be avoided forever, and sooner or later the dreamer must 'return' to face his or her difficult predicament. In most cases, we make an attempt to escape from ourselves. In which case, we must turn around and face our own reality, as difficult as it may seem. If we dream of a successful escape, we may be reflecting on our own luck in having avoided consequences deserved in waking life. The Unconscious may be daring us to confess our 'evil' doings and setting the stage for personal and social forgiveness. (see Drug) (see Regression) (see Wish-fulfillment) (see Run) (see Chased)

ESP There exists a rather large ongoing record of study focusing on Dream Telepathy which has yielded promising results. The successful percentage for supplanted rational suggestions (in the mind of dreaming individuals,) would suggest the mind in REM has the ability to become highly receptive of metaphysical data in the material framework of its dynamic brain waves (see Alpha & Delta). Whether this synopsis of research supports Carl Jung's theory of the Collective Unconscious or a similar physiological communication (or memory) inherent in DNA information codes, is speculative. Notwithstanding, and in the dream sense, an episode involving ESP, may refer to an intimate connection with another individual. For instance, if in our dream a young person becomes lost in the forest, we may be concerned about the 'natural' curiosities growing within this adolescent and fear for their well-being and overall safety in a chaotic world. We wish to make room for both interpretations of extra sensory perception, or ESP. We realize the brain itself and its various levels of consciousness allow for huge gray areas of comprehension. This would suggest that ESP may in fact exist in all of us, but is not stimulated in the great majority of our species' numbers. Perhaps its normal appearance in our species' peception is dependent on the evolutionary advances we gradually obtain as a society. If the Unconscious and the Collective Unconscious is indicative of God and an infinite universal potential, then ESP is only natural and actually expected. We find a rich history of ESP case studies and personal acounts. Can they all be fabrications? Furthermore, we must ask ourselves why diverse cultures the world over possess similar mythologies and expressions of divine intervention. Why does every culture possess an ideology about paradise, penance and humanities use of one to achieve the other? Why has every culture practiced some form of dream interpretation or at very least, dreaam understanding? Why do we sense each others emotions with such determinate skill? All the questions of mankind's power relates to its 'extraordinary' presense in reality. Why shouldn't a product of infinte creation possess infinite comprehension? ESP is merely another hazy part of the overall human condition. (see Clairvoyance) (see Magic) (see Ritual) (see Bar)

ETERNITY The dream of life Eternal, may involve a witnessing of life in CRITICAL transition, especially the life of others. This may imply that we are either stuck or stolid in our worldly perception. Accordingly, we need to determine our own self-worth and our own reactions and responses to eternity or being eternal. Moreover, is the eternity found on earth, or on some other-worldly or heavenly plane? We must ask ourselves if we find contentment in an eternal plane? If not, our Unconscious may be illustrating that our fixed and unshakable point of view may be alienating us from the fluid and ever changing world around us. Moreover, the safety of our opinion, has left us unscathed by life, but at the same time, unaffected by life's true instruction. We have refused to grow. As such, we must ask ourselves if our fear of honestly facing life has caused us to miss out on life's necessary lessons? In this sense, the lesson of life may only be valid when it involves the experiencing of that life. Conversely, if we find contentment in an eternal plane, we may be alluding to a personal spiritual peace, which we have achieved by the merits and pointed conviction of our own daily life: a life fully experienced and then conclusively transcended. We must address the nature of our own soul and its journey back into the source of its creation and 'ongoing' being. Are we worthy of eternal life? Have we proven our relative necessity in the grand scheme of things? I suggest the reader carefully observe the entire section dedicated to the Tarot and 'spiritual paths' in general. (see Engrave) (see Heaven) (see Tarot Major Arcana: Judgement (20) and The World (21)) (see Butterfly) (see Mouth) (see Sacrifice) (see Christ) (see Buddha)

ETHEREAL The Ethereal body which floats above our sleeping and very physical body symbolizes a 'spiritual' overview on material life. In the philosophical sense, all human qualities are invisible to the naked eye. For instance, our emotions, faith, life-force, even our thought constructs are 'formulated' inside our brain. All these aspects are abstract, immaterial entities, or 'components', which nevertheless, define the very essence of the human machine. Appropriately, the ethereal body may be perceived as the embodiment of our invisible, yet 'highest' gifts. In the dream sense, this spirit body may be 'watching over' our primal, physical selves, a kind of archetypal 'astral guide' to a fully realized life. It must be recalled that our ethereal self is not however, our spiritual self. It does however entail our first and perhaps most crucial path toward spiritual enlightenment, or at very least, supernatural achievement. (see Tarot) (see Element) (see Magic)

EUCHARIST The taking in of a supernatural body has aspects of ancient symbolism concerning personal sacrifice. When we ingest the figurative flesh of a deity, or demigod, we become 'purified' in the name of that holy personage. Therefore, in the dream sense, we may be experiencing a deep 'taking in' of spiritual wisdom and a dismissal of our own sins, through penance. We are cleaning the moral slate. However, in the truest sense, we are absorbing ourself in this figure of the euchariat and hence, ingesting, or accepting, the humility of our own fragile humanity. This implies the transfiguration of self into a force HIGHER and greater in meaning than the individual himself. In this, we may be witnessing a connection with the

EXCREMENT   71

union of altruistic love, (as well as yet another advancing stage in our own spiritual development.) We are accepting God (or a Spiritual Center) into our personal life. (see Ethereal) (see Cannibalism) (see Mouth) (see Eat) (see Christ) (see Sacrifice) (see Adam and Eve) (see Bread)

EUNUCH   In the dream sense, a Eunuch represents a lack of drive, sexual, or otherwise. He is the embodiment of false contentment. We may be expressing in this dream symbol a rather complex form of sexual alienation as well as disaffection with life. Accordingly, we need to analyze the behavior of the eunuch and understand fully in which way (if at all) he seems to resemble ourselves. Have we grown fat and lazy in life? What force has erased our drive and are we submissive to this force? Is the eunuch free of emotions, or is he the victim of emotions? (see Emaciate) (see Cut)

EVERGREEN   The primary symbolism of the Evergreen is everlasting life. The strong scent and hard resilience of pine needles echo this revitalizing nature. A pine tree is beautiful and robust all year around. In dreams, evergreens may represent our highest human potential in ALL of life's endeavors. When we 'push' ourselves and strive for our greatest possible performance, we may dream of sprinting up an immense mountainside, opulent with tall and thick evergreens. It is said the pine needles of an evergreen are extremely magical and may have several medicinal purposes. We find a great strength in these tiny needles. As such, the tree also represents power in numbers and all forms of social union. A christmas tree is covered with glitter, surrounded by gifts and topped with a shining star. This christmas pine tree represents the gift of life, the joy of life and the ultimate transfiguration of life. The trees straight moral character and appreciation of life is undeniable. Are we dependent on the tree? Do we lean on its sturdy trunk? Are we cutting down the majestic tree ? Our relation with the tree represents our 'relative' feelings about love, strength and spirituality. (see Tree) (see Adam and Eve) (see Green)

EXCAVATE   To remove something (or someone) from the earth itself, implies revealing a hidden aspect of oneself. Since the earth is symbolic of mother and womb, we may be referring to a deeply repressed instinct which became buried from the symbolic light of day. As such, we may have planted some deep seed of conscious awareness into our Unconscious and now we are preparing to finally face up to its TRUTH. Aspects of self-revelation are often treasures in disguise. (see Dig) (see Earth) (see Seed)

EXCREMENT   The waste we leave behind is primarily linked to situations which we desire to see removed from our living experience. However, given the recycling and regenerative nature of Excrement, we may be alluding to a transition and reworking of a particular situation, perhaps even, a relationship. Perhaps we are now disgusted by something, or someone, which we were once attracted. May involve a 'seed' of personal change. This change is linked with the ancient concept of 'good luck'. (see Feces) (see Seed) (see Dirt)

EXPLOSION In the dream sense, an Explosion rather dramatically represents a fear of personal destruction or painful disruptive changes in ones life. The key element to this dream imagery is sudden and unexpected 'jolts' in ones fragile construct of reality. For example, should a ten year old boy visualize himself walking through a mine field in his school's auditorium, he may be expressing anxiety pertaining to how his classmates will discern his actions or ability in gym class. Other important elements of this dream figure involve surprise and an unseen threat. We are displaying a complex form of fear and perhaps even paranoia. We cannot allow ourselves to go through life fearing the next 'explosion'.

EXTRATERRESTRIAL The aboriginal people of Australia believe that Extraterrestrials once came to earth in the 'Dreamtime' and transformed themselves into all 'life' on the planet as we know it. Moreover, the aborigines maintain that 'one day' the Dreamtime will return and the extraterrestrials will mutate into new and reanimated life forms which will remarkably complete their dream cycle and return into the heavens. Appropriately, in the dream sense, the ET or alien archetype refers to help from an 'outside' force, in the aboriginal case, hope for mankind, in our case, hope for ourselves. In this sense, to dream of being captured and analyzed by aliens may strongly represent a personal need to be heard and understood. As such, the aliens may illustrate a 'wiser' social power whom 'recognize' our true worth and incomparable ability. In this world of diminishing spiritual faith, aliens have become our new figurative angels and saviors. (see Angel) (see Foreigner) (see Stranger)

EXTROVERT In our dreams, we sometime illustrate personal 'masquerades' which display wish-fulfillment by revealing our passionate sense of personal expression. In this sense, a dreamer must examine his or her own 'feelings' about personal Extroverted behavior which appears in his or her dreams. Conversely, and rather hypocritically, if an 'associate' or 'family member' emerges overly 'outgoing' in a dream landscape, our Unconscious may be depicting particular apprehension, concerning aberrations in that particular individual's recent behavior. In other words, what's good for the goose is not (in this case,) good for the gander. We can express our own (usually subdued) fantasies in dreams, but others seem to be revealing a personal problem if they do the same. Why do we perceive other people in society as being more 'normal' or 'together' than ourselves? Is this why THEY must remain rigid, while we can go 'all out' and loose our behavioral mind? Does society reflect our own sense of sanity? What happens when society goes crazy? (see Aboriginal) (see Ape) (see especially Demigogue)

EYES In the dream sense, Eyes symbolize being observed or analyzed and causing insecurity or fear. Consequently, they lose the humanity of the 'head' in which they function. As such, they become simple and focused embodiments of our paranoia. We may need to 'stare down' our Unconscious and perhaps volatile eye, to bring back the predominance of our own clear mind and faithful spirit. As such, we must question whether we can believe everything we see? In another avenue of interpretation, since eyes reveal a great deal about our emotions, what do the dream eyes tell us about our mood or the moods of others? Are the eyes red and tearing or are they small, crinkled and amused? Are we gazing at some aspect of ourselves? Eyes in a dream may represent the Unconscious vision itself, or the survey of God. (see Image) (see Mirror) (see Round) (see Ring) (see Glass)

F

FABLE A Fable is a story with an underlying philosophical or moral message. This singular message is conveyed through the art of analogy. The analogy in turn is enacted by fantastic characters which represent our separate choices or unique states of mind. A main character moves step by step through a 'gallery' of such characters and experiences, each of which demonstrate a diverse aspect of himself. As the main character experiences these successive stages of self-awareness he learns more and more about himself and generally gains a deeper philosophical outlook on life. Given that most fables begin with the words "Once upon a time...", they are primarily constructed as a 'narrative'. As such, a narrating, or 'all knowing', voice describes the significant adventure of our own main character. Interestingly, this narrative voice seems to signify our own highest consciousness. We are in essence 'remembering' or 'relating' this tale in order to instill its meaning deeper into the fabric of our own understanding. This is why every aspect of the fable illustrates a unique shade of our own consciousness. The fable is attempting to bring order and priority into our active conscious awareness and decision making. The fable's construction embodies a moral lesson taught by the hardships of human experience. The adventure of the fable parallels a spiritual journey of personal enlightenment. Since the Unconscious utilizes dreams to uncover personal revelations, the fable within the dream seems to represent a crucial and decisive turn in our own personal outlook on life. Perhaps we are questioning our entire belief system, or some aspect of our normal behavior, or certain rules of organized society. The fable signifies our initial learning. We are looking deep into the memory of our own self-developmetnt. Can we find these answers with ourself? A predominant number of therapists believe we not only can, but absolutely should! (see Landscape) (see Colors)

FABRIC In a dream sense, we must analyze the color and respective 'feel' of Fabrics upon our skin. For example, wool may represent warmth or hot irritation, while silk consistently symbolizes cool, comfortable sensuality. On the other end of the spectrum, polyester garments mark artificial environments and constricting personal experience. In other words, dream fabric represents emotional moods and our ability to remove them from our immediate experience. (see Image) (see Drapes)

FACTORY The image of a pollution-creating, pitiless fortress which 'constructs' thousands of identical products on an essentially dehumanizing assembly line, may certainly be representative of a modern world, a world separated from nature and the true nature of creative man. In the dream sense, the factory represents personal alienation from our 'connectedness' with our spirit, (offset by greed,) our neighbors, (offset by competition and contempt,) and the land beneath our feet, (offset by contamination.) On the other hand, the factory dream vision, may be a warning us about poor health conditions in our own immediate environment, (including our homes,) which may need to be 'cleaned up' and made sanitary immediately. (see Form) (see House)

FAN The endless rotation of a fan on a hot, sweltering day, refers to repetitive thoughts and actions which lead us nowhere. The fan simply blows hot air all around. It cannot cool the heat and therefore, it only seems to add to the heat's irritating quality. When we find ourselves rolling a thought, or memory, over and over in our minds we are refusing to 'let go' of that memory. As such, we are interfering with times ability to heal the memories devastating wound. We must not get caught up in the paralysis of our emotional disturbance. We must endure our emotional heat until our body is ready to cool itself down. We must go through our hottest fever, before we can be finally healed. If given the chance, our body will eventually build up its own best defence. There is no point in fooling ourselves. Miracles ONLY happen to those who help themselves. (see Fever)

FAITH A conscious contemplation of Faith deeply involves the interrelationship between human belief and human inertia. Does our belief in divine intervention cause us to stand back and do nothing at all in dire situations? Will we let a loved one die because we believe God's will defies the advances of modern medicine? Must there be a separation between God's will and man's will, or does God help those who help themselves? When we explore faith in a dream setting, we must ascertain the psychological causes and consequences of our belief system. A spiritual journey involves the deep, physical labors encountered in profound experiences. These experiences are ONLY THEN transfigured into a personal and spiritual sacrifice of self. But we must remember, the spirit finds its focus in the active and material (that is to say, physical) body. In short, we must go through hell, before we can get to heaven. Is our faith denying a profound trust in self? Are we afraid of failure? On every level, we must learn to find a working balance between our faith in God (spiritual center) and our faith in ourselves. Blind faith only concerns the invisible. The visible world must be handled on a daily basis with wisdom and reason. (see Tarot) (see Ritual) (see Christ) (see Heaven)

FALLING When our emotional or psychological balance is thrown off, because of recent and drastic changes in our life, we may experience a falling away from 'ourselves', into an unknown and therefore, terrifying condition. However, the pivotal objective of these dreams seems to emerge in their present application, or performance. In other words, we have not fallen, yet we are in the act of falling.

The implication being that we are at the crossroads, betwixt regaining our balance, or falling flat on our face. Therefore, in a dream, our Unconscious may be offering us a symbolic support beam. (If we are wise enough to understand its meaning!) Hence, in clarifying our waking emotional dilemma, in the model of an accurate dream explication, we may be prevented from falling unnecessarily. To help us make this decision we must analyze in what place are we falling, what causes us to fall and what will happen to us if we do in fact fall. Does our falling represent some form of personal failure? Are we moving too fast? Are carrying too heavy of a load? Are we attempting to perform too many tasks at the same time? All of these symbolic references may pertain to our own particular condition. Hence, we must observe our fall in slow motion, frame by frame, until we are able to deliberate EXACTLY what fctor in our waking life has thrown us completely off kilter. (see Balance) (see Juggle) (see Blood)

FAMILY Our Family represents our closest ties and 'immediate' social safety net. As such, we carry a responsibility to guide and protect this group as well as gaining support and protection from within its gregarious confines. This social safety net loosely represents our own sanity in its configuration of family sanctity. Is this sanctity disturbed by some outside force? Appropriately then, in dreams, any small group which we 'feel' an instinctive need to protect, may be representative of our not just our family, but also our self. Therefore, we need to analyze in our dream environment, the needs of this small collection of people (or animals,) and conversely, any personal message or warning they may collectively (or individually) convey to our dreaming consciousness. We must determine what they are lacking and otherwise asceertain how we can increase their potential for growth. In short, we must allow for our own self-growth to best assist those around us. If we find that we ourselves have become young children again (in an ancient familial setting,) we may be expressing some form of regression or elaborate wish-fulfillment. Are the responsibilities of adult life beginning to get to us? (see Table) (see Child) (see Baby) (see House)

FARM A Farm represents health, harvest and the honest work necessary to successfully achieve them both. Naturally then, any aberrations in this symbolism, for instance, barren fields, sick livestock, or sluggish farm hands, may represent a cessation in personal growth, health and individual ambition. Along these lines, we need to analyze all the 'effecting' factors and characters in the farm landscape to interpret the impetus for our waking regression and degeneration. (see Seed) (see Earth) (see Tree) (see Water) (see Cow) (see Corn)

FAT The symbolic imagery of obesity varies from jovial or 'jolly' old souls, to high-powered, cigar smoking bosses of industry. The similarity in both examples is centered around 'excessive' behavior. The reality of obesity is much more complex and involves in many cases, physiological and social imbalances, which have little (if any) to do with the choices or behavior of the individuals themselves. Nevertheless, and unfortunately, in the symbolic sense, 'overweight' persons are thought of as weak willed, obsessive or lethargic. Hence in the dream sense, viewing oneself as extremely corpulent, may involve feelings of guilt about excessive, self-fulfilling behavior. In the sexual sense, viewing ourselves as obese may imply a repression of our own eroticism and desire. As such, we may be placing a layer of cellulite around ourselves to protect us from the difficulties of courting, romance and relationships in general. (see Table) (see Emaciate) (see Eat) (see Abundance)

FATHER In many ways, a Father represents the masculine and authoritative natures within ourselves. Appropriately, how we view the behavior of the father figure in a dream, may be reflective of personal feelings about our own 'recent' behavior effecting the society of individuals around us. This is especially true of persons believed to be subordinate to us, for instance children, employees or service laborers. Are we a guiding force, or do we exercise power and unjust punishment upon those below us? (see Authority Figure) (see Demagogue) (see Fraternity) (see Bar) (see Sibling)

FATIGUE In the dream sense, Fatigue may represent emotional or psychological exhaustion. As such, our Unconscious may be illustrating a necessary surrender concerning a difficult personal situation. We may need to stand a few steps back from the living experience of our emotional or psychological realities. We need to do this (simply) in order to readjust ourselves to their complex intricacies. If we refuse to rest, our judgement will be clouded and disorientated. We need to observe the 'big picture' and hence, establish the real consequences of our relativistic behavior. (see Sleep) (see Falling)

FEAST Primarily, Feasting involves a joyous absorption of life. In this, we see a fulfillment of our waking experience, both physical and spiritual. However, a primal factor of hunger and the reality of the food as a life force, may also be implied. In other words, the feast image in our dream may involve the conclusion of any survivalist behavior. As such, the feast may involve sexuality or relationships in general which have flourished before us because of our own personal actions and behavior. Accordingly, we are celebrating not only ourselves but our connection with society on the whole, which enables our real fulfilment of joy and moral abundance. (see Eat) (see Celebration) (see Table) (see Fat) (see Emaciate) (see Abundance)

FEATHER Because of its 'lighter than air', fragile beauty, the archetype of the Feather indicates wisdom, freedom and peace. As opposed to the collection of feathers which make up a bird's wings and aids in flight, the single feather 'floats' up 'spirit-like' into the breeze, and remains airborne in the perfection of its developed form. This is why we write down our 'wisdom' with a quill, and why a 'feather in ones cap' is observed as a credit for a great and nearly divine achievement. In the Egyptian Book of the Dead, a deceased man's heart, or Ba, was weighed against a feather, which the ancients represented as divine love. This comparative measurement determined whether or not that particular individual was worthy of eternity. If the person's heart was (unfortunately) weighed down by the immoral nature of his worldly character and behavior, the feather would deny his entrance into the infinite realm of the afterlife. In Native American tribes, such as the Shawnee and the Cherokee Nations, feathers were worn by warriors to represent the strength and swift flight of their spirit guides. The force of a warrior was only as powerful as his wisdom and spiritual devotion to his guide. (see Tarot Major Arcana: The World (21) arcana.) (see Flying) (see Eagle)

FECES In a dream, Feces may represent the purging of unwanted feelings or situations intruding in ones life. For example, we may be experiencing regret or guilt pertaining to our pugnacious
behavior toward someone once close to us. Alternatively, we may feel violated by a person who refuses to keep his or her distance. In our dream, we may be symbolically removing this person from our immediate lives. Is the experience of this removal healthy, or unhealthy? (see Excrement) (see Dirt) (see Earth) (see Stomach) (see Vomit)

FERRY BOAT In the dream sense, a Ferry boat symbolizes a slow emotional transition toward a new 'state' of being. Moreover, in medieval Europe, and further back into ancient Egypt, it was believed that a 'ferryman' paddled individuals from the death plain, into the netherworld. Taking all this into account, we may interpret a ferry boat journey, as a voyage with poignant consequences and deep meaning in our waking lives. The relative roughness (or tranquility) of the 'river crossed' may need to be analyzed for this dream's complete interpretation. However, Because a ferry boat follows a similar path over and over again, we may, on the other hand, be expressing an emotional rut which may need to be altered, at least slightly. (see Boat) (see Ocean) (see Float)

FETAL POSITION To find oneself in the Fetal position, reminiscent of womb warmth, safety and nurturing, may dramatically symbolize hiding within oneself. We may be expressing an emotional or psychological regression into a dark and silent past where ALL of our needs were provided for. In the dream sense, we may be expressing difficulty in our 'adult' roles replete with the complex anxieties of personal and/or family responsibilities. (see Womb) (see Baby) (see Family)

FETISH A precious Fetish (hope) which is clutched in a person's hand, may be representative of harnessing ones own strength and personal 'magic'. Moreover, we empower ourselves via the 'force' of this image or idol held in our hand, or placed under our pillow at night. Therefore, in the dream imagery, the possession of a fetish represents deep faith in our ability to succeed when 'set' under the guiding light of our loyal spirit familiars. Accordingly, we need to analyze where the fetish is found (or positioned) and determine how the symbolism of that particular fetish offsets our waking psyche and ANY personal dilemma which we may be working through. (see Magic) (see Faith) (see Image)

FEVER The body temperature which is raised in the heat of Fever, may symbolize a complex mixture of passion, aggression and fear. Appropriately in a dream, our Unconscious may be revealing a physiological change effected by a hot emotional situation which needs to be immediately resolved. To further interpret this symbolism, we need to analyze all physical changes represented in the body. Furthermore, we must study the separate meaning of these respective body parts relative to passion, aggression and perhaps, internal anxieties. (see Ablaze) (see Body)

FILM Some of the best selling points behind photography and video tapes in general, have always revolved around the concept of 'capturing' life's joy. Conversely, many primitive people feared photography, believing that images captured were the parallel of souls stolen, or 'possessed', in our own 'modern' terminology. In both cases, the key is a detailed attempt at 'capturing' and holding 'life' as we know it. This very well may represent the starting point of Film symbolism in the dreaming sense. Since dreams can recreate individuals or places 'at will', one needs to question why 'pictures' or 'reproductions' of characters (or places,) are displayed by our Unconscious at all. The answer may lie in the imagery of a 'missing person' photo, and our frozen memory of that particular person. Our Unconscious, like a private investigator, seems to say, where is this person (or place) and why is he or she no longer involved in our own active relations? Moreover, have we done anything to harm or push away this person? These are questions which must be addressed in order to interpret these unique dream revelations. We must also determine whether the film is faded, or conversely, sharp and crisp, in other words, brand new. This will help us determine whether we are examining an old memory or a recent development. (see Fable)

FINGERS Equipped with opposable thumbs, our human hands manipulate our immediate environment like no other creature on earth can. Our Fingers coordinate to perform complex operations and intricate (even astounding) procedures which, by and large, we take for granted. Therefore, when these fingers appear in dreams, we need to examine their message which may involve our greatest human potential or simply our multifarious sexuality. For instance, should our fingers appear injured and immovable, our Unconscious may be illustrating an anxiety involving our ability to function or execute demanding tasks in our professional, or personal, arena of waking experiences. Conversely, a hand which incessantly runs fingers over curved and smooth (or silky) surfaces, may be communicating a desire for sexual contact and erotic wish-fulfillment. We must determine EXACTLY why are our fingers are doing the walking? Why are we pointing toward a particular person? What is this persons relation to us? (see Hand) (see Tarot, The Wheel of Fortune)

FIRE In each case of intense emotion, we seem to find a reference concerning Fire. In another sense, fire may refer to highest civilization in the form of protection from a cold, wild and decidedly inhuman, landscape. Capturing and utilizing this fire demonstrates power over our own fears and subsequently opens a door to our own creative potential. In a rather peculiar, yet poetic twist, much of the creative invention which hones our modern existence was forged by fire itself: (laser, electric etc.) Hence we see a combination of our deepest emotions and most potent creative faculties. Figuratively, both our heart and our mind can burn and their unique fire can either create or destroy our complete sense of Self. (see Ablaze) (see Hot) (see Dry) (see House) (see Lightning) (see Candle) (see Tarot, The Tower)

FISH Fish swim in lakes, rivers and oceans, each of which is symbolic of separate states of emotion. Accordingly, we need to analyze where a fish swims, its color, species and behavior, in order to properly determine its significance within our emotional paradigm. For instance, if a school of hungry shark(s) swim in a river under a narrow bridge which we happen to be crossing, we may be depicting an intense fear concerning a present relationship AND the course of action necessary to change this painful relationships more dangerous or harmful aspects. On the other hand, if a school of Angel fish appear in our in-ground swimming pool and circle our bodies, we may be illustrating a new emotional or spiritual love in our active waking life. In a strict literary sense, a fish may also represent our ideas and memories which swim, dive and surface in the universe of our Unconscious. (see Dolphin) (see Shark)

FIST A Fist represents violent power and straight-forward aggression. When we make a fist we are saying we are prepared to fight for our cause. However, are we prepared to be 'beaten' for our cause? Are we prepared to hurt innocent people caught in the 'crossfire' of our cause? Moreover, have we determined EXACTLY who is our enemy, and EXACTLY in which direction we are shaking our fist? Is our violence in self-defence? If so, does our violence end violence? If not, can we open our fists and turn them into hand-shakes? Can compromise bring us nearer to our goal? (see Fingers) (see Hand)

FIT In our dream, when something Fits well, we generally imply a feeling of unity and cohesiveness with certain aspects of our reality. On the other hand, if another person's things (clothing, car etc.) seem to fit us well, we may be referring to a desire to become like that person. In this case, we usually desire opposite attributes, or possessions, from those we call our own. However, our Unconscious may be telling us, we can never know a man or woman's perceived reality, until we have walked a mile in his or her shoes. Good fit or not, we may be in for a few unexpected revelations. Everyone suffers in life, in one way or another. Furthermore, appearances can be very deceiving! (see Fabric) (see Clothes) (see Image) (see Choke)

FIT The Fit primarily involves indecisiveness and the frustrated reality of behaving in two or more worlds. Moreover, in a symbolic sense we witness the energy which the body transports fluidly and with great symmetry throughout the body from brain to spine, suddenly finding reason to impede or cut off from normal patterns of regulation. As such, we may need to examine the relationship between mind and body in the waking experience of the dreamer. Our thoughts in certain situations may seem entirely removed from our behavior. If so, why. In the fit imagery, we have many deep and probing questions to ask ourselves. However, the presence of the dream itself, may illustrate a healthy key toward regaining our balanced individuality. (see Epilepsy)

FIVE In the Tarot deck, and in folklore 'magic' in general, the number Five is symbolic of 'man' equipped with two arms, two legs and a head. Notwithstanding, a pentagram is often thought of as a Satanic symbol, while its actual representation is of 'man', (the five-sided star), inside the infinity of being, (the circle). Another example of this ancient archetype is the Pentagon in Washington DC, representational of the power and order-keeping ability of man. Taking all this into account, the number five appearing in a dream may refer to 'marks' and directives meant specifically for the dreamer's waking awareness and strength. How will ones character and soul carry them further in life? (see Tarot, The Hierophant and The Wheel of Fortune) (see Hand)

FLAG A Flag is symbolic of a nation or social movement. Therefore, a flag may represent an action taken for what we believe is the 'greater good' of the 'people'. As such, a flag is a powerful symbol of unity and order. It embodies the axis which a nation (or society) radiates out from. In our dream, our Unconscious may be calling us to action, or warning us about our demagogue-like social behavior. We may need to analyze whether we 'lead' or 'follow' our social group and whether we believe in the motivations and goals of our assembly. Will we abuse our power? (see Father) (see Fist) (see Color) (see Demagogue)

FLOAT When we obtain the inner-faith of self-confidence and its accompanying psychological quiet, we may 'experience' a temporary freedom from the weight of life's problems. In this peaceful state of mind, we may encounter the ability to Float in the heavens, at one with our 'higher' qualities of spirit, love and elation. Comparatively, if we float on a tranquil sea, our Unconscious may be signifying a profound 'emotional calm'. However, if we perceive our sea becoming stormy and our body floating too far away from land, we may be depicting anxiety and panic over our good sensations coming to an end, as we realize we've moved too far into the unknown and immeasurable depths of our own psyche. (see Boat) (see Dive) (see Dolphin) (see Fish)

FLOWER Flowers symbolize the highest, yet most fragile, human receptions of love, union and a peaceful death, or afterlife. As such, we need to interpret the color, type and number (bouquet?) of flowers observed in the dream, and our specific and detailed 'feelings' about their presence. Are the flowers wild? Who might the flowers, or flower, represent? (see Daisy, Rose, Wreath) (see Dirt) (see Earth) (see Womb) (see Seed) (see Butterfly)

FLY As opposed to floating, Flying represents psychological and emotional power, direction and control. In a dream sense, if we are able to 'steer' ourselves through our dream horizon and landscape, we are indicating successful management over the actions we take in waking life. On the other hand, if we are flying out of control, our Unconscious may be warning us that we have gained too much force and upward momentum too quickly. In a myriad of ways we may not be ready to 'fly' over life's obstacles. We may in fact be in for a crash landing. We need to determine what event has caused us to fly, where we are flying, what force interferes with our flying, (if any,) and if we possess the skill and self-determination to land safely. (see Mountain) (see Sky) (see Bird) (see Tarot, The Star) (see Feather) (see Butterfly)

FLY (insect) The Fly has many connections with demonic or immoral fears. In fact, the name Beelzebub literally means Lord of the flies. The reason for this allusion to evil forces involves the living condition and behavior of the tiny and relatively harmless bug. The fly is annoying, persistent, resilient, fast and its young are brought forth from putrescence. As such, our dream implies that our irritating and persistent condition of reality, may involve the passivity of our own actions. Perhaps we sit with our guilt when the moral aspect of our psyche feels we should be undoing our wrongs and purifying our reality. Moreover, we may be envisioning a hot and sweltering place, which may allude to a torrid situation involving iniquitous and perhaps even, profane behavior. (see Unclean) (see Devil) (see Tarot, The Devil) (see Dirt)

FOG In the dream sense, a Fog may represent a fear of the unknown. Furthermore, it may symbolize a difficulty in understanding the exact boundaries and/or 'heading', or direction, of a particular waking situation. We need to analyze therefore, why we harbor such personal fear and uncertainty, regarding certain conditions or circumstances in our life. Moreover, we need to interpret any and all objects which literally appear in our field of vision, in spite of the dense fog. These objects, or characters, may represent agents of 'clarity' which may in fact, throw light upon our (perhaps irrational) foreboding. (see Sun) (see Light) (see Eyes) (see Blind)

FOREIGNER The complex image of a Foreigner includes exotic behavior, far away lands (themselves symbolic of promise), and a strange new experience. Nevertheless, while we are inevitably 'drawn' toward the unknown, we also may fear its actuality. Appropriately, we need to interpret our exact emotions 'felt' upon meeting this particular character in our dream landscape. Yet another way of comprehending this dream figure regards the dreamer himself. The foreigner may be a representation of changes found in ourselves. We may be indicating that we are no longer recognizable to our friends, our family, even to ourselves. The latter example may necessitate some form of professional counciling, unless we are absolutely and unequivocally certain why we appear 'foreign' to our own natures. For example, if we formulate changes in our life which are unique to us, solely to appease our loved ones, we may experience ambiguity and strangeness in our normal self-perception. (see Abroad) (see Image)

FOREST   The archetype of the Forest resides deep in our species memory. The symbolism of the landscape 'rich' with utterly wild plant and animal life-forms beckons to our immeasurable Unconscious conceptualizations upon fear, aggression, desire and (spirit) magic. In fact, the mythological journey into the forest has often represented the sacred and often necessary trip into our deepest selves. We realize in this archetype a rather balanced perception of personal light and darkness, good and evil. The successful journey through the forest primarily involves a total acceptance of the primal itself, in other words, a surrender of human control. Accordingly, in the dream sense, we are welcomed into the Unconscious when we leave our 'static' view of the world behind us: far back in the light of day and ordinary waking consciousness. We are in essense returning to our innocent and naturalistic behavior. We have lost the calculating skill of our species and we exist instead in a moment by moment deliberation of hard reality. The trip through the forest reveals the magic of our warrior selves, our spiritual selves, and our soulful selves. We cannot conquer the forest, we can only become one with its all-encompassing life-force. This figure involves our deepest instincts. (see Tree) (see Shadow) (see Wild) (see Aboriginal) (see Ape) (see Adam & Eve)

FORESIGHT   There is a great ongoing debate between neurologists, philosophers, psychologists, metaphysicists and almost anyone else you can think of, about the true nature of time and our relative perception of it. To grossly oversimplify the matter, time may be looked at as linear, or arrow-like, leaving a past behind, and heading straight ahead into an uncertain future. Conversely, it can be perceived as a circular or spiral matrix which overlaps itself, and in doing so, creates a continuum of space and time which may be 'theoretically' criss-crossed. In another conceptual sense, theories involving the Collective Unconscious demonstrate an infinite web of knowledge, which each living being possesses and programs into personal and evolutionary existence. Naturally, this theoretical construct involves an infinite substance which is thought to transcend any and all limitations and restrictions which time may set upon us. Therefore, taking all this into account, we may NOT want to dismiss a dream involving Foresight in which a loved one is injured simply because it may be a projection of our own worries. In no way is this dream out of the realm of physical and metaphysical possibility. Hence, the dreamer should not feel stupid in making all the appropriate calls which provide some measure of reassurance. (see Clairvoyant) (see Time) (see Collective Unconscious) (see Jung)

FORGE   The symbolism of Forging creations with mallet and fire, may be representative of 'shaping' ones future with the fortitude of passion. While this masculine imagery may seem healthy and vital, the reality may be a bit more complex. For example, a condition of intense emotion, as in a loving relationship, may revolve around a 'giving up' of oneself. Consequently, personal strength may be necessary to surrender the guard around oneself. However, anger and aggression, which seeks to break down a person's barriers before they are ready to be broken (if at all), may be extremely dangerous for both parties, and should be avoided at all cost. As such, we need to analyze the nature of the creation which we forge into shape with all our 'hot pounding'. In this sense, we need to 'see' if the forger completes his or her creation and then cools its red- hot metal in water, or simply and endlessly pounds the shapeless object throughout the duration of the dream into an unrecognizable blob of personal anguish. Accordingly, we need to interpret the metal sculpture forged and its 'effect' upon our emotional perception in waking life. Is the forged metal useful to us in some obvious way? Conversely, are we creating armour to protect us from a fearful reality? If so, which body part do we 'protect' with our newly forged armour? (see Fire) (see Ablaze) (see Form) (see Hand) (see Hammer) (see Body)

FORM Disparate Forms possess extremely different and diverse meanings. For example, a circle may represent infinity, God, and the universe, while a square represents a person's body and four-cornered psychological approach on reality in general. Two shapes in juxtaposition may represent conflict or an engagement into unification, while parallel lines infinitely mirror, yet never fuse together in affiliation. The particular assignment of joining worlds belongs to the archetype of the cross, or intersecting lines, which carry the responsibility of psychological, emotional and spiritual balance and unity. (see Circle)

FORM, PAPER When we are forced to 'list' personal information on a form, we may be expressing concern, or anxiety, about how we are being perceived, or accepted, by society. A form reveals our age, sex, race, financial status and personal skills. This stark revelation of self removes our real humanity and reduces us to our physical attributes and concurrent achievements. The strength of our character, our moral righteousness and even our innovative potential, is entirely overlooked in this dream representation. We are judged by our appearance and performance like a common consumer product, for instance: a car, boat or household appliance! We find ourselves with a number and a file. We are neatly 'packaged' into a social order. If we find ourselves covered, or buried, in such forms, we are expressing another aspect of 'dehumanization'. We are being forced to sift through a 'catalog' of human beings, or human actions, without REALLY knowing the individuals behind these actions. This procedure reduces us to robotic judges of human character. All in all the figure combines feelings of personal guilt and contempt for a 'soulless' system. We must determine whether our own behavior parallels this seemingly inhuman behavior. If so, why have we allowed the pressures of society to alter our own conscientious decisions? On the other side of the coin, if we ourselves are victimized by this inhuman behavior, we must determine ways to battle back. We must figure out ways to expose our more valuable characteristics to an interactive society which includes our friends, family and peers. We may need to take a long, hard look at ourselves to determine whether or not our better qualities are hidden from others due to our own fears and petty distrust.

FOUNDATION   The Foundation upon which we create and build, clearly symbolizes our psychological and physiological strength, poise, and creative potential. If our foundation is solid, well thought out, and resistant to destructive outside forces, we may be prepared to erect a poignant edifice reflective and thankful of our place in the cosmos. We have faith in our position and purpose in the society of our fellow human beings. On the other hand, a shaky foundation represents anxiety concerning our ability to grow, either psychologically, or, emotionally. We need to interpret why a particular dream foundation is not too sturdy and look for ways to improve the buttresses, columns, supports and entire substructure. To do so, we must find balance within our own psyche. In the location of the dream structure itself we will find clues to our unstable 'conditions' in life. Where can we find support? Conversely, why do we allow some outside force to shake us up in the first place? Has our childhood effected our position in the world today? How so? (see Balance) (see House) (see Earth) (see Seed) (see Child) (see Womb)

FOUNTAIN   A Fountain equipped with high spraying jets of water and brightly colored lights is symbolic of emotional joy and elation. In a dream sense, a fountain may represent a deep and entirely unrestrained outpouring of sensitivity involving a new relationship in waking life. Conversely, if the fountain runs dry, we may be experiencing the intense sadness of 'coming down' from the delicate euphoria and exhilaration found in a full and passionate relationship. In another sense, a fountain is often representative of the gushing, internal human soul. In this imagery, we fruitfully combine the separate interpretations of light and water to signify a swelling metaphoric enlightenment. (see Water) (see Baptism) (see Float) (see Light) (see Color)

FOUR   The number Four symbolizes the balance and entirety of being, including the compass points: north, south, east and west and the ancient elements: air, earth, fire and water. Furthermore, all intersections of perfect balance create four perfect and all-encompassing segments of reality. In the dream sense, the number four symbolizes the finite parameters of the material world and our psychological place within that world. (see Square) (see Tarot Major Arcana: The Emperor (4) arcana) (see Magic) (see Elements) (see Table)

FOWL   A Fowl is a bird which cackles, lays eggs and leaves the serious flying to other birds. As such, it is a bird attached to mother earth. Symbolically, a Fowl is sole representative of the maternal wisdom of reproduction. Accordingly, in a dream sense, viewing ourselves with chickens may imply wish-fulfillment concerning the bearing of children. On the other hand, we may be depicting ourselves as cacophonous hens in order to reveal guilt over spreading rumors, or simply gossiping too much. Perhaps we are overly concerned with the physical world and as such, we are missing out on the real joy of spirituality and an infinite number of our own intellectual flights of fancy. (see Tarot, The Devil)

FRATERNITY   In colleges and universities, we find Fraternal Orders which court students to become life-time members of their particular organizations. These fraternal orders represent a support group which the individual can turn to at any point in his life, even far beyond the 'college years'. However, these orders only accept applicants, or 'pledges', if they can withstand the difficult and harrowing process of 'initiation'. This 'initiation' is designed to test ones strength, character, determination and loyalty. The 'hazing' involved in this process can run the gamut from psychological humiliation to outright physical torture. The permanent memory of the crueler aspects of this hazing seems to fuel a self-perpetuating system of aggressive and violent behavior. The initiate bears through his own torture in single anticipation of unleashing his own brand of sadistic violence upon the next initiate down the line. This endless system of imposed power (sometimes!) seems to outweigh the true meaning of the fraternal, or brotherly, order. The personal sacrifice involved to become a member of certain orders is strikingly similar to the brainwashing initiation of certain 'fringe' cult groups. Some of these cults attempt to remove individuals from the larger society. When an individual becomes isolated from all other structures of society he may become wholly dependent on the 'cult system'. We are not condemning fraternities, or even 'cults'. We are merely commenting on some of the psychological dangers of certain of these 'sadistic' and 'intrusive' groups. Hence, in our dream, we must be able to differentiate the positive and negative aspects of the fraternal order itself. Are we being tortured by our own peer group? Is some force alienating us from 'normal' society? On the other side of the coin, the dream may in fact be exploring healthy, life-long relationships which were earned with sweat, pride and above all, true 'fraternal' loyalty. (see Family) (see Demagogue)

FREEZE The action of Freezing involves alienation, isolation and an utter stagnation of self. This hesitation involves a slow process of restriction and a subsequent hardening of fluid, yet uncontrollable, emotion. Will we allow ourselves to heal in order to 'feel' once more? Can we hide from life forever? Life is ours to face, endure and finally, overcome. This is our mission on earth. Life has its own miraculous rewards for those of us who give it a fair chance. (see Antarctica) (see Water)

FREUD, SIGMUND Dr. Sigmund Freud, born in Vienna, Austria 1856-1939, is considered to be the father of modern psychanalysis. His early research involved intense dream analysis which centered around the belief that 'phrases' and 'ideas' slip into the consciousness of dreaming subjects. This theory was witnessed in patients involved in word associations. These patients revealed truths about themselves which were found to be repressed in their own Unconscious. However, his theoretical concern with the Unconscious shifted gears when Freud developed a three-tier system of human consciousness, namely the ID, Ego and Superego, each of which supported a level of human development from infant wish-fulfillment, (ID,) to self-awareness, (Ego,) to moral restraint, (Superego.) In limiting dream consciousness and dream interpretation to the confines of an individual's mind, Freud differed from his student Carl G. Jung. Jung believed in the infinite temporal and spatial reach of the Collective Unconscious and its revealing archetypes. Freud was strictly scientific and analytical in his research and (for the most part) denied any metaphysical realm of the human Unconscious.

FROG   In the dream sense, the complex symbiology of a Frog may represent sacred riddles, elusive truths and hidden beauty. Yet another aspect of the frog is its squatting ease, floating on a lily pad, which may be representational of spiritual tranquility and emotional wisdom. In our dream, we need to pinpoint which facet, or behavior, of the frog is highlighted. If the frog calmly disappears into the murky pond, we may be witnessing a figurative trip into our own Unconscious. On the other hand, a frog which swims and frolics with grace and beauty may symbolize inner resplendence in ourselves, or some other persons in our social environment, which may not be immediately recognized. As such, we may need to pay extra attention to our slippery friend the frog.

FRY   The dream of Frying may involve a longing for home and the good, hot emotion of its pointed resolve to feed, nourish and protect. In this sense, we see the frying as a completion of love and family which we take into ourself. On the other hand, frying may refer to being 'captured' within the inescapable confines of a certain situation and beginning the process of being burnt to a crisp. In other words, beginning to accept our own punishment. Accordingly, we need to determine the intent of the frying which is nevertheless, and in either case, a pointed, poignant and emotionally driven metaphor. (see Burn) (see Eat) (see Fish) (see Metal) (see Forge) (see Table) (see Family)

FUMES   The dream involving Fumes may indicate a fear of silent, creeping evil intent which threatens to build up and eventually devastate our waking existence. We may need to wake up and check our gas lines! However, if the dream is symbolic, we may need to evaluate whether or not our fears are based on realistic observation or simply paranoid distrust. The working mechanism in this dream landscape is the invisibility of fumes. As such, we need to determine exactly how (and why) we detected the presence of the vapor in the first place. The reference of smelling or feeling 'evil', may indicate an internal predisposition about a situation or a group. We may need to explore our own prejudices versus our actual experienced encounters. Are our instincts in this personal situation sound, or based upon our own simple and close-minded ignorance? (see Invisible) (see Faith)

FUNERAL   The image of a Funeral may be symbolic of preparing oneself for the change of renewal. Buried into the womb of the earth, our bodies depict the seed which bursts and allows new life to enter the world. The funeral procession and the flower wreaths all signify the social blessing of our parting, replete with memory and love enshrouding our resting place. In the dream sense, we may be expressing division from our group and absolute renewal in our waking environment. Conversely, if we attend a funeral of another person, we may be indicating that this person is figuratively 'dead' to us. In other words, we have become disassociated with this individual. All characters in the funeral dreamscape should be analyzed in terms of their relation to us. Have they motivated our need for transition, or do we miss their presence and their overview upon our own life and our crucial decision making process? The Unconscious may be warning us that eventually we must learn to stand alone in life. (see Corpse) (see Flower) (see Earth) (Death) (see Tarot, Death)

FUNGUS Fungus thrives and grows rich away from direct sunlight and drenched in a moist environment. As such, a fungus may flawlessly symbolize strange, and perhaps dark, emotions 'hidden under the surface' of our day to day consciousness. Moreover, a mushroom is a fungus with deep archetypal significance elucidating 'visions' and 'hallucinations' from the deepest part of our own psyche. A number of ancient cultures employed the sacred mushroom in ceremonial rituals. The visionary or 'medicine man' consumed the mushroom, or peyote button, to 'bring' him into the world of spirit (Unconscious), where he hoped to learn the 'brightest path' for his people, and the answers to their tribal concerns. This of course included finding the cures for all their various forms of illness. Accordingly, in the dream sense, we need to determine EXACTLY who locates the fungus (if not ourselves), and furthermore, in what secret place is the 'revealing' fungus discovered. We then may need to decide how this place and/or person correlates with our own undisclosed emotions. What has triggered our repressed ideas and emotions to come this close to the surface of our awareness? Are we growing as individuals? Have we entered a new state of vibrant and explorative consciousness? (see Earth) (see Plant) (see Water) (see Rock) (see Clairvoyant) (see Parasite)

FUR In the dream sense, the archetype of Fur may symbolize 'protection' from the outside world of sensations. Our Unconscious may be revealing an ancient memory of harsher, colder times when we certainly required thicker 'coating' upon our hide. Appropriately, in a dream incarnation, the vision of possessing, or hiding under, fur, may allude to an outside person or place which alarms our human fragility. It must be noted that dream fur may only be significant if it materializes in a place, or on a person, where it would not 'commonly' appear. For instance, if we dream about a bear, it is only natural that it should have a thick coat of fur and we should instead gear our interpretation toward the animal itself and not its pelt. If we happen to be an animal rights activist, the fur may sharply indicate the merit of our cause. However, will our own violence stop the senseless violence of others? Awareness may be the best and only real weapon against ignorance. Hence, an individual who wears a fur coat may need to address his or her own highly irrational fear about a cold and creul world where only the 'financially secure' can survive. (see Hair) (see Fabric) (see Wild)

FUTURISTIC The vision of a Futuristic world in our dreams may represent wish fulfillment, or, an intense fear of the immediate future, dependent on whether the fantasy is crystalline, bright and inviting, or conversely, torturous, dreadful and dehumanizing. In either case, we may be expressing an Unconscious projection of reality, based upon our perceptions of a current reality and our repressed desires or repulsions within that reality matrix. As such, we need to clearly interpret our dreaming futuristic worlds as the visceral landscapes of our emotional psyche. All colors, shapes, characters and numbered layouts, need to be cross-correlated to provide us with the significant and pertinent understanding of Self. What does the future tell us about the past? (see Fable) (see Child) (see Hallucination) (see Fungus)

G

GADGET The image of a useful Gadget in our dream may be representative of a rudimentary procedure or skill necessary to realize a difficult, yet desired, goal. We may need to analyze the exact use of this device and ascertain our skill in using it. For instance, if our skillful use of a dream gadget, opens locked doors, we may be reflecting on a new found personal ease in staging (formally difficult) meetings and interrelationships in our life. On the other hand, if our gadget looks fancy and complicated, yet is totally useless, we may be illustrating personal ineffectiveness in certain situations in our waking life. As such, the gadget is symbolic of our own relative competence and the frustration we nevertheless feel, because our competence, or mastery, is not recognized, or even accepted.

GALLERY The dream landscape of a Gallery, or exposition, is representative of an unveiling of personal creativity and novel imagery. In our dream display we may find images alien to our immediate experience which our Unconscious deems to be explored. Conversely, we may find portraits which echo memories deeply embedded in our psyche which perhaps need to re-enter our living day to day actualization. Taken together, the gallery environment may be a revelation of symbolic windows opening out into the vast expanses of our perception. What are we revealing about ourselves? (see Landscape)

GAME In the dream sense, a Game represents psychological and/or physiological competition with another individual or group. Accordingly, we need to interpret what sort of game we are engaged in, how do we perform within that game, and what are the 'stakes' involved in 'winning' this particular game. Naturally, as it contains so many separate symbols, the game imagery can be indeed complex. However, The key aspect remains in the 'challenge' itself. As such, we need to interpret our relationship with our respective competitor. Having done so, the complex symbiology of the game may become clearer and point toward an understanding involving this perhaps confrontational relationship. What are our feelings about winning and losing? Do we deliberately lose the game in order to 'win' the love of our competitor?

GARBAGE   The dream symbolism of Garbage is highly dependent on what we do with that refuse. For example, if we push heaps of trash into another room and lock the door, we may be expressing difficulty in letting go of someone or something which may be harmful or distasteful to our living experience. On the other hand, if we burn our garbage, we may be illustrating a passionate consummation of a difficult past experience or relationship. Consequently, we find the significance in both these dreams is not merely the garbage, but how we 'deal' with the garbage. (see Dirt) (see Feces)

GARDEN   In the dream sense, a Garden is symbolic of growth, beauty and nurturing. Because we refer to a garden and not simply a 'field' of flowers, we imply the labor, toiling and love involved in cultivating such resplendence. As such, a garden may be representative of how we view ourselves and moreover, the 'fruits' of our labor. Accordingly, we need to analyze the condition of the garden. Is it laid out creatively and lush and magnificent, or is it covered with weeds and wilting flowers? We may need to interpret the specific flowers and plants as well as the geometrical layout of the garden for more detailed symbolic meanings. (see Eden) (see Apple) (see Farm) (see Earth) (see Seed)

GARGOYLE   The image of the horrible, winged Gargoyle which guards our dwelling, may well be representative of our human recognition of a shadow Unconscious. As such, we assert and reveal a part of ourselves which may be considered 'evil', in order to fend off the greater evil inherent in an unbalanced psyche. Furthermore, on roofs of buildings, we find that gargoyles are primarily designed as rain-spouts. Viewing this in the symbolic sense, we observe a commanding imagery of 'channeling' the flooding rains of our more fervent emotions, which otherwise could prove disastrous. Does our own anger and aggression protect us from emotional, or psychological, harm? (see Drain) (see Water) (see Monster)

GARLIC   In the conception of Garlic, we find a potent, absolving agent, which literally conquers anything in its path (including nostrils). As such, ancient men and women hung cloves of garlic on their door to ward off disease and other evils of an unknown, unclean environment. Accordingly, in the dream sense, the use of garlic may represent a cautious attitude involving a corrupt or contemptible situation in our waking life. On the other hand, if we fear garlic in our dream, we may be expressing guilt about our own poisonous behavior, including perhaps, social vanity. Lastly, since garlic's potent odor is able to revive an individual who has fallen unconscious, we may be indicating a necessary awakening from a charm or enchantment which is damaging our better judgement.

GATE   The symbolism of the Gate involves entrance into a visible world. However, while this world or place is discernible, we nevertheless must be welcomed into its confines. As such, we need to prove the merit of our worthiness to gain passage. However, we may come to realize that gates so eagerly crossed, may close behind us and subsequently trap us in the forceful world of our own deepest aspirations and desires. In this case, our wishes, once realized, may prove to be entirely destructive to our own better nature. Look before leaping. (see Door) (see Window) (see Tarot, The Sun)

GELATIN   In the dream sense, Gelatin may refer to sweet and easy, hence, immediate gratification. As such, gelatin may indicate the desired fulfillment of child-like needs and/or wishes. However, these aspirations are not primarily infantile, and may involve a complex craving to complete oneself through relentless sexual behavior. In the dream interpretation, we may need to explore several aspects of the gelatin such as color, taste, movement, place where we find the gelatin, and who serves us the gelatin. Taken together, these aspects and characters, may reveal the exact nature of our need for immediate gratification. (see Child) (see Eat) (see Color) (see Form)

GENITALIA   In the dream sense, Genitalia may not merely imply carnal knowledge, but an elaborate expression of joy (or anxiety) concerning procreation. In the symbiotic sense, the human body illustrates aspects of our own personality. Appropriately, genitalia refers to 'conscious' masculinity and potential. Hence, we may need to interpret the condition of the genitalia and explore the activity of the procreative function for signs of atypical, or unhealthy, behavior. Do we fear for our genitalia? Is our sexual desire placing us into peril?

GEOGRAPHY   The physical extremes and real elements displayed in a dream image figure prominently in its psychological interpretation. As such, the enormous mountain may be seen as an obstacle to overcome and once surmounted, a revelation of ones personal triumph. Conversely, a harsh, flat wasteland may be viewed as emotional isolationism. (see Water) (see Desert) (see Landscape)

GESTALT THERAPY   Therapist, Frederick (Fritz) Perls, developed a technique for dream interpretation which involved a re-enactment of the dream itself with active participation from the dreamer as well as other individuals acting as the 'supporting' characters in the dream scene. The word Gestalt comes from the German tradition and translates as an 'entirety' so complete, that it cannot possibly be obtained from the sum of its parts. Accordingly, Gestalt Therapy searches for whole 'segments' of self and personality which cannot be reduced further. For example, a dreamer may act out a dream sequence where she is in a hospital bed surrounded by young girls who are healthy and vivacious (played by the support group.) After a short time, she may find herself suddenly angry and hostile toward these girls. When the girls (support group) ask her why she is angry, she may (in that instant) gain the entire realization that she is furious at them because they reveal herself and her own unfeeling treatment of her mother, who has recently passed away. We see in this example, a clear example of guilt which cannot be easily discounted. (see Jung)

GHOST   In the dream sense, the complex symbiology of a Ghost, involving memory, guilt, fear or repression, seems highly dependent on the 'personage' of the apparition itself. For example, if the ghost is a deceased friend or relative who appears sad or disheartened, we may be expressing guilt concerning our past relationship with this person. Conversely, if the deceased specter seems warm and friendly, our Unconscious may be illustrating support for a recent action enacted by the dreamer whose moral basis may be rooted in a parallel history with the departed individual. On the other hand, if the apparition is unknown to us, we may be depicting a complex symbol of our own repressed fears. Appropriately, we may need to come face to face with our fears by interpreting the full expression, and any verbal message possibly conveyed, by our ghostly guest. What does this wise apparition need to tell us? (see Clairvoyant)

GIANT The archetype of the Giant may involve a testimony of the human struggle against nature and his other competitors, a battle which was 'won' with man's use of 'brains over brawn'. As such, a number of cultures, including and especially, the ancient Greeks, incorporated giants into the core of their mythology. Greek mythology relates the tale of a world ruled by giants for a 'thousand years' until the Gods (and 'man') defeated their numbers and assumed 'rightful' control. In the Biblical tradition, fragile, young and yet brave David, slays Goliath the giant and becomes leader and king of his people. In today's world, where man has significantly dominated his environment, symbolic giants are no longer feared and are readily embraced in myth. Hence, figures like Paul Bunyon, Babe the Ox and the Jolly Green Giant, are but a few of our gargantuan allies. Accordingly, in dreams, we either encounter angry giants which may indicate physical fear and personal insecurity and a need to 'think' our way beyond their apparent ferocity, or friendly giants, which remind us of our human potential and far-reaching capacity of kindness and warmth.

GIBBERISH In the dream sense, Gibberish may represent personal, or social, confusion. As such, we need to interpret our 'correlation' with the person who chatters the unintelligible language. Conversely, should the dreamer find him or herself speaking gibberish, it may be an indication of frustration concerning the dreamer's ability to communicate ideas, or perhaps, self-worth. (see Noise) (see Foreigner)

GIFT The meaning, or purpose, of Gifts exchanged remain expressions of mutual joy and intimate acknowledgement. As such, a gift given, or received, in a dream landscape, may represent a 'reward' for hard work or personal achievement. However, if the gift turns out to be something unwanted and loathsome, we may be embodying preposterous fanfare and an entirely false hope. We must interpret not only the gift and the giver, but also where the gift is given, and for what purpose. Do we expect the gift? In ancient times, the gift dream was taught to foretell a pregnancy. Depending on our feelings about the miracle of birth, this ancient adage still may ring extremely true. (see Box) (see Evergreen) (see Square) (see Present) (see Baby)

GLASS   The transparent image of Glass may refer to a desired object, or person, 'behind the glass' which is within view, yet firmly out of reach. Moreover, the reflective quality of glass may represent varying 'feelings' which accompany our separation from the object or person behind that glass. Appropriately, we need to analyze three distinct aspects of the glass imagery in our dream landscape. First, the shape or form of the glass (see Form), second, the image and/or color reflected upon the glass (see Color), and third, and most importantly, the image 'seen' through the glass itself. Taken together, these three components of the dream vision may uncover the impetus for any 'transparent' barriers we may suffer in waking life. (see Mirror) (see Image) (see Window)

GLUE   The image of Glue may refer to a fear of being trapped and the subsequent permanence of this entanglement. We may be referring to the cautiousness necessary to maintain a relative freedom of movement. However, a fear of partnership, or commitment, may also imply a distrust of people around us in waking life. In this case, our Unconscious may be implying our need to create a social cohesion concerning the people involved in our reality. As such, we may need to formulate a collage, or unity, of communal experiences. Perhaps, this unity of perception may aid us in the balancing of our own psyche and the desired anchoring of our own fundamental self. If our friends learn to trust one another, then the entire group will be allowed to support each and every member with strength, loyalty and altruistic comradeship. (see Fraternity)

GNARLED   The image of a Gnarled face may imply knowledge and wisdom gained from experience. The wrinkles of age may also illustrate the worries and concerns of a complex reality which must be endured before gaining its appropriate lessons. In another variation, spiritual idealism may be represented in the surrender of ones smooth, unblemished facade, which may be viewed as superficial and as such, motivated only by material concerns. With age and experience, we move closer to the truth of life. Sometimes the truth can be very ugly, but must nevertheless, be faced. (see Gargoyle) (see Aging) (see Frog)

GOAT   In the dream sense, a Goat may symbolize excessive or mindless behavior. As such, the goat in our dream landscape may be an expression of guilt concerning our greedy and/or 'obsessive' actions in the recent past, or (planned) and immediate future. Moreover, the raw quality of a goat's manner may carry a sexual indication which cannot be ignored. Accordingly, we need to analyze the location where the goat is seen, and observe all his habits, especially 'material' chewed and swallowed. Do we fear the goat? Is the goat competing with another goat? Is the goat cognizant of its actions? (see Horn) (see fat) (see Eat) (see Fur) (see Beard) (see Devil) (see Fowl)

GOD/GODDESS   Contrary to popular contemplations on the old, white haired, caucasian look of the 'supreme being', the image of God varies dramatically according to culture. However, there are certain common denominators in the universal figures of Gods and Goddesses. Perhaps the most 'central' aspect of these supreme beings is their 'separation' from man. In order to get around this factor, gods and goddesses utilize messengers, prophets, angels and spiritual envoys (including their own sons and daughters). Hence, in the dream sense, the image of a god or goddess usually symbolizes an untouchable, unreachable perfection which we hope sheds a figurative 'light' and 'protection' upon our mortal, physical and very vulnerable selves. We may be illustrating wish-fulfillment in our projection of ourselves in conjunction and synergy with such a perfect, unblemished being. Spiritual leaders recommend people to 'walk with God' as much as they possibly and humanly are able to. (see Tarot Major Arcana) (see Christ) (see Buddha)

GODZILLA The giant, radiation-blowing lizard from the Japanese cinema of the late 1950s comments upon the use of nuclear weapons by the United States to bring an abrupt end to World War II. In no uncertain terms the creature symbolizes the monstrous and unnecessary effect of these two massive bombs upon a primarily innocent populace of Nagasaki and Hiroshima. The unstoppable force of Godzilla represents technical advances which threaten a mankind unable to control and philosophically 'accept' the towering responsibility which comes with these advances. Godzilla is the 'reptilian brain' which emerges from the dark sea of our primitive consciousness. When technology is placed into the hands of 'instinctual', rather than 'reasoning' man, the results can be devastating. Furthermore, Godzilla represents an absolute measure of power. He is Hitler, Napoleon, Ghengis Khan and Nero all wrapped into one super-enormous dinosaur with bad breath and a worse attitude. At the same time, he is in one sense innocent. He cannot be blamed for his size, strength and fury. He is merely a victim: a product of our own poor judgement and bad reasoning. In the end, the tormented monster is obliterated in a boiling liquid. A meek scientist (who can't even keep his own girlfriend) invents the liquid which reduces the mighty Godzilla reptile into a pile of crumbling bones. This scientist represents the last bastion of reason and rational thinking. The scientist is the pure intellect which balances the great urges of the body. (Little wonder his girlfriend 'initially' decided to leave him!) In the strange and ironic world of movies and media, Godzilla became something of a hero in later American-produced versions of the film. In the 1960s, Godzilla was fighting fierce creatures such as Giddra, or Monster Zero, in order to save the earth and mankind. In this, we see a primitive brain which finds refuge in the name of mythology. The new Godzilla mythology rationalizes our NEED for primitive aggression and forceful technology in order to fight off bigger and badder participants of the same ideology and conscious processes. Interestingly enough, the United States and (then) Soviet Union were struggling in a staggering nuclear arms race at this approximate point in history, each in the name of protecting itself from the other. Eventually, they jointly agreed to decrease and eventually end this mindless stockpiling of doom weaponnry. In later years, combining reason, friendship and vision, Russia and The United States were able to join two space satellites in a unique waltz through the heavens. This union wholly represented technology and philosophy existing on the same level of experience. Now, taking all this into consideration, we turn to the dream imagery of Godzilla. Is the monster out of control and not at all our protector? If so, have we misused our own power, or knowledge? Are we victims of a technological existence which we are not wholly prepared to accept? Have we hurt someone we love dearly in an unnecessary, or sadistic, manner? (see Demagogue) (see Ablaze) (see Lizard)

GRAB The concept of Grabbing in the dream sense refers to an attempt to capture someone, or something. We may be expressing insecurity in our waking life involving a situation which has recently ensnared us, or plans to do the same. Accordingly, we need to interpret the person, animal or plant which 'seizes' us. We also may need to analyze which part of our body is clenched in the formal act of the apprehension. For example, if our arm is grabbed by an authority figure, we may be indicating an anxiety concerning an older person (perhaps a father) who seems to usurp our strength, by treating us as a subordinate, rather than an equal. (see Fry) (see Glue) (see Chase) (see Run)

GRASS The lush green 'covering' of Grass may be representative of rich and ample living. Hence, we need to analyze the relative condition of 'our' dream grass and the location of its appearance. For example, if the grass is patchy in our own backyard, we may be expressing concerns about the 'togetherness', or general health, of our family and/or significant others. Conversely, if the grass in our backyard is tall, wild and unkempt, we may be depicting a lifestyle which has become lackluster and lazy. In this case, we may need to wake up and push our symbolic lawn mowers over the excess swelling of our personal creature comforts and create instead a streamlined, balanced and well organized blueprint for our own waking lives. After all, we don't want our neighbor's lawn to look better than ours, do we? By the way, are we in any way concerned about our own social appearance? (see landscape) (see Garden) (see House)

GREEN The color Green symbolizes life and growth. Therefore, when a focused object in our dream appears bright green, we may be referring to an enhancement in the significance of that object. In essence, it has 'grown' in importance. Green may also be representational of envy or the immaturity of a novice. It is no coincidence that in both cases the conceptualization of 'potential' (revenge or completion) is decisively suggested.

GRIFFIN The mythical creature called a Griffin possessed the body of a lion, and the head and wings of an eagle. Its fantastic presence referred to the protection of a great 'treasure', designating it as a glorified 'guard dog'. The combined symbolism of the 'spirit' of the eagle, and 'strength' of the lion, implied the moral fortitude necessary to resist greed and temptation (symbolized by the treasure). Accordingly, our Unconscious may be demonstrating a caution to exercise moral restraint in a waking situation. As such, we need to analyze exactly 'what' the griffin protects, and from 'whom' it protects it, (if not ourselves.) (see Lion) (see Eagle) (see Tarot, Judgement) (see Bull)

GROW In a dream, the image of Growth is as complex as the phenomenon itself. The conceptualization of an increase in size and strength based upon an internal DNA/RNA program of potential is fully reflective of life on the whole. Life, or reality, is rooted in the repeated material realization of its understood design potential. Whether or not this 'plan' is previously laid out, or learned through time, is a matter of great philosophical debate. Nevertheless, the fact remains that there is a blueprint and the fulfillment, via physical manifestation, of this basic plan occurs, over and over again. However, since exact growth may vary according to behavior, we witness how this design is rooted in variable probabilities and possibilities. As such, the dream may reveal various aspects of potential, either previously achieved or probable, and then again, merely possible. Furthermore, we need to interpret the position of growth, rate of growth and whether or not the growth is desired. Therefore, if a particular body part or unique object grows, we need to analyze its individual symbolism and determine how the factor of increase may directly effect it and our overall relation to it, especially concerning our waking talent and future promise. Is our growth physical, or metaphysical? (see Garden) (see farm) (see Grass) (see Giant)

GUARD In the dream sense, a Guard may symbolize a denial of entry. As such, we may need to interpret the meaning of the location or entrance which is respectively shielded. We may find our Unconscious is illustrating a barrier, or block, (repression,) against our own wishes, or desires. For further information, analyze the color and clothing of the dream guard or sentinel. (see Bull) (see Tarot, Judgement) (see Gate) (see Door) (see Authority Figure) (see Brick) (see especially Wall)

GUMBO SOUP In the dream sense, the image of Gumbo Soup is one of fusion, or the placing together of separate entities and their emotional 'flavors' (if you will.) Consequently, we need to examine social gatherings and/or collections of diverse incidents which seem to be merging, or colliding, in our waking life. Moreover, we need to interpret our relative position in this 'coming together' of disparate, and perhaps esoteric, souls. (see Family) (see Table) (see Glue)

GUT We may refer to the removal of essential living materials in the Gutting dream. As such, our Unconscious may be illustrating a reduction, or elimination, of ones basic humanity. Furthermore, to cut into an animal's vital body, we may represent the absorption, or taking in, of that creature's particular strength and/or skills. Unfortunately, this acquisition is symbolically obtained at the expense of that living being. Hence, we need to interpret the direct effect of our desire to possess an opponents' goods, or well being. Is our forward progress dependent on the failure of others? If so, we may be displaying an insecurity about our own ability to succeed solely by our own talent and/or merit. In all cases, we need to ask ourselves, is accomplishment EVER worth the loss of humanity? (see Abdomen) (see Cut) (see Blood) (see Fur) (see Fist) (see Demagogue) (see Form, Paper)

GYMNASTICS In a dream, the action of Gymnastics involves the solo performance of an individual in tune with his or herself. Moreover, the conceptualization of human potential is clearly presented in this powerful, yet fluid display of physical movement. As such, the balance achieved by the gymnast reflects all the merits of a symmetric psychological and physiological union. Consequently, in the dream sense, we may be referring to our relative performance and poise in waking life. (see Balance) (see Ballerina) (see Falling)

GYPSY The Gypsy represents movement, freedom and magic. Accordingly, we may be depicting a need to escape from the rigors of waking life. Moreover, because of the magic and carnivalesque life-styles of the free-spirited gypsies, we may be indicating a need for psychological and/or physical challenges in our life. We may need to analyze whom the gypsies represent (if anyone) in our waking life, and discover how these individuals figure into our real and active personal freedom. Why do we wish to continue our movement? Do we fear planting roots? (see Magic) (see Tarot Major Arcana) (se farm)

H

HADES As opposed to a Christian conceptualization of hell, which is an eternal landscape of misery, constructed only for evil men and women, the ancient greeks viewed the land of eternal death for ALL human beings and named it Hades. As such, no deceased person returns from Hades ever, no exceptions. (Unless you're in very special favor of the gods and ask for a momentary visit). In any case, this harsh eternal plane of the dead, may symbolize more than straight forward moral concerns. The dreamer may be implying a stagnant, exhausted and lifeless existence which reveals no change, or hope of escape. As such, the dreamer may need to critically analyze and interpret all the characters in the Hades landscape. In this regard, the Unconscious may reveal certain individual/s (indicative of ourselves and our own actions) and situation/s which have caused this feeling of existing in a death-like trance. In a psychological sense, a series of repressions and/or depressive behavior, may cause an individual to sink into this particular comatose state of reality perception. In such extreme cases, the dreamer must come to realize (via therapy and/or continual social support) that he or she IS in very special favor of the gods (self), and may return to the quality of life and the land of the living, any time he or she pleases. Moreover, this LIFE is where they belong and fully deserve to be. (see Hell) (see Tarot, The Devil) (see earth) (see Womb)

HAIL In the Hail landscape we witness a slow, painful and obstacle-ridden movement, or experience. Since hail is primarily frozen rain, emotional difficulty or hardship may be involved. Accordingly, we may interpret the hail dream as an expression of anxiety concerning difficult emotional situations or misgivings concerning psychological metamorphosis. For further information, we need to analyze the symbolic location of the falling hail and its physical effect upon our material body.

HAIR In the dream sense, Hair implies virility, strength and sensual ease. Accordingly, we need to analyze the color, texture, length and relative fullness of the hair revealed in the dream imagery. For example, long flowing red hair may symbolize fiery passion while unending black hair may symbolize mystery and extreme sensuality. On the other hand, short hair may imply aggression and swiftness, in other words, 'purpose' and 'freedom' in movement and action. Conversely, a loss of hair primarily indicates insecurity about sexual performance, old age and descending levels of self-esteem. However, the act of having ones hair forcibly cut off may indicate an attack on ones vigor or potency by an aggressive or otherwise intimidating outside force. (compare Baldness)

HALLOWEEN Their are two separate representations of the Halloween imagery in our dream landscape, which are nevertheless fundamentally connected. The first concerns our childhood ability to fulfill role playing in the form of costumes and disguises. As such, the child is able to become someone other than him or herself. Moreover, the child is allowed to become anonymous (unknown) and in this pretense, is allowed to throw off the shackles of responsibility and pointed consequence. In this sense, the children become akin to wandering spirits who cannot be directly blamed for their deceit. Hence, the game and the playing of the game become one in the same. The second representation involves the adult regression into childhood, which itself implies a disguise used to avoid the natural obligation and accountability of adulthood. So we see an adult, disguised as a child, who in turn is disguised as an imposter, who in turn becomes an invisible or ghost-like force. Hence, in a very elaborate illustration of continually transcending bodies, we witness the revelation of a repressed desire for unlimited freedom. Perhaps this is why we allow for the democratic release of candies and other sweets to quench the passionate thirst of this newly realized autonomy and its subsequent and nearly anarchistic realization. If only for one night. (see Mask) (see Child) (see Ape)

HALO The symbolic image of a Halo, or spiritual light, radiating from a person's body and head, refers to an unearthly intervention in the 'purpose' or 'motivation' of that human being. As such, these individuals emanate 'divine' or 'spiritual' integrity. In the dream sense, an illuminated person or entity may be drawing us into his or her experience of love, happiness and/or glory. A halo visualizes the absolute, and usually not seen, real worth of an individual. (see Aura) (see Circle) (see Ring) (see Ethereal) (see Christ) (see Frog)

HAMMER The ancient Nordic symbolism of the Hammer of Thor, referred to the powerful and instantaneous 'order' inherent in total authority. In the modern world, judges bang their gavel to indicate a verdict ruled and therefore finalized. Accordingly, in the dream sense, a hammer which pounds once with great authority may refer to an absolute conclusion in a waking situation. Conversely, an incessant pounding of hammers may refer to the pounding of our heart, (emotion) or in our head, (psychological.) This refers to an unresolved situation which needs to find some sense of immediate closure. As such, we need to interpret the nature of the 'hammering' which pounds upon our psyche. Are we attempting to break down walls which we ourselves have created through our own apprehensive behavior? (see Explosion) (see Lightning) (see Wall)

HANDS Hands represent ones absolute manipulation of the world around them. In fact, the latin root of the word manipulation is 'movement of hands'. Moreover, a person 'handles' situations, which means THAT person either fixes or copes with the problem at 'hand'. Naturally, we see how hands are fundamental archetypes of our overall behavior, both psychologically as well as physiologically. In the spiritual plain, the movement of fingers represents magic as well as music. The hand, in the archaic sense, became the map of our entire life, allowing palm readers, (otherwise known as palmists,) to read the future of our love, health, family and creative disposition. The hand became so prominent in our historic and psychological expression of self, that rings (made specifically for fingers) and scepters (made especially for hands) were chosen as the instruments fully indicative of 'divine' royalty and 'holy' matrimony. Taking all this into account, we need to examine the use and intent of all hands which figure into our overall dream landscape. (see Fingers) (see Tarot Major Arcana: The Wheel of Fortune (10) arcana)

HANG The symbolism of Hanging refers to being forced or 'choked' out of our normal existence. As such, we may need to analyze which aspect of our waking behavior has become restricted and otherwise cut off. Moreover, we need to interpret why this conduct or internal mental construct has left us 'dangling' and powerless. Once we have discovered the grounds for our symbolic hanging, we may begin the process of forgiving ourselves and returning to the natural 'flow' of our lives. However, if the hung person fights against his or her predicament, the Unconscious may be signalling a warning against resisting the consequences of our own fate. The hanged man represents our 'acceptance' and 'tolerance' of social opinion. We can ONLY be true to ourselves and our own heart. Public opinion should have very little effect upon our crucial decision making. As such, we need to determine the exact 'feelings' of the individual being executed upon the dream gallows and the nature of the 'crime' which has brought them here. (see Tarot Major Arcana: The Hanged Man (12) arcana)

HARBOR In the dream sense, a Harbor represents a home or haven for our deeper emotions. Appropriately, we need to analyze the calmness of the waters in the harbor and the condition of the vessels anchored in that close proximity. If the crafts are safe and well kept in sunny smooth bay waters, we may be depicting 'comfort' in our family relationships. Conversely, a rough harbor which tosses around neglected ships may imply a deep anxiety about our affiliations (not so close) to home. (see Boat) (see Ocean) (see Crash) (see Family)

HARVEST The symbolism of the Harvest is highly dependent on the weather found in the season. A cold spring and summer may leave hard soil and feeble growth, representative of sickness and cold, distant emotionalism. On the other hand, a hot, wet season may bring forth a sturdy and robust harvest indicating good health, a considerable sex drive, or perhaps, the birth of a child. Accordingly, we need to examine the symbolic contents of the harvest, as well as, the representative climate of the harvesting season itself. (see Farm) (see Earth) (see Seasons)

HAUNT The concept of Haunting revolves around ones own fears. The unstoppable figure of a ghost or demon may reflect our Unconscious and its long list of repressed realities. As such, we need to determine why we are haunted in the dream and what harm, if any, can befall us. A majority of psychoanalysts believe that a dreamer, under normal conditions (i.e. not suffering from psychosis) should challenge the spectral image which does the haunting and question its intentions. In this manner, the dreamer may come to understand the symbolic meaning of this nightmarish figure. Especially, if it answers! (see Ghost) (see Grab) (see Chase) (see Run)

HAWK The Hawk is known for its precise eyesight, soaring speed and keen instincts. As such, a hawk may symbolize accurate judgements and/or keen decision making. Furthermore, flying high above the landscape akin to the eagle, the hawk possesses spiritual insight and divine affectations. In ancient Egypt, the ruling messiah Horus, the son of the sovereign gods Osiris and Isis, possessed the head of a hawk and the respective body of a pharaoh. As such, he symbolized the 'ideal' visionary ruler of mankind. (see Eagle)

HEAD The Head possesses six crucial characterizations, one being the mind, the second the face, and the last four being the individual eyes, ears, nose and mouth. Appropriately, we need to determine which aspect of the head is pinpointed in the dream imagery and examine the symbolism of that respective 'part'. However, if the entire head is focused upon, we need to turn to the psychological structure of the dreamer's self-image and perception of the world experienced. For example, if in a dream, our own head was screaming on the 'chop block' of an ax-toting executioner, who looked remarkably like ourself, we may be rather dramatically illustrating how our own personal actions have 'severed' our own personality and life-style. Case in point, our Unconscious may be demonstrating how we have needlessly cut ourselves off from society by adopting radical new methods of existence with no social merit whatsoever. (see Face) (see Image) (see Headdress)

HEADDRESS The ancient practice of adorning a shaman or temple priest's head with an ornamental Headdress, symbolized an invitation to the spirits into the tribal psyche. In ancient Egypt, and later in Greece, individuals wore similar headdresses within the chambers of dream incubation temples to encourage the entry of guiding dream spirits. Hence, in the dream sense, the vision of an ornamental veil worn by a dreamer, may represent an enticement to outside forces to influence or enlighten ones waking life. Conversely, if an individual other than the dreamer wears the headdress, evidence of personal guidance may be presented in the form of that person. (see Halo)

HEALTH   Health may concern an acknowledgement of ones strengths and/or limitations. As such, we need to determine the symbolism of certain parts of ourselves which may appear unhealthy and otherwise dysfunctional. Conversely, if the body part appears healthy, our Unconscious may be signalling us to call upon its metaphoric specialization, right here and right now in our waking life. (see Garden) (see Grass) (see Family) (see Fever)

HEARTH   The image of Hearth in general terms, may refer to a feeling of overall contentment, stability and peacefulness in ones life. This tranquility may come with the wisdom of age, which teaches to slow down, plan and foster caring, mutual and therefore ongoing, relationships. (see fire) (see Warmth) (see Chimney)

HEAVEN   In the dream sense, the Heaven landscape, or perfect bliss, primarily symbolizes compensation, and consequently escape, from our imperfect and harsh reality. However, every so often, a dreamer may be depicting harmony and fluid movement in his or her actual waking experience. Dreams often serve as reflections of our more passionate moods, as such, heaven may be perceived as absolute joy. In order to determine on which side of the emotional line we stand, we may need to honestly assess our waking life and compare its relative 'bliss' to our dream's visual jubilation. If they seem to represent an utter contradiction, we may need to address our escapist behavior by seeking professional counciling. (see Tarot, The Star) (see Hades) (see Hell) (see God) (see Angel)

HEEL   The connotation of the Heel involves power and subservience. In the sense of the foot which crashes down with authority, we see control (of mother, primarily). In this Freudian sense, we witness a correlation with sexual commands and domination in general. Hence, to be placed underfoot seems to symbolize ultimate submission. Conversely, in the sense of our Achilles heel, we see vulnerability and metaphoric pain which never leaves us. Accordingly, we need to determine the position and intent of the heel in its particular dream orientation. (see Achilles Heel) (see Authority Figure) (see Mother) (see Amazon) (see Lawyer) (see Father) (see Godzilla)

HELL   The archetypal image of a world of pain and punishment, sometimes labeled Hell, represents expressions of personal torture and guilt. Accordingly, when our emotions and passions painfully smoulder within our psyche, we may need to create the landscape of our suffering in the form of a hell-like spectacle. Providing our deeper emotions a location, may enable us to move, react (and, in the case of self-guilt), 'accept' our own relentless castigation. (see Hades) (see Tarot, Judgement) (see Devil)

HEMP The ritual smoking of Hemp, in order to propel into the enigmatic world of our Unconscious, may be representative of hiding from ones commonplace, monotonous, or thoroughly onerous reality matrix. As such, we may need to analyze the location of our hemp experience and any and all visual or hallucinatory signs revealed. This way we may better understand wishes which remain unfulfilled in waking life and may need to be compensated for. Does the hemp open up a reality which is hallucinatory, or entirely possible? Are we returning to a primal sense of self? With whom do we smoke the hemp? What is our social relation to these individuals? (see Fungus) (see Drug) (see Escape) (see Authority Figure) (see Bar) (see Ritual)

HERMAPHRODITE In ancient times, a significant number of tribes exalted Hermaphrodites into sacred social status because of their unique possession of both male and female reproductive organs. In the modern world, people are beginning to understand the necessity of a balance in their masculine and feminine attributes. As such, the combination of strength and sensitivity is considered futuristic and ideal in our social and personal behavior. Accordingly, the hermaphrodite dream image, may refer to a completeness and balance in our gender-related characteristics. For example, a woman who controls a corporation with fierce (and sometimes harsh) executive power, while tenderly raising three children at home, may well dream herself into the body of a hermaphrodite. As in ancient times, this dream imagery remains normal, powerful and self-advancing. (see Anima/Animus) (see Jung) (see Amazon) (see Mother) (see Queen)

HERO The archetype of a Hero/ine refers to an outside force which has the ability to save us from evil. The hero/ine provides physical and psychological courage in place of our own mortal vulnerability. In the dream sense, we may be supplanting our own responsibilities into the hands of another. As such, we may be exemplifying detrimental forms of personal regression and escapism. Our need to be saved prevents us from saving ourselves. On the other hand, if we ourselves are heroic in dreams, we may be declaring personal strength and the ability to move far beyond our own limitations. (see God/Goddess) (see Godzilla) (see Faith) (see Flying) (see Griffen) (see Eagle) (see Extraterrestrial)

HEX The feeling of a curse placed upon us by some person dabbling in black magic, may symbolize a fear of our own powers and/or harmful intentions, (which may have come full circle and now return to us in a devastating manner.) This is primarily because a curse, or Hex, involves revenge or a unique blend of retaliation for some grotesque act of disrespect. In this, we may witness a fear concerning our own impertinence toward certain or all tenets of magic or witchcraft itself. These may include naturalism, feminine instincts, free sexuality, elemental forces and otherworldly spiritual influences, (or, all of the above.) In any case, our dream indicates that we have crossed, or annoyed in some way, a force which is perceived to be, greater than ourselves. In this, we explore a form of abstract domination over our individual being. In the psychological sense, this control is projected from the self, back toward the self. This is accomplished by the most horrendous, fearful form of torture imaginable, (namely: self-torture). Furthermore, counter-magic, or the protection of self, can only occur when the plagued victim harnesses enough personal strength and force of will to match and neutralize the initial self-inflicted negative force embodied in the shape of tormentors. Herein, we witness how black magic is similar to other practices. Its strength lies in the force of our belief and faith in its words of truth, or conversely, under its 'accepted' spells of potential disaster. (see Witchcraft) (see Magic) (see Green) (see Griffen) (see Godzilla) (see Demagogue)

HIDE, ANIMAL   In the Native American and otherwise aboriginal sense, to be covered in the Hide of a dead animal, symbolizes taking on its peculiar medicinal and spiritual properties. As such, what we wear becomes who we are, and moreover, who we are able to become. We are experiencing a conscious movement into our primal selves. Like the shamen, we are gaining intimate wisdom from the world around us. (see Gut) (see Blood) (see Cut) (see Headdress) (see Fur) (see Mouth) (see Teeth) (see Eyes) (see Womb) (see Bar) (see Ritual)

HIEROGLYPHICS   In the dream sense, Hieroglyphics may symbolize an unknown language or knowledge which may need to be deciphered. Hence, we may be alluding to desired information which has eluded our immediate understanding. Moreover, the historical significance and rarity of hieroglyphics may demonstrate a form of dream information which is indicative of ancient truth and/or wisdom. Taken together, we find our dream imagery may in fact symbolize a quest for truth and/or unique knowledge which may expose the wisdom of our own elaborate and prehistoric Unconscious. (see Jung)

HIGHWAY TRAVEL   In the dream sense, Highway Travel symbolizes speed, movement and sexual freedom. Moreover, since a highway stretches across the landscape moving us from old locations to new locations, we may be depicting fast and exhilarating psychological changes. Plainly, the concept of potential is inherent in this far-reaching dream landscape. However, if our dream highway is loaded with traffic, potholes and illegible road signs, we may be expressing difficulty in movement, or a dull, routine waking life, which seems to be heading nowhere. (see Landscape) (see Road)

HOAX   In the dream sense, a Hoax or chicanery, may symbolize a fear of deception in some formality in our waking life. Our Unconscious may be issuing a warning about being misled in our beliefs or planned actions. Accordingly, we may need to determine the nature of the subterfuge, or joke, played upon us, and the motivation of the trickster. Moreover, do we know this person, or group of people, who deceive us? What exactly is our working, or personal, relationship with these people? Are we deceiving others? What are our feelings about the concept of a 'trickster'? Is the trickster a 'fool', or a 'devil'? (see Tarot, The Fool, The Devil) (see Devil) (see Deception)

HOLE   The concept of a Hole, or absence of space, involves the double-sided reality of the unknown. As such, a hole may be something we fall through, or conversely, a hole may be a void which allows us to see another landscape of reality, (other than the one in which we are now fixed.) In another sense, the circular nature of a hole implies a relation to rings and perhaps provides a physical space for the insertion of an axis, or center pole. As we have seen, spiraling electromagnetic energy creates a center around which we can perceive three hundred and sixty degrees of reality. This hole is oriented neither north, nor south, not west, nor east, it is merely a circular vortex of potential. Accordingly, physical manifestations of living creatures allow for holes, or cavities, which provide plausible growth. Human Beings possess eyes, ears, nostrils and pelvic sockets, each of which allot for the development of the specialization of our own peculiar human adaptation. In the dream sense, we may need to determine the possibility of the hole. Will we fall through its drafty abyss, or will it harness our psyche into a multifarious wonderland of twisting and turning promise? (see Ring) (see Circle) (see Den) (see Axis) (see Empty)

HOLSTEIN   (see Cow)

HOME   As opposed to a house, which represents our psychological make-up and overall characteristics, a Home symbolizes our emotional stability. As such, the home is a far less fixed concept. In fact, the feeling of home may change from day to day, even minute by minute, dependent on our relationship with others and our sanctity of self. In laymen terms, the house is in our head, while the home is in our heart. Moreover, (in the sense of gender,) it is the father figure who creates the house and mother figure who creates the home. Accordingly, disorientation of home may involve difficulty in ones feminine aspect. This is why a shy recluse, who hides from psychological masculinity and outside relationships, may be thought of as 'homely.' The term has little to do with appearance and centers rather around a basic imbalance of masculine and feminine principles. (see House) (see Grass) (see Family)

HOOD   In a dream sense, the Hood implies the undoing of the head and all its neurological senses, both symbolic and material. As such, the hood erases our psyche and therefore, our unique individuality. This being the case, we may feel anonymous in society at large. Moreover, we may seem dangerous to others in the diminishing of our responsibility and furthermore, levels of sensitivity. In the realm of this conceptualization, the Grim Reaper represents the insensitive, anonymity of death which steals away life regardless of individual status. Illustrating this idea one step further, we find the covering of heads executed in the 'jacketing of' corpses. We cover their faces to 'release' them from this world. Instead, they are introduced into the ranks of the dead. Accordingly, in a dream, we may need to understand who wears the hood and for what purpose. The death of our own individuality is usually a paramount factor. (see Death) (see Bury) (see Fabric) (see Head)

HORIZON A Horizon symbolizes the psychological parameter of our landscape, a celebrated beginning, or a somber conclusion. Furthermore, the horizon represents our goal, or future plans, it is the product of a world in absolute transition. As such, it represents continual rebirth and regeneration. In our dream, we may need to analyze the terrain leading toward the distant horizon and the colors and mood of the skyline itself. It may also be critical to interpret any person or creature which moves, or interacts, within this imagery. For instance, a high flying hawk soaring across a brilliant sunrise may indicate a direct and positive outlook on the future. The spiritual significance of this dream figure cannot be ignored. Does the horizon represent our highest potential as individuals? (see Tarot, The Moon)

HORNS Primarily, Horns indicate fertility and productivity. However, the action and relative condition of the horns translate their inherent meaning. For example, horns on a charging animal may symbolize speed and steadfastness in purpose, while a broken horn on a caged beast may represent a departure from physical, or sexual, interest. On the other hand, when horns present a dream threat, there may be an indication of repressed passion and an inability to let go of oneself. Interestingly, within the Unconscious terror of being 'pierced through', exists the very real possibility of self revelation. This honest revelation exposes the 'innocence' and 'purity' which is also associated with horns. (see Bull) (see Elephant) (see Tarot, Judgement)

HORSE In the Chinese zodiac, the symbolism of the Horse individual involves independent natures, attractiveness and enormous popularity, combined with a cheerful intelligence. The horse itself has always implied powerful freedom in the grace of gallop, majesty of leap and outright force of kick. Man naturally feels a connection with the mighty horse because the animal is willing to work and merge its regal energy with the balance and skill of a rider/provider. The mutual benefit of man and horse raises to a unique level of freedom, power and grace blended with discipline, balance and artistry. As such, we have come to love our four legged friend, every bit as much as we love our self. The horse represents our emotional and psychological balance, as well as our individual and social stability. (see Centaur) (see Equestrian)

HOUSE In the dream sense, a House may represent the structure of our entire psychological self-perception. As such, separate rooms within the house symbolize diverse characteristics. For example, a bedroom may imply marriage or sexual relationships, while the bathroom may represent feelings of cleanliness and purification. Following along this train of thought, we find the kitchen representing family togetherness and/or bodily sustenance and the living room expressing lifestyles and general psychological perceptions (TV,VCR,LIBRARY etc.). As such, we need to interpret the relative condition, shape or state of each of the rooms which comprise our house and determine which idiosyncratic room of our self may need repair or reorganization. (see Grass) (see Home)

HUNCHBACK The symbolism of strength, loyalty and determination, all tempered with a humble submissiveness represents the Hunchback figure in our dream landscape. It is crucial to understand the symbolic disfigurement of the hunchback allows for his endearing humility and faithfulness. Accordingly, we may be revealing a personal or perceived distortion of self, either physical or psychological, which renders us eternally compliant to our peers. Perhaps our Unconscious is indicating that we should use the strength of the 'hunchback' to finally free ourselves from the subservience of our peer group and regain our personal freedom. We must ring the bell in the high tower of our individualism in order to obtain the people we truly love. (see Gnarled) (see Frog)

HUNT The archetypal symbolism of the Hunt, refers to the struggle of survival. Consequently, the lone predator, whether it be a man or a hungry lioness, must outperform and out-think the desired prey. In order to live another day, either the predator, or the prey, must emerge victorious. In the social sense, a group of hunters may represent a dreamer's ability to work with others toward a common goal. In addition, this band of trackers may refer to the dreamer's family, or coworkers. Conversely, the notion of being hunted oneself, may represent feelings of being stalked by life's challenges. In other words, our fearful struggle for survival may be wearing us down and we desperately may covet a halt in the excruciating pace. Accordingly, we need to analyze the landscape of the hunt, the hunter/s themselves, and the motivation behind the hunt. In the latter example, we may need to determine exactly what or whom pursues us, and why. In most cases, the dreamer is hunted or pursued by his own fears, which need to be faced and categorized in the waking psyche. (see Chase) (see Ghost) (see Eyes) (see Gut) (see Cut) (see Blood)

HYBRID The concept of two or more beings which are combined to form a new model of living creature through genetics or metaphysics is known as a Hybrid. In a dream, these hybrids, man or animal, (while existing as unique life forms,) nevertheless possess traits and behavior of all (its) fixed ancestry. As such, we need to examine the symbolism of the separate components which comprise the hybrid itself. Once knowing this, we may determine if these aspects negate each other, or combine to form a kind of super-being. For example, crossing a wolf and a human creates a fearful, yet tortured creature, who is more powerful than we may care to think about. Conversely, a wolf and a dove may combine to form an animal with powerful spiritual influence, which is nevertheless ferocious in the determination of its composure. Accordingly, these hybrids may reflect internal struggles which either strengthen us, weaken us, or render us completely immobile in our waking behavior. (see Animus) (see Transmutation) (see Zoomorphism)

HYGIENE The act of meticulously cleaning oneself, may involve guilt about ones actions. In this, we witness the dream illustration of purifying oneself from influences of negativity. In the archaic sense, evil is nearly always equated with unclean objects and persons. This is why the name Beelzebub is translated 'Lord of the flies', as we know flies are inexorably drawn toward refuse and bacterial substances. Moreover, we find a slight variation of this cleaning involving the wishes of mother and home life. If we cleansed ourselves, we were rewarded with love and attention. Naturally, girls relished in this behavior, formulating deep relationships of equality with mother, while boys struggled with gaining independence from the mother figure. In this sense, we find an allusion to sexuality, especially in males, who may find themselves concerned about love of mother, yet in parallel discernment, struggle with a socially unapproachable love of the feminine aspect within themselves. (see Cleaning) (see Baptism) (see Unclean) (see Fly,Insect)

HYPNOSIS In the dream sense, Hypnosis may refer to an uncontrollable psychological suggestion which may become an obsession. Our Unconscious may be revealing our folly in being reined in by an individual, or group. Conversely, if we hypnotize another dream character, we may be illustrating self-guilt involving the personal manipulation of a friend, or relation, in waking life. Moreover, the symbolism of hypnosis seems to contradict the powerful conceptualization of autonomy altogether. As such, we may find ourselves invoking a call to freedom, or emancipation, from some outside force which seems to possess an extraordinary influence over us. (see Halloween)

I

ICE The symbolism of Ice in the dream landscape, refers to frozen or paralyzed emotional states. However, melting ice, may imply a re-entry into the warmth of spring, romantic love and the welcoming, yet sometimes wild, world of nature. Along those lines, dislodged icebergs symbolize the slow, yet gigantic movement of emotional passage into sexual or psychological maturity. We need to interpret where the ice settles in the dream and what warm and uniting event will dissipate its continued existence. (see Antarctica) (see Hail) (see Freeze)

ICEBERG The Iceberg defines an enormous amount of emotional pain in the vastness of its cold landscape, or conversely, the intensity of its hot dislocation from an even larger mass of cold, harsh existence. In either case, the potential of the ice mass is unfathomable and WILL cause major devastation if underestimated. Hence, the Titanic remains the eternal reminder of human frailty and fallibility. In this larger sense, the iceberg is symbolic of man's ultimate subordination to nature. Accordingly, a dreamer may need to contemplate the wisdom of his or her forward progress against nature, or natural forces; which may be far greater than they appear to the naked eye and physical senses. (see Ice) (see Mountain)

ICON The dream of an Icon suggests a personal bridge between an image and the spiritual reality which that image conveys. In other words, our Unconscious may be presenting a physical reality, (representational painting or sculpture) and asking us to discover the abstract reality behind (and beyond) that symbol. In so doing, we may come to realize that there exists within the context of consciousness genuine steps into deeper and truer reality which become more apparent and more tangible with time and discernment. In the icon example, we find first a painting (object,) then a representation, (or symbol,) and finally, an ultimate meaning, (or significance to our very own worldly condition.) Accordingly, the dream icon represents the process of gaining a deeper understanding of the visual world around us each and every day. We must find the spirit of nature and the Soul within man. (see Elememts) (see Unconscious) (see gallery) (see Archetype)

IGUANA In the dream sense, the archetypal Iguana may epitomize cold, fierce and above all, inhuman poise. The iguana represents an ancient time when the world was sweltering, harsh and hostile toward animal life (including human beings). However, in this unforgiving terrain, the iguana stood motionless, without fear, and arguably noble, (almost, surreal.) Taken together, the Iguana in the dreamscape may represent an almost unstoppable, inhuman (yet very human) determination, which we may find appalling and terrifying, yet nonetheless, awe-inspiring. Appropriately, we may need to determine if the iguana represents a certain individual or group in our waking life whose behavior has us frightened and/or spellbound. On many levels, our 'reptilian brain' is reminding us of our very real 'primal' potential. (see Hypnotism) (see Godzilla) (see Ape) (see Aboriginal) (see Frog) (see Gnarled) (see Gargoyle)

ILLNESS In ancient incubation temples in Greece (see Aesculapius), patients were encouraged to search their dreaming mind for possible remedies and cures for their various illnesses. Conversely, in modern dream interpretation, we find the physical imagery of illness, representational of a psychological or emotional breakdown in the dreamer. Accordingly, we need to analyze the severity of the illness and which part of the body it primarily effects. For example, a painful stomach affliction such as an ulcer, may indicate greed in procurement, or the acceptance of bad, or inappropriate, psychological nourishment. We may have received a huge helping of 'bad food for thought'. (see Health) (see Fever)

IMAGE A dream which reveals a person, place or thing as a direct Image, either on a screen, or in 'thin' air, may be focusing on the meaning of the form of that particular manifestation. This conceptualization of a 'meaningful' shape, may seem strange in this contextual sense. However, each and every day we create and modify a particular 'look' which we hope speaks volumes about our character, or active characteristics. This image represents who and what we would like to be associated with, either directly or indirectly. In other words, we present an image of self, roughly matching our internal hopes, passions and drives. This rule does not simply hold true for persons who dress well or fashionably, but also to casual, traditional or simply uninterested styles of appearance. Every appearance, like it or not, is appraised by society, along with physical mannerisms and articulation; the slang of our speech. Being aware of this basic tenet, our speech, manner and dress usually conform to one another, creating a basic image of self. Accordingly, in a dream, a viewed image reveals the psychological meaning within an exposed person. As such, our Unconscious may be referring to the connection between our inner self and the self we expose to society. Are the two coinciding, or are we disguised and therefore, hiding from our own beliefs and/or desires. Conversely, if the image uncovers a person known to us, we may need to compare this image with the clear image we know of that person. The dream image may represent our own desires placed upon the form and subsequently, the psyche of that person. In this sense, we may be recreating this individual to fit into our own desired projection of our relationship. Moreover, this reworking of another, may reflect a yearning for that particular human being to become more involved in our own life and lifestyle. Can we separate the truth of self from the image of self? (see Hybrid) (see Mask) (see Halloween) (see Hang) (see Deception)

IMBRUE The symbolism of Imbruement, which entails a physical staining of the body with blood, refers to forced spirituality or a sacrificial ritual which brings one closer to the sensation or presence of God. In the biblical story of Exodus, Moses covers his people (the Hebrews) doors with sheep's blood to protect them from God's wrath against the first born (male) children of Egypt. In this sense, the stained doors drew in the reality of God, just enough to placate his essence, yet send it off in the direction of the Egyptians. In ancient warrior traditions (universally,) the blood of the warrior's victim, man or animal, ended up smeared upon the face or body of that warrior. As such, the blood became a sign and justification of the sanctity of the spirit released in battle. Hence, in a dream landscape, the staining of blood refers to the sacrificial embodiment of spirit to flesh, soul to reason.

IMITATION In the dream sense, Imitation refers to flattery and idolatry. As such, it is crucial to note if the dreamer is the imitator, or the person imitated. If the dreamer finds him or herself imitated by another person, an expression of intrusion may be indicated. Plainly, we may feel our creativity or style has been wrongfully stolen and used unjustly by a competitor. Conversely, if we imitate someone else, we may desire someone or something which that person possesses. While appearing harmless, this escapist dream mimicking represents a difficulty in accepting oneself and may lead to a detrimental self-catharsis. We must regain our individuality, regardless of how mundane it may seem to our (wholly biased) perception. (see Image) (see Ghost) (see Hunchback)

IMMERSION The archetypal symbolism of Immersion comprises the ritualistic preparation for thorough, and absolute, change. Accordingly, the nature of that transformation is dependent upon the representational medium in which one is immersed. For example, to be immersed in a foul, trash-like substance, may be an illustration of anxiety, involving a forced entry into a suffocating, unpleasant and perhaps, immoral situation (or new position) in our personal occupation. Conversely, to be immersed in a hot, liquid medium may involve a dreamers surrender and complete consummation into physical libidinous reality. On the other end of the spectrum, immersion into cold liquid, may symbolize harsh celibacy and a purifying act of regeneration and rebirth into the solitary self. Lastly, we examine immersion into blood, which may represent the dreamer coming to terms with his internal needs, honest desires and soulful direction. (see Imbrue) (see Blood) (see Water) (see Baptism) (see Hygiene)

IMPALE   To be run through, or Impaled, symbolizes a violent or passionate release of ones own repressed and sequestered emotions. In other words, a person is symbolically set free from the physical limitations of their own psyche. Furthermore, because the lance or sword remains intact in our body, that weapon's own symbolism, including directness, aggression and sexuality come into immediate play. Appropriately, we need to analyze which part of the body, including vital organs, is penetrated in the symbolic impalement. Is this forceful invasion of self the only way to release pent up emotions? Have we finally released a repressed passion which has refused to set us free? Has a deeper love impaled us? (see Horn) (see Cut) (see Blood) (see Bull) (see Arrow) (see Hole) (see Heel) (see Sword) (see Hammer) (see Explosion)

INCENSE   In the dream sense, Incense is symbolic of spiritual warmth, sanctity and inner peace. The burning flame or ember, which originates the incense plume, is representative of the radiating source of love which permeates our being. To whom we offer up this inner devotion, is entirely up to our own personal sense of purpose (and perhaps desire.) Accordingly, in the dream landscape, we may need to determine the location of the incense and decide why this location is consecrated. Why does this specific place need to be anointed in our waking experience? Whom did we come into contact with, in that place? Who do we pray for: a loved one...ourselves? Will we allow our spirit to burn bright and transfigure our devoted mind? Is our faith strong? (see Icon) (see Ablaze) (see Chimney) (see Faith)

INCEST   The conceptualization of Incest may involve a restriction of outside influences and experiences. To find ourselves drawn toward a reflection of ourselves, in the embodiment of relatives, signifies a fear of strange new desires, passions and emotions. To respond only to that which is familiar, may be reflective of a deep and unhealthy sexual repression. Moreover, a lopsided narcissism (as in ancient royalty) may be overcoming our natural craving and physical sensibilities. As such, in our dream landscape, the witnessing, or participation in incest, may reveal a limitation in our openness to the outside world of experience, and perhaps an escapist egomania, (which could in fact, prove harmful.) (see Image) (see Imitation) (see Hunchback) (see Ice)

INCONTINENT   This dream may illustrate a fear involving a personal loss of control. The management of ones own body is critical in our symbolic understanding of mind and spirit. Therefore, when our bodies act on their own, we fear the demise of our own powerful human will and hence, our basic humanity. This dream seems to illustrate more than a fear of old age, it illustrates instead, a phobia about losing our 'real' strength as an individual. As such, persons suffering from extreme emotional and psychological anxieties may question their primary sense of self and social worth. We seem to be useless to both ourselves and society. It is interesting to note, being out of control is not at all like being wild and destructive. While both examples display chaotic behavior, the anarchy of the latter is 'freely let loose' and therefore enjoyed in a mental release of all responsibility. On the other hand, the anarchy of the former is 'torn away from any and all command' and releases responsibility much to the individual's chagrin. In a sense, the former example may be a direct consequence of the long standing repression of the latter example. The body has taken matters into its own hands, leaving will, spirit and even soul, far behind. How do we recover what is truly ours? The Unconscious tells us it is high time for serious and honest self-assessment. (see Diarrhea) (see Gnarled) (see Gargoyle) (see Feces) (see Excrement)

INCUBUS In medieval times, an Incubus was believed to be an evil spirit which descended upon a sleeping woman and performed sexual intercourse with her. This convenient belief explained sexual explorations, or passions, which may have overcome a sleeping woman in the course of her dreams. Naturally, this incubus reflected the sexual repression of an entire society. It was far easier to believe an evil spirit possessed the body of a sleeping righteous woman, rather than accept the fact that this upstanding woman was still a sexual being. Nevertheless, these puritanical images remain with us, when we practice sexuality in dreams and abstinence in waking life. Our Unconscious may be demonstrating a need to balance our feelings of desire with our absolutions of self purity. (see Devil) (see Demon)

INDIAN, NATIVE AMERICAN In the dream sense, the Native American refers to honesty and quiet wisdom. Moreover, the culture of the American Indian is highly representative of personal power and a union with nature and all her elements. In this noble figure we find the perfect transcendence of earth and spiritual worlds, traveled freely back and forth by one human being. Appropriately, in this dream imagery, our Unconscious may be alluding to personal dedication. The figure may also refer to social situations in our life which are graced with sublime, inner peace and divine simplicity. The image of the young warrior refers to personal stages of spiritual transcendance. (see Bar) (see Feather) (see Aboriginal)

INDUSTRIAL In a very real sense, Industry has become the unmatched nightmare in the world of man, and especially nature. The inhuman speed and sheer number of goods manufactured into the world has enabled society to quadruple in less than one hundred years. Society grows faster than the availability of land able to support its basic needs. All this coupled with the reality of greed, which expands exponentially and drains resources further and further, has created an angry an callous environment. The new social standard is one in which we are forced to thrive as best as we can. We are programmed to 'win at all cost'! Taken together, the dream of Industry may indicate an individual life of mounting complexity and competitiveness funneled into a single-minded working condition. This repressive combination has caused the dreamer to lose the spirit AND the will necessary to thrive in a progressive and naturalistic direction. We may feel ourselves becoming the inhuman offspring of a cold and unfeeling technology. This illusion is not only escapist, but defeatist as well. This dream nust be taken seriously and must be addressed immediately, both socially and individually. (see Gadzilla) (see Form, Paper)

INFANT The Infant dream, involves the reality of early life. In this early life, all of our basic needs are provided for and our stress and responsibility levels are nonexistent. In this sense, we may be expressing a form of regression into a simpler time where the absolute difficulty of adulthood is pretty much, nonexistent. However, if in our dream an infant is in danger, our Unconscious may be illustrating our maternal and paternal instincts to protect our children. In this, we find a connection between our fragile self, requiring attention and affection, and our protective self, fearless in its dedicated resolve. Our Unconscious may be telling us to quench our irrational fears with the sound strength of our adult logic and reason. (see Baby) (see Womb) (see Child)

INFESTATION The symbolism of Infestation involves a terrible intrusion upon oneself, both physically and psychologically. The idea of the body of self becoming host to parasites, may be indicative of mortal vulnerability and weakened defense mechanisms. Our Unconscious may be warning us against individuals who seek to invade our autonomy with their influence and powerful presence. In order to stop this infestation, we may need to immerse our bodies into the cold water of purification and isolated retreat. Once we have regained our solitude and cloaked our bodies in self understanding, we may be able to withstand the encroachment of others upon our (bared) souls. (see Fly, Insect) (see Impale) (see Immerse) (see Hypnotism)

INFINITE In the dream sense, Infinity refers to limitless potential. The landscape which goes on forever and ever may be the living reflection of our own Unconscious. As such, we need to gain a detailed account of all objects, characters and layouts of the infinite panorama and decide which relative direction and/or figurative path we may need to follow. If we choose this path we may be able to find our maximum creative facility and primary visionary goal. Do we seek some form of spiritual enlightenment? (see Landscape) (see Horizon) (see Unconscious) (see Sky) (see God/Goddess) (see Tarot Major Arcana)

INFLATE The act of Inflating, may be representative of growing tension and stress-related anxiety. As we blow up our figurative balloon, we increase its relative force while decreasing our own. Plainly, we must reach a point where the balloon can no longer become inflated and finally bursts. This bursting is symbolic of our own mental breakdown into depression and listlessness. Accordingly, our Unconscious may be warning us to inhale and release the hot air of our tension balloon. As such, we may need to liberate our pent-up anxiety and divide the previously inmost components of our daily concerns into rational compartments of achievable obligation. We must learn to relax. Pent-up energy may not be only effecting our general health, but also may be distorting our personal outlook on life. (see Baloon)

INK The image of Ink in our dream landscape, may refer to permanence, as in an unwanted stain. Moreover, since ink is used to convey language and subsequently thought and wisdom, we may be referring to a misunderstanding with long term consequences and/or a mistake in our own judgement. This latter example is explored each and every time we witness spilled ink. Conversely, the coordination of mind and hand with ink and paper, may reflect the lasting and unchanging value of the written word. The truth of the written word gives form to content and otherwise manifests our abstract mental processes. This being the case, we should take great care in analyzing the position and form of all ink markings in our overall dream narrative and its determinate physical landscape. Does our mark embrace the world and society? Does our John Hancock carry 'weight' and a 'trustworthy' agreement? Has inked spilled on our contracts and made our word seem questionable? Are we in fact able to fulfill our promises? (see Contract) (see Form, Paper) (see Imbrue) (see Color)

INSECT The relentless, exacting, nearly robotic activity of an Insect may be symbolic of an anxious psychological state of mind. However, the species of a specific insect and the focused action of that particular creature, may be extremely significant in the analysis of our own process of psychological exertion. Is the insect's movements reminiscent of tiny anxieties which slowly disturb our sense of well being? (see Bug) (see Fly) (see Parasite) (see Butterfly)

INSTRUMENT Each Instrument has its own peculiar tone, ornate color and honed material, (out of which it is constructed.) Accordingly, we need to determine our emotional attachment to unique sounds, notes and melodies associated with certain instruments. Solo performances are often associated with unique emotional experiences which must be 'released' and 'integrated' into the world of our peers. Our instrument is always reflective of ourself and moreover, our deepest internal passions. Music is said to calm the savage beast because it can awaken repressed emotions which suddenly become clear and present in our memories. We must stop at these moments, and listen. (see Accordion) (see Beat) (see Dance) (see Noise)

ISLAND An Island is defined by its watery boundaries, as such, the effect of its geographic isolation offers a unique set of symbolic images. For example, odd and wonderful life forms which flourish within the confines of an island epitomize creative distinctiveness. Conversely, the circumstance of being 'stranded' all alone on an island may refer to being lost or trapped, in which case the island becomes a symbol of alienation or solitude. Along those lines, if one is trapped with others upon a desolate island, the Unconscious may be hinting at a lost cause within which we suddenly find ourselves ensnared. Whatever the particular circumstance, the dreamer should keep in mind, that ultimately, the island is a symbol of a tenacious, reliant, individuality and the propagation of unique, unrestrained creativity. (see Image) (see Sand) (see Ocean) (see Beach)

ITCH Since our skin symbolizes how we sense the world, any complication or discomfort involving the skin, may imply psychological disarray. Accordingly, in the dream sense, an Itch may be representational of a painful psychological or emotional complexity which has become enmeshed in our daily realization of the world around us. Moreover, attempting to scratch the itch and rid ourselves of its pain, may cause distress upon healthy surrounding parts of our body (psyche). Our Unconscious may be telling us to stop reacting sluggishly and otherwise becoming further enmeshed in a particular problem. Instead, we need to isolate the 'source' of our psychological or emotional wound, and purge it once and for all. In other words, we need to face our difficulties and determine a course of action to deal with them as effectively as possible. The itch dream illustrates the grave error in begrudgingly accepting, or attempting to ignore, our more sensational quandaries. Instead of disappearing, they tend to grow bigger, and far more irritating. (see Skin) (see Parasite) (see Eczema) (see Bridge)

IVORY TOWER The symbolism of the Ivory Tower refers to an intellectual retreat which heightens our awareness and stimulates our future aspirations. In the dream sense, the image of the pure, ivory edifice is both naturalistic and noble. Its wisdom is gained through our honed and honest virtue and not shadowy, abusive deceit. Consequently, an ivory tower would teach man to love and honor the great ivory-tusked bull elephant and never destroy its numbers. In a dream landscape, the ivory tower may epitomize a moral and honorable decision which needs to be made in the very near future. This decision may assist the physical, psychological and emotional well being of certain individuals around us. However, the dream also reminds us of our own humility. If we believe ourselves unworthy of our friends and family who exist 'below' our high, moral and intellectual tower, we will surely fall and we will surely fail. We must build the ivory tower only for our neighbor, never for ourself. (see Tarot, The Tower) (see Elephant) (see Edifice)

J

JACKAL The symbolism of the Jackal pertains to petty and unscrupulous, yet crafty, behavior. As such, in our dream landscape, we may be expressing guilt over devious actions perpetrated. On the other hand, since the jackal is primarily a forager, we may be illustrating an aimless search for something useful, or challenging, in our life. Consequently, we may be masking anxiety over a lackluster existence without practical goals. We must determine whether or not our clever nature interferes with our real needs. Do we procrastinate and even falter, simply because we have no real understanding of social order and social institutions? Does our hunger for life seem strange, even to ourselves? This figure questions the merits of a strong sense of self. However, a jackel is no fool. He has a method to the madness of his search. Can we say the same? (see Wolf)

JACKHAMMER In the dream sense, a Jackhammer's pounding may represent breaking through deep foundations of reality. The fact that the Unconscious uses a jackhammer, may be representational of forceful influences in our life who may be involved in a process of harshly breaking the 'cohesiveness' of our vital psychological infrastructure. Consequently, we need to determine who operates this jackhammer (if not ourselves,) and interpret this person's influential control over our social awareness. Why does our perception of the world now seem fragmented? Do we need to break apart our old view of reality? If the jackhammer is operated by a stranger, or runs itself, we may need to examine recent upheavals in our life which may ACTUALLY BE beyond our control. (see Hammer) (see Bang) (see Noise) (see Break)

JACOB'S LADDER In the bible, Jacob had a dream vision consisting of a staircase which led up to paradise and God, upon which, angels ascended and descended freely. In biblical times, the fully believed interpretation of this dream, was the undeniable existence of an elevated path to heaven, which was open to all righteous souls. In today's world, the dream vision of Jacob's Ladder, may imply a spiritual hope, or wish, to raise oneself up and out of the sometimes cruel and harsh misery of an earthbound reality. What do we make of the angels and spirits who ascend and descend the ladder beside us? Do we feel guilty about our upward progression? Conversely, are we frozen in a particular place upon the ladder? Is this journey into heaven too difficult, or too easy? Have we examined our own worthiness to enter paradise? Are we escaping earth prematurely? (see Tarot, The Star) (see God/Goddess) (see Angel) (see Ghost) (see Ladder)

JAGGED EDGE The symbolism of the Jagged Edge refers to a painful and otherwise unclean emotional transition. In the dream sense, we may be expressing difficulty in adjusting to a new and perplexing situation. Furthermore, this new situation may be reinstating old and painful, (hence jagged,) memories. Our Unconscious may be warning us that in order to adjust properly, we may need to sharpen our senses by executing clean breaks (and unequivocal entries) in the pinpointed and detailed schemes (of ALL our forward progressions.) We must clean up the mess of our emotional past, simply in order to strive forward into the future: as well-balanced individuals. (see Cut) (see Bridge) (see Window) (see Door) (see Gate) (see Fence) (see Glass)

JAR In the dream sense, a Jar symbolizes a transparent enclosure in which we store psychological, or emotional, perceptions for an elongated period of time. Like a child observing a captured moth, we casually observe our own painful memories. As such, witnessed through the glass, we remain fully aware of our painful emotions, yet persist in our inability to change them. In this isolated condition we also find ourselves utterly powerless to alter any of their overall effects upon us. Accordingly, we must determine whether the emotional contents of the jar should remain preserved, until the proper time of their return engagement, or whether the jar should be shattered in sudden and shocking revelation of Self! Both options eventually surrender a more complete, and perhaps well-balanced, fulfillment of Self. We must remember, a jar is made to be opened! (see Glass) (see Window) (see Bottle)

JAW The image of the powerful Jaws of an animal, which desire a tearing of our flesh, involves our fears about personal destruction and more exactly, a loss of conceptual wholeness. Our intact and unbroken sense of self, may involve any number of perceptive realities including economic status, spiritual tranquility, or physical health. The sharp teeth which deem to penetrate and tear at our well being, (fragmenting the very core of who and what we are,) may be reflective of influential realities which we deeply fear and which have invaded our social structure. We need to determine who these forces are and what real, or perceived, control they hold over our waking life. Ironically, if the jaws belong to a pet dog, we may be referring to a reversal of trust and loyalty, or conversely, our own psychosis, or neurosis, which impedes the sanctity of our daily life. (see Bite) (see Teeth) (see Penetrate) (see Cut) (see Bleed) (see Jackhammer)

JAZZ The single and unique feature of Jazz as a musical style, involves its open range of improvisational expression. In this sense, jazz demonstrates an inordinate display of physical, spiritual and psychological dexterity and potential. Moreover, since music expresses our passions, we find in the jazz dream a rather intense range of emotional latitude. Perhaps in this interpretive sense, we begin to see the magnitude of a musical style which signals a grand, metaphoric 'reassurance' of our own free and unique individualism. (see Island) (see Instrument)

JELLYFISH In the dream sense, a single Jellyfish may refer to cowardice, while a school of jelly fish, may refer to barely visible, or altogether unseen danger. The connection of these two representations is not coincidental. The danger presented in social cowardice, or individuals who refuse to act, is indeed invisible. As such, in becoming 'blind followers' of some demagogue (ex: Reverend Jim Jones,) we place our entire society in peril. Appropriately, our Unconscious may be projecting a jellyfish into our dream awareness to remind us about our own stagnant, and otherwise fearful, behavior. This dream symbol may be a clear indication of a personal need to assert ourselves more in the communal spectrum of our waking experience, including our home, occupation and other social gatherings. (see Demagogue) (see Godzilla) (see Sheep)

JESUS The dream image of Jesus, or any deity which we fully believe in, may involve our feelings of guilt, or conversely, our feelings of spiritual joy. Naturally, this depends upon the self perception of our moral ethic combined with our moral behavior. How exactly, do they correlate? Accordingly, an evil person may fear Jesus, while a pious person may cherish and adore his presence in a dream. However, the dream may reveal hidden truth, wherein, the devout person realizes hypocrisy in his deportment and is guilt-ridden under his figure of the Lord. Conversely, a criminal may find love, or compassion, within him or herself and may deem to change the course of their life. In any case, the dream is extremely subjective and equally effectual. When we face a figure who is primarily associated with goodness, we cannot help but examining our own righteousness, or lack thereof. (see Christ) (see God/Goddess) (see Angel) (see Abbey) (see Church)

JOB Our place of business, or the location where we perform our occupational duties, may be symbolic of the perception of our own self-worth and self-reliance. Accordingly, in a Job related dream, we need to interpret the circumstance involved, any and all characters present, and the physical condition of the work place itself. For example, if everything seems to be functioning normally in our occupational landscape, yet we are not present, we may be experiencing a feeling of uselessness IN OUR OWN JOB ENVIRONMENT. Conversely, if we find ourselves working exceptionally hard, while our co-workers sleep peacefully, our Unconscious may be revealing a bad workaholic habit, which may be threatening our overall well being. We must dertemine the social dynamic of our peer group. Do we share the same goals and desires as the people around us? Are we respected within this group of our peers? We must also determine whether the goal of our relative dream job, (such as it is depicted,) reflects the goal we have set for ourselves. Does our individuality interfere with our social structure? (see Jackal)

JOKER A Joker symbolizes a sly, yet powerful character. In the dream sense, the joker may refer to a sudden change of luck, either good or bad. Accordingly, we may need to interpret the moment of the joker's appearance, and what cards we held prior to this riveting and perhaps fortunate, entrance. Was the Joker wild? (see Clown) (see King) (see Tarot, The Fool, The World)

JOSHUA TREE The image of the Joshua Tree, with its limbs spread out in prayer, is one of complete and unshakable faith. Additionally, the plant's upright stature and green and white flowers epitomize purity and natural achievement. Plainly, in this dream imagery, we are gazing upon a spiritual life. At this point, we need to determine our relationship with God and the tenets of our spiritual belief system. Does the Joshua Tree provide us with strength and courage, or, are we (unlike the tree,) crooked and entirely ashamed of ourselves: hiding under long shadows beneath its sacred boughs? We must question whether we are able to stand tall and righteous in our commited faith? (see Tree) (see Adam & Eve) (see Plant) (see Wood) (see Green) (see Faith)

JOURNAL The act of recording the events of our life in a Journal may be representative of saving (and otherwise encoding,) those events into our permanent memory of our self and family's history. As such, in a dream scenario, we may be illustrating a need, or desire, to engrave recent and vital 'happenings' into our permanent recollection. However, our Unconscious may be warning us against the possibility of rewriting history, or inventing history, to satisfy our own vanity and conceit. Accordingly, we need to interpret the clear recorded message in the journal and compare it, (to the best of our memory,) with the actual events experienced in our life. Is our memory of the truth synonymous with the truth itself? Are we creating a fantastic life to make-up for our own mundane existence? Do we trust our peers and business associates? (see Ink) (see Contract) (see Form) (see Book)

JOURNEY The mythical Journey is fully representational of a voyage into the unknown regions of an infinite human consciousness. As such, the journey through our dream landscape may be seen as a search for new and unconditionally unique experiences. At the same time, the voyage into a new world of reason is entirely reflective of an escape from another world, perhaps, an old world of hardship and personal pain. Hence, we may need to determine the symbolic similarities between our waking reality and our dream expedition. If we find ourselves incessantly fleeing from familiar terrain, we may need to address our escapist behavior which offers no real solution to our waking obstacles. In an ideal sense, the journey into the unknown pertains to a collection of PROGRESSIVE experiences, each new experience expanding upon our limitless reality base. As we grow, we gain wisdom about our background history, our present dynamics and slowly create a long list of our future possibilities. As such, in a true spiritual journey, instead of escaping reality, we are able to build a sturdy bridge which transgresses our past, focuses upon the present and provides us with a valid aim for the future. The jouney into Self provides SPIRITUAL CLARITY in a single moment of fully realized existence. (see Tarot Major Arcana) (see Highway Travel) (see Road) (see Landscape) (see Horizon) (see Infinity) (see Claivoyant)

JUGGLER The image of the Juggler may involve the balancing of many situations and/or social relationships in the scope of our waking life. As such, we need to observe the relative skill of the performer. If our juggler is adept at what he or she does and displays flare and passion, our Unconscious may be revealing a steady, healthy and exhilarating balance in our life. In such a case, we need to determine to what end the juggler performs. Who are we performing for? Who do we wish to impress, with the mastery of our skills? Is the execution for oneself, or others: perhaps our peers, or love interest? Examining this in a real sense, we need to determine if our personal worth is devised to impress others and not in fact, a WORTH true to our own natures. Are we ignoring our own needs to appease the needs of others? If so, why are we martyring ourselves? Do we lack self-esteem? Only the dreamer can know the absolute worth of his or her balanced perception of reality. A well-adapted individual is not tense exploring the 'rainbow' of his varied interests. Conversely, if the juggler is failing at his or her craft and balls are flying in every chaotic direction, our dream may be warning us that our hands are over-full. We must now focus our skills and knowledge upon a goal which carries 'weight' and 'meaning' in our life. (see Acrobat)

JUNCTION A Junction in the road may refer to a choice which needs to be made in our waking life. The severity of this decision is demonstrated in the long term future derived from this particular choosing. In another interpretation, our Unconscious (in the junction dream,) may be implying that our decisions in life may be too extreme and that in waking reality, some roads run parallel or occasionally weave in and out of each other. In either case, we need to determine the reason for our confrontation with our own decision making. Have we executed bad choices in our past? Do we lack confidence in our ability to judge? We must learn to believe in our choices, at the same time, we should realize that our own judgements can never be absolute. We must leave room for change and always allow for a measure of forgiveness. (see Journey) (see Road) (see Tarot Major Arcana)

JUNG, Carl Gustav The Austrian, Carl G. Jung, began his career as a protege of Sigmund Freud. Eventually however, Freud and Jung parted company with a divergence of fundamental points of view. (see Freud). Jung, disagreeing with Freud's theoretical approach to the human Unconscious and utilizing his own studies and observations, theorized that the entire population of humanity shared a universal, or Collective Unconscious. Furthermore, Jung believed the human Unconscious contained the entire primordial memory of human existence and revealed this ancient wisdom through archetypal or universal symbols. He believed and eloquently explained in the course of his life-time how (and why) these archetypes were innately understood by all men and women of every race, creed and geographical locality. He also elaborated upon theories which expounded why diverse cultures the world over taught and transcribed to their people Universal Symbols via their own diverse and infinitely varied forms of expression. Jung's spiritual motivations enabled his science to reach, embrace and include all people, in all times: past, present and future. (see Unconscious) (see Collective Unconscious) (see Freud) (see Clairvoyant) (see Archetype) (see Infinity)

JUNGLE In the dream sense, the Jungle archetype symbolizes the wild and untamed side of our Unconscious nature. In the primordial jungle, man operates exclusively via his instinctual drives and desires. Therefore, any impulse which carries us into activity without the express consultation of reason, may refer to this unrestrained component of the psyche. Accordingly, the jungle dream, may involve feelings of passionate drives which may have been repressed in our own Unconscious, but may finally need to emerge. Hence, it is crucial to interpret which features of the jungle landscape we are drawn toward, and which facets we fear. Do we experience a loss of reason? (see Aboriginal) (see Wild) (see Ape) (see Elements) (see Trees) (see Forest) (see Sun) (see Green) (see Teeth) (see Bar) (see Iguana)

K

KANGAROO In the dream sense, a Kangaroo may symbolize a complex connection of maternal and paternal protection and an otherwise balanced psychological development. Since the female kangaroo carries her young in a physiological pouch, we may be expressing the mothering and decisively female aspect of our own nature. Conversely, the marsupials' reputation for fighting with fists, legs and tail, clearly represent the aggressive, masculine component of that same psyche. Taken together, the dream image of the exotic kangaroo, may refer to the creativity needed to enable naturalistic and well-balanced decision making in both ones personal and professional life. (see Hermaphrodite) (see Infant) (see Anima/Animus)

KAYAK In the dream sense, a Kayak may represent an isolated and individual struggle against our own emotions. Accordingly, if the Kayak spins out of control in rough breakers, we may be expressing a difficulty or confusion in handling our deeper fears and/or emotional desires. Conversely, a solitary kayak operating smoothly and efficiently on course with rapid flowing river, may illustrate the heightened experience of our individuality and singular sensation of the world within. (see Boat) (see Balance) (see Float) (see River) (see Water)

KEY, SKELETON The Skeleton Key is symbolic of potential, freedom and personal accessibility to previously unreachable goals. In all cases, the dream key illustrates a hopeful future and a real position to gain the benefits offered by an unknown future. In this sense, the key echoes a new-found faith and a sudden discovery of personal confidence. Accordingly, we need to interpret where we find the key, which specific locks can be opened, and which thresholds are subsequently crossed. However, if our key fails to open any locks whatsoever, our Unconscious may be revealing false hope witnessed in a (transient) waking situation. (see Door) (see Gate) (see Bone) (see Faith) (see Hole) (see Impale)

KILL The act of Killing in a dream is primarily a straight forward symbolic reference to change and drastic transition in life. Therefore, we need to understand the full metaphoric allusion involved in the context of who or what is killed. If we ourselves are killed, we need to determine who kills us and exactly how we die. This disclosure will hold clues to aspects within ourselves which may need to be concluded in order to 'move on', in a new and healthy direction. There is a common MYTH which holds that if a dreamer dreams of death, he or she will die. Naturally, the dead do not (normally) speak, and so, do not relay their pre-death dreams. Moreover, millions of individuals dream of their own death each day and night and live to tell about it, time and time again. In fact, death in ones dream is quite similar to death in the Tarot deck, which is looked at as a sign of 'revelatory' change in ones experience. In the devout or religious sense, we may think of dying as the physical transfiguration from bodily or worldly life, into the intangible life of ones holy spirit. (see Death) (see Impale) (see Cut) (see Blood) (see Hunt) (see Chase) (see Coffin)

KINDLING   The symbolism of Kindling wood involves a psychological breaking down of our problems into their smallest parts. Naturally, this systematic fragmenting is done in order to render our whole 'reality' compliant to a point by point understanding of our relative states of experience. Examining the separate aspects of a complex reality (one step at a time) enables our mind to construct a rational order of assessment and a valid system of detailed decision making. Moreover, the representation of burning wood may involve passion, or an otherwise emotional, undertaking: including marriage and the raising of family. The long, dedicated work of chopping a 'log' into its 'kindling' may itself be symbolic of child rearing and responsible parenthood. (see Ablaze) (see Hearth) (see Wood)

KING   In the dream sense, a King may be representational of absolute authority and the apex of social order. As opposed to tyrants or dictators, who lead their respective empires by force and the conquering passion of lust and desire, the heralded king assures tranquility and a code of morality in the ranks of his own dominion. Accordingly, in a dream, the image of a king may refer to taking charge of a particular situation, or mediating a dispute, with an organizational, ethical and spiritual wisdom. We must determine our exact relationship with the 'dream' king. Do we believe ourselves to be in charge of a particular situation? Are we able to deal with this responsibility? Have we abused our power and in so doing, acted more like a tyrant, than a king? What are the 'parameters' of our kingdom? Are we just in providing the answers, rules and needs of our relative kingdom? (see Ring) (see Queen) (see Tarot, the Emperor) (see Castle) (see Demagogue) (see Authority Figure)

KITCHEN   In a dream, a Kitchen refers to both physiological and emotional nourishment. As such, we may be expressing concern for the needs of our family and/or significant others. For example, the image of a clean and well-stocked kitchen may illustrate personal health, or a caring, loving family. Conversely, a dirty, rancid kitchen, lacking food or drink, may clearly indicate a depressed and needy emotional status. In either setting, we need to analyze our acceptance, or dissatisfaction, within the 'vivid' dream imagery itself. (see House) (see Home) (see Color) (see Table) (see Eat) (see Family) (see Knife)

KNEECAP   In a dream, a kneecap may refer to ones physical pain in symbolic, hence spiritual, traveling, or similarly, the exertion involved in making psychological leaps. Moreover, the kneecap may indicate ones ability to stand up straight, once again symbolic of moral integrity and furthermore, self-confidence. In a rather complex interpretation, we may also examine the injury of water on the knee. In this dream imagery, we may witness emotional realities (water,) which interfere with our own forward progress and ability to 'move' into higher realms of social and personal existence. (see Heel) (see Bone) (see Leg) (see Body)

KNIFE   The symbolism of the Knife refers to psychological or emotional separation. The image also may involve some form of release, or personal revelation. As

KNOWLEDGE

such, the meaning of the knife image is highly dependent upon the action and placement of the sharp instrument itself. Appropriately, a kitchen knife which slices a loaf of bread, may be representative of sharing, equality and community; while a dagger, hidden in the pocket of a stranger's jacket, may represent potential and very real danger.(see Jagged Edge) (see Impale) (see Cut) (see Kitchen)

KNIGHT   In a dream, a Knight may represent chivalry, courage and honor. In this sense, we find the embodiment of the spiritual warrior, an individual who gathers strength to battle the relentless forces of evil. Therefore, he is able to love and honor a fair maiden, but unable to perform sexual union with the poor girl, (for that base carnal act would prove entirely hypocritical to his true spiritual cause.) Hence, we may be expressing moral and spiritual strength, including chastity, in our dream vision of the mythical Knight. The figure traces a line around our fortitude of spirit. (see Castle) (see Dragon) (see Forge) (see Metal) (see Bar) (see Fist) (see Lance)

KNOCK   The sound of Knocking in a dream usually refers to expectations either welcome, or conversely, dreaded, with deep and perhaps even repressed, consternation. In this sense we understand the allusion of opportunity knocking on our front door, and of course on the other hand, death, who also comes knocking on our front door. We need to note the extremity of good (or bad) fortune which this representational outside force desires to bring into our life. However, interestingly, the house (i.e. the door), represents the psyche of self. In this, we begin to see how this knocking force must nevertheless, in spite of all its power, yield to our human will, in the form of our choice to allow (or deny) its ultimate entrance. In clinical studies involving the terminally ill, practitioners find, (time after time,) that death only comes when the patient has DECIDED to let go of life. In this sense, we witness the metaphysical testament of the human mind. Therefore, in a dream, we need to fearlessly determine the source of the knocking, and once found out, choose to permit or deny its influence over our waking reality. (see House) (see Beat) (see Explosion) (see Hammer) (see Jackhammer) (see Door) (see Key, Skeleton)

KNOT   In the dream sense, a Knot may be representational of an emotional or psychological entanglement. We may find ourselves unable to move or free ourselves from a predicament in our waking life. Accordingly, in our dream, we may need to interpret the physical location of the knot, the character who tied the knot and any attempts to loosen the knot. Plainly, the nature of a knot causes it to tighten as we pull and tug attempting to escape. Hence, we may need to stop and calmly reason our way out of the intricate overlapping bonds of our symbolic entanglement. (see Glue) (see Web) (see Rope) (see Itch)

KNOWLEDGE   In finding a loss of Knowledge in our dream, we may fear the ability to properly express our skill and wisdom. As such, our presentation, or image, of self, may be involved in this dream interpretation. We may be nervous about an interview or social situation in which our relative intelligence, as perceived by another party, may effect our future. Conversely, an increased knowledge in our dream, may involve repression of ideas and opinions due to social intolerance. Therefore, women all over the world are still taught to speak with their eyes instead of their mouths. The romantic allusion to 'knowing eyes' however, fails to cover the limitation and repression of an individualized self. (see Gibberish) (see Invisible) (see Mouth) (see Ink) (see Juggler) (see King) (see Queen)

L

LABORER The image of the Laborer may involve our feelings about work and alternatively, tasks which we may need to complete. In the sense of the creative laborer, (who builds something which functions as more than the sum of its parts,) our dream may be illustrating the potential of our hard-earned efforts. However, if the laborer is trapped in a mindless, repetitive activity, with little chance of change or transfiguration, we may be indicating our own feelings of personal obscurity and mundane achievement in our daily existence. The essential difference may be located in the desire to work toward an achievement, versus, being forced to work to maintain 'basic' survival. In a forced situation, we are rarely able to express our full potential and feel therefore, entirely stagnated by the personally 'fruitless' enterprise. In this sense, our entire life may become a laborious effort and it may become increasingly difficult to maintain normal social and interpersonal relationships. On the other hand, when our work thrives, our sense of self thrives, and therein lies a major component of a well-balanced and self actualized individuality. (see Industrial) (see Form, Paper)

LABYRINTH The complex symbolism of the Labyrinth involves the dead ends and open passage ways towards life's goals. As such, we find ourselves driven toward an unseen purpose. The dream may be illustrating the necessary obstacles and pointless roads which we must traverse in order to find the fulfillment of our own wisdom. In the mythological sense, the labyrinth's goal is guarded by the Minotaur who represents the last bastion of our own repression. In order to overcome his base influence and aggressive behavior we must place our spiritual quest far above our mortal fear. Accordingly, the labyrinth dreamscape may illustrate the complex and obstacle ridden path explored faithfully by the guiding enlightenment of our deepest emotional, psychological and spiritual convictions. (see Maze) (see Path) (see Tarot Major Arcana) (see Tarot, The Sun) (see Bull) (see Horn) (see Journey) (see Tarot, The Fool) (see Junction)

LACE The symbolism of fine Lace is reflective of the sensual and erotic qualities of our physiological and psychological selves. The frail fabric of lace depicts the nearly vulnerable surface of our visible, carnal desires. As such, we need to analyze who wears the lace and what promise that person beckons. Are we vulnerable

LAMB   **123**

to the powerful influences of this individual? Furthermore, we need to interpret the condition of the fabric itself. Is it torn, tattered or otherwise affected in some strange, or atypical, fashion? Moreover, If the lace is worn or displayed on some specific part of the body, that body part's symbolism, may need to be interpreted as a crucial component in the dream's entire landscape involving repressed sexuality and our vulnerability to some form of emotional devastation. (see Fabric) (see Bikini)

LADDER A Ladder in our dream landscape, may involve climbing to new heights of reality and/or perceptions, either psychologically or emotionally. The interesting facet of this particular dream image, involves the steep vertical ascent and conversely, descent, of the ladder itself. This physical reality may imply a rapid ascent into our new perception or emotion. At the same time, there may be an equally obvious risk of falling from these same exaggerated heights. As such, we may need to consider the relative soundness of each rung and what we perceptually find at each level of experience. In any case, the ladder may imply a social, sexual, economic, or even spiritual, rise, which needs to be scaled very slowly, and with extreme caution. (see Jacob's Ladder)

LADYBUG The Ladybug represents beauty, innocence and mirth. The insect's tiny non-threatening size, combined with her bright red coloring and sudden bursts of flight, seem to epitomize unexpected pleasure and joy. As such, in a dream landscape, the ladybug appearance may symbolize a sudden and optimistic revelation which changes some aspect of our outlook on life. Conversely, our Unconscious may be illustrating a desire for creative and fluid spontaneity. In this figure we explore intuition and an acceptance of personal magic (or charm.) Accordingly, it is crucial to note the landscape wherein the ladybug first emerges and any character which she (quite unexpectedly) lands on. She has made a choice! In ancient times, the ladybug symbol became associated with a sensation of new love, especially among the young and innocent (in those times called: virginal, or chaste.) (see Insect) (see Orange) (see Flying)

LAGOON The image of the Lagoon reflects a warm, personal and creatively unique emotional state of consciousness. Hence, in a dream landscape, we may be expressing the rare quality of our deeper sensitivities, including the fulfillment of our sexual and individual yearnings. Moreover, the womb-like nature of the lagoon signals a rebirth into our primal consciousness. In this sense, we may be indicating a new incarnation for ourselves which involves accepting the raw purity of our actual 'feelings'. We are immersing ourselves in the purifying waters of our own deepest truths. (see Immerse) (see Water) (see Beach) (see Sun) (see Tarot, The Sun) (see Baptism) (see Elements)

LAMB Today, as in historic times, the Lamb symbolizes peace, innocence and social tranquility. Moreover, because of its wool coat and easy manners, the lamb has provided man with warmth, milk and various other forms of physiological sustenance. Traveling back to biblical times, the lamb's innocence and white fleece combine to serve as the ideal sacrificial animal to a mighty and benevolent God. Following this tradition, the early Christians called Jesus the Lamb of God, who suffered the sins of the world by sacrificing his own life in order to grant ALL righteous members of humanity a place in heaven, beside God. Consequently, the lamb in the dream landscape may represent a form of self-sacrifice which ultimately strengthens the living society of our peers. However, an entirely opposite interpretation may be offered. Hence, our Unconscious may be warning us against running with the herd and opting instead, for the complete establishment of our own unique identity. Even as spiritual men and women, we cannot be complacent in our individuality. We should never be 'sheep' led to the slaughter. Accordingly, we need to fully analyze any and all symbolism found in this complex and rather peculiar, lamb dreamscape. Offering ourselves to God, does not mean offering ourselves up to fanatical leaders. (see Jackal) (see Sheep)

LAME The conceptualization of Lameness may involve insecurity about ones mobility, or a fear of standing up for what one believes in. This is primarily because the dream image of our legs, represents our ability to choose whether we will charge, flee or 'dance' around our confronted obstacles. The dream likeness of our sudden lameness, involves the limitation of our overall potential. In this sense, we become frozen in fear, akin to a deer in the headlights. Our Unconscious may be revealing on outside force in our waking life which has narrowed our decision making and subsequently hampers our creative fulfillment. The dream, like a messianic figure (who heals the lame,) may be telling us to get up and walk. It may hurt a little at first, but eventually, we will have learned the sturdy balance and potent forward progress of our own abilities. (see Ice) (see Run) (see Walk) (see Kneecap)

LANCE The projected rod, or Lance, symbolizes the aim of our intentions. The exertion with which we handle the lance may represent the resolve of our position. Moral concepts involving 'an aim which is true', are deeply imbedded in this dream imagery. Moreover, this natural metaphor of sexuality transforms into a 'value system' within the context of our social relationships: including romance, marriage and inevitably, family. Accordingly, if the lance is broken, or launched without power and determination, we may be witnessing a symbolic breakdown of our own faith in a chosen commitment. In a rather complex combination of the former and latter representations, we may be exploring a competition, a kind of sexual 'rites of passage'. As such, when males demonstrate physical and sexual potency, they display an ability to propagate the species, which is in fact, their evolutionary aim. This aim is 'accomplished' via hormones and our unique, individuated DNA/RNA structures, but, on the other hand, 'advertized' in our overt physicality. In this revelation, we explore the inbred competition between ALL potential mates. It should be noted (that) in human beings, BOTH GENDERS participate in this ritual of sexual projection and social posturing. (see Arrow) (see Impale) (see Blood) (see Bar)

LANDSCAPE Its extensive use in dream interpretation demonstrates the significance of what is termed, the dream Landscape. In fact, the entire 'dream scene' is referred to as the landscape, or 'dreamscape', of the psyche. Our environment defines us in a way that is understood on a plethora of representational levels from our physical, material and economic status to our enigmatic and diverse psychological development. Accordingly, the world presented in our Unconscious is a visible icon of symbols which defines our singular, yet complex uniqueness in the world of human experience. In other words, a dream reveals our vital comprehension of self. The lanscape is the psychological 'scene' of our specific level of consciousness, or more exactly, our level of comprehension. What we 'see' in a landscape is our 'perception' of the world. (see Horizon) (see Infinity) (see Elements)

LANTERN As a path is symbolic of a course taken in order to find our truest selves, a Lantern implies the enlightenment, or spiritual guidance, necessary to safely and accurately traverse that passage toward the inner most self. In the mythological sense, the hermit holds high his lantern of wisdom and spiritual truth. His pondering, cryptic figure accepts the darkness of the Unconscious yet places trust and spiritual faith in the embers of his burning lantern. The lantern represents the measure of his faith. Appropriately, in the dream sense, the lantern may symbolize a moral quandary which may need to be focused upon with the light of a personal conviction. Moreover, the lanterns presence within our dream may be indicative of a new and clear direction in our waking life. Should the lantern be snuffed out, our Unconscious may be illustrating a loss of honorable principles, which may be affecting our true heading in life's long and complex labyrinth. Our lantern guides us through our 'darker' moments of reality. (see Tarot, The Hermit) (see Light)

LATE The concept of being on time demonstrates accuracy in planning our affairs. When we are on time we are demonstrating our adeptness at projecting allotted times necessary for each undertaking and social responsibility. As such, we are subtlely indicating our respect for our peers. This act of maturity and altruism avoids any unnecessary interference with a group, or individual's, own sensitive schedule. We are going with the flow of life's smooth flux. The act of being Late may involve the exact reversal of any, or all, of these dedicated social components. The most prominent interruption of life's flow entails insecurity about our ability to understand, organize and perform in a social setting. Our fear stops the momentum of life's infinite potential. In this sense, we isolate and alienate ourselves from 'groups' by arriving late for their communal events and relinquishing the smoothness of the experiences themselves. This is known in psychological terms as Reaction Formation, or the self-creation of our own deepest fears. Because we fear being noticed, we suddenly become all the more noticeable. Our passionate desire to fit in becomes the motivational force for our 'nerve-wrecked' social 'rift'. The alternate side of this tardiness details our lack of concern for the social meeting altogether. This lack of responsibility illustrates expressions of emotional stagnation and a general disruption of our natural maturation process.

In the clinical sense, this can include ongoing levels of personal regression experienced over and over in various degrees throughout ones life. However, the goal of personal freedom may also be immersed in this complex participation of social organization. In this connotation, we need to examine how late we (or other individuals) appear in the dream itself. For example, we may find ourselves 'fashionably late', which in some circles, is considered a very good (social) thing. Its all in the timing! (see Self) (see Image) (see Clock) (see Calendar)

LAUGHTER   In this dream image, we find a dualistic expression of extreme elation, or dire embarrassment, dependent upon which side of the Laughter one happens to fall. As such, we need to examine the impetus for this release of psychological, or emotional, control. In other words, what's so funny? Furthermore, we need to determine if the humor is good natured, or mean spirited. We also need to determine in what capacity is it geared: as a weakness, or as an absurdity? Do we wish to mock, or share familiarity, with our slandered victims? In this sense, we may need to carefully search the dream for the EXACT source of our humor. Once discovered, we may analyze the symbolic reasoning for all this UPROARIOUS amusement. We need to understand why we need to 'expose' and then 'explode' our perception of reality. For example, we may be reacting in the form of compensation, to a very serious and solemn issue. Conversely, we may have linked social and personal absurdities in life which gratify us because they undermine the supposedly 'unshakable' order of humanity, (and the great society.) In all cases, we need to find the appropriate analogy for an emotional outburst in our waking experience. In this sense, the Unconscious may be asking us not to take something too seriously, or, warning us about not taking certain issues seriously enough. Moreover, we may find a representational connection to madness, or unhinged, behavior in this dream figure. If this is the case, we may need to examine the full range of our dream emotions and compare their diverse catalysts in waking life. We are exposing and exploding every aspect of life. This recourse can leave devastating emotional, or psychological, damage. The dream may illustrate the nature of our overall and focused perception and as such, reveal a great deal about our repressed desires and outright fears. Therapy may be highly recommended if this dream is a recurring one, AND, if the behavior of Inappropriate Affect begins to appear in our daily life. Inappropriate Affect involves abnormal emotional responses; for example, laughing at a loved ones funeral, or becoming depressed after winning the lottery.

LAVA   The hot threatening liquid which emerges from the womb of the earth and covers our symbolic landscape may illustrate a flood of sensual emotions which dictates our waking behavior. As such, we may find ourselves tortured and paralyzed by our own newly revealed 'emotional currents'. The rumbling volcano which blows out the Lava may represent an Unconscious which suddenly 'vents' our hidden drives and desires. Conversely, the lava may be symbolic of female cycles and regenerative principles. Accordingly, in the dream landscape we may need to interpret the location of the lava flow, any and all characters effected by the lava and the full destructive capabilities of the lava itself. Is the emotional swelling symbolic of an intense form of personal sacrifice? Are we destroying the colder features of our present emotional armour? (see Blood) (see Hole) (see Explosion) (see Impale) (see Womb) (see Tears)

LEAF In the dream sense a Leaf may be symbolic of rich, swaying and delicately animated life. Moreover, the leaf represents the fragile mortality of nature which must return to its origin or source. Consequently, the leaf illustrates the potential of cyclical and eternal rebirth. Furthermore, a leaf may symbolize skin and the utter sensation of experienced life. Taken together, the dream image of a leaf, may indicate a fragile encounter in our waking life which may have ignited a personal transfiguration in our day to day existence. We must learn when to surrender ourselves to a higher cause. We must accept all the stages of our life well-lived and teach those who come behind us. (see Tree) (see Joshua Tree) (see Adam & Eve) (see Apple) (see Fall) (see Green) (see Earth)

LEAK The image of Leaking represents a fear of loss. Since water is primarily the substance which is lost, we may be referring to an emotional loss which seems irreversible and irretrievable. Naturally, we need to determine the severity of the leak and compare it to the relative force of the catastrophe. In a rather interesting rationalization, a slight leak of water which falls drop by drop, has become an archetype linked with madness and the slow loss of ones mind (Chinese Water Torture.) Strangely enough, studies show that wives commit their own husbands to psychotherapeutic hospitals, only after THEY CAN NO LONGER TOLERATE their loved ones psychosis and otherwise, abnormal behavior. This climax represents the final outburst, or culminating psychotic 'episode'. However, when the wives are routinely asked when the extraordinary behavior of their husbands first began, they have extreme difficulty in pinpointing any exact moment in time. In this, we witness the gradual dripping of sanity as it slowly drains away with the ongoing obstacles found in everyday life. Is our dream reminding us that we are letting it all 'slip away'? (see Basin) (see Water) (see Drain)

LEATHER The image of worn Leather elicits a tough, rugged hide and an otherwise thick and impenetrable psychological skin. The visual media has enhanced this perception by portraying erotic, anti-social and entirely untamed individuals sporting leather regalia, from cowboys to young street gangs to underground, sadomasochistic (sexual) deviants. Appropriately, the dream image of leather symbolizes a complex conceptualization of extreme physicality which unfortunately, may lack a bit of emotional maturity and/or responsibility. Are we exploring the connection between our unique expression of (anti-social) individuality and our simultaneous (and entirely confusing) desire for social acceptance? (see Fabric) (see Black) (see Sadomasochism) (see Image)

LEMONADE STAND The image of the Lemonade Stand may imply another time and place where trust and simplicity were commonplace in small communities nationwide. Furthermore, this image may involve our earliest concepts of value and a sense of responsibility about fairness, hard work and a sacrificing of the present moment, for a slightly belated gain. These concepts are very much a part of adulthood and the slow developmental process of social maturation. In fact, in a fair example of absolute symbolism, we find the lemon itself to be an 'adult fruit'. This conceptualization is clearly witnessed in its bitter taste, a taste which satisfies a thirst far longer than any of its sweet, fruity counterparts. Sweet alternatives produce a nonsensical requirement for repeated intakes of their sweet, sugary base because their quenching properties are short-termed and short-lived. In lemonade, we witness a long term gratification, rather than an immediate, (or in Freudian terminology,) Id, gratification. As such, what better soft drink for the (Superego's) instructional Stand, than good old lemonade? (see Freud)

LETTER In a dream, a Letter may represent communication with, or feelings about, individuals outside our immediate experience. Furthermore, the symbolism of the love letter refers to a revelation of deepest emotion transcribed in hopes of capturing a significant love interest. As such, the idea of potential may be inherent in the letter imagery. This, of course, is supported by the reality of cover letters, query letters and resumes, all created in hope of some desired future fulfillment. Accordingly, the letter in our dreamscape, may refer to an Unconscious longing to bring a distant reality into its truest fruition. Conversely, the image of a "Dear John" letter, may represent a preparation for separation due to 'irreconcilable differences', in certain aspects of our waking relationships. This particular anticipation may involve a fulfillment of personal 'freedom'. (see Language) (see Contract) (see Form, Paper) (see Ink)

LIE In a dream, dishonest behavior enacted by persons known to us as 'honest' in waking life, may be representational of growing feelings of distrust, or an otherwise lack of faith in a once trusted individual's recent actions. On the other hand, if we find OURSELVES willfully engaged in Lies in the dream landscape, our Unconscious may be revealing various levels of our own personal deception. In other words, we may be involved in activities which are unnatural to our basic instincts, or perhaps even our long held beliefs. As such, our 'twisted' smiles may be giving up our calculating insincerity as we continue 'lying through our teeth'. In order to interpret this dream properly, we need to analyze the exact nature and particulars of the lie/s perpetrated. We need to accurately determine who is being lied to and what precisely motivates this act of duplicity. Are we hiding something from ourselves? Are we hiding something from others? In either case, what is the consequence of revealing the truth? Will our lies damage our friends or family? How so? Is the dreamer involved in some form of addictive behavior which NEEDS to be exposed? (see Deception) (see Mask)

LIGHT The complex symbolism of Light, may involve an intricate combination of illumination, warmth and hope. Examining the primary source of all light, the sun, we observe the full embodiment of representational images concerning light.

For example, a shimmering and warm sunrise may refer to hope promise and furthermore, a fulfillment of personal aspirations. Conversely, a hot midday sun may refer to exposure, difficult labor and a relentless psychological or emotional struggle. Lastly, the brilliant and captivating western sunset may illustrate a feeling of deep reverence, personal enlightenment and the realization of a burning persistance of faith which will remain within us, long after the sun has set, leaving a dark and unknown future to enshroud us in her mysterious folds. Light can also be blinding. In the symbolic sense, this occurs when we stare directly into the source of a guiding light, rather than the path it is fully meant to illuminate. This occurs with religious fanatics, who avoid God's moral laws in the name of God himself. Their quest to become God-like supercedes their basic humanity. 'Inquisitions', 'religious wars' and enacting the 'wrath of God' are all too familiar examples of this 'blind' behavior. Let the light act as a guide and you will find it burning and emanating from within yourself. According to several ancient (and globally crisscrossing) teachings, we can never be blinded by the truth, (turned to stone, maybe,) but never, ever, blinded. (see Tarot, The Sun) (see Tarot, The Moon) (see Lantern) (see Lighthouse)

LIGHTHOUSE A Lighthouse may represent a warning of impending hazard or outright danger. Moreover, since the lighthouse is situated near the sea, our dream may be implying an emotional adversity, which can, (and perhaps, should at all cost,) be avoided. Naturally, the other side of this symbolism involves real hope in the face of perilous diversity. Once again we need to determine if the light is guiding us, or blinding us in her glaring rays of delusion. We need to determine what emotional aspect of our waking life has the potential to damage us. Is the threat coming from dry land, which represents psychological firmness, in other words: HARD REASON? Hence, are we attempting to use the 'light' of 'logic' in order to understand our highly illogical 'matters of the heart'? Conversely, have we lost sight of land, in which case the lighthouse represents the comforting light of familiarity and firm ground. Light is the guide of our own humanity, we must make ceratin our own human potential doesn't carry us too far away, (or bring us too close to,) our 'neutral' sense of a 'balanced' Self. (see Water) (see Boat) (see Light) (see Lantern)

LIGHTNING The archetypal symbolism of Lightning refers to God-like and otherwise superhuman power, and the reality of its threat. As such, mortal human beings are reminded of their ultimate submission to God and/or nature herself. However, in the dream sense, the massive electrical potential of lightning, may be indicative of a brilliant new idea or a powerful new direction found in the high frequency spark of a 'radical brainstorm'. Accordingly, we need to examine our emotional reaction to the lightning and the physical location upon which the bolt strikes its devastating, yet illuminating blow. (see Electricity) (see Tarot, the Tower)

LION The ancient symbolism of the Lion combines two separate representational facets, that of the wild and powerful beast and the converse nobility of a ruling king. As such, the complex lion archetype represents the focused aggression, outright power and ferocious behavior necessary to overcome ones own disabilitating emotions and the endless obstacles found in ruling (or at least maintaining some semblance of order,) in an otherwise chaotic environment. The lion icon is sturdy enough to rule its own psyche and maintain significant influence throughout its pride, (or society,) without the use of 'destructive' aggression. Its power is established without the actual use of force, but rather by its direct and forceful presence. Accordingly, our Unconscious may be indicating a need to establish honorable leadership in our own personal or social life, without petty anger or gratuitous (and entirely unnecessary) violence. We lead by example, solely by the strength of our unique and straight-forward character. (see Tarot, Strength) (see Wolf) (see King) (see Joshua Tree)

LIZARD The Lizard is a cold and poised reminder of our primal instincts and predatory beginnings. Scientists often refer to the brain stem as the reptilian brain. This is because it enacts our basic functions, without which, we would 'immediately' cease to be. In as much, we begin to see the correlation between our 'automatic', or innately triggered, deep consciousness and the further evolved, decision making, surface consciousness. Accordingly, we witness the Unconscious expression of our basic primal drives including sexuality, hunger, pleasure in the tropical sunlight, and of course, fear. In short, the initial use and virgin examination of all of our five senses is explored in this age-old archetype. This dream involves experience over thought, excess over slow lingering deliberation. (see Iguana) (see Lighthouse) (see Aboriginal) (see Landscape) (see Ape)

LOCK The concept of the Locked door entails closing oneself off from the world, or conversely, having the symbolic doors of life slammed shut and locked in your face. In both cases, an internal mechanism of fear is implied by our Unconscious. Appropriately, we need to examine the fundamental roots of our own fears, or conversely, the repeated and fundamental doubts and suspicions we seem to inspire and bring forth in others. In other words, what about our behavior causes our dream passage-way to close before us? What, or whom, is shutting us out? Questions of our worthiness may be illustrated in this dream, as well as complex associations involving our relationship with nature, or our own 'not-so- civilized' environment. In the latter example, being INSIDE a house and behind its locked door, may imply harsh lessons learned about civilization's right of passage and the manifestation of our Superego itself. Conversely, being outside the locked door, may reveal our natural, yet anti-social and entirely Id, self. In this sense, we relish in our lack of reason and conveniently use this argument for an excuse not to succeed. We are the starving artist, tortured by a society which cannot understand us. Yet we refuse to work for minimum wage to buy our paints and canvas! The dreamer needs to determine which side of the door he or she may be on, and exactly what his or her intentions are, for crossing over to another side. In other words, where do we wish to go, and why? Once again, we need to determine who exactly has locked the door, (if not ourselves.) The Unconscious always exists on both sides and prefers free access either way. It teaches us that the key to our humanity lies in the entirety of our being and the fullness of our potential. Can we open the doors of perception? (see Door) (see Key, Skeleton)

LOCUST Since Locust invade land and crops, we may symbolize them as an interruption to the union of man and nature. Locust, like tornadoes, indicate to man that nature, (like man,) has a bad side, and that (that) side, may strike out at any time and absolutely ruin our well being. In as much, the dream may illustrate the fallacy of permanence and indestructible methods (and strategies) meant to preserve life (and livlihood.) This forced realization of human vulnerability may have the dual purpose of keeping mankind humble, as well as, pushing him to strive for a better and more respectful confederation with his natural environment. In the Biblical tradition, when God became angry at the Pharaoh, he took the form of locust, to break the back and spirit of the Egyptian people. In this (perhaps mythical) imagery, we see the archetypal connection between God and nature. In fact, even today, a government relief claim, involving locust devastation, would certainly be considered in print, a justifiable 'act of God'. When we respect nature we respect God's creation and hence, we respect ourselves. The cycle is complete. Locust remind humanity of its rightful place in the scheme of things, not on top, but somewhere snug in the middle. (see Infestation) (see Circle) (see Lightning)

LOTUS The Eastern symbolism of the white petaled Lotus, which indigenously occurs in low lying areas, involves an intricate collaboration of tranquility, sensuality and metaphysical transcendence. Furthermore, its connection with calm pools of water illustrate emotional maturity and a serenely feminine union with nature's enlightened blueprint. Appropriately, the appearance of the lotus in our dream landscape, may depict emotional comfort and spiritual grace in our conceptualization of a certain situation, perhaps even, our entire perception of the world around us. Conversely, if the lotus is threatened, or becomes submerged, we may be expressing anxiety over our own loss of individual faith. This conceivably may involve a sinking emotional interrelationship with a person still considered to be a loved one. (see Water) (see Float) (see White) (see Flower) (see Frog)

LUCID DREAMING Lucid dreaming entails a semi-consciousness within the framework of the dream itself, which enables the dreamer to manipulate his or her surroundings by force of imaginative will. In other words, the dreamer may decide a horse in his or her dream should instead become a Ferrari, and immediately this transformation occurs. Naturally, the concern here centers around the supposed elimination, or expansion, of the intended dream itself and also its Unconscious message, which in this example (initially) chose to picture a horse. So we say, as interpreters, we NEED that 'horse' and its symbolic reality, to learn something 'true' about our intrinsic selves. That's all well and good. However, an alternative argument is that the Unconscious (aware of all states of consciousness) is fully aware of the individual who practices lucid dreaming and therefore chooses to present ordinary, or undesirable, objects to create a direct negative pathway toward the 'suggested' imagery, which the dreamer may then follow in a personalized and fully 'corrective' succession. In this sense, the Unconscious is actually pinpointing its intentions far more accurately than in a normal dream scenario by offering colorless hues which beg to be sharpened and focused into the dreamers truest colors and most unique shades of experience. Naturally, this debate continues. In any case, for those interested in the practice of lucid dreaming, let us say that perception and meaning are intertwined. Our neural picture of the world fully encodes the world in which we live and comprehend. Keeping this in mind, the dreamer may initially need to view his or her waking reality as a living dream, placing meaning on objects and intensifying these meanings until they (perceptively) transcend the objects themselves in the waking world. He is incorporating the 'truth' of his imagination into the 'truth' of his internal worldly perception. In doing so, the fusion of perceived objects/meanings become the true 'language' of a distinct and entirely lucid memory. The dreamer must then learn to recognize this unique language as it appears and is utilized by the language of the Unconscious. The awareness of self, provided through recognition, allows a fundamental entry into the deep and abstract layers of the dream. At this point, the lucid dreamer travels into the dream image itself, with comprehension, and moreover, a heightened sense of curiosity about the nature of the perceptive reality of his or her overall dream symbolism. In this faculty, the lucid dreamer may come to witness that fact and comprehension are in this (waking) world, one in the same. (see Memory) (see Collective Unconscious) (see Clairvoyant)

LUMBER   The symbolism of Lumber may refer to the natural construction and formulation of our psychological makeup. Accordingly, we need to determine the condition of the lumber and the soundness of our architectural layout. For example, sturdy oak planks criss-crossed to form a stable rustic cabin may be symbolic of a well-balanced psyche, replete with ancient, naturalistic and reasonably oriented sensibilities. On the other hand, termite ridden lumber, may represent psychological stagnation and a break down in our perception of self, including social cohesiveness, personal worth and moral integrity. (see Wood) (see House) (see Parasite) (see Infestation)

M

MADONNA   The archetype of the Madonna figure involves the mesmerizing combination of maternal nurturing and divine spiritual love. The madonna icon, (or vision,) illuminates a bridge between earth and sky, birth and transcendence, creation and animated life itself. In the dream sense, the imagery of an eternal mother, may imply trust, warmth and hope in an uncertain future. She is the guidance and care of the cradle of humanity. She is the world and the womb of (its) reality. Because of the unconditional love associated with motherhood, the madonna figure represents forgiveness and divine tolerance. She will care for the sick, lame and mentally abandoned. Is her figure a reflection of our own highest aspirations, or a gross contradiction of our own self-serving and callous behavior? Are we tolerant of a harsh and imperfect world? Can we be? (see Womb) (see Earth) (see Mother) (see Queen)

MAGIC The symbolism of Magic refers to illusions, surprise and impossible feats of reality. Accordingly, in a dream sense, a magic act may represent an enactment of the seemingly impossible. In other words, we may be expressing extreme self confidence or conversely, a delusional sense of our superreal personal ability. In either case, we may be illustrating (via compensation) a basic fear of failure. We may have a deep insecurity about being labeled 'ordinary'. However, magic, or witchcraft, involves our 'shaping' of the world. In the (up to date) elaborations of modern physics, we learn that the world exits in our perceptive awareness and memory of that world. This implies, that a so-called 'hard' reality is actually our fundamental perception of that 'hard' reality. A world can only be perceived through the lens of Self. Therefore, when we combine our aspiration, imagination and insight, we approach a reality with fortitude, confidence and faith in its inclusive completeness, we celebrate the 'magic' of being. Furthermore, we realize that we are a working part of reality's construction. When we believe in the highest purpose of ourselves we 'work' the highest magic in existence. Casting spells simply involves projecting the confidence of an infinitely potential existence. When we become aware of the infinite measure of reality, we become modern-day magicians combining reason, faith and (what is today called) personal power. Appropriately, we need to analyze the nature of the magic involved and all the characters effected by our respective magic. We need to deetermine whether or not we wish to cast these spells? Is our 'manipulation' of the world really warranted? Are we prepared to dabble in a magic which already old us steady in its limitless sway? (see Witchcraft) (see Clairvoyance) (see Collective Unconscious) (see Crystal) (see Pyramid) (see Hand) (see Tarot, the Magician) (see Mandala) (see Ring) (see King)

MAILBOX In the dream sense, a Mailbox may represent expectation, desire and hope. Furthermore, the mailbox may be compared to a womb which accepts the combination of procreative life and delivers a new life into truest fruition. Each day we explore the confines of the mailbox to find news which may change our reality and hence embody our physical, emotional and/or psychological rebirth. We wish to hear news from 'outside' our immediate field of experience. Ae we dissatisfied with our present community, or our relative social position within that community? Do we feel trapped by the geography of our physical existence? We must remember that the psyche's truest geography exists and is created from deep within oneself. In this sense, we must understand our needs and our desires. What, or whom, are we searching for? What do we wish to accomplish? Must the reward of our accomplishments come from outside our own field of experience? Why? Do we feel our friends and family limit us by casting us into one particular 'shade' of existence? Must we break the role of our peers? We may find that 'individual freedom' can be its own reward, and ALL societies (even our very own) are made up of unique collections of individuals. Our mailbox dream may be reminding us to experience the truth (not of an outside world) but rather right here at home with our friends and neighbors. The Unconscious tells us, the news is not in the mailbox, but (right here at home) within ourselves. To this significant end, we need to interpret the color, condition and naturally, contents, of the dream mailbox. We will often find it empty, for this very honorable reason. (see Letter) (see Womb) (see Child) (see Form, Paper)

MANDALA The archetypal image of a Mandala, replete with a square within a circle, symbolizes the infinite radiance of microcosm to macrocosm. Used in Hindu and Buddhist traditions to represent the foundation of universality, the mandala embodies the form (see Circle) of its own all-encompassing meaning. Appropriately, in the dream sense, we may be referring to the limitless potential of our own Unconscious; the infinite mind, within the finite body. We are also referring to the connection and superimposition of our infinite, immaterial soul and the immeasurable parameters of an unimaginable existence. We must ascertain if our belief in self is as strong as the promise of our existence? If so, is there a meaningful place for us within the boundaries of a soulful world? (see Infinite) (see God/Goddess) (see Magic) (see Ring) (see Collective Unconscious) (see Lucid Dreaming)

MARBLE In the dream sense, articles constructed of Marble, may symbolize fragile beauty, inspired artistry and superhuman eternal adoration. As such, we need to determine the form and/or character depicted in the contour of the marble. If the sculpture is recognized as someone we know, we may be expressing an everlasting fondness for this individual, tinged nevertheless, with a personal estrangement from that person. Perhaps the person has grown larger than life in the grandiosity of his or her own self-perception and pretentious exploits, and hence negated our admiration. Conversely, if we ourselves become marble statues in a dream landscape, our Unconscious may be illustrating a well-defined mockery of our own overblown ego. We may need to eradicate this particular image of ourselves by replacing it with the proven operation and fulfillment of our true goals and aspirations. We are not immortal in this world. Eventually, (akin to marble sculptures,) we must all turn to dust and continue the great cycle of life. Sculpture represents the immortal spirit of man, but never man himself. Only an icon can fulfill the 'best' meaning of an ancient memory. Moreover, we must remember never to worship false idols, especially if those idols happen to be ourselves. (see Icon) (see Hands) (see Sculpture) (see Image) (see Elements) (see Stone) (see Epitaph)

MARCH A March may be symbolic of a political, (or spiritual,) cause which requires the impact of social unity to display the merit of its validity to the 'whole' of society. Accordingly, in a dream, a march may refer to a solid position, or belief, which we and our social group join together in strengthening. However, the march scenario may indicate a deep insecurity regarding our own opinions, which may require organizational support in order to remain valid in our individual consciousness and belief system. Does a single idea hold our group together? Are the members of our march truly united? Will our march enble society to comprehend the straight-forward, force of social unity. Examining some of these interpretations, we must determine whether our particular 'dream' march fulfills 'all' the tenets of its 'true' purpose. Lastly, and perhaps most importantly, does our march fail to fulfill our own purposes, but instead fulfills the purposes of a virtual demagogue? Do we stand together in moral strength, or scream together in the vengeful agreement of our own hatred? (see Demagogue) (see Godzilla)

MARIJUANA The conceptualization of drugs in general, may involve various forms of escapism. The longing to enter into the potential freedom of ones mind and its active imagination, has long characterized our human kind. However, the social reality of Marijuana has created diverse limitations which are in direct contrast to our modern forms of personal freedom. The use of hallucinogens by archaic cultures operated as forms of social ritual meant to bring together tribes in peaceful union. In today's world, the isolated use and underground culture of pot may separate individuals from family and other instrumental social organizations. As such, it operates as a 'compensation' for serious forms of alienation, which could in fact, effect personal development. The culture of drug-use creates its own self-fulfilling prophesy of social abandonment. In this, marijauna loses its true archaic value of communal transcendence and symbolizes instead, a personal difficulty which has forged a path into a rather elaborate, yet nevertheless repressive, fantasy. We must explore our true visions and avoid shortcuts which limit the absolute potential of our absolute 'becoming'. Additionally, drugs can only bring out 'that' which is already sparkling within ourselves. No-one will ever place a law against knowing the infinite parameters of oneself. (see Hemp) (see Fungus) (see Infinite) (see Bar) (see Indian, Native American)

MARIONETTE The Marionette may refer to a loss of control in ones life. As such, we may feel like a puppet manipulated by the strings, or attachments, of the people around us. Accordingly, we need to analyze the suggestive movements and the style and color of the clothing worn by the marionette itself. This interpretation may reveal the reason for our suppression and subjugation by certain individual/s in our life. However, if we ourselves are NOT depicted as the marionette/s, but rather these marionettes resemble our own subordinates in waking life, (including spouses and children,) our Unconscious may be signalling our own (completely unnatural) rule over these persons. It may be time to 'cut the strings'. (see Puppet) (see Demagogue) (see Godzilla) (see March) (see Authority Figure) (see Lawyer) (see Incontinent)

MASK The ancient symbolism of the mask used in divine rituals from the preparation of tribal warfare to the unification of marriage vows, refers to the spirit we present in the face of super-real events. Moreover, a majority of archaic religions, (including Judaism and Shintoism,) believed that supernatural forces entered into, and resided inside, the head and face of human beings. Consequently, a Mask worn over a face served as either a greeting to, or barrier against, spirit messengers. In the dream sense, the mask may represent the personal spirit and animated face we present in certain situations in our life. For example, a big, burly man, may become docile and remarkably tender in order to win the affections of a very feminine, young woman. As such, he may dream himself wearing the mask of a fragile and delicate child. (see Image) (see Face) (see Ritual) (see Icon) (see especially Tarot, The Moon, The Sun)

MASON In a dream, a Mason may refer to the building of ones own psychological and social development. As such, the relative skill and adeptness of the mason needs to be determined in the dream landscape. For example, a foolish and inept mason who builds a shabby log cabin on top of a lake, drastically depicts a psyche unable to handle, or otherwise deal with, an ever-present emotional reality. Conversely, a master builder who crafts a sturdy chapel on top of an exalted elevation, may be indicative of growing spiritual, emotional and psychological strength and forbearance. this figure illuminates the entirety of self. An ancient religious order known as Freemasonry continues to exist in todays world. This order believes in the concept of sturdy spiritual building. Its members are schooled in exact techniques of movement, prayer and meditation. Their goal is to build a 'true' house of worship witnin their own humble beings. (see House) (see Home)

MAZE The age-old symbolism of the Maze involves the closed pathways and open roads we traverse in order to find our deepest desired goals. As such, we witness the trip through the Maze as the journey into self-understanding. The overall conceptualization of the maze illustrates a layout which is predetermined by some greater force who in turn, observes the choices made by the traveler within the elaborate puzzle. We may view the 'greater force' as God, but the symbolic force of the maze lies in the lone traveler within the labyrinth, who begins dimly aware, but over time, through negative and positive (associations), begins to understand the distinct sequential paths necessary to arrive at his or her desired goal. The goal is primarily God, or Spiritual Enlightenment. Accordingly, we need to ascertain our own forward progress (or lack of it) in the dream, determining precisely, what pushes us, or conversely, hold us back, in the day to day experience of our waking life. We must also be well aware of the final obstacle within the maze, often represented as the half man/half bull creature called the minotaur. This figure symbolizes our ability to come to terms with our own worthiness to find a form of 'ultimate peace' in our life. (see Labyrinth) (see Path) (see Tarot Major Arcana)

MEAT In the dream sense, the symbolism of Meat may refer to physical desires and/or cravings. Conversely, if the dreamer happens to be a vegetarian, the image of meat may refer to aggression, suffering and/or immoral behavior. In either case, if the meat appears rotten, our Unconscious may be illustrating a degradation in our physical health or psychological drive. The meat in many ways parallels our own physical being. It is a metaphor for our own body and our bodies health.

Therefore, if we carry, or punch, a side of beef in our dream, we are referring to a physical exertion which may be necessary in the very near future. We are testing the limits of our external strength. Often times, our external physical strength mirrors our inner tenacity and conviction. However, if we become obsessed with the 'meat' of our physicality, we may begin to lose sight of our 'highest' values. (see Eat) (see Table) (see Bikini)

MELODY When a melody is repeated in a dream it may be symbolic of a particular feeling, or specific time, which is etched in our memory. The precise physical and mathematical beauty of a musical motif, may embody an otherwise fragmented, recollection of a significant event in our distant past, perhaps even our childhood. As such, in the dream sense, a melody may refer to a regressive state of mind, or an elaborate fear of a future which bears momentous, yet foreboding, changes in our life. In the psychological sense, it is far easier to remain in familiar territory, than to venture out into an alien unknown. A melody is symbolic of the accepted, intimate and deeply embedded world of our past. What memory does the melody bring forth? Are there situations in our waking life, (at this point in time,) which may have 'prompted' this deep recollection? Are we repeating some form of history in our new relationships? Do we live to replay and old tune? The words, 'Play it again Sam', were never spoken in Bogart's Casablanca, however, their emotional significance caused a nation of movie-goers and fans alike, to repeat their resonant truth, over and over again. Emotions are forever. (see Memory) (see Instrument)

MEMORY The conceptualization of Memory is crucial in the dream sense as it draws from the infinite pool of the Unconscious itself. Hence, the recollection of repressed memories, returned to waking consciousness, may reflect a growth in our human awareness. In theory, we instinctively (and rather innately,) understand the universal balance of our own psyche. Accordingly, recalled dreams guide us in our ongoing experience of life. Moreover, dreams which leave a strong impression on us, (and are remembered in detail,) are decisively more significant than forgotten dreams, whose recollections are (not at all) important to our intimate sense of self. We need to determine the connection between our distant memory and our present occurances. Have we learned from the past? In terms of emotions, we will find that history often repeats itself. The important consideration in the memory dream involves the dream itself. Why has our Unconscious chosen to reveal this memory in a dream scenario? Does a 'dream' revelation lesson the shock of the memory's exposure into the real world? (see Instrument) (see Collective Unconscious) (see Melody) (see Dream)

MERMAID/MERMAN In the dream sense, a Mermaid/Merman may be representational of ideal beauty, fluid emotions and unexpected wish-fulfillment. As such, we need to determine the symbolism of the location where the mermaid/merman is discovered, his or her intentions and motivations and our own behavior toward the zoomorphic dream figure. However, if a known person becomes a mermaid or merman in our dream, we may be illustrating an almost abnormal desire for the affections of that person. This sort of singular drive, based primarily on the physicality of an individual, may indicate a lack of personal self-esteem and an immature outlook on the affinity of 'real' persons involved in a loving relationship. The fact that the mermaid lives underwater may be loosely symbolic of our emotional attachment to her 'actual' personage. The mermaid/merman figure lives and breathes in a deep (and perhaps unknown) part of ourselves. In this sense, the figure knows us better than we know ourselves. Hence, we must learn to live and breathe in alternate levels of our own consciousness. We must become ever more aware of ourselves, our strengths and our abilities. Does he/she signal a unique chance of emotional freedom? Has he/she released us from our earthbound (and harsh) intellect? Will we swim with her? (see Ocean) (see Fish) (see Zoomorpism) (see Beach) (see Centaur) (see Dolphin) (see Water) (see Immersion) (see Breathe) (see Diver) (see Tarot, The Star)

MERRY GO ROUND Primarily, the Merry-Go-Round represents hypnotic, childish glee, and perhaps, the beginning stages of romantic love. However, the symbolism of the merry-go-round, may also involve a complex connection of regression, psychological stagnation and the fear of reliving the up and down experiences of childhood. We feel we are going nowhere, and we want to get off, but the ride refuses to stop. Like life's obstacles, the merry-go-round never slows down its tragic pace. Accordingly, we need to determine our personal feelings as we turn atop the carnival apparatus. Moreover, we need to analyze the look and pose of the imitation horses upon which we ride on the merry-go-round itself. If we feel alienated by the endlessly rotating ride, replete with toiling horses and infantile music, (yet find ourselves too afraid to jump off,) we may be expressing anxiety concerning the harsh transition from reckless youth to opresive adulthood. This dream may occur if we are nervous about forthcoming nuptials, or any other adjustment into adulthood and responsible behavior. (see Child) (see Horse) (see Marionette) (see Infant) (see Circle)

METAL The archetypal symbol of Metal may involve a hardness, or coldness, of character. In the dream sense, we may be depicting a shield, or barrier, against personal and entirely human, heartache. We are replacing soul and emotion with cool reason and innovative spirit. In this sense, in the image of cold metal, we are observing the force and accuracy of man's mind and 'hard' logic. However, if our dream reveals metal which is rusted, cracked, or frayed, our Unconscious may be illustrating a weakness in our personal meddle and intellectual refinement. On the other hand, a fluid combination of metals and organic materials, may represent a healthy balance of intellect, emotion and spirituality. For example, the dreamscape of a glass and metal greenhouse thriving with life, may epitomize an articulate understanding of nature and all her fervent creation. Because we 'manipulate' metal it becomes a crucial impression of our own self-development. However, its hard, angular shape provides a defined contrast with our own smooth and soft flesh. This paradox imparts the relationship between our sensitive mind and our sensitive body. We must ask this question: 'Are we creating in order to sustain life, or, are we creating in order to destroy life?'. Is technology, (in our unique perception,) good or evil? The metal dream explores this question and the many facets of our own positve and negative attitudes about human life. (see Sculpture) (see Godzilla) (see Demagogue) (see March) (see Leather)

METAMORPHOSIS In a dream, any and all acts of Metamorphosis, involve our feelings about forthcoming personal changes in our life. In this sense, our Unconscious illustrates transitions from one state of being, into other (and perhaps opposite,) state of being. If in the dream, our physical 'transformation' is fluid and natural, we may be expressing a necessary and planned modification in our formal awareness which will enhance our ability to readily adapt to a new situation. On the other hand, a complicated transformation into an unpleasant, or unkind, entity, may signal erroneous conduct in our preparation and even our acceptance of a new reality. This behavior may potentially harm ourselves and/or others very close to our personal lives. As such, we need to determine the nature of the change and any and all effects it causes in our overall dream landscape. Furthermore, it is crucial to compare the characteristics and symbiology between ourselves and the creature/persons we change into. (see Zoomorphism)

MILK The symbolism of Milk refers to nurturing, maternal purity and emotional sustenance. As such, the image of milk in our dreamscape, may refer to an endearment and compassion for new acquaintances in our life. Moreover, the serving of milk may imply an aspiration to strengthen our relationship with these respective individuals. However, the vision of spilled milk may negate all these representations and symbolize instead a loss of faith, opportunity and trust. Nevertheless, if this same milk is spilled, and an unrecognized animal comes along and laps it up anyway, we may be epitomizing the loyalty of a friend, who unbeknownst to us, returns our love and care in a humble, yet naturalistic, fashion. In yet another dream imagery, we may find ourselves choking on milk. This dream figure involves overprotectiveness and a desire to smother another individual with our love. This behavior works against self-development. Individuals must learn to 'weather' life's experiences. When we shield our loved ones from experiences we limit the 'true' shaping of their character. In this sense, it may be indeed harmful to 'cage' our loved ones. (see Family) (see Table) (see Mother) (see Tarot, The High Priestess, The Empress) (see Nest)

MIRROR The Mirror pertains to the image of oneself and how that image may compare to the inner perception of oneself. The truth is, we live in a society which places all too much emphasis on superficial images. Hence, we sometimes project the realities of our recent behavior upon our own physical appearance. We note the 'anti-hero' in modern movies who continuously observes his face in the mirror as he falls deeper and deeper into the horrific territory of his ultimate demise. In this same mythical sense, when we commit atrocities, or, if our life begins spiralling into a veritable nightmare, we may find ourselves searching in the mirror for the familiarity of who we are. We are searching for who we once were. More importantly, remembering that person, we explore how (and why) our current (and presumably difficult) reality could have happened to us in the first place? We seem to ask, is this face guilty, or innocent? The image in the glass offers a silent answer which is gravely understood. In a variation of this mirror reality, we examine the tenets of beauty. Can inner beauty be witnessed in the external reflection of the glass? In other words, can we reveal our true psychological and emotional make-up in the symmetrical expressions of our face and soulful gaze. The answer, as any psychotherapist concerned with the psychology of Self knows, is absolutely and positively, NO! Therefore, beauty (as well as bitter ugliness) is anything but skin deep. (see especially Image) (see Double) (see Self) (see Beauty)

MISSILE In the dream sense, a Missile may represent the immanent and inevitable destruction caused by prejudice and directed aggression. When we practice a fixed and entirely intolerant idealogy concerning others in a social group, it becomes predetermined that we will eventually cross paths with these individuals and lock symbolic horns. The image of the missile reflects this anger and/or vengeance we feel toward another individual. In another sense, a missile may represent the symbolic outburst inherent in new romantic encounters, or furthering the stages of love in long-term relationships. As such, our intense emotions drop a 'bomb' on the world we once knew. This figure describes our direct emotanal aggression. Are we trying to defend ourselves against individuals, or groups, (who in our perception,) represent an immediate disturbance to our general well-being? (see Penetrate) (see Candle) (see Explosion) (see Godzilla)

MIST The notion of Mist revolves around mystery, enigma and the exotic lure of the unknown. Naturally, many dream landscapes seem to find themselves shrouded in these B-Horror Movie clouds. In any case, the reality of mist is rising moisture, and as such, both representations of water and floating are rather dramatically presented. Accordingly, we need to examine the more comforting, yet fragile emotions, emotions which may lead us into danger. The big screen werewolf always seemed plagued by a surrounding mist, because we, (the viewer,) needed to feel his eternal anguish and pain. Here was an individual who loved, and who loved life, yet due to his misfortune, was now forced by the full moon (i.e. lust, madness etc.) and the bite (i.e. primal awareness) of a wolf (i.e. the loner), to devour and kill the very life he cherished. In this sense, large night clubs spray clouds of mist into large crowds to disguise the complex emotions of our exotic, 'wild' and largely hypnotized, behavior. We are delving into the cerebral world of the isolated unknown. Are we prepared to learn these (perhaps disturbing,) aspects about our deepest selves. (see Fog) (see Water) (see Float) (see Wolf) (see Bite) (see Hybrid)

MOAT The Moat is symbolic of emotional barriers placed around oneself. In other words, we may display our harsher emotions, such as anger and apprehension, to approaching strangers, (who we fear may otherwise invade the inner sanctum of our fragile being.) Accordingly, we need to determine on which side of the moat we appear in our dream. Are we dispalying threatening behavior to others, or, are we unfortunate victims? Furthermore, we must analyze the creatures which live in our dream moat and appropriately find the symbolism of these menacing emotional passions. If we find ourselves outside, trying to enter a precious castle, (but find ourselves halted by a perilous moat,) our Unconscious may be warning us to honorably wait for the proper invitation of a drawbridge, before forcing ourselves upon the sanctity of others. (see Castle) (see Bridge) (see River) (see Shark) (see Dolphin) (see Dragon) (see Knight) (see King) (see Queen) (see Door) (see Penetrate)

MONEY   The image of Money, as it appears in dreams, may refer to concepts of social status and our relative'power' within a group. However, the acquisition and our personal handling, of money, play a big part in the perception of our (not so material) worth. Did we earn, steal or borrow our money? Are we used to handling (or seeing) this amount of money? If not, we may be examining a form of wish-fulfillment. Conversely, do we appear broke in our dream? Why might this be? Did we give our money away to the poor, or, did we steal it from the poor and invest all of it into our own corporate share holdings!? In this sense, are we revealing guilt and perhaps a sudden surge of our own better conscience? The look and feel of the money itself may reveal something about its exact nature in our waking consciousness. Is it dirty money which we count in our (perceived) 'grubby little hands'? Naturally, we begin to see how our own behavior patterns and our complex self development prominently figure into our overall dream/economic reality. (see Accountant) (see Abundance) (see King)

MONGREL   The image of a Mongrel may concern inner feelings of social alienation, combined with low self-esteem. However, the Unconscious may simultaneously be revealing the stealth, cunning and longevity of the mongrel, who survives against all odds with the commendable resolution of his place in the cosmos. As such, we need to interpret the mannerisms and direction of the wayward animal. This figure involves the glory of the underdog. It also examines the complex figure of self-confidence. The mongrel is not applauded by society like the purebreed, however, the animal illustrated in this figure knows his true worth in existence, regardless of social acceptance. In spite of his detractors, he lives a long and healthy life. Furthermore, in its longevity and health, the figure represents the error of inbreeding and separatism. It expresses instead, a blending of cultures and diverse worlds. The mongrel is the strongest union of an interactive humanity. (see Dog) (see Tarot, The Hanged Man)

MONKEY   In the Chinese zodiac, a Monkey personality refers to practical and clever genius which generates popularity and in some cases, even fame. Similarly, in the western sense, the natural coordination, intelligence and kindness of the monkey in general, is almost certainly symbolized in our deliberate dream imagery. The wild nature of this primate is offset by its nearly human aptitude, including and especially, its communication skills. Therefore, we find in the monkey conception, a deep language of union entailing the attachment of our intellect and emotions. Thus, we find the genius of understanding what we feel. However, knowing our emotions, does not mean controlling them, or their effect. Knowing what we feel, merely transcends the meaning of who we are, and furthermore, illustrates how our unique personal life reflects and therefore, may co-exist, with our understanding of a 'universal' society. Herein, lies the genius of the figure. (see Ape) (see Dolphin)

MOON The symbolism of the moon pertains to romance and wild behavior. Moreover, the moon may be indicative of madness. These intense emotional patterns may occur because of the moon's effect upon oceanic tides. In the dream sense, we may need to determine the phase of the moon in order to ascertain its relative impact upon our psychological and emotional demeanor. As such, a new moon may represent young and virginal love, or a delicate transition into womanhood. Conversely, a half moon, waning or waxing, may be symbolic of psychological and emotional balance, a sort of physiological Yin/Yang. Finally, the imagery of the full moon represents our extreme passion, the high tide of perhaps our deepest psyche. Appropriately, In this last example, we need to interpret our personal motivation for howling at the big, bright moon with open heart and flaring teeth. This figure represents our emotional potential and our ability to surrender these passions for a higher purpose. Hence, all three concepts of femininity, true love and spiritual enlightenment are all intensely explored in this powerful imagery. (see Tarot Major Arcana: The Moon, The High Priestess, The Devil) (see Mist) (see Queen) (see Ring) (see Seasons) (see Wolf)

MOTHER This figure explores altruism and our working levels of tolerance. If in our dream the mother figure is healthy and intact, we may be examining our own ability to nurture and care for individuals around us. However, if the dream-mother appears cold and distant, (especially to her own young,) we may be exploring complex feelings of social alienation. When the archetypal mother figure acts this contrary to the behavior with which we ordinarily associate her, we need to examine social interrelationships in our waking life which seem to be unfolding in an odd and wholly unexpected fashion. Are we, for example, experiencing feelings of betrayal enacted by persons who are (usually) close to us? Has our own insensitive behavior motivated this act of betrayal? The strong image of the mother figure examines (in great detail) the opposite spectrum of our own interactive tolerance. When we 'accept' others and exercise forgiveness, we strengthen our own moral character by surrendering our own selfish needs. When we move beyond ourselves, we begin to absorb the truest meaning of our soulful union with a higher power. In this sense, we see why our truest love 'seeks no 'reward' other than the support of its own enactment. (see Tarot, The Empress) (see Madonna) (see Milk) (see Queen)

MOUNTAIN In the dream sense, the mountain landscape symbolizes the hope of our highest reason and in some cases, our highest spiritual truth. The seemingly infinite vision found atop a mountain may be reflective of our dynamic human potential and never ending quest for knowledge, (both physical and spiritual.) However, if the oxygen is lacking in the dream altitude of our mountain, we may be indicating a delusion of grandeur which may need to be confronted by a humble and rather low-lying reality base. In climbing a dream mountain, we explore the uphill struggle of our best determination. In this sense, we need to determine whether the dream mountain climber climbs far too fast and hence, risks falling. This imagery may represent a mindless rush to succeed. On the other hand, the slow, sturdy and calculating mountain climber may be in tune with the 'pace' and 'mastery of skills' necessary to achieve ones highest goals. In another dream image, we find a skillful mountain climber who seems to effortlessly move up the mountain by leaping on stones, deftly twirling himself from ledges, and virtually floating to the high peaks of his furthest aspirations. In this figure, the Unconscious may be examining 'spiritual faith' and our sound moral integrity. In this conception we recall the adage, 'Our faith will keep us from falling and lead us on our best path'. We are, in this dream archetype, 'floating with angels'. Naturally, the mountain archetype is highly dependent on the dreamers own vision of his or her possible futures and the hopes and dreams which complete (that) unique vision. (see Float) (see Sky) (see Landscape)

MUMMY The Mummy figure may be symbolic of our Unconscious and its ancient unknown world of exotic and timeless beauty. Consequently, if the mummy chases us in a dream, we may in some sense fear the archaic wisdom of our own consciousness. Conversely, the mummy imagery may be indicative of a need to preserve and otherwise save, some rare aspect of ourselves. Furthermore, the quest for eternal life which has daunted man from the beginning of time, may be alluded to in this antediluvian Egyptian answer to the riddle of life, death and immortality. As such, we may be expressing a concern about our own mortality and the lack of a permanent and personal legacy left behind for our future descendants. However, in a general sense, we may simply seek to safeguard a personal item or belief which is outwardly threatened by time, custom or novel fashion. (see Heaven) (see Epitaph) (see Time) (see White) (see Chase) (see Run) (see Lame) (see Pyramid)

N

NAIL In the dream sense, a Nail may refer to an intimate bond and a connection of diverse 'emotional' symbols. In the portrayal of Jesus nailed to the cross, we find a masterful nexus of flesh and wood, epitomizing an ephemeral and ethereal fusion, which satisfied monastic, as well as paganistic, sensibilities. The archetypal Jesus was brought down from heaven to join the world of man. In the symbolic gesture of his crucifixion he reunited man and God with the shedding of his own blood and sacrifice of his own life-force. The nail represents the release of

Jesus's forgiving blood and the 'ultimate' union of body and spirit. Similarly, the nails which seal a coffin, provide permanence to our coupling with earth, maintaining the stillness and peace desired in our ultimate dissolution. As such, in the dream, the 'driven nail' may symbolize a healthy, permanent 'morally correct' union of opposites. We are nailing together, (in good faith,) entirely diverse principles in an 'inspired' effort to create a working 'whole'. When we bang our dream nail with our swift dream hammer, (the hammer of authority,) we are exploring our present ability to judge fairly, both sides of a conflicting argument. (see Wood) (see Flesh) (see Skin) (see Impale) (see Bleeding) (see Coffin) (see Cut) (see Hammer)

NAKED The symbolism of Nakedness in the dream sense, may refer to a feeling of being exposed and consequently, vulnerable. The protection offered by clothes in most cultural traditions, includes sexual concealment, economic assurance and social inclusion. As such, the absence of these clothes may represent a stripping of civilization's attire and the promise of safety which comes along with it. Accordingly, we need to interpret our own feelings concerning (peculiar) aspects of ourselves which have been exposed and/or lost in our sudden (and perhaps startling) moment of dream nakedness. Conversely, in this revelatory imagery, the wild and primitive freedom offered by a baring of self, may in fact be desired in our waking life. In fact, this exposure may reveal the deepest desires of our being. Since skin and flesh represents our sensing, or experiencing, of the world, our nakedness explores our truest hunger for life's raw potential. We seek to erase the original sin of personal guilt and experience creation in all its fully illuminated glory. In this event, our nakedness is normal, emancipating and entirely healthy in our own perspective. However, other characters in our dream, may express confusion and moral quandary over our personal choice, (and expression,) of freedom. In this sense, we may find that our immediate peer group is at odds with our own individualistic yearnings. We need to determine the 'real' intention of their judgemental behavior. Do they act in our best interest, or conversely, do they try to limit us simply due to their own short-sightedness? (see Skin)

NATURE The conceptualization of Nature involves everything which is untouched by man and is (in this logic,) virginal. Moreover, the wilderness which underscores our primal beginnings, illustrates the harshest truths of reality: including and especially, our ability to survive on our own. Taken together, we find a representation of resilient integrity which fights and otherwise wards off, all forms of man-made, and hence unnatural, personal contamination. The question we must ask ourselves is a simple one. Is our knowledge of self strong enough, and dedicated enough, to fend off civilization's contamination of our natural self. In this sense, have we become dependent upon technology? Conversely, is our own disrepect of nature a subliminal act of our own self destruction? Are we examining Freud's theory concerning 'The Death Instinct', in which the famous analyst postulated that an exclusive aspect of man's consciousness actively attempts to destroy (the man) himself? Clearly, when we destroy nature, we destroy ourselves.

We observe Freud's theory in action when we witness how this obvious statement seems to allude so many (apparently rational) human beings. Accordingly, we need to analyze our interaction and appreciation of the natural environment revealed in the dream landscape. Do we fear its unknown potential for danger, or do we welcome its delicate fruits and unspeakable miracles? (see Aboriginal) (see Elements) (see Seasons) (see Virgin) (see Kill) (see Wood) (see Joshua Tree) (see Green) (see Forest) (see Bar) (see Godzilla)

NAZI A Nazi soldier may represent the potential for our anger and aggression. Moreover, the blind passion of prejudice plays a major part of our overall dream symbolism. The third Reich itself was quite aware of the influence of symbols upon the human psyche. The movement utilized internal archetypes in well-programmed methods of propaganda which have been repeatedly used in political power plays throughout the world. In this sense, our dream may be warning us against being blinded by symbols which only represent singular distinctions about our waking reality. (see Demagogue)

NEEDLE The concept of pinpoint accuracy symbolizes the Needle. Moreover, the tiny manifestation of the needle may be indicative of a minuscule difficulty, including a complicated solution, which cannot be discovered without exhaustive and nearly impossible exertion. Furthermore, the image of a needle and thread, may illustrate a deliberate weaving, or restoration, of torn emotional, or psychological, skin. Consequently, in the dream sense, we need to analyze the position and operation of the needle in order to determine its conceivably significant message.

NEST In a dream, a Nest may refer to ones home and family. Consequently, we may need to determine the condition of the nest and the hatchlings inside its confines. For example, if we observe a little, red bird attempting to build a nest in a heavy rainstorm, we may be illustrating frustration concerning the emotional, psychological and economic difficulties involved in starting, or simply supporting, a family in today's world. (see Matriarch) (see House) (see Child) (see Falling)

NIGHT The complex symbolism of Night involves mystery, danger and erotic seduction. Accordingly, when our dream landscape takes on a nighttime flavor, we may be alluding to darker and decisively concealed aspects of own nature. Hence, the image of night may allow for a smooth reappearance of repressed desires and impulses. Furthermore, this escape from the scrutiny and exposure of light, may reveal a creative faculty which has been ignored, or otherwise pushed aside, by the pressures of our day to day reality. Hence, in our dream, the star-filled skies of night, may provide a safe haven for our ancient and articulate passions, alive and well in the pool of our unconscious memory.

NINE The archetypal symbolism of the number Nine, pertains to individual horizons, their subsequent finality and a preparation for rebirth. Furthermore, the end of numbers signifies the apex of understanding. Consequently, to move further, would entail a new beginning in another plain, or novel field, of cognizance. The cycles of life and learning, must possess points of entry and departure, the numbers 0 and 9 respectively, suggest these finite positions. Accordingly, the appearance of nine objects, or the numeral nine, may refer to a culmination or completion of plans, which allows for a fresh beginning in ones perceptual awareness. (see Tarot Major Arcana: The Hermit (9) arcana)

NOCTURNAL ANIMALS The symbolism of Nocturnal Animals found in the dream landscape, may involve a restless and relentless psyche which searches for fulfillment in the darker hollows of the unconscious. Moreover, the tiny, camouflaged night creatures, may be indicative of the dreamer's apprehension about social discovery and subsequent admonishment. As such, in their subterfuge, these animals serve to elucidate the dreamer's preference to appear normal and otherwise complacent, in other words to become obscure, in the fully exposed landscape of waking reality.

NOISE In the dream sense, Noise refers to the unexpected and the unknown. Consequently, we may be expressing fear and confusion concerning up-to-date developments in our waking life. For example, if we hear a series of loud crashes within a house, yet cannot find who or what causes that sound, we may be depicting anxiety about the underpinning of our psychological or spiritual beliefs. Our unconscious may be informing us that our convictions may be radically and disturbingly changing as we become older and gain more experience. Conversely, noise may represent a breakthrough in our personal struggles. Perhaps we have burst through a barrier of resistance which has held us back for a prolonged time. In this sense, noise may represent freedom and vindication. Accordingly, we need to analyze the exact sound and determine its effect upon our symbolic dream landscape representative of our entire psyche.

NOMAD The complex symbolism of the Nomad involves incessant travel and transient goals. As such, nomadic peoples may be representative of a creative spirit which forever searches new and fertile ground. Moreover, a band of travelers may be identified with a spiritual journey. Consequently, the dream image of a nomadic tribe, may imply a quest for truth and higher meaning in our lives. On the other hand, archaic nomads practiced a slash and burn method of agriculture where grounds were cultivated until they were exhausted and entirely useless. In this sense, our unconscious may refer to our waking opportunistic behavior, which seizes everything nature and society has to offer, without offering anything in reciprocation. (see Journey) (see Vulture)

NUMB The symbolism of the Numb body, may refer to our own indecision and/or incapacity to function in certain situations. Moreover, in the dream sense, this feeling of helplessness may be complicated by the immobile reality of our concurrent sleeping status. Consequently, our stagnation in waking life, compounded by our motionless state of sleeping, may combine to portray a dream image of paralysis. Hence, it should be understood that this paralysis is not physical, but entirely emotional. In truth, we may become numb simply because we can no longer endure the pain of a complicated reality. (see Antarctica)

NUMBER Numbers are alphabetically listed in the analytical course of this text, as such, please see One through Nine. Moreover, study the Tarot Major Arcana for ancient wisdom upon numerology and its startling effect upon mankind's spiritual journey.

NUN The image of a Nun is rather complex, involving as it does, the ritualistic denial of sex and motherhood, in favor of a spiritual union with God (a patriarchal figure). In this, we find either a miraculous affiliation of natural femininity and spiritual masculinity which ordains a saintly earthly presence, or, a person who has negated their natural maternal drive with a paternal control of instincts. Naturally, these are two vastly opposing representations of the same figure. Once again, we must ask our dream itself. Is the unconscious illustration of our nun, selfless and holy, caring for children and the family of God, or, is she an angry and misunderstood soul, who takes out her emotional frustrations on young girls and boys under her strict and quite corporal supervision. Which image reveals something about ourselves, or persons known to us in waking life? (see Abbess)

NURSE The image of the nurse embodies motherly caring and a sensual form of bedside comfort. The impression given by a normal, healthy young man or woman administering to our ailing needs, is one of promise and wish-fulfillment. Accordingly, a nurse dream, may refer to hope in the face of desperation. On the other hand, our unconscious may be illustrating personal regression involving the dream nurse as mother figure.

O

OAK In ancient nordic tribal tradition, the mighty Oak tree was seen as the center, or power point, of divine transfiguration. Accordingly, tribal elders performed religious ceremonies, including ritualistic sacrifice, in the husk of the tree itself. Moreover, since the old trees seemed ageless, their spirit familiars offered a promise of eternal life to mortal worshippers. Appropriately, in the dream sense, an oak tree may refer to stability, permanence and rich spirituality. Hence, we need to determine our feelings in conjunction and close proximity with the tree in the dream landscape in order to ascertain its symbolism concerning our own peculiar psyche.

OASIS In the dream sense, an Oasis may imply a renewal of hope. Moreover, since the gift of the oasis is primarily fresh water, we may need to analyze the aspects of a revitalized emotional involvement in the context of the dreamer's life. Accordingly, we need to consider if the water is cool and refreshing, therefore welcome, or bitter and murky, representing a form of false hope. (see Heaven) (see Water) (see Barren) (see Desert)

OBELISK   The tall tower which tapers into a pyramid at its very apex, in other words, the Obelisk, symbolizes divine strength, moral direction and infinite potential. As such, its appearance in the dream landscape may imply the spiritual strength of a certain direction in life which may now stand before us, for example, the birth of a child. Conversely, the imposing tower may represent a monolithic presence which surveys and judges our wayward behavior. Along these lines, if the obelisk is destroyed in our dream landscape, our unconscious may be revealing a complete loss of personal development and the spiritual guidance which may be necessary to continue in the sound path of that maturation. (see Ivory Tower) (see Tarot Major Arcana: Lightning Struck Tower (16) arcana)

OCTOPUS   The multifarious symbolism of the Octopus involves the use of its eight legs and their objective. When all eight legs are used together we may revert to the symbolism of the numeral 8, which represents completion and organizational strength. As such, the octopus which captures and encompasses its prey, may represent the forbearance of our emotional or psychological convictions. Moreover, this particular cephalopod is known for its ink-cloud defense mechanism and solitary existence. Taken together, the octopus in our dreamscape may imply an individualistic tenet which empowers our vital experience. On the other hand, if the octopus uses its arms to perform a variety of disconnected tasks, we may be illustrating the anxiety of spreading ourselves out too thin in the daily undertaking of our numerous endeavors.

ODOR   Our olfactory senses originate in the brainstem or 'reptilian brain'. In other words, our ancient sense of smell is an integral part of our most primitive and archetypal remembrances. As such, in a dream, Odor may elicit a powerful memory. Therefore, the presence of a peculiar odor in our dream landscape may refer to the time and original event of its experience. For example, if the smell of cotton candy recalls a painful childhood memory of sickness, its appearance in a dream may imply feelings of uneasiness and disorder involving the visual symbolism underlying its presence in the dream landscape. (see Memory)

OGRE   In myth, an Ogre is a huge, brutish creature who happens to eat human beings. Nevertheless, the ogre is not literally evil, but simple-minded and animal-like. Consequently, he eats human beings because they are significantly smaller than himself, and thus, easy prey. As such, in the dream sense, the image of an ogre may represent our own unintentional, yet nonetheless, cruel behavior. For example, an elementary school teacher who harshly admonishes a tiny child for disobedient behavior, may dream herself as an ogress terrorizing a wayward human being who foolishly crosses her path.

ONION The Onion represents the harsh reality of purity, which must in its faculty, eliminate persistent contaminants. As opposed to an apple, or a loaf of bread, an onion will not spoil for an unusually long period of time. Hence, we see how the onion is far stronger than most forms of bacteria. Moreover, we witness in the course of this book, how impurities have become archetypes of evil and more accurately, immoral behavior. As such, the onion is pure, healthy and virginal (untouched). It is the embodiment of dedicated virtue and rectitude. It is not fun, but darn decent, nevertheless. The onion reminds us about the difficulty required to stay the moral path. In fact, one may make the biblical analogy, that once Adam and Eve ate the apple, mankind has been forced to eat onions ever since! (see Garlic) (see Unclean) (see Vampire) (see Apple)

ORACLE The symbolism of the oracle involves the decision-making faculty of the mind itself. As such, the oracle is shrouded in the mystery of infinite possibilities. However, some potentialities may prove to be harmful to our well-being. Hence, we find the brutality of the mythical sphinx who guards the oracle and administers its punishment. The sphinx possessing the body of a lion and the head of human being, accurately symbolizes the destructive strength of our own bad decisions. Taken together, we may need to pay serious attention to the oracle vision in our dreamscape, primarily because its riddle, or forthcoming choice, may prove to have significant ramifications in our waking life. (see Tarot Major Arcana: The Wheel of Fortune (10) and Judgement (20) arcanas)

ORCHID The Orchid is a plant which grows wild and brazen in a harsh landscape. Accordingly, the orchid may be symbolic of a resolution for freedom, choice and autonomy. The color of the orchid and direction of its growth, may represent certain facets of our desire for liberation and self-sufficiency in waking life.

OUIJA BOARD In the dream sense, a Ouija Board may represent the language of our repressed feelings which return to us by way of an apparition, otherwise known as our unconscious. Accordingly, we need to fully interpret any messages revealed on the ouija board itself. Moreover, since the board is primarily used for divination, we may be yearning for the insight of a loved one who has passed on. Hence, the message the unconscious provides on the board, may be indicative of wisdom once gained from this highly regarded individual. (see Clairvoyance) (see Telepathy)

OUTLAW In the archetypal sense, the Outlaw represents the potential of our immoral or anti-social behavior. Moreover, the criminal figure may represent the embodiment of all the functions which have been prohibited in our moral education and/or learning experience. As such, in the dream sense, an Outlaw may illustrate our personal frustration regarding everyday society and our normal and possibly tiresome, lifestyle. Our dream may be expressing our wish-fulfillment to seize all the goods which life has to offer.

OVERFLOW   The image of an Overflowing tub may entail an excess of emotion (water), which has a powerful effect upon our psychological outlook (house), and therefore, floods our floors, representational of our normally quiescent state of mind. In other words, our feelings in their complexity, may be interfering with our normally 'reasonable' methods of judgement. Similarly, the view of a flooding river, may allegorically demonstrate our wilder passions which can no longer be restrained in our waking experience. In a still larger symbolic sense, nature herself, accepts this overflowing river's pulsing waves as they irrigate the once arid land and bring fruitful life to the seeds of her creation. Moreover, the overflowing cup of cheer, profoundly illustrates the celebration, joy and thankfulness for the a bountiful existence fraught with miraculous wonders. (see Basin) (see Water) (see House)

OVERSEAS   The image of strange and far away lands, may reflect a deep longing for exotic and sensational experiences, not found in our ordinary life. In this, we witness an apparent limitation in the fulfillment of our mental capacity and overall potential. As such, our unconscious portrays the richer colors, deeper sensations and incredible variations of the collective human experience. Doing so, we may begin to see the uniqueness of our own mind and its fascinating individuality. In this sense, we understand the universality of Da Vinci's Mona Lisa, Michelangelo's David, The Taj Mahal and the Great Pyramid of Giza. Universally, They each unveil the limitless potential of mankind. Thus, the unconscious fully illustrates, that the world of experience out there, regardless of how far Overseas, remains the same world of experience found right here at home, in the soul of each and every human being, who dreams the infinite potential of self. (see Abroad) (see Path)

OWL   The archetypal symbolism of the Owl involves the keen insight of true wisdom. Furthermore, the owl flying and hunting at night, may suggest its knowledge is amassed from the dark recesses of an enigmatic unconscious. Fittingly, this sapient dream figure may represent a reflection of our own insight. In other words, the dream owl is reminding us that we instinctively possess all the necessary solutions to our own questions and personal quandaries. Accordingly, we may need to analyze the color of the owl and symbolic meaning of all characters and backgrounds which exist in conjunction with it, to fathom the presence of our obscured waking wisdom within the boundaries of the dream landscape itself.

OX   In the Chinese zodiac, the Ox personality is considered to be alert, intelligent and easy going. However, their is a tendency for quick temper tantrums and otherwise, angry mood changes. The western symbolism of the ox is quite similar. The image of a hard working animal who asks for little and returns much, is firmly rooted in the physical nature of the domestic ox. However, if the beast is mistreated or becomes agitated due to complex external situations, it may become indeed become angry and quite dangerous. Moreover, we may find an allusion to

PARALYSIS 151

awkwardness and a general lack of the mental or physical tact involved in movement through delicate and fragile situations. Accordingly, we need to determine the temperament and behavior of the ox in the dream landscape and interpret whom the animal symbolizes in our waking experience. Furthermore, our unconscious may be revealing our own stubbornness and inability to find comprehensible compromises. (see Bull)

OYSTER   In the complex imagery of the Oyster, we find a plain and ordinary shelled creature, which may or may not be hiding a rare and beautiful pearl. In the symbolic sense, this mystery of the tightly shut shell may refer to an immense hidden potential. Moreover, the oyster's opening and closing shell, revealing a delicate and soft internal body, may be indicative of sexual copulation and an otherwise erotic intimacy. Taken together, the oyster dream may represent the potential of gaining love if not rare passion in ones waking life.

P

PAPER   In the dream sense, Paper symbolizes the physical communication of our modern world. Consequently, huge piles of paper may represent our anxiety about the 'red tape' of everyday life. The complexity of maintaining records for a huge society requires mountains of documents, which is why the 'computer' age is accompanied by the 'printer' age. Our dream therefore, may be expressing a return to a smaller, simpler and more naturalistic way of life. On the other hand, if we lack paper in a dream, we may be illustrating an insufficient vehicle, or social blessing, to fully express our creative potential.

PALM   As opposed to the hand itself, the Palm is primarily linked with aspects of our future potential. This kind of palm reading is associated with the concept of predetermination, which views life as a destiny preordained in the higher order of reality. Hence the term, 'things happen for a reason' or 'it was their time to go' etc. The palm lines themselves, represent the fundamental concerns experienced in the course of a life, those being love, family, health, creativity, productivity and finally, longevity. (see Hand) (see Fingers) (see Tarot Major Arcana: The Wheel of Fortune (10) figure)

PARADE   A Parade may be symbolic of a communal commemoration of personal or moral convictions which are allowed to exist in a free society. Consequently, we may be expressing neighborly support for a unique system of belief. (compare March)

PARALYSIS   The symbolism of Paralysis involves an inability to function in certain situations found in our waking experience. This tendency to freeze up may involve repressed fears, firmly rooted in developmental incidents of our past.

Moreover, we immediately grasp how the decision not to 'act', essentially frees us from incorrect (and therefore socially alienating) behavior. This dramatically illustrates the major social component found in the overall dream analysis. Exploring this further, we find the concept of our 'act', or performance, carries with it the very real perception of acceptance and popularity, or conversely, disapproval and rejection. As such, we appraise the social reality and decide the stakes are just too darn high and so, we symbolically stop and hope to become unnoticed in the whole reality of the situation. However, the unconscious refuses to waste its wisdom on statues and thus, illustrates the pain and vulnerability of utter stagnation and dire paralysis. As such, the dreamer is compelled to rise and move forward, slowly at first, then gradually with increased momentum and self-confident determination, into the full 'act' of a life lived, for better or worse. In short, the paralysis dream whispers faith in the effort and movement of self. (see Numb) (see Ice) (see Antarctica)

PARASITE The rather undesirable image of a Parasitic creature may reveal the rather undesirable reality of a parasitic nature. As adult human beings, we pride our individuality above all else, because it demonstrates better than anything else, our utter uniqueness. Moreover, this distinction of our peculiar self is created and thrives in the arena of the specific choices we make throughout life. These decisions naturally, propel the free movement of our destiny. In other words, we understand how our ability to choose and make decisions, gives us independence in our living experience. When we lack this confidence in our own decision making, we may look to another person (or being) for guidance. This may in fact be normal, and expresses the full value and basic need for society and its elaborate rituals. However, when this (social) dependence erases ALL motivation to decide ones own faith, we may be witnessing a deep regression into infantile dependency, or even deeper into prehistoric lower life forms fully dependent upon outside hosts. Furthermore, when this parasitic form of blind dependency, or idolatry, sways an entire group, community or nation, the results can be devastatingly savage and entirely inhuman. Accordingly, we may need to examine and temper all parasitic behavior as it appears in our waking life. We need to realistically determine why this behavior persists and develop objectives which lead us, or others, into the gradual confidence of self. Professional counciling may be recommendable for extreme cases of dependency. (see Infestation) (see Ego)

PARK The complex symbolism of the Park primarily involves a temporary escape from reality. The escapist trappings of the park include a tiny version of the natural environment, the make-believe world of child's play and an overall carnivalesque, essentially unreal, microcosm. Accordingly, in the dream sense, we may need to determine the intentions and motivation of all characters and situations which occur in the park landscape. For example, if we find ourselves lost in a park and nobody seems to know the way out of the park, we may be illustrating a temporary straying from society and the evident struggle in returning to that society and our old way of life. This dream may occur after a sobering transition in our life, for example, the end of a passionate affair, or readjustment after a serious addiction.

PARROT The image of a Parrot may involve repetition, emulation, or conversely, mockery. The colorful plume of the bird combined with its permanent smile, seem to indicate jovial characteristics in all the potential representations. (see Bird) (see Color) (see Double) (see Mirror)

PARTY In the dream sense, a Party may represent the microcosm of our social universe. Accordingly, our behavior in a party may be indicative of our relationship with our peer group or family. Moreover, the casual nature of a party may serve as a foil for the unrestrained expression of our true selves. In this sense, our unconscious may illustrate among other things, our deep connection with, or separation from, a diversity of individuals in our life based upon our unique idiosyncrasies.

PATH The symbolism of a Path involves a way of life and the direction, or steps, taken toward that particular method of personal enlightenment. Accordingly, we need to interpret any obstacles in, or deviations from, the path itself. (see Tarot Major Arcana) (see Labyrinth)

PEARL A Pearl may be symbolic of the perfection of beauty, affection and love. Its luster being smooth and reflective, it may also represent the spiritual wisdom of self. (see Oyster) (see Light)

PENDULUM The back and forth swinging of a Pendulum may be symbolic of ambivalence concerning a difficult choice in our life. Moreover, the movement of a pendulum is associated with the governing function of antique clocks and other various timepieces. Hence, in the dream sense, we observe a wavering which may involve a long and seemingly endless passage of time. In other words, our indecision and hesitation may be causing distress for ourselves and moreover, for others, who may be anxiously awaiting our decision. This vacillation may serve to block the normal process of transition and any subsequent emotional or psychological healing which may be necessary in readjustment.

PENETRATE The conceptualization of Penetration involves a complex insertion into another reality to release a part of what is known as the 'life force' in general. We seek to create a pathway from this symbolic source into our own vacuous need. Furthermore, this forced synthesis, or union, may serve as a catalyst for the newly animated 'vitality' which surges between beings, a dialectic creation all its own. (see Impale) (see Bleed) (see Imbrue)

PENIS The overt image of male sexuality, or the Penis, may also involve complex representations of masculine characteristics. These may involve an insensitivity to elusive and fluid emotions, as well as, feminine principles of fragile earth (flesh).

The depiction of the penis nevertheless, represents the potential for union between man and woman, yin and yang, sky and earth; in short, the linking of opposites. (see Genitalia) (see Vagina) (see Womb)

PERPETUAL MOTION As opposed to the pendulum symbolism which involves decision making, objects in Perpetual Motion may imply anxiety and/or nervousness in general. The conceptualization of perpetual motion involves the constant and incessant duration of a phenomenon in time. However, real life consists of a transient series of ever-changing events. This is primarily because the human mind adjusts well to new and different stimuli. Consequently, perpetual motion, or any fixed stimulus, torments the brain whose normal function is the continual formulation of new data. In the dream sense, we may desire a change in the repetitive and/or predictable behavior found in an occupation, a relationship, or the robotic operation of modern life itself.

PHOENIX The mythical image of the fire-bird, also known as the Phoenix, symbolizes passionate burning freedom. In the dream sense, we may witness the vision of a phoenix corresponding with the onset of personal emancipation, which wholly expands our emotional and psychological horizons. The phoenix burns down to ashes which scatter and then reorganize into the eternal rebirth of the majestic winged creature. As such, our unconscious may be illustrating the parallel and consistent reincarnation of our spiritual self which burns and flies on the divine wings of an infinite consciousness.

PIG The symbolism of a Pig involves base actions, whether they be hygiene-related or sexually orientated, the little hog lets loose. In this sense, we must observe the sloppy, muddy appearance of the swine first and lastly examine it as a possible food source. Regarding the slop, our friend the pig may represent a fusion with earth and nature from which it came and returns daily. Contemplating the naturalistic and thus, erotic aspects of this animal's behavior, we observe a parallel with uninhibited sexual conduct in human beings. Lastly, as a food source, we interpret pork as a rich, thick and flavorful sustenance, symbolically based on the animal's free-spirited temperament. Hence, in the dream sense, we may be fully embodying our desires and earthy fervor. Alternatively, in the Chinese zodiac, the pig personality is linked with chivalry and honesty. Perhaps it is the straight forward manner of the animal, which provides us with the necessary courage to reveal truth and stand by our deepest convictions.

PINE TREE The Pine Tree which remains green and healthy throughout the year is symbolic of eternal and transcendent spirit. The seasons which change our activity and behavior, nevertheless, cannot change the continuity of who we are. In this, we witness the unconscious revelation of the soul of life, of which the unconscious itself, is an inexorable part. Furthermore, pine needles are taught to be therapeutic by many archaic cultures and in the tradition of Wicca, or witchcraft, they are viewed as receptors of pure elemental energy. Perhaps this is why the pine tree remains forever impervious to the elements themselves. (see Evergreen)

PIRATE As opposed to the symbolism of the outlaw, the Pirate lives out his immoral potential on the high seas upon a naturalistic vessel constructed of hardwood planks. Consequently, his iniquity garners a more emotionally disturbed and overtly sexual temperament. In the dream sense, the image of a pirate may involve a complex wish-fulfillment pertaining to dangerous and perhaps sexuality and an equal lust for freedom and adventure. In other words, our unconscious may be expressing a desire to take on more risks and chancy ventures in our waking life.

PLAY The natural tendency of many young animals to Play, involves their inbred understanding to develop the coordination necessary for adult skills needed later in life. Therefore, in a rather complex dream sense, we may be exploring the fundamental beginnings of our own unique skills and conversely, our unfortunate limitations. In this, we may need to determine our strengths and weaknesses within the context of the games played. Moreover, we may need to analyze our social place within the group. Are we one of the gang, or a hanger on? Are we an outcast? The overall symbolism of playing involves every aspect of our memory. Accordingly, we may need to explore the restructuring of our relative abilities and real reactive potential. (see Child) (see Wall) (see Lemonade Stand)

POISON The symbolism of Poison may be entirely dependent on who administers the toxin, and who ingests it. For example, if we ourselves are the recipient of the poison, we may be illustrating a symbolic slow death pertaining to a certain aspect of ourselves. However, if we ourselves administer the venomous substance to a known party, we may be signifying the violent release of an otherwise suppressed hostility, and perhaps retaliatory aggression, toward this individual. In both cases we may need to address the overtly violent and turbulent behavior of our conscious invention.

POLICE In the dream sense, Police represent our own morality and conscience (Superego). In this capacity, the dream flat-foot may reinforce the internalized programming of an authority figure which guides us down the straight and narrow path of social benevolence. (see Authority Figure) (see Guard)

PORT A Port may involve emotional, as well as, psychological opportunities for us to discover. We may need to determine whether our ship or plane is preparing to leave the dock, or has just returned. Is the dock sturdy and able to withstand a violent storm? Naturally, we need to interpret the subtle connections of earth and sea. (see Dock) (see Depot) (see Water) (see Boat)

PREACHER The symbolism of a Preacher may involve a harsh personal lesson. Accordingly, the internal lecture may center around our feelings of guilt and subsequent self-admonishment. On the other hand, a fanatical fire and brimstone rant which seems to indicate obsessive behavior in the embodiment of the dream creature, may be an unconscious illustration of our own extremist demeanor. In the dream sense, this conduct may reveal intense over compensation and an absurdly hypocritical personal stance.

PRIEST The image of a Priest may involve the symbolism of chastity and abstinence. In this, the dreamer may view sexuality as immoral, or in any case, removed from the tenets of spiritual life. (see Abbot) (see Preacher) (see Nun) (see Virgin) (see Church)

PRIZE As opposed to a gift, a Prize is won for some personal achievement. Therefore, our unconscious may be revealing either one of two things. The first may entail a form of congratulations for a job well done, due to perseverance and dedication. The second may consist of a warning against material lust, which may sway us from our real goals, which should provide reward enough in their mastery and fulfillment. As such, we need to determine the nature of the prize and our reaction to its relative personal value. (see Gift) (see Greed)

PROPHESY (see Clairvoyance) (see Telepathy) (see Foresight)

PROSTITUTE The modern symbolism of Prostitution may involve a lack of self-esteem. However, the selling of ones body may be indicative of sexual power and an otherwise extreme separation of emotion and intellect. In this sense, we may be consciously concealing the frailty of our own emotions and replacing them with a rugged and calculating physical and psychological hide. As such, strength gained from an absence of passionate turbulence is expressed in the symbolic guise of finances. Furthermore, this wish fulfillment of open sexuality may imply a serious and perhaps fanatic repression of our natural drives and desires.

PUPPET The Puppet is thought of as a cute, animated, highly spirited reflection of child-like and innocent life. However, with the exception of Pinnochio, who in fact became a boy; Puppets possess no soul and have no life of their own. They are controlled and manipulated by outside forces, who use their innocent and sometimes wholly inanimate charm, to convey real (live) human ideas and ideals. This is why many politicians and appointed leaders are symbolically viewed as puppets, existing at times within puppet governments. In this capacity, they are given wordy speeches written by spin doctors, which are public orations chock full of the agendas and beliefs held by a powerful organized party. Moreover, these words may not agree with the internal belief system of the speaker him or herself. Accordingly, our unconscious may be warning us against proclaiming ideals which are not even our own. Conversely, we may be wrongly seeking control of others who are to young and/or naive to resist our influence. In this sense, do we fear reciting our own message/ Are we lost without support, even it happens to be weak-minded? (see Ventriloquism) (see Parasite)

PURPLE The symbolism of Purple involves riches, sensuality and fullness of life. As such, its presence in the dream landscape may be indicative of excess and/or erotic encounters.

PYRAMID The image of the ancient Pyramids involves enigmatic magic and the lure of the unfathomable. Moreover, the exact architecture and compass-coordinate layout of the great structures reflect the mystery of an ancient human wisdom. Accordingly, the pyramids in a dream landscape, may represent personal power based on the faith of our metaphysical ancestry. In the vision of the pyramid we find a naturalistic union with the physical landscape, human intellect, and the expanse of the heavens. Taken together, this dream figure effectively bridges the trinity of mind, body and spirit. (see Tarot Major Arcana: Judgement (20) and The World (21) arcana) (see Mummy) (see Pharaoh)

PYTHON The complex symbolism of the Python involves danger, overt sexuality and seductive, sinister evil. As such, we need to determine the location where the python slithers and what motivates its movement. Furthermore, the coiling of the python around its victims and their subsequent suffocation may be indicative of emotional pressure and anxiety associated with modern living. Conversely, the power of the snake's body may refer to an almost incredible physical or mental determination. Moreover, to be bitten by a snake in our dream may refer to a drastic change in life which may lead to a profound spiritual transfiguration. (see Impale) (see Bite) (see Apple) (see Satan)

Q

QUARANTINE In the dream sense, a Quarantine may refer to a personal isolation from someone or something. Our unconscious may be illustrating the difficulty and/or emotional and physiological hazard involved in interactions with certain human beings. As such, we temporarily force them or ourselves from the shared social mainstay. Consequently, the dream of the quarantined landscape involves short-term alienation which is well intentioned but is nevertheless harsh and emotionally painful.

QUARRY As a mountain symbolizes spirituality, a Quarry dug deep into the bowels of a mountain may represent the rich depths of our earthbound soul. In this sense, we combine the embodiment of earth and sky to unearth the rare gifts of an infinite unconsciousness. Furthermore, these man-made valleys may refer to the tireless search into the self for jewels of wisdom, metals of courage and fossils of symbolic archetypal truth. As such, the dream quarry may illustrate the potential depths explored within ones own psyche.

QUARTZ The symbolism of bright crystalline rock found in the substrata of earth may be representative of a hidden and vital potential. Moreover, this buried capacity may involve emotional or psychological clarity of which we are only barely aware. Consequently, in the dream sense, the image of Quartz may refer to a budding realization of personal enlightenment and a growing wisdom in crucial decision making.

QUAY   A Quay refers to our emotional transitions and elaborate transformations made in our waking reality. (see Dock)

QUEEN   The symbolism of the Queen pertains to mature, enlightened and otherwise supreme femininity and womanhood. As such, the queen embodies matriarchal wisdom, strength and stature. Moreover, the queen symbolizes the completion of the kingdom within the undeniable aspect of her sensitive and sympathetic sovereignty. Consequently, in a dream, a queen may represent the moral and altruistic determination of the archetypal mother figure. (see King) (see Amazon)

QUESTION, THE   When our unconscious poses a Question from its own memory banks, the implication is that we already KNOW the answer within ourselves. The dream uses the interrogation as a direct rationalizing agent of our own knowledge. Similarly, we understand how thought itself is a product of reflection and self examination. In this so called 'reasoning', we piece together the meanings of separate concepts in order to find a larger and primarily unifying, theme. As such, the dream acts as a private investigator delving into our personal behavior and belief system in order to comprehend why we may or may not enact certain responses to life's diverse predicaments. Moreover, the unconscious may become aware of our future intentions and pointedly ask us why we have made this particular choice. In this manner, passionate responses may give way to calculated reasoning, including the realization of possible backlashes. (see Oracle)

QUICKSAND   The symbolism of drowning in Quicksand may imply a stagnation in ones psychological development. In other words, we may be clinging to old ideas, or ideals, however forcibly we may be coerced into change. This resistance to a new awareness may prove to be the very catalyst which pulls us deeper into the transition itself. Accordingly, in the dream sense, quicksand represents our phobia and struggle against inevitable changes in our life.

QUIET   The dual symbolism of Quiet, or silence, in a dream may refer to inner peace or conversely, the maddening stillness of the proverbial calm before the storm. Appropriately, we must determine our relative feelings within this soundless landscape. Are we aware of life in repose or dimly cognizant of hidden life forms? If we experience anxiety in the dreamscape we may need to determine the nature of the violent storms which threaten to break in our waking life. (see Numb)

QUIZ   A Quiz may be representational of being tested by some group or individual in our waking life. Appropriately, we may need to determine who quizzes us, the nature of the questions, and our self confidence concerning our ability to meet the challenge. For example, the dream of the pop quiz which catches us off guard and in a state of panic, may be indicative of our insecurity involving a lack of preparation and/or neglectful behavior. Moreover, the regressive image of the failing grade school examination may represent adult anxiety reflecting self-worth. (see Test)

R

RABBIT   In Lewis Carroll's novel Alice in Wonderland, the white Rabbit represents the embodiment of curiosity which entices Alice into her surreal adventures. In the mythological sense, a rabbit is thought to be the purveyor of good luck, good news and good health. Moreover, the prolific characteristic of the rabbit combined with its benign nature may signify sound childbirth. Taken together, we realize the hare symbolizes a genesis of new and wondrous events, Accordingly, in the dream sense, the image of the rabbit may represent the ingenuous faculty necessary to step through portals of new and novel worlds. Supporting these tenets, the Chinese zodiac views the rabbit personality as extremely lucky, talented, intelligent and naturally, affectionate.

RABID DOG   The symbolism of the Rabid Dog, with foaming mouth and glaring eyes, refers to confusion, madness and dangerous uncertainty in ones waking relationship/s. The image of a canine is usually associated with loyalty, trust and friendship. Hence, this conversion of a faithful emblem into a violent, distrustful and aggressive creature, may be indicative of a reversal in fraternity and a sudden and complete loss of amity and goodwill demonstrated by a close comrade. In the dream sense, this separation of a once powerful union illustrated by our unconscious' paradoxical puppy, may entirely epitomize unwarranted and unjustified actions on the part of the dreamer against his or her social peers. Conversely, if a rabid dog threatens a friend or family member, the dreamer may be reflecting his or her own feelings of betrayal involving the deceptive and deceitful behavior of significant others.

RACCOON   In the dream sense, a Raccoon may embody a restless search through the darkness of our unconscious for goods, or objectives, which satiate our hunger. Furthermore, this inquiry into our passionate motivations may involve personal heroics and reckless behavior in general. Accordingly, the raccoon may symbolize the hazardous quest and/or painful initiation of overt physical, emotional and psychological maturation.

RACE   The symbolism of the Race may refer to a heated contest to prove oneself worthy of social praise and the attainment of life's prizes. Moreover, the nature of competition and rivalry may be inherent in this ancient archetype. For example, if a man strives for the singular affections of a particular woman, he may dream of a race wherein he is pitted against all the viable suitors of that lady. Normally, winning the race, may be an expression self-confidence, pride and conceivably, conceit. Conversely, finishing last in the race, may imply a lack of self-esteem and/or a difficulty in wholly applying oneself. Lastly, a close finish may imply the dreamer's personal and psychological struggle in the exploit of this goal. Consequently, the dreamer may need to interpret if the toil of the race in the dream landscape is worth the price of its goal and moreover, if the contest, is really necessary in the first place.

RAGS The symbolism of Rags may refer to poverty and the otherwise insufficient wrapping of our psychological skin. In the image of tattered rags we find fragmented components of a psyche which may lack the individual cohesion of a fully realized self. Moreover, in the group sense, rags may represent a fundamental alienation from the society at large, which is primarily recognized by its communal costume. Consequently, in a dream landscape, rags may refer to feelings of hardship, self-abasement, or personal estrangement, in the interwoven fabric of our waking interrelationships.

RAIN The archetypal symbolism of Rain pertains to psychological extinction, emotional purification and natural regeneration. As such, our unconscious illustrates the torrential skies as a tearful acceptance of death's transformation into rebirth and the eternal cycle of renewal. Hence, we are continuously cleansed in the new, yet remembered, realizations of our psyche. Accordingly, rain in the dream sense, may refer to a harsh, yet emotionally beneficial, alteration in our waking life. (see Boat) (see Baptism)

RAINBOW Occurring after the transfigurative rains, the Rainbow represents hope and reward for prolonged sacrifice. Accordingly, the rainbow is the bridge to personal illumination. Consequently, since the rainbow contains all the primary colors, our unconscious may be illustrating the paramount gift available to humanity is the embodiment of the full spectrum of our emotions. Furthermore, since a rainbow is a direct refraction of sunlight, we may interpret the dream rainbow as pertaining to the arrangement of wisdom, guidance and perceptive clarity in our waking life.

RANCID We often find disagreeable elements in our dream landscape. Accordingly, we need to examine the exact nature of these repellent objects. In the case of Rancid foods, we find an allusion to neglect, alienation, or a movement away from normal human concerns about health and security. As such, this rancid environment may refer to slipping into ones mental neurosis and leaving the rational (social) world behind. However, since in the dream itself, an illustration of awareness of this 'bad' food is apparent, we may be referring to an individual or situation outside of our DIRECT experience and/or involvement. Nevertheless, we may fear being drawn in by this person and/or situation and subsequently, entering his or her world of chaos. Conversely, we may seek to free this person from his or her dysfunctional, or abnormal, behavior and the intolerable price of its possible consequences.

RAT The symbolism of the Rat pertains to shrewd faculties and their corresponding capacity for survival in horrid and utterly reprehensible conditions. Unfortunately, in human beings this instinct may sometimes involve relying on the selfish, backhanded or back stabbing temperament of oneself. In other words, a betrayal of allies in order to personally survive, may be indicative of the 'stool pigeon', or rat, (or the entire rat race) itself. In the dream sense, our unconscious may be warning us that our personal interest in survival may be suspending, or outrightly obliterating, our basic human compassion for others. In a rather interesting variation of this imagery, the Chinese zodiac finds the rat personality as charming, honest and ambitious, yet, sometimes unable to maintain long friendships and/or relationships!

RATTLESNAKE The symbolism of the Rattlesnake involves the shrill pierce of its rattle. Hence, the snake may represent a warning of physical, psychological or emotional danger involving a recent encounter or occurrence in ones waking life. (see Python)

RAW In the dream sense, Raw meat may refer to carnal knowledge and/or physical desires. Moreover, the freshness of the flesh may represent its vitality and still present potency. As such, our ritualistic devouring of this physical potential, symbolically enhances our own vigor, vivacity and endurance.

RED The color Red is symbolic of intense passions including anger, lust and shame. Moreover, its association with blood manifests deep emotional and spiritual connotations. Consequently, any and all red figures found within the dream landscape may refer to a raise in the entire propensity and fervor of the symbols revealed.

REFLECTION A Reflection involves the complexity of self image and self understanding. Are we who we appear to be? In the shimmering and swaying image we catch of ourselves on the surface of water, we may refer to explorations of self, as it pertains to our elusive emotional realities. Do we remain intact in these pools of self-discovery? (see Double) (see Mirror) (see Water)

REGURGITATE In a dream, the image of Regurgitation refers to the expulsion of entities or individuals who are venomous and otherwise malevolent to our sensibilities. Hence, we reverse our acceptance of these people, or ideas, and symbolically send them away, in other words, back from whence they came. Conversely, the regurgitation dream may involve our inability to accept, or swallow, a difficult truth or reality. Accordingly, we need to examine the exact nature of the individual, or concept, which seems blatantly noxious in our overall discernment of reality.

REINCARNATION Reincarnation in our dream, may represent direct associations with the tenets of this religious view. As such, reincarnation involves a continual return to worldly experience in diverse living forms. This relative formation is dependent upon ones previous incarnation. As such, a lowly, greedy person may return as a snake or algae eater. Conversely, a loyal dog or cat may return as a human being. This hierarchy of animals (including humans), links behavior with moral and spiritual uprightness. Consequently, a person who lives a moral, ethical and spiritual life will not return into the animal (or human) cycle, but will instead become pure spirit and subsequently part of heaven (the realm of eternity). In a dream image where our spirit is embodied in another form (human or animal), we may be expressing concerns about the relative 'level' of our devout behavior. (see Transmutation) (see Zoomorphism)

RELIGION In the dream sense, Religion may refer to our moral path and resolute belief in a higher power. Accordingly, we need to comprehend the ethical message produced in the dream vision. Moreover, if the dream landscape involves a ritual, we need to examine its procedure for further unconscious illustrations. Essentially, the religious imagery pertains to our feelings of guilt concerning our straying from a moral path, our converse sensations of somber mortal humility, or passionate, nearly escapist elation, involving ethereal rewards for our devout behavior. (see Christ) (see Heaven) (see Hell) (see God)

REMEMBER   (see Memory)

RESTRICTION The act of sleeping involves a relative degree of paralysis and the subsequent Restriction of certain body parts. As such, the dreaming mind often rationalizes for this physical restraint by creating scenarios involving various and elaborate forms of bodily limitation. For example, if we happen to be sleeping on our right side, with our full weight on top of our right arm, in our dream imagery, this right arm may appear lame, broken, or perhaps, in a great deal of pain. In the symbolic sense however, restriction in a dream landscape may reflect a struggling, burdensome reality which we have difficulty in escaping in our waking life. For example, if our everyday clothes suddenly do not fit us and we experience pain and anxiety about this dilemma, we may be alluding to concerns about weight gain (obesity or bulimia) or oddly enough, pregnancy. Another example of restrictive dreams invokes a room or building whose doorways and windows are too small to traverse completely through. This dream may elucidate waking relationships or situations which are arduous in exiting or entering, dependent of course, on which side of the respective doorway we happen to be positioned upon. Are we in, or are we out? In all cases, we need to examine the exact nature of the limitation (doorway, clothing) and interpret appropriate analogies in our day to day experience. (see Hang)

RICE When a couple is married, Rice is thrown on them to symbolize the acquisition of a new and strong social foundation. As such, rice refers to a basis or cornerstone of human endeavors. Moreover, since rice is a basic and necessary nourishment, its presence may imply an indispensable requirement or consummate building block recently instituted in ones waking life.

RING   The archetypal symbolism of a metal circle, or finger Ring, involves the eternal shielding, or protection, of mortal human liturgies. This is why a king, magician and ordinary husband and wife all become consecrated with a ring. Moreover, the ceremonial kiss of a king's regal band, represents the acceptance of his total authority and eternal sovereignty. Accordingly, in the dream sense, a ring may depict an emotional or psychological confirmation of responsibility, status or honor in ones waking life. (see Circle)

RITUAL   In the dream sense, a ritual represents the physical enactment of our symbolic language. As such, a ritual, or ceremony, may refer to any number of deep, passionate transformations of self. Moreover, the determining manner of rituals are their repetitive and therefore, worshipful nature. Accordingly, in a dream, we may be expressing faith in the criterion of our beliefs to bring valid, vital and absolute meaning into our lives.

RIVER   The symbolism of the river refers to the psychological and emotional continuity of our existence. As such, violent rapids may represent difficulty in our everyday interrelationships. Furthermore, swimming against the current of a river, may be indicative of unproductive and wearisome actions, which exhaust our drive, yet lead us nowhere. (see Bridge)

ROAD   The overall symbolism of the Road involves freedom, movement and travel. It is the long existence into the unknown. However, unlike the highway which is impersonal and seems to go on forever, the road often carries with it aspects of familiarity in the shape of houses, street signs, people, in other words, entire neighborhood vistas. In this sense, the road may promise a new way of life which is not entirely alien to our own subtle sensibilities. Alternatively, a lone, empty road in the middle of the night, might reflect darker and perhaps frightening choices which we have made in the not too distant past. As such, do we desire this 'road less taken' , or do we find ourselves entirely lost. In another interpretation of the road dream, we examine the idea of continual movement whence we (as driver or hitchhiker) never stop to plant our roots firmly into a single way of life. This dream rather eloquently illustrates an internal restlessness which may reflect our interrelationships and social moorings. In this dream landscape, our unconscious may reveal certain images of people or places which momentarily appeal to us. We may need to explore these metaphorical offerings from our sleeping mind. (see Highway)

ROCKS   In the dream sense, Rocks may represent our own obstinate behavior, which must be avoided, or conversely stockpiled, to use as a form of psychological or emotional protection. Moreover, in the image of our resolute rock pile, we may find valuable gems and crystals of honor, courage and hope. Consequently, a dream of breaking rocks, may refer to a profound sacrifice necessary to reveal our hidden resplendence. Furthermore, the chiseling and shaping of hard stone may epitomize the sculpting and perfecting of our human psyche. (see Wall)

ROPE The symbolism of a Rope represents help and the possibility of climbing to new summits in waking life. However, the dreamer may be referring to the tangibility of physical or emotional capture in the embodiment of a rope or lasso. (see Knot) (see Hang)

ROSE The archetypal symbol of the red Rose refers to passionate desire and/or a deep and mature level of love and intimacy. Furthermore, the unconscious illustration of a bouquet of roses may indicate a grand gesture of hope, joy or formidable applause. Additionally, dried-up roses may refer to a flame which still burns in a love affair which has come to an unceremonious end. Appropriately, we need to analyze the condition of the roses and the initiation and motivation of the person who gives or receives the flowers.

ROUND TABLE The Round Table of King Arthur lore, refers to spiritual equality in all men. There is no head at the table and all men figure equivalent in the decision making process. At the center of the table, we primarily find a flame, which is symbolic of God as the nucleus of creation and the universe. All men identical under the Almighty and fortified in their circuitous union of faithful humanity. (see Tarot Major Arcana)

RUN As opposed to walking in a dream which refers to a search for the self, Running may symbolize an elaborate escape from ones internalized fears and anxieties. In other words, the dreamer may be expressing misgivings about stopping and 'facing the music'. Moreover, our unconscious may be indicating the physical, psychological and emotional breakdown inherent in this continual and anxious movement. As in the chase dream, therapists recommend the 'marathon' dreamer to stop and confront the source of his or her terror. More often than not, the trepidation may prove to be nothing more than a Catch-22 side-effect of the self-imposed distress.

S

SACRIFICE To give of oneself completely, or to Sacrifice oneself, may involve a surrendering of ones symbolic body, in place of ones spiritual concerns. This form of martyrdom may illustrate a deep commitment to ones beliefs, or conversely, an overcompensation for a personal belief system which is not socially recognized. The question is, 'Are we saintly, or do we want to be remembered as a saint'? In the sense of a human offering, the age-old concept of the human sacrifice, not only satisfied the totalitarian gods, but also eased the blood lust of a human community, number one in the food chain for no small reason! The unifying theme in both cases is appeasement, the submission and limitation of one part of ourselves, in order to raise up high, another and yet deeper, part of our complex perceptive reality. Accordingly, we need to determine what aspect of our life is sacrificed and moreover, what is our greater reward for the ordeal and/or inconvenience, endured. (see Cannibal) (see Imbrue) (see Impale)

SADISM   In the dream sense, acts of Sadism perpetrated by the dreamer, may be indicative of repressed anger and aggression which re-emerges as a passionate and violent form of wish-fulfillment. Moreover, the infliction of pain upon captive individuals may symbolize a complex construct of psychological revenge involving forced paralysis (see numb). Conversely, sadistic behavior performed on willing participants, may be an unconscious illustration of dominant and forceful sexuality (see Leather). Accordingly, in a dream involving victimization, we may be unleashing the emotional and psychological pain carried within the depths of ourselves.

SAINT   The conceptualization of a holy man or Saint may be paradoxical in nature, yet the terminology conveys a bridge from ordinary human frailty to profound inner strength. This leap of human potential is accomplished by a total conviction and dedication to faith in a supreme being. In the dream sense, we may be utilizing the image of the saint to metaphorically relate moral fortitude and/or deep faith in something (not necessarily religious) in which we profoundly believe. It should be stressed that a saint, unlike an angel, began his spiritual journey as an ordinary man or woman. This undeniable aspect of sainthood appeals to our very own mortal humanity. In the religious sense, we attribute certain saints to their particular worldly deeds. Therefore, if the saint is known in the dream landscape, we may be able to gain some insight into our own particular nocturnal vision. (see Icon)

SALT   In the dream sense, Salt may represent added flavor and a new found flare in the experience of life. Moreover, in the biblical sense, salt is symbolic of the greatest stature of life itself. Hence, the salt of the earth, represents the very pinnacle of creation. Accordingly, in a dream, salt may refer to increased zest and vigor in ones life and an elevated sense of individual worthiness. The dream may also refer to our truth, dedication and creativity in every day life.

SAND   The complex symbolism of Sand refers to the transient impermanence of being. Moreover, sand may be indicative of the dualism of the microcosm and the macrocosm, representing simultaneously, a single grain of sand and a mighty desert. Additionally, the diverse illustration of comfort offered by a beach and the sudden violence of a sandstorm, both pertain to this enigmatic dream imagery. Accordingly, we need to interpret our interaction with, and manipulation of, the dream sand, in order to understand how its multifarious and elusive nature may figure into our current waking circumstance and/or predicament.

SATAN   The devil Satan is often depicted as ingenious, deceitful, smooth and entirely full of evil. In this extremity of behavior, we witness how influential this personage can be upon our mortal being. In the spiritual and intellectual sense, this dark demon is able to prey upon us via the large array of our weaknesses. It is interesting to note, while a saint or angel motivates our personal inner strength, the devil asks us nothing but the indulgence of our worldly desires. He is happy to speed down life's low road, laughing crazily behind the wheel. The interpretation of this dream image is split, dependent on our reaction and interaction with this powerful allegorical being. Are we drawn within its charms and ease, or are we repulsed by its lack of any and all restraint. In the psychological sense of the former example, we in fact be overcompensating for the mundane reality of our day to day existence. (see Demon) (see Tarot Major Arcana: Devil (15))

SAVAGE   The wild individual who practices little or no restraint whatsoever, may be indicative of our own need to figuratively 'bust loose'. Moreover, the Savage illustrates darker proponents of our psyche which may be repressed in our waking experience. Furthermore, in a not entirely separate interpretation, the wild man may illustrate a spiritual visionary or shaman which guides us with the eccentricities of his naturalistic movements, gestures and elaborate dance. With this in mind, we may need to determine the symbolism of the savage's mask, clothing and other adornments. (see Aboriginal)

SCAR   The symbolism of a Scar, may represent old wounds, or bad feelings, which never entirely heal and linger in our memory. Primarily, these psychological and emotional injuries occur in our youth and remain repressed and buried in our unconscious. However, when personal regression develops, a dreamer may call upon these memories to support his or her irrational behavior. Accordingly, in the dream sense, a scar may be representative of a deeply seated insecurity which may be holding us back from accomplishing our adult endeavors and fulfilling our well-deserved goals. Conversely, a scar may epitomize the struggle we have gone through to become self-realized individuals. In other words, do we display the scar as our personal badge, or does the scar display us, as its hapless and defeated victim?

SCHOOL   In the dream sense, a School may represent the foundation and beginning stages of our earliest social skills. As such, we need to honestly confront the memories of our shy, awkward and painful, or conversely fun, lively and animated scholastic interrelationships. The appropriate memory depicted in a dream landscape, may be entirely reflective of these identical emotions rekindled in a dreamers waking life. (see Academy) (see Quiz) (see Scar)

SEA   The complex symbolism of the Sea represents the embodiment of our entire emotional matrix. Moreover, an endless body of water which reflects the sun and sustains a multiplicity of wonder below its depths may be indicative of our unconscious. As such, all movements directed into the sea may imply an immersion into our unconscious. Conversely, physical movement rising out of the deep waters may refer to memories recalled from our own personal depths. Accordingly, in the dream sense, a sea may refer to the symbolic transition from our unconscious to our conscious and vice versa. In so doing, the sea may represent the plateau between our waking mind and our dreaming mind. (see Drown) (see Baptism) (see Unconscious, the) (see Water)

SEASONS, THE FOUR   The Four Seasons may be symbolic of the entire cycle of life. As such, spring refers to birth, youth and potential, while summer alludes to the zenith of life in full bloom and blistering enterprise. The fall, or autumn, represents a gentle dismissal from the climax of young adulthood, into the wise, reason of weathered maturity and steady industry. In the end, gentle winter numbs our bodies into a lingering detachment of worldly concerns and prepares us for the profound transfiguration of our own death. In turn, this passing allows for the completion and new beginning inherent in the eternal cycle of divine renewal.

SEED   The image of a Seed involves potential for life generation and growth in general. As such, everything in the realm of hope and possibilities may find a symbolic allusion to the living seed. In the judgement that a seed once planted, needs water and sunlight, we witness a representation of the wise acceptance of emotions in order to grow to ones fullest potential. Furthermore, the memory of seed gives primary strength to the mighty tree. In other words, transformation is not separation, but rather, transcendence, which is the goal of existence and unequivocal completion of being. (see Acorn) (see Garden) (see Growth) (see Overflow) (see Water) (see Sun) (see Light) (see Earth) (see Womb)

SEVEN   The archetypal symbolism of the number seven refers to chance, luck and the divine animating power of God. If these representations seem too diverse and radically opposed, the reader may want to consult modern theories of quantum physics. In quantum theory, the only provable certainty is uncertainty, or randomness. Another branch of modern physics called Chaos Theory wholeheartedly agrees with this random, or arbitrary, approach to the workings of our material existence. In other words, theorists exclaim, 'God plays with dice.' (see also Tarot Major Acana: Charioteer (7))

SHADE   The dream imagery of Shade illustrates a temporary relief from the heat and exposure of direct sunlight. However, since sunlight is symbolic of reason, clarity and revelation, shade may refer to mild deception, harmless subterfuge and sensual foolishness. Moreover, shade may represent an elusive union of light and dark which may reveal a peculiar conglomeration of good and bad intentions. Accordingly, we may need to analyze the individual and combined natures of these consorted feelings and decide if they are well-balanced in our psyche, or thoroughly muddled and consequently, alienating.

SHADOW, THE Carl G. Jung referred to a person's dark, and perhaps repressed, inner self, as The Shadow. In the figure of the shadow we find the intense passions of self which are too powerful and too individualistic to reveal in normal society. In Robert Lois Stevenson's short story entitled: Dr. Jekyll and Mr. Hyde, the author reveals the physical embodiment of ones repressed self through chemistry; a sort of anti-reason elixir is created by the good doctor, which involves opening portals into the dark regions of the human psyche. The tragedy of the story is not found in the form of the evil Mr. Hyde, but rather in the unbalanced natures of both Jekyll and Hyde. The same lesson holds true in the dream sense, which reveals the shadow as a figure who is overtly repressed and must emerge, at least partially, to complete the balanced psyche of the dreamer.

SHAMAN In ancient times, Shaman, or the spiritual messengers of tribes, looked to dreams to guide them in their social instruction and inspiration. The visual quest of the shaman became the singular embodiment of the spiritual needs of the entire clan. Accordingly, in the dream sense, the vision of a journeying shaman, may represent the incarnate motivation of our own spiritual search. As such, any and all gestures and rituals performed by the shaman, should be interpreted for their appropriate symbolic meaning in our own life.

SHARK The symbolism of the Shark refers to swimming in dangerous emotional waters. The several million year old shark species is known for its fierce aggression and razor sharp teeth, but not for its colorful body or physical nature. In fact, the cold predatory eye of the shark displays no emotion whatsoever. Accordingly, this large-jawed creature may represent a lack of sensitivity concerning our own sentiments and the inherent danger involved in this behavior. In the dream sense, the unconscious may be displaying our own cold and ruthless insensitivity, or conversely, warning us against the actions of a known individual whose intentions may be less than noble.

SHEEP In the Chinese zodiac, the Sheep personality is thought of as being elegant, artistic and religious, yet shy and sometimes baffled by life's complexity. In the west, the symbolism is not entirely different. The sheep is thought of as innocent and vulnerable in a harsh and complex world. Unfortunately, this longing for belief and understanding may lead sheep into slaughter, their own, or someone else's. As such, the concept of blind trust, or faith, while admirable in a certain sense of humility, may also spell disaster. As human beings, we are not sheep, and have the ability to think for ourselves. We have the ability to reason and estimate the repercussions of our behavior. When we blindly follow, we negate our foresight into the forward future, instead relying on trust and the ensuing of rear ends before us, in the herd at large. The dream drastically illustrates the nature of our own behavior, or conversely, the nature of others who follow our lead. Sheep or shepherd, we still rely on some form of hidden truth. (see parasite)

SHELL Because of its bright color, feminine shape and proximity to water (ocean beaches etc.), a Shell is intricately associated with emotional relationships which transcend the normal tenets of lust and desire. The nature of the shell involves pure love, spiritual ascendence and a mystical union with nature. In the ancient Kabbalah, the tree of life is generated and enlightened via the transfigurative associations of archangels, otherwise known as 'shells'. From still another point of view, the sea shell tells the story of an entire life, its once cephalopod inhabitant. Taken together, we understand the poignancy of the shell dream. As such, we need to determine all the factors surrounding the discovery and employment of the shell in the dream landscape. For example, the image of walking upon broken shells may symbolize the caution we exhibit in relationships, fearful of the heartbreaks or disillusionments endured in our past. (see Oyster)

SHELTER The image of a hiding spot which momentarily saves us from the harsher elements, may be directly symbolic of real hope amidst violent chaos. However, what makes this imagery unique, as opposed to a house or apartment sanctuary, a Shelter is not permanent and will eventually deny stability. In this sense, we must interpret the short-lived extension of hope offered by its dwelling. The unconscious may be alluding to much needed assistance offered in waking life via a person, family or organization; however, a conscious realization asserting a re-emergence of self-determination may equally be implied in this dream communication. accordingly, we need to analyze the condition of this shelter, either man-made or natural, and examine the steps we take to prepare for our emergence back into the real world. (see Den) (see Cabin)

SIX In the Tarot deck, the number Six major-arcana, refers to naturalistic and divine love which is not based upon simple carnal desire. Moreover, the Star of David in the Hebrew tradition, illustrates a balance of strength, counterbalancing as it does, the powerful triad forms. Accordingly, in the dream sense, the number six may represent the fortitude and solid prosperity of family and otherwise, consecrated union. (see Tarot Major Arcana: The Lovers (6) figure)

SKY The archetypal symbolism of the Sky refers to infinite vision and/or wisdom. Moreover, the masculine aspect of spirit resides in the sky above and compliments mother earth below. Furthermore, the light blue reflection which veils the atmosphere is indicative of boundless potential and eternal grace. Consequently, all entities which move through the vast horizon, illustrate freedom and the zenith of existence. (see Fly) (see Light) (see Blue)

SLAVE In the dream sense, a Slave may be indicative of our servitude to individuals who forget, or ignore, our basic humanity. Moreover, the representation of slavery may involve our unconscious illustration of a sudden personal loss of individuality and inherent liberty, for no justifiable reason. Consequently, we may need to analyze our lack of autonomy in our working relationships, including our own family life.

SLEEP CYCLES (see Alpha & Delta waves)

SLOW MOTION As opposed to dream paralysis, which involves an entire loss of movement, including escape or retaliation, Slow Motion dreams seem to focus our mind on the temporal unfolding of symbolic events. In this sense, our unconscious may be revealing minute peculiarities and subtleties in our behavior. This may be an indication of slight personal changes occurring in our waking life which may be causing us anxiety. Moreover, slow motion imagery seems to add a poignancy to our dream situations. Accordingly, we may need to determine if certain waking events are exaggerated in our consciousness and justifiably, need to be placed in their proper psychological or emotional context.

SMOKE The complex symbolism of Smoke is innately involved with flame and therefore carries all the tenets of danger, passion, deception and creation which one associates with fire. In the realm of sensuality, smoking continues to induce feelings of calm, cool control and an almost emotional toughness. This lure of smoke is so powerful and humanly transcendent, it causes teenagers to begin smoking even though they are deluged with information about cancer and the string of other respiratory illnesses linked with the use of tobacco. Far from being a defense for smoking, one finds a far superior alternative in the Native American practice of smoking the peace pipe to mark social unity and tribal bonding in sacred ceremonies. In a single instant, these people (especially the Dakota Sioux) combined ritual, creation and communal sharing to incorporate a powerful, reasonable center of human wisdom. So, we must ask our dreaming mind; is our smoking a healthy religious experience, or just a 'cool' deceptive fog? (see Fog)

SNAKE In the Chinese zodiac, the Snake personality is considered deep, wise and romantic. These individuals are also thought of as being strong-willed and very determined, despising nothing more, than their own failure. The western image of the snake is not entirely different. The natural allusion to stealth and sexuality infer quiet wisdom and an almost hypnotic romanticism. The strength of the entwining serpent, illustrates a kind of gradual and building determination, which finds little room for real compromises. Taking all this into account, our dream may imply something about our internal force of will, which may move beyond our ability to stop its sometimes damaging effects. (see Python)

SNOW The complex symbolism of Snow involves purity, childhood and rudimentary pleasure. Moreover, the image of a silent and tranquil snowfall, may be indicative of spiritual peace and/or somber wisdom. As such, we need to determine our exact feelings in and around the snow.

SPIDER The image of a Spider may represent a loner, or lone being, whom it may be wise to keep away from, even though he or she may be extremely alluring. In another sense, a spider's danger is aimed primarily at unwanted pests. Therefore, the stranger referred to in the form of the dream spider, may in fact illustrate a positive force eradicating the prevailing infestation of negativity. In the connotation of a female, Black Widow etc., we may be revealing fear or uncertainty concerning relationships and their intricate ensnarements. (see Vampire) (see Bleed)

SPOTLIGHT   In the dream sense, a Spotlight may refer to the strict focus and intense concentration upon our actions. As such, we may be expressing a desire to be noticed by a particular individual, including a parent, or romantic interest. Moreover, this spotlight may be an indication that we have perfected some behavior which may have been previously ordinary or nondescript in our waking character. Along these lines, our unconscious may be illustrating overcompensation regarding the nature of our own insecurity.

SQUARE   The Square shape implies strength, stability, honesty and a conservative outlook on the future. Furthermore, we see the sound foundation for building upon ones own physical, psychological, emotional and spiritual development. (see Form) (see Eight) (see Four)

STAGE   As opposed to the symbolism of the spotlight, which focuses individual attention, the Stage refers to the social choreography of our interrelationships and the subsequent reaction from our audience of peers. In this sense, the stage is representative of our communal behavior. Accordingly, we need to analyze our relative success, or failure, upon the dream stage. Furthermore, if we find ourself on the side stage, our unconscious may be elucidating the reality of our introverted behavior. Consequently, we may need to storm the stage of our interpersonal existence with style, poise and confidence.

STAIN   As opposed to the symbolism of a scar, which refers to a deeply seated and difficult memory, the mark of a Stain may allude to the remembrance of a superficial and therefore, wholly reversible mistake in our life. Accordingly, we may need to analyze the substance and color which stains our clothes or body, and the clothing or body parts, themselves. (see Imbrue)

STARS   The symbolism of Stars, or celestial bodies, refers to the hopes, dreams and aspirations of man immersed within the boundless reaches of creation. Moreover, since light represents wisdom and clarity, flickering stars reflect enigmatic, unfathomable and incomprehensible cognizance. As such, star gazers, star readers and especially, star travelers (aliens), are consulted for knowledge and guidance. Accordingly, in the dream sense, a starry night may typify future knowledge and the potential to use that wisdom in a peaceful, benevolent and steadfast manner.

STOMACH   The food we eat and the desire with which we consume it, illustrates a great deal about ourselves and our respective needs. In the conceptualization of the stomach, we examine foods (or information) ingested, and our digestive (acceptance) of them accordingly. Hence, the feeling of our stomach reveals the temperance of our belief system or relative way of life. When certain situations appear before us which are entirely unacceptable and lack the basic humanity we are accustomed to in life, we find ourselves nauseated and wanting to purge the entire matter. We are therefore, in a very real sense, ruled by what we are able to stomach. Consequently, in our dreams, we need to analyze all effective stimuli concerning our stomach, otherwise known as our 'gut' instinct. (see Abdomen)

STORM Used extensively in art. literature and film, Storms eloquently symbolize internal turmoil and seething anguish. The combination of dark skies, harsh winds and flooding, drowning torrents of rain, illustrate the instability of emotion and the relentless punishment and ruthless unanticipated effect they unleash upon our psyche. As an archetype in human consciousness, the eruption of elemental forces signals caution and danger. This is the time to hide and find shelter. In the wisdom of the animal world, the calm BEFORE the storm, is the time to work and make preparations for the impending havoc. Therefore, our unconscious may be implying, we are too late for carefree preservation and now we must 'weather' the symbolic storm before us. Once again, similar to the animal world, the survival against the elements builds our character and strengthens our life force. (see Boat) (see Rain)

STRANGULATION The restriction of breathing essential to the process of life, signals an innermost danger which we feel may harm, not only ourselves, but our loved ones as well. As such, our own Strangulation may involve a sickness in our family or a threat to our livelihood in general. In this sense, any stress related to ones survival, including and especially the aforementioned, economic failure or accomplishment, implicitly reflect this nightmarish dream imagery. Alternatively, a strangulation may imply a suffocation of ideas, passions, and otherwise suppressed instinctual drives. Events which produce shortness of breath, including eroticism, may be illustrated in a suggestive sense. (see Hang)

SUCCUBUS (see Incubus)

SUGAR In the dream sense, Sugar may be representative of instant, yet short-lived, gratification. As such, the sweetness of sugary pleasures may be symbolic of a compensation for the true happiness found in love, charity and devotion. Moreover, the sweetness of sugar may be indicative of personal, and therefore selfish, enjoyment and/or debauchery. In any case, sugar can be used as an exceptional ingredient in healthy and nutritious cooking. Accordingly, the symbolic sweet crystal can be used in good measure toward sound and meaningful relationships. In the dream landscape, we may need to determine the amount of sugar used and the nature, and motivation, of the individuals who produce and serve the confectionery substance.

SUN The symbolism of the Sun dates back to earliest stages of human development and involves the hope of a new day, the alleviation of our fear of night (more appropriately the unknown) and a basking in the warmth and sensory brilliance of creation. Primitive cultures world-wide, including the Aztecs, Celts and ancient Greeks, held elaborate ceremonial rites of worship to their SUN deities who reserved great force and aided mankind in an almost day to day, interpersonal fashion. Today, as in the countless millennium past, the sun dream indicates immense radiance and outright wonder, the eternal exploding energy of the ceaseless fire bearing star which sustains life and illuminates being. Naturally, the negative or flip side of illumination is exposure. In this sense, a blazing desert heat might evoke a fear of being seen, discovered, revealed and thusly ravageed by elements out of our human and/or immediate control. (see Light) (see Tarot Major Arcana: The Sun (19) figure)

SURGERY In the dream sense, Surgery implies a radical intrusion into the foundation of self. Appropriately, we need to interpret whether this encroachment is for our own emotional or physiological benefit, or conversely, an attack upon our stolid psychological meddle.

SUSPENDED ANIMATION The surreal image of floating in Suspended Animation, may involve various levels of alienation and isolation. However, in this circumstance, the detachment and seclusion experienced, may not be entirely unpleasant. When the external muscles of the body relax, we may become aware of our internal processes. Gradually, all biological operation is accounted for, and otherwise overlooked. When this separation from our physical self occurs, we begin to be able to move directly into our neural imagination and the full repertoire of its deepest memory. In this externally motivated journey into the unconscious, we may or may not find what we expected. Herein, lies the paradox of suspended animation. We may feel a desire to surrender ourselves to the vast internal world of perception, however, we may not be stable enough and secure enough, to relinquish ALL external physical control. In fact, we may panic at the thought of a situation without means of physical escape. In this sense, we become suspended, immobilized and entirely vulnerable to all forms of perceived danger, which of course increases with the steady rise of our irrational panic. The panic may become so violent and taxing to our central nervous system, that we awake from this nightmare physically exhausted and utterly entangled with anxiety. Conversely, the biological release which leads us into the unconscious, and otherwise spiritual awareness of self, may bring memorable elation and inner peace which lasts a life time. Taking all this into account, we need to understand our relative ability to animate ourselves without the control of our usual faculties. Moreover, is our fear too overwhelming, to allow for the full disengagement of body, absolutely necessary to explore the uncharted worlds found in this so-called, suspended animation? (see Float) (see Numb)

SWAMP The symbolism of a Swamp may refer to an unstable foundation in ones waking endeavors. Moreover, a swamp may represent murky and obscure emotional involvements, which may in fact, be confusing and desperate in scope. Taken together, we see how the swamp landscape in our dream, may be indicative of an unconscious warning concerning the shaky groundwork of a recent emotional undertaking. (see Drown)

T

TABLE   The image of a Table may represent the potential for a meeting or gathering. In this sense, our unconscious may be signifying a need for talks, to perhaps bring together social unity, or in any case, purposeful unification of some kind. Moreover, the contents upon a table may symbolize a person, or an entire group's psychological makeup. For example, a lone plate, full glass and burnt-out candle may symbolize lonliness, or the lack of human socialization, while on the other hand, a map, pointer and ashtray full of cigarette butts, may certainly indicate an organized plan involving a considerably large group of people. (see Dinner)

TABOO   In the dream sense, any personal behavior which is strictly Taboo, may be referring to actions repressed in our unconscious. Along these lines, a tribe, or cluster, may be indicative of our moral and social code. Accordingly, we need to determine the tribe's grounds for the suppression of this behavior. Does the dream clan's taboo match our own social prohibitions? If the group's restriction is radically different from those of waking society, we may need to interpret all of their public and community differences. Hence, when we build a psychological awareness of the group and its motivations, we will have begun obtaining an accurate description of our own psyche.

TAIL   In the dream sense, an animal's Tail may refer to our feelings of happiness, fear and/or sexual arousal. The latter example may allude to the symbolism of the male phallic. In yet another sense, our tail may refer to our point of vulnerablity. As such, we may be taking risks, for which we are not prepared to pay the full consequences if caught. In this case, we may place our tail between our legs, symbolizing fear and outright embarrassment. The tail as hind quarters, may refer to a form of sexuality which is hidden and unable to face up to its true reality. Furthermore, when we view objects of desire from behind, we may be illustrating voyeuristic tendencies and perhaps a coy form of repression.

TANGO   The passionate dance known as the Tango, may have little to do with rhythm and music and everything to do with the hypnotic nature of sensuality. In its torrent, wave-like repetition, we find the building of carnal heat and an almost burning sexuality. Nevertheless, the tango adheres to rules of society and gathers its strength from mutual sexual tolerance. Therefore, should one partner lose the passion found in the ritual, the tango becomes no longer relevant. In a dream tango, we may be reflecting the building passion of a particular situation, especially involving opposing forces who are attracted by the measure of their mutual emotion. The dreamer needs to analyze the direction of this passion and its metaphoric connection with waking realities.

TAPESTRY The combination of disparate materials and diverse color woven into a Tapestry may be symbolic of community unity and the lengths we as human beings are willing to go, to achieve these ends. Accordingly, we need to analyze the condition of the tapestry, as well as the colors and material chosen. We also need to determine if the tapestry is completed. Understanding these precepts, we may begin to understand the organization of parts (people, situations) in our life toward a greater and grander whole.

TARGET The Target dream may involve dualism depending on whether we view ourselves as the symbolic victim of life's arrows, or conversely, the active and brave archer reaching the bull's eye in admirable achievement of self. To ascertain this distinction, we need to uncover all the representational tenets and images in both the arrow as well as the launcher. Moreover, do our emotions signal fear and anxiety in this dream landscape, or thrill and exhilaration. (see Arrow)

TAROT The complex symbolism of the Tarot, refers to a language of divination and a multi-dimensional mirror into our own unconscious. As such, we see a random selection of cards, each pertaining to a facet of our human psyche, laid out before us to illustrate the past, present and future. Appropriately, we analyze the meaning of the cards, which in theory, reflect the arbitrary reality present in our concurrent awareness. This essentially means, a Tarot card reading performed two days hence, may be radically different than one performed today (in the present), simply due to the new arrangement of thoughts and worldly attitudes which are ever changing in our perceptive awareness. Consequently, in the dream sense, a Tarot layout may involve a description of a dreamer's current, yet entirely changeable, feelings concerning reality, or some specific point effecting his or her waking life. The four respective suits of the Tarot: Wands, Swords, Cups and Pentacles are synonymous with the four elements: Fire, Air, Water and Earth. In this sense, the fire element of the Wand represents inspiration and the spiritual, psychological and physical reality of action and initiative. The air element of Swords refers to the determination and strength of an individual who conquers fear and inner paralysis with complete faith in oneself and ones purpose. The water element of Cups refers to ones emotional capacity and furthermore, the purity of ones soul and spiritual outlook in general. Is the cup of love shared with others in the hope of interactive communal hope? Conversely, is the cup spilling, or empty and void of the fullness of life? Finally, we come to the earth element of Pentacles where we find a concern about worldly experience including and especially money and social influence. However, the Pentacles may also refer to our ties with the natural world around us, in other words, man and mother nature. Is the connection mutually fulfilling or one-sided and thereby destructive overall? We will explore each of the twenty-two major arcana in the course of this publication beginning with the Fool and culminating with the World. (see Seven) (see Collective Unconscious)

THE TAROT MAJOR ARCANA

TAROT

The TAROT DECK (Major Arcana) The Tarot deck is fundamentally used as a system of divination, however, many historians and theologians worldwide have agreed that within the boundaries of the Tarot deck, ancient belief systems and (otherwise lost) spiritual doctrines, are encoded in a picturesque series of symbols. These symbols were fashioned into the Tarot deck by ancient luminaries in order to preserve the ancient priestly texts; texts which were, at that point in history, threatened by outside forces. Turning the ancient system of faith into a simple card game hid its authentic (and highly volatile) value and moreover, enabled ALL members of society to gain insight into an ancient labyrinth-like system of spiritual wisdom. (On every street corner in fact, as was very much the case!) Occultists sight the beginnings of Tarot law in Egypt's Book of Thoth, whose followers pursued the Royal Path of Initiation. This initiation led a devout individual toward the complete physical, mental and spiritual contemplation of divine order. Tarot, Rota, and the Hebrew Torah, all reflect this conceptualization of the Path of Existence which reveals its truth in repeating spiralling steps of ascending and descending events of experience. These paths serve as a compass, or guide, in our appropriate (or not so appropriate) personal decision making process. (We can loosely compare this spiral guide to Jacob's biblical vision of the Ladder.) Perhaps, the controversial seed of the Tarot deck's absolute beginning will never be found, nonetheless, the esoteric structures of faith which the deck has wholly influenced throughout history can also never be denied. These powerful traditions include the Kabbalists, Pythagoreans, Astrologers, Alchemists, Enochians, Rosicrucians, Old and New Testament (literal) followers, as well as the Hermetics. We also find Eastern Incarnations of the spiritual labyrinth in such diverse faiths as Zen Buddhism, Hinduism, and (in its color-coded system of symbols,) first stage Shinto.

In examining the 22 major arcana, from the (0) Fool card, to the (21) World card, we will explore the central idioms and ideologies, as well as the generic social dynamics, which the cards represent. These are Living Symbols which continue to tutor the scope of our universal culture. Therefore, as the ancients intended, they will forever figure prominently within our psyche and overall dream consciousness...

Sequentially, in our initial viewing of the deck, we find the four respective suits of the tarot: Wands, Swords, Cups and Pentacles, which are synonymous with the four elements: Fire, Air, Water and Earth. In the first link, we discover that the Fire element found in THE WAND depicts INSPIRATION and the spiritual, psychological and physical reality of INITIATIVE, the SPARK of creation. Secondly, the Air element of SWORDS refers to the DETERMINATION and mental STRENGTH of an individual who conquers fear and inner paralysis with complete faith in oneself and ones own purpose. The Water element of CUPS beckons to ones EMOTIONAL CAPACITY and furthermore, the PURITY OF ONES SOUL and SPIRITUAL DEPTHS. A question is posed: Is the cup of love shared with others in the hope of interactive communal charity, or conversely, is the cup SPILLING, EMPTY and otherwise DRAINED of the fullness of HUMAN kindness? Finally, we come to the Earth element of PENTACLES where we find a concern about WORLDLY EXPERIENCE including and especially MATERIAL GAIN and SOCIAL INFLUENCE. However, before we color this suit in an entirely negative cast, we learn that Pentacles and Earth also refers to the natural, organic, and highly visible world all around us. In this sense the suit asks: can the connection of man and nature be mutually fulfilling, or is it one-sided and therefore, doomed to be forever destructive? The question becomes ever more pertinent as we roll full steam ahead into an uncertain ecological future.

One last point should be made. In the examination of each of the twenty-two major arcana in the tarot deck, we will reveal color, shape, numerical, and all other coded symbolic meanings, inherent in the face of the card itself. It is our aspiration not to overlook any of the subtle wisdoms and criss-crossing details encoded therein by the ancient seers. Hence, by stepping directly into their vision we provide a gateway to share the unique perception of these immortalized ancients. In the process, we slowly unearth our own dream consciousness within the fool's journey (0 Tarot Card) into a complex spiritual awareness. Armed with this particular brand of enlightenment, we systematically justify (via) the interpretation of the cards, the timeless wisdom of the archaic Tarot, the uncompromising Royal Path...

THE FOOL (0) (Tarot Major Arcana) The Fool figure does not begin with the number 0 merely to symbolize nothingness, in the sense of loss. In fact, quite the opposite is true. The emptiness of the fool represents his potential to obtain all the wisdom which the world around him has to offer. However, he can accomplish this feat only by operating on his instincts and fundamental innocence. In this way, he must remain fearless and fixed within his faith. As such, he wholly WELCOMES ALL EXPERIENCES, which surely must await him. Similarly, when we ourselves play the fool, we instinctively follow our raw, (or sensational,) emotions, rather than our own intellect. In other words, we sometimes charge blindly (yet devotedly,) into the world of experience.

On the card itself, the fool figure is about to step off a cliff with all the assurance of a man stepping into his own garden. He is at peace in his own absolute faith in a reality which supports him and drives him forward. In this fashion, the fool is potential energy awaiting the spark of active life. The fool is associated with the element Air because of this stealth determination to acquire the full-blown experience of existence.

Observing the fool arcana further, we find the figure focusing all his concentration upon the future. The past is behind him and he has no concern about it. His eyes, (the eyes of man and other such predators,) are fixed forward. This is the point where he needs to stay, the point of potential and all possible encounters. (In other words, the fool is not concerned with the kill, but the thrill of the chase.) The card tells us any musing or reflection whatsoever, will be saved for another day (and another card!)

In the Jungian sense, this point of the fool's potential is roughly comparative to the limits (which are actually limitless) of the unconscious. He (the fool) is the collective unconscious before it collects data and focuses on discriminate solutions. He is the unseen law behind a physical system which produces actual and viable results. In this, he represents the onset of the initiate (the tarot card reader) into the folds of spiritual reason and the path of enlightenment. As we prepare to begin a journey, we find ourselves happy, healthy and bursting with energy. The same holds true of the fool as he begins the Tarot. The exuberance of the fool is reflective of his absolute purity. Life has not yet punished him (and in fact cannot punish him,) because he is the lure (and initial push) of life. He can accept in an instant the whole of the world and then again reject it, without batting an eyelash. He can do this because he is the beginning and the end of physical existence. When at long last, he has gained all the wisdom in the world, you will not see him resting his britches in spiritual satori, because he will simply begin anew the search for greater experience. After all, he is not a fool, he is THE FOOL!

In this fearless/impenetrable riddle we find an association with the mind of God. Accordingly, the gods associated with the fool are Jupiter and Zeus. The animal linked with the fool card is the eagle who sees all and yet cannot be reached. In the truest sense, the fool is ever matched up with the individual who uses the deck, whether for divination or serious philosophical study. The initiate needs to remain the fool in order to move through the wisdom of the tarot, which may seem frightening through the eyes of ordinary reason, but gains force in spiritual faith. The card itself depicts this constant approach to faith and enlightenment with the shiny yellow sun which seems to continuously fill the fool with warmth and encouragement, while lighting his way into the great beyond.

In some decks, a dog is pictured yapping at the fool as he begins his perilous journey. This simple representation symbolizes leaving home and the familiarity of friends and family, who sometimes bind us with their own emotional ties. In spite of this COMFORTABLE haven, the initiate understands that he or she must experience the realm of existence ALL ALONE in its fullest and purest sense; in all its splendor, harshness and outright severity. Only by tackling and overcoming life's hardships again and again armed only with FAITH, can an individual gain the true meaning of the Royal Path of existence, the ancient ROTA known as the Tarot...

THE MAGICIAN (1) (Tarot Major Arcana) The Magician represents the spark of the fool's potential. In this, the white robed figure brings all of life's possibilities into full physical existence. Accordingly, he possesses control of the four suits which lay horizontally on a table before him, they are: Wands, Swords, Cups and Pentacles. As stated earlier, these four suits are symbolic and synonymous with the four elements which are: Fire, Air, Earth and Water. It is the magicians SINGULAR PURPOSE to REVEAL THE WORLD and the promise of its abundant application. This is why he stands below the figure-eight infinity symbol which demonstrates the boundless (or, infinite) reality surrounding mankind.

As he points simultaneously to the heavens above, with his right hand and earth below, with his left hand, he becomes the incarnate symbol of man existing directly between heaven and earth, a yin/yang axis between spirit and body, SELF and WORLD. The magician acutely understands that all these levels of perception embody the oneness of being. Naturally, he is the beginning of self awareness and social awareness. This is why, on most decks, the figure is depicted on-stage performing to an outside physical world. However, unlike the fool, the magicians confidence upon this world stage is reflected from the fullness of the knowledge of his enterprise, not upon blind faith. The magician has become the full EMBODIMENT of the fool's potential. Life has become manifest.

The magician in some decks is portrayed as young and virile. There is a two-fold application for this rendering. First, his youth represents the initial 'spark' of life, previously mentioned, and second, the young magician indicates an individual who has only recently gained knowledge and reason through the attainment of ALL experience. In so many ways, he is Adam, before the fall. This sudden accumulation of organized knowledge, or 'reason', shows us an objective perception of the world, rather than a personal, self-orientated and entirely subjective perception of that same world. This immediately connects the magician figure with the infinite capacity of pure mind. As such, he sees and comprehends the path which the fools has undertaken and allows entry into each of its portals of experience. In this sense, the hebrew letter Beth is attributed with the magician. Beth means house, and as we have come to learn in the course of our study, house is symbolic of the world. Hence, the magician, (being master of the household,) welcomes us inside his home, (the world!) and moving through its rooms swiftly and effortlessly, (with the speed of thought,) he is able to grant us the one and only GRAND TOUR of existence.

In yet another connection with the magician's REASON, we find the figure associated with the gods Mercury, Hermes and Thoth who are known for their speed of thought and infinite vision. In fact, the Hermetic order, followers of Hermes Trismegistes, (or thrice great Hermes,) believed that the forty-two books of their master revealed the secret knowledge of both the ancient Greeks and the ancient Egyptians. It was said that Hermes Trismegistus was the divine incarnation of both gods: Thoth and Hermes, who were similarly associated with the universal wisdom, otherwise known as, (as we have come to discover,) the MASTERY OF MAGIC(K). The swiftness and completeness of thought born in the art of magic, correlates with the shaping and shifting of reality, Naturally, this bending and shaping of energy fields has a GREAT DEAL to do with physical (or, hands on) healing and the symbolic power of the T-shaped Caduceus. Historically, this T-shaped bar entwined with snakes, dates as far back as early as Mesopotamia, 2700 BC. Throughout that time, its symbolic representation of the magician's balanced force of will, has been linked with the metaphysical powers of all forms of healing. In a similar correlation, the Hindus believe the caduceus to be symbolic of the kundalini force which travels up the spine over and betwixt the six major chakras in every human being on the course of becoming whole. Fully involved in this life flow, we find the magician associated with ALL the elements, but especially the element Air, which is once again synonymous with mind. In this, we find the position of his experimentation and its subsequent learning. In other words, his power of healing is not incarnate, but a product of his swift and curious mind. MOREOVER, he is not afraid to fail in his attempt to discover implicit truths about his elemental reality. This is why the element Air is linked with the suit of Swords, or cutting knowledge. This viewing of the life potential in all its harshness is fundamentally what separates the Magician and the Fool. Yet, at the same time, their co-existive nature binds them together forever as one in the same, they are collectively THE EYE and THE BOW AND ARROW. Enduring at two separate levels of existence, one always follows the other, CAUSE (THE FOOL) ensued by an entirely inevitable, MANIFESTATION (THE MAGICIAN.)

In as much, we see the absolute, albeit austere, purity of life in its beginning stages, eloquently represented here in the Magician card. Exactly how this relates to our own initial perception of the world, replete with its four symbolic elements and infinite possibilities, we must gradually assess for ourselves. Nevertheless, the confidence and assurance of the card cannot be ignored and may serve as a starting point in our own concrete understanding of the conscious world around us. Combining faith and an infinite imagination, we too have begun the task of becoming 'thrice great' purveyors of a new world.

THE HIGH PRIESTESS (2) (Tarot major Arcana) Following cause and manifestation, it is only natural to find separation and ALL its subsequent developments. The High Priestess represents the first division of the whole world necessary to bring a return or reunification of that world. This destruction and restoration produces the birth of an ever evolving cyclical creation.

Seated between the negative and positive pillars of Solomon's temple, respectively Boaz and Joachin, the High Priestess becomes the manifest duality (or, splitting) of the magician's replete and whole universe. In the depth of her calm introspection, she seems to pull the world into its absolute opposition of physical realities, especially male and female (which she is both and neither,) generating a chasm of infinite potential. In this dynamic separation of the life force, she brings about the inspirational and flooding torrent of inconceivable attraction and miraculous union. In her beauty, youth and perfection, she forms the deepest well of first love, romantic love and eventually spiritual love. Strange, how all these powerful emotions are born from simple opposition and attraction: an ocean created from drops of rain, swelling emotion energized upon a dry and anticipating human psyche.

Naturally we see how the High Priestess figure is associated with the element of water and its multiplicity of forms and expressions. In this vain, the Hebrew letter connected with this card is Gimel, which means camel. The camel brings life into the desert because of its ability to store water and reserve its force and vitality. Moreover, the shape of its hump also implies a potent sexual ability and survival cunning. The High Priestess too has demonstrated her cunning, by separating the world in order to continuously rejuvenate its essential being. In her wisdom she fashions both a CUP and WATER to form life's completion, providing thirst and emptiness with celestial quenching and deepest fulfillment.

The figure is often associated with inspiration and the divination of DREAMS, in particular. She accomplishes this by existing in harmony with the deepest pool of the unconscious, with which she is synonymous. In this way, her resplendent, yet deep tranquility, teaches the tenets of wisdom honed carefully by reflection and abstract musing. Still further, in many ways, she is the combination of the Fool's faithful instinct and the Magician's keen intelligence. As such, she is our own consciousness taken to our deepest levels of awareness.

The color associated with the High Priestess is sky blue because of its infinite scope and welcoming clarity. As such, the figure seems to stretch her arms under the light of wisdom and warmth of love and fashions the very sky in the doing. At the same time, night brings darkness and moonlight, (i.e. emotions) and this too is symbolic of the High Priestess, for she is the beginning of the Yin/Yang struggle of all cyclical opposition. HOWEVER, it is crucial to note, unlike The Empress, The High Priestess offers no way of bridging these apparent opposites, she is and can only be, the POLARITY of opposites. She is to the Empress, what the Fool was to the Magician. Instead of the spark of BIRTH, she is the spark of REBIRTH. In short, she is the regenerative PRINCIPLE masterfully and forevermore embodied.

As such, the High Priestess is connected with Adam, Eve and the serpent, Pandora and her famous box. She is also linked to the gods Rhea, Isis, Shiva and of course, Venus (Aphrodite). The universal and common denominator of these female archetypes is their involvement with evil or evil forces (i.e. separation) in order to regenerate the order of the world such as it (factually) exists. These figures become a rationale or disclaimer for the tragedy of life. However, in the process, they equally assume credit for the perceived peaks of human existence, crowned by the emotion of love and the bearing of life itself.

In this, we understand why the figure is seated between the pillars of Solomon's temple and possesses the sacred Torah (which she solemnly holds in her lap.) It is SHE, the High Priestess, who has caused the great chasm in reality, therefore, it is SHE who must hold the 'rules' required to return to spiritual wholeness.

This is our final clue concerning her symbolism in the unconscious of our own dreaming awareness. Her presence clearly involves and invokes the patience necessary to disassemble an object simply to learn its proper function as a reconstructed unit. Accordingly, the High Priestess may be the architect and engineer of our deepest psychic understanding of the world. She has single-handedly, in her symbolic appearance in the Tarot, set the cycle of infinity into motion...

THE EMPRESS (3) (Tarot Major Arcana) The Empress in her feminine principle, seeks to join all states of being (divided by the High Priestess) in the stolid faith she holds in mature, natural and spiritual love. In this sense, she champions Acceptance of reality, regardless of its multiple contradictions, and as such, hopes to bridge the separate facets of the world together in fluid harmony. She is a sovereign in this: her singular desire to reunite social order and maternal cohesion into the reality of existence.

Her Hebrew name is Daleth, which means door. A door joins isolated rooms of meaning and provides an interchange of ideas. In the deepest philosophical sense of this wisdom, all that is necessary is the absolute joining of two rooms (or, entities.) Herein, we find her connection with mother nature and the living chain.

It is her contention that when we account for the balance of ALL complex elements of existence, these disparate realities will find a way to coexist without complication. Hence, her symbolic DOOR, becomes a passageway into entirely separate worlds and an invitation from each respective side to unite the other.

We find in this card a desire to control the impassioned love of the High Priestess and then generate it into a COMMON GOOD. This moral and common denominator is understood as MATERNAL LOVE. The Empress cares for the miraculous child (life) she has been allowed to heal and nourish into physical rebirth. The mother, child and their mutual bond (for example, safety, warmth, affection etc.) represent the completion of The Empress's three-fold nature.

Reviewing this trinity of spiritual families, we find associations with the three fates of ancient Greece: Clotho, Lachesis and Atropos, as well as the Hindu trinity: Brahma, Vishnu and Shiva. In Egypt we find: Osiris, Isis and Horus, and of course, in western Christianity, there is the trinity of Father, Son and Holy Spirit. All of these trinities form a single bond and become ONE unshakable force. In the scientific sense, we may compare this three-fold unification with our own worldly perception of past, present and future. In other words, the Empress creates a present which absorbs ALL of the past, to prepare for the future (which is NOW.) For this act of genius, she is forever connected with the planet Saturn, as well as its cohorts: time and music, which connect physical reality and experiential man in the infinite realm of conscious logic.

In fact, since the Empress exists in perfect harmony with all the planetary spheres, she is linked with the twelve signs of the zodiac, which not surprisingly, appear as solar rays emanating from her matriarchal crown. Hence, she is a master of light, especially the color emerald green, which is representative of infinite (and therefore, cyclical) life. Moreover, she is linked with the swan and the scorpion, both creatures noted for their acceptance of the variables of death. In this, she finds herself in continuous transcendence and transformation of life. This is her WORK and her reason for being. Only SHE can bridge the chasm (created in the master plan by the High Priestess,) by embracing HER simple and straight forward maternal love. Naturally, her elements consist of earth (the physical world of reality,) and water (the emotional world of spirit,) creating soil which nourishes the SEED OF LIFE. The world is hers to nourish and guide, absolutely...

Her three-fold strength, visualized in the triangle (pyramids, geodesic domes, etc.,) underpin her glorious balance of universal mind, body and spirit. Like Atlas, she supports the natural world of being in all its harsh complexity. She is a door and passage into perceptive awareness, providing a level, fertile ground for sober and entirely subtle, reasoning. She has embraced the world in its astounding and limitless measure, culminating the infinite love of the High Priestess herself, whom she cherishes and humbly follows in the eternal dance of the spiritual path.

Therefore, in our dreams, the maternal Empress figure demonstrates an acceptance of a very difficult situation, including pregnancy, or conversely, the passing of a loved one. The capability of collecting facts and reasoning a valid position is also suggested in the naturalistic world of the Empress. She, who sits calmly in the seat of life, in her long flowing robe of patience, tolerance and above all, absolute mercy...

THE EMPEROR (4) (Tarot Major Arcana) A suitable mate for the material grounding of the spiritual world embodied in the Empress is the Emperor, who provides order, stability and purpose in life. Here we find the beginning of law and self-discipline. The Emperor exists in the logic of mind, laying down its foundation upon the randomness of physical reality. As the Empress grounds the spiritual world, so the Emperor grounds the physical world. He accomplishes this by utilizing his old, wise and virtuous mind. In this sense, he is the FIRST PHYSICAL COMPLETION of the Fool's quest for worldly experience. HIS knowledge is not instinctual, but rather learned over a life-time. Therefore, he moves BEYOND HIS OWN LOGIC, into that of his mate, the Empress. He has learned from her in the course of time both SPIRITUAL ACCEPTANCE and MORTAL HUMILTY.

The Hebrew letter for this figure is Tzaddi, which means to lie in wait. The wisdom of age comes slowly, and age itself prepares us to accept its gradual unfolding. Hence, we learn to 'lie in wait.' The stages of good and evil which define a life are indicated in this card only when their lessons have sunk into our world view and behavior. Only then, have they become wisdom.

Rulership over the spiritual and material world can only be described as judgmental. Since only God may judge, the Emperor merely interprets the will of God through the vehicle of his experiential knowledge. In this, we witness the beginning of social structuring. The Emperor must create limitations of behavior, in the form of social rules, to provide the most beneficial good possible for all of his subjects. These limitations or 'cultural norms' become law and should be obeyed by all. In as much, to disobey the law of the Emperor, is to defy both God and Man, by refusing to accept the responsibilities of social human life. Herein, we see why the mineral associated with the Emperor is the Crystal. Intact, the crystal is rare, precious and reflects equal light in all directions. However, when the crystal is broken, shards of glass fragment reality and deceive perception. We are left in an unbalanced kingdom with little direction and even less spiritual value. In order to retain our sense of worth, we need to establish both SELF and SOCIETY: Individuality and Equality. As such, the Emporer illustrates the fine distinction of self-awareness, in the free society we willingly create as individuals.

The color bonded with the Emperor is violet which symbolizes royal splendor. The animal linked with this same imperial format is the peacock. To this end, we understand why the element associated with this figure is Air. All encompassing, life-giving AIR, demonstrates the free range and valor of the card proper. The Emperor gazes his noble face and steadfast principles into the multiple angles of the four cornered world. Akin to the square, (and number 4,) the figure is fair and just and acknowledges the rightful place of the four elements and four cardinal points of the world. He has set the macrocosm into order and within it, justified all human productivity and subsequent interaction. In short, he is recreating the catalyst of the Magician in the physical plain of mankind's equal and balanced discernment of reality.

In the dream scenario, the Emperor figure demonstrates a need for brave decisions in life. He symbolizes the world of LOGIC and a WISE, OLD UNDERSTANDING of that logic. He states 'Our emotions have led us where we are; but NOW, we need to organize a plan to lead us forward to where we actually need to be.' In this sense, the necessity of self-discipline in life, is squarely laid out before us in the assurance of the Emperor. We exist in a world of free choices, when we choose with reasonable wisdom, we crystalize who we are and where we want to be. The Emperor welcomes ALL into the clearest light of logic, fairness and moral conduct.

THE HIEROPHANT (5) (Tarot Major Arcana) In many ways, the Hierophant is the extension and in fact the completion, of the Emperor. This is because the creation of physical laws which pertain to FAITH and SPIRITUAL LIFE in general, fulfill the purpose of the Hierophant. In this, the figure logically (and with personal and social authority,) returns us into the purity of the Fool's world of absolute faith. We have completed the four corners of the physical world around us. Now we are able to return to a fifth point within the center of the square. This point represents our spiritual center, or SOUL. In this, we note the symbolism of the pentagram (and the number five in particular,) as pertaining to Mankind. Man is balanced life, infused in spirit. (Thus, $4+1=5$.)

The journey into high initiation, or the path of God, is indeed difficult and at times, self denying. We must surrender the material world in order to claim the spirit within that world. In this sense, the Hebrew letter for the Hierophant is Vau, which means 'nail'. We must nail (or stop) our forward progress on the physical plain in order to see, feel and know God: who is omnipresent and without direction. The purity of martyrdom is implied in the 'nail' translation, as many prophets, (and more exclusively, the Christian God, Jesus Christ,) were ALL crucified with nails upon an upright and extremely symbolic, cross. In as much, we all have a cross to bare with humility and a higher power to answer to; higher than either the Emperor, or the Hierophant. This is the honesty within oneself, the Soul which must face God.

The sign which vibrates within this figure is Taurus and appropriately, the animal linked with the card is the bull. We find in this connection, a stubbornness of faith and will, a vision of charging ivory horns (purity) which defy the obstacles of a physical world and penetrate instead, the very heart and mind of a soulful humanity. We will later see this image of the bull as the Minotaur which blocks the exit (or goal) of the labyrinth-like Spiritual Path. In this final confrontation: WE WILL FACE THE TRUTH of our own worldly behavior. WILL WE be worthy to pass beyond?

The element associated with the Hierophant is Earth. In this, we see a figure in the physical realm, preparing to transcend it via spiritual and moral faith. This wisdom, reached by a humble acceptance of love and mercy, dictates the surrender of Self in the next ascending step in the path of enlightenment. In fact, the number five is often depicted in occult texts as the foundation of light. Hence, in the Astral world, we become 'Beings of Light'. Furthermore, the color orange/red of the Hierophant is synonymous with the radiance and illumination of the heart.

In this we find the passage, 'See with the heart and not thine eyes.'

In music, the fifth tone of the octave produces the initial stage of the next cycle. Musicians worldwide, learn to recognize (early in their instruction) the infamous Circle of Fifths. Concluding the conceptualization of 5 as a Spiritual Form, we examine the human hand whose five digits (including an opposable thumb,) virtually separate him, from ALL other species of life.

However, we cannot confuse the position of the Hierophant, with the humility of His purpose. In this sense, we must constantly challenge the veracity of organized religion, which may (in some cases) fall prey to the surrounding physical world. In the past, all too many kingdoms had allowed churches absolute POWER and SOCIAL CONTROL, which led to horrific results. Legitimately, this was NEVER GOD'S PLAN. Observing this statement, we look to the Hierophant as spiritual guide and not vainglorious ruler of the pulpit. The temptation on this level of the Royal Path of the Tarot is perilous indeed. The message may indeed warn against the lust of power and greed: in the name of God (no less!)

In the dream sense therefore, we come in contact with a figure who takes the whole of man and the physical world and attempts to lead it forward (a rather dangerous task) into the enlightenment of God and spiritual faith. Hence we must ask ourselves, are we strong enough in our heart and in our mind (decisions) to follow this difficult path of love, charity and at times, relentless self sacrifice? From another perspective, the dream may be asking us if are we able to transcend the sometimes contradictory beliefs of organized society and personal faith? In short, can we remain honest within ourselves even in the sphere of a social and sometimes wholly seductive world of sensations? The unwavering Hierophant re-establishes the deepest faith of the Fool. When the Soul faces God, we cannot fail.

THE LOVERS (6) (Tarot Major Arcana) In the journey of the Tarot, the initiate must come to terms with his or her own sexuality and the responsibility of intimate union with a partner who may represent a mate and the eventual source of family. Inherent in this understanding, we witness the initial innocence and shame experienced in first attraction and the choices which inevitably develop around it. Furthermore, as the relationship grows, we find the struggle and jubilation of the mature loving commitment, replete with physical desire and emotional responsibility. In the extent that these principles are balanced, we find a merging of two individuals into one higher realm. This provides the impetus for birth and the subsequent continuity of life. However, when any one AGREEMENT of mind, emotion, or spirit is not REACHED in the relationship of two people, hardships, deviations and misunderstandings slowly replace the true sanctity of the domain of the Lovers.

The Hebrew letter for this figure is Zayin, which means sword. The prominent symbolism of this association refers to the double-edged nature of the sword itself. The Lovers, akin to a medieval saber, become one unit with two separate (and unique) sides which cut in two different directions. In this, we find a reference to the painful aspects of unrequited devotion, or desire. Likewise, the sharp blade of love can inspire, and even motivate!

In a sense, the figure itself depicts both physical and spiritual opposition. The division of male and female is most prominent in this plain of experience. In childhood (and old age,) the CARNAL feminine and masculine aspects of our being are less harsh and play a smaller role in our direct interrelationships. The Lovers however, are attracted by their split and seek to explore the elaborate connection of their intense differences. On the spiritual side of this investigation, male aspects (including logic and determination) come into contact with feminine principles (such as deep emotion and maternal sensitivity.) Joining these aspects into a social union can indeed be hazardous, and has been a vocal point of deliberation, at least since organized society began.

In this we see the struggle or double-edged sword inherent in the Lovers. Love may become a shameful battle ground when power and misdirected passion directly interferes with the natural alliance of the couple's masculine and feminine principles. In this circumstance, we may find a constant wrestling of personal ideology, which may turn into bitter animosity and outright hatred if not properly diffused and given ample opportunity to heal. In another very serious sense, we may find within the context of an unbalanced union, situations where lust or material gain utterly dominate altruistic caring and emotional commitment. In the complexity of these relationships which 'drop' out of kilter, we find painful pitfalls which can run the gamut from psychological abuse, to battering, and yes, even murder.

The other side of the double-edged sword demonstrates the love which most people prefer to think about. The affiliation of man and woman represents the chosen joining of spirit and the consequent initiation of family. As such, the cycle of life, death and rebirth vibrate in complete harmony in the earthly sphere of this stage of human enlightenment. We witness the mental, spiritual and physical fulfillment of two separate individuals who celebrate in their wedding of Yin and Yang. This merge in The Lovers (6) Arcana represents our Emotional Force on the Earthly Plane.

The astrological influence of The Lovers is Gemini, the twins. The secret of the twins lies in their strength together. Apart they lose their cyclical cohesion, little is left but utter imbalances, demonstrated in evils such as distrust and deceit. This is why The Devil card (15) (1+5=6) displays a smaller version of the lovers chained below the devil himself, prisoners of his lustful and chaotic revelry. Due to the nature of the double-edged sword which allows an equal opportunity to elevate to spiritual oneness, (or drop into the pit of physical and psychological loathing,) the element we find associated with The Lovers is Air. We envision the sword as it slices through Air, on its way toward self sacrifice and purification, or doubling back, cutting through human sanctity and destroying (even the strongest of) hearts. In the modern jargon, we may utilize in the place of Air, the conceptualization of Time and Space (respectively,) to further confuse the opposing connection. Time, is the abstract notion of mind, order and reason; in other words, MALE. Space, on the other hand, is physical, infinite and ever changing; in other words, FEMALE. Neither Time nor Space can be perceived without the other, and Einstein made it clear that space and time are in fact continuous, via the perception of measurement and our relation to that measurement. We call this the 'Space/Time Continuum'. We clearly see the riddle of The Lovers, opposites who are in fact inseparable. Split like the world itself, they must come together and become whole.

In the dream sense, all of these tenets need to be explored to unravel the complexity which is love and relationships. The dreamer needs to thoroughly reflect on the card itself and determine which aspects of the figure foremost stand out. On a superficial level, the cards appearance in the dream may reveal the coming of a significant other to share in the revelation of ones individual contentment of being. Then again, perhaps love appears to unravel life, soley, to begin the next cycle of spiritual learning...

THE CHARIOT (7) (Tarot Major Arcana) The joining, and more importantly, disciplinary control, of spirit and matter, brings great potency to the initiate on this paticular path of the Tarot. Accordingly, the individual on this path seizes the reins of life and immediately and confidently moves forward in the conquest of life's fulfillment. In this, we visualize how The Chariot figure represents perseverance, determination and direction in particular. Herein, we have completed the growth of our personal and social self. In other words, we now utilize the power we have been given, striving to bring this ability into action, a mortal composite of The Magician, who once brought the spark into the potential world of The Fool.

We must, however, avoid the temptation to lose ourself in the capacity of our labors. The loss of our spiritual center is at risk in the building edifice of our material ego. We witness this in the Arcana displayed in The Tower of Destruction (16, 1+6=7). The tower is hit by lightning signifying that man has built himself, (and more significantly the belief in himself,) too high and must now suffer the consequences of a displeased God. We witness a crowned king and ordinary man both falling from the destroyed tower. This demonstrates the potential corruption of all men (regardless of social standing and relative authority.) The lesson to be learned therefore in The Chariot figure is a PROPER USE OF POWER. The Charioteer harnesses a white and black sphinx and wears a vestige insignia of a triangle within a square. The images represent MENTAL FORCE on the Earthly Plane; initially seen in the sphinx/steeds, which are held together and work in unison rather than veering apart into chaos. Similarly, the triangle, synonymous with spirit and maternal acceptance, is firmly centered within the square, synonymous with an ordered physical universe. In short, we see the coupled force of Emotion and Intellect.

The Hebrew letter associated with The Chariot is Cheth which means fence. On first analysis, we may believe the visual conceptualization of 'bridge' may have been a wiser choice of symbolism in this arcana due to the presupposition of the charioteer as bridging opposite states of being. However, this is not entirely, (if in fact at all,) the case. The Charioteer harnesses his steeds so that they cannot veer away from one another AS WELL AS not crashing into each other. As such, he does not merge, or 'bridge', opposing states of being, but rather allocates their separation and dictates the unity of their meeting. In other words, he builds a fence between their respective plains of reality. In placing this sound FENCE between spirit and matter, he is able to move swiftly and efficiently between the two, managing both in the process. His direction on the Royal Path is insured by this MENTAL AXIS which he firmly plants into the Fool's world.

The astrological sign associated with The Chariot is Cancer, the crab. In this symbolism we witness the durable (masculine) shell which is also brilliant in color, (wholly suggestive of femininity.) Moreover, we find an amphibious creature who is equally at home in the water (emotion), or dug deep within the dry land (logic.) In both cases a fluent and well controlled (not to mention purposeful,) balance of elemental reality is exhibited. Moreover, the patience of the crab whispers another secret of this figure. The initiate on this path must be SERENE in order to build a proper fence, and in so doing, plants his posts upright and firm into the central nucleus of his goal.

The element linked with this arcana is Water. This is primarily because water as a substance exists in all three states of matter: solid (ice,) liquid (water,) and gas (steam.) Moreover, water is able to easily pass from one state to another via environmental conditions, (hot or cold,) which connects it to the other three elements: Fire, Air, and of course, Earth. Furthermore, while water may easily transfer through each of these states of matter, it remains separate and unique in each relative state. In this, we find another reference to Cheth, the fence, which in its boundaries becomes the prime character of The Chariot Arcana.

Placing all these tenets together, we see in the context of a dream, how the card represents a desired goal, (or achievement,) which may be imminent in our experience. The card tells us to hold strong in our determination and jurisprudence of a worthy purpose. Above all, the card is indicating that we should never lose our sense of Self by maintaining an equal balance of Logical Reason and Emotional Compassion in our personal strategies toward attaining our highest goals. Consequently, the card straight out tells us, our success is impending upon our steadfast and just integrity. In as much, we are the Charioteer and our INTENTIONS ARE PARAMOUNT in the highest fulfillment of our highest ASPIRATIONS!

STRENGTH (8) (Tarot Major Arcana) The Strength Arcana brings the initiate yet further down the path of Self. It is at this point that the individual learns inner calm and quiet. This picturesque path represents the Fool's attainment of SPIRITUAL FORCE on the Earthly Plane. The tranquil female figure which serenely tames the lion on the Arcana depicts Celestial SPIRIT gathering up Earthly MATTER into its folds. As such, this path is the first lesson in the release of our manifest Ego. Strength (8) demonstrates a deep faith in the perfection of divine order which prevails over our own earthbound ambitions and passionate crusades.

The figure eight, which sits halo-like atop the peaceful young girl in The Strength card, depicts the infinity of creation and reality itself. It is to this end that finite physical endeavors, while being noble, (represented as the courageous and powerful lion,) are ultimately limited. In this sense, the physical world must humble itself before the successive planes of Absolute Existence. Human perception merely reflects the omnipotence of Celestial Creation and its various levels of Being. The next plane, (the Ethereal Level,) provides the undeniable undercurrent of everything perceived in the material world. Higher levels increasingly know Absolute Reality in clearer revelations. The Royal Path thus, brings ever more focused perceptions of Existence, closer to hand. As we have seen, this wisdom is not developed in a series of hard calculations, but rather, felt and understood, in a comprehension void of all earthly presumptions. Hence, a man may only become Infinite, through his own release of Self.

The Hebrew letter for The Strength Arcana is Teth which means snake. The biblical association of the snake in the tree of knowledge is a rather elaborate labyrinth of symbolism. It involves Man disobeying God in order to gain material knowledge. However, a fascinating two-fold meaning of this archetypal image involves a return path as well, a return to grace. It is necessary for the tree and the snake to be close to God, for they exist as prime archetypes in the garden of eden. Therefore, we find their presence inevitable in the Return to His celestial plain. Herein, we find the symbolism of Teth. The tree, which is silent and therefore wise (wisdom, as well as knowledge,) carries the serpent which depicts both knowledge and Self awareness. In the royal path of the Tarot, the initiate learns to traverse both paths of emotional and intellectual force in the forms of The Lovers and The Chariot, respectively. The Fool overcomes the downfall of the serpent's desire for lust and blind ambition in man, replaced instead by the love and honest perseverance found in the same Arcanas of The Lovers (6) and The Chariot (7). Carrying this numerology one step further, we see how 6+7=13 vibrates with The Death (13) card. Naturally, having overcome these first stages of the material plane, we begin to feel confident in the transfiguration of death, the ability to transcend our physical and mortal conquests in favor of a spiritual redemption, or absolute faith. In this well ordained transition, we are allowed to finally approach the Tree of knowledge once more. We have RETURNED to the Garden of Eden. However, in this cycle we are equipped with the certain realization which involves the unconditional surrender of our knowledge to the higher, celestial wisdom of spiritual faith. Accordingly, we are able to return to God and the source of reality, intact once more. We have withstood the test of our own empowerment upon the earthly plain of reality and its elaborate temptations. Conclusively, we are allowed to focus and master the purpose of our existence once more, simply by justifying the original purpose of our being.

In the dream sense, we approach a dramatic cessation of our physical force in this figure. Accordingly, the unconscious reminds us to reflect on the higher purpose behind our passionate and otherwise ambitious drives. Calm meditation upon the overall social merit of our personal achievements may transcend the initial vainglorious gratification of our individual megalomania. Stated yet another way, if we believe our physical accomplishments separate us from ordinary men and deem us God-like; we certainly will be in for a rude awakening when we inevitably fail in the physical imperfection of our own mortal nature.

On the contrary, if we gain wisdom from our serenity, we will comprehend humility and the frailness of our being. Doing so, we will find the real strength in silent stillness and work in earnest toward the purity and craftsmanship of the Celestial Plan. A plan known to our very own Plato, as the Ideal Form of all creation. In this, we realize the master design, blueprint and purpose is Silent and Unseen. Yet, it provides all life forms with a balance of equality and innate perfection which simply could not flourish in the isolated vacuum of individual physical separateness and otherwise foolish, material selfishness...

THE HERMIT (9) (Tarot major Arcana) The Hermit arcana continues the journey away from the Earthly Level which is begun in the path of The Lovers arcana. The deepest form of meditation depicted in this card reflects the complete removal of our physical self in place of a humble ETHEREAL awareness and the selfless prostrations involved in the ego-defying entrance into this higher plane: The Ethereal Plane, third plane of the Tarot. In as much, The Hermit, as man, is bent before his God and relies only upon his staff for support and his antique lantern for real and purposeful vision. The upright staff is symbolic of righteous faith and the will necessary to link the straight and narrow line between heaven and earth. The staff remains continuous and direct, even when the mortal body bends and falters. Further into the representation of this figure, we find the Hermit's lantern which reveals the spiritual light of truth. This ethereal light (held high by the Hermit) shines a brilliant path through the darkest corridors of human ignorance. Unfortunately, the lantern also throws shadows upon our remaining worldly and physical reality. These shadowy delusions must be expelled by The Hermit in his curved, yet unswerving, destiny into the purity of truth.

Accordingly, the Hebrew letter for The Hermit is Yod, which loosely translates to foundation and 'firm' truth. In this, we find the fulfilling aspect of this figure in the royal path of the Tarot labyrinth. Numerologically speaking, the very last numeral, that being number nine, is fundamentally linked to this arcana and path. It represents the stability and finality of the three threes, or three triangles. After the number nine, we only find combinations of the previous numbers. Therefore we see how nine is the highest single number in material existence. In the symbolic sense, this is the subsequent realization of the necessity of final, or last, Death in order to return, or emerge, into the soul of God and Eternal being. In other examples of this numerals significance, we find the Eleusinian Mysteries which involved nine spheres, through which the consciousness of the initiate needed to pass, prior to becoming born again. Similarly, we pass through nine months (moons) of gestation in the womb of our mother before we are born into the physical world. Moreover, in the strict mathematical sense, we see how the numeral 9, when multiplied by any number, becomes 9 once again. Some examples: $9 \times 3 = (27)$ in turn $(2+7)=9$; $9 \times 6=(54)$ in turn $(5+4)=9$; $9 \times 38=(342)$ in turn $(3+4+2)=9$; etc. Furthermore, any number when added with the numeral 9, returns to ITSELF once again. Some examples: $9+(4)=(13)$ in turn $(1+3=4)$; $9+(138)=(147)$ in turn $(1+3+8=12)$ and $(1+4+7=12)$; $9+(6)=(15)$ in turn $(1+5=6)$; etc. In this mathematical exposure, we find the fixed and conclusive reality which is the number 9, a definitive and mystical number indeed!

Accordingly, the transfiguration of The Hermit (9) Arcana overcomes both our fear of death and the reality of death itself, in the intrinsic sense. This empowerment over mortal trepidation prepares the initiate for the necessity of isolation from the outside world. As such, the journey into the Tarot at this point becomes one of total solitude, the symbiotic return to the purity of new born innocence. In this pristine state of native consciousness, (unclouded by personal and social preconceptions,) we are able to fully meditate on the oneness, completeness and truth of being, AND, our inexorable role within THAT divine drama. Furthermore, we see in this figure the predisposition toward a personal relationship with God. This is quite removed from the normal form of enlightenment found in organized religions, (which we comprehend through rituals and accepted ethical standards.) The ancient theological argument examining the whereabouts of the true house of God, whether in the human heart, or human place of worship (church, temple; etc,) is approached in this high spiritual arcana. The Hermit recognizes God as absolute within and without. As such, the residence of God has no physical location, instead, GOD becomes the invisible, underlying principle which animates the whole of the physical world. In Plato's point of view, this unseen life source is known as the Ideal Form. Curious, yet logically sound, this idea of God as the perfect underlying principle of life dates back to the earliest aboriginal cultures known to civilization. It was understood, then as now, this luminous infrastructure of God, cannot be perceived by our wholly material and earth-bound five senses. The Spirit world can only be comprehended in our purest and most inviolable Visionary Experiences.

Reaffirming this statement, the astrological sign which vibrates with The Hermit is naturally Virgo, the virgin. Hence, only in our purest state of acceptance can we comprehend the absolute necessity of matter's dissolution, or death. Only in the innocence of our birth, can we enter deaths finality and transcend its plain into the Ideal Form of God's foundation. Furthermore, the element associated with this figure is Earth. In this, we find a very crucial point about this particular path in the Tarot. The Hermit (9) illustrates the earthly plain of existence which the initiate must transcend in order to begin his consummate and unequivocal transformation into the ETHEREAL world. This rite of passage is common in the primitive world and reflected in young warriors sent out into the natural world to brave the elements and test their ultimate faith. In these ornate, (and at times bloody,) survivalist functions, or Vision Quests, the young warrior witnesses the extreme heaven and hell of physical existence which changes his fragile character forever. The young warrior enters the Ethereal Plane as he gradually moves beyond his own physical needs and desires. In fact, in traversing this hypnotic state of physical exertion the initiate embodies the entire cycle from the Material to the Ethereal world beyond. In this meditation he learns to comprehend visions beyond his own sight, walking effortlessly and puposefully within his own dream-like state of a new found higher consciousness. (In this we find a precursor to the next full cycle of the Tarot path, beginning appropriately with The Wheel of Fortune. In this path we will approach the need for acceptance of a soul centered within the material world, a silent vortex, or hub, which rotates the great up and down wheel of our earthly existential experiences.)

Taking all this into account, what we experience in the dream appearance of The Hermit concerns our ability to sink into the deepest part of ourselves. In so doing, we finally may be able to leave our material concerns behind. Why do we feel the need to do this? Do we find ourselves way too involved with the every day trappings of our physical world, or, are we losing sight of who we really are as individuals? The arcana demonstrates our need to stand back and become isolated and self-sufficient once more; secluded enough in fact, to lose our artificial sense of personal grandeur and emerge into ever-higher states of being. May we finally move beyond the reality expressed in an infinity of material charms and earth-bound diversions? Alas, will the old, curved Hermit (9) deliver us from ourselves?

THE WHEEL OF FORTUNE (10) (Tarot Major Arcana) The next cycle of the major arcana begins with The Wheel of Fortune. We visualize in this arcana, a wheel of physical, mental and emotional ups and downs centered by a spiritual axis which is neutral concerning the position of the wheel itself. The neutrality of the Wheel of Fortune's spiritual axis demonstrates how today's hardships will be replaced by tomorrow's triumphs (and vice-versa.) There can (and will) be no control over this random selection. Appropriately, we must endure the present and remain as spiritually centered and faithful of life's innate order, as we possibly can.

Let us delve into the symbolism of the axis. This concept of the axis, the unifying principle of all matter, holds true in living biology, planets and entire universes. We observe in material reality a helical rotation which creates a circuit from negative to positive and back to negative once more. This binary loop allows for elaborate patterns of life which interweave in their relative codependence. From the human brain, to radios, satellites, star clusters and movable joints; to tires, arch-ceilings, audio equipment and every day alarm clocks, we depend on the end result of the unifying principle of the AXIS. In as much, we witness in this axis, or vortex, the behind-the-scenes foundation of an infinite reality.

The clear symbolism of the Tarot Axis relates to the underlying divinity centered within all earthly reality: high, low, good, and bad. This is what is meant by the antique phrase 'God works in mysterious ways'. We speak of a God who exists behind all worldly realities, regardless of their relative difficulty. In this sense, the strength of faith is tested in the harshest of times, not in joyous days when worship and thankfulness come easy. The biblical story of Job encapsulates this spiritual lesson. It is also paraphrased by Jesus Christ in the New Testament: wherein is the quote, 'What gaineth a man who inherits the world, but loseth his soul?' Job, in the Old Testament, loses his entire world, both his family and possessions, but nevertheless, maintains his complete faith in God in direct resistance to Satan. He has overcome the dark side of the outer wheel of material existence.

The pointed symbolism in these narratives elucidate the necessity of both good and bad fortune. The path of the initiate in the Tarot maze is fortified explicitly with obstacles which need to be overcome before transfigurations may occur. Hence, the movement of the wheel is synonymous with life and the continuous nature of an enigmatic future. Accordingly, transgressing and transcending each successive stopping point of The Wheel of Fortune as they occur, brings the initiate that much closer to its spiritual center, the axis mundi of all creation.

This rather abstract conceptualization of the physical world spinning indeterminately around an unchanging and central spirit, may be difficult to assimilate in every day life. However, the key to this elaborate figure's symbolism absolutely relies on the initiates understanding of the wheel's relation to himself. Hence, where the initiate finds anger, jealousy and hatred in his own heart, he must remain strong in his faith that God continues manifest beyond the immediate reality of all physical weakness. Likewise, where the initiate finds joy, pleasure and contentment, God is here too, as always, the unmistakable catalyst beyond. As such, the student gains the wisdom that all actions, all behavior and all movement, each step and each breath, animate the spiritual center within us all. In as much, each gesture we make and every word and deed we express, becomes a prayer to the infinite source of creation. In addition, we perceive this thinly disguised divinity in the human beings who share the earthly plain with us. Accordingly, we gain the realization that we are blessed in their presence, regardless of their mortal standing and relative behavior. In our humanity, we may feel offended and antagonized, and conversely, flattered and intoxicated, by interactions with our fellow men and women. The Wheel of Fortune reminds us to weather ALL social storms, good or bad and look far within the ornate shell of mankind in order to find the heart-beat of soul which resides there. Our soul effortlessly ignores the emotional gradations of color which displays the material world in its brightest and darkest hues. In other words, when we allow for God's (Ain Soph Aur) ongoing creation in the acceptance of our own heart, we begin to move closer to that God which permeates being. In this understanding, we begin to feel the presence of our own ETHEREAL SPIRIT, as we walk, talk, eat and sleep with the infinite reality of a divinity which transcends each moment of our entire life.

The Hebrew letter for this figure is Kaph, which means palm of the hand. Palmistry, once called Chiromancy, is the oldest form of divination and long predates written history. In ancient Persia, the palm was believed to hold an individuals relation to the stars, planets and other mystical spheres. The future was preordained in the intricate lines, curves and shape of the hand itself. In Asia, Zen masters practiced the shaping and proper aligning of the contours of the initiate's hand to gain inner wisdom. In another example, the ancient Chinese healing art of acupuncture recognized the palms relation to ALL internal organs. In this, we witness the ancient (and ongoing) belief of individuality and fate, laid bare in the palm of our hands.

How we choose to use these hands in order to fulfill our respective destiny reflects our awareness of self. Accordingly, we see how our physical manipulations, (the Latin 'mano' meaning hand,) shapes our continuous opportunity to return to spirit and enlightenment. Furthermore, only with a firm grasp of reality, can we perceive the course of our ongoing existence and internalize its progressive lessons. Should we deviate from our preordained (innate) wisdom and lose our 'hold' upon the world around us, we may radically effect our individual destiny. The phrases, 'He is not himself', or 'She isn't her usual self.' are based upon this confusion of purpose. Free will (unfortunately) may allow a dislocated journey away from ones natural path of beneficial existence. In this wayward semblance of potential reality, the initiate may lose the balance of his or her acquired experiences and become drawn toward some form of excessive behavior. This unbalanced scenario may involve sickness, drug abuse, mental neurosis and a host of other mutilations of self. Painfully, the firm grip of a steady, well-adapted individual, becomes the shaky, numb and ravaged hand of an individual in dire need of help. Thankfully, this hand may be clasped by an outside influence (or concerned force) and returned to its former passage. If the initiate transcends free will and regains inner realization he or she may be able to rationalize him or herself once more. As such, the student allows himself another chance to vibrate in perfect balance and harmony with his own natural destiny. He has returned to the soul-centered world.

We observe in this formulation, how The Wheel of Fortune operates in its full complexity within the reasonable compass of each human being. Additionally, we have seen how we are rewarded for this insight of our unique destiny in the universal scheme of things. We are blessed with a perception of the world and a place within its confines. The Wheel of Fortune elaborates upon this primary knowledge, a knowlede absolutely necessary before the initiate can transcend the next stages of spiritual wisdom.

Within this figure, we find the Sphinx depicted, a figure who represents the ambiguous riddle of universal existence. The Wheel of Fortune also reveals the paradoxical nature of the ultimate question of existence which can have no direct and material answer. The Sphinx represents the last stop in the cyclical and winding labyrinth of all material experiences and their gained spiritual insights. Hence, the fierce looking Sphinx dramatizes the lesson of The Wheel of Fortune (10) itself. Symbolically, the Wheel and the Sphinx are one in the same. They are the gained experiences of all worldly existence. This is why the Sphinx promises death to the seeker who answers its final and paramount riddle INCORRECTLY. Put simply, to live unaware of the Soul within Matter, is to have no connection with the divine creation at all, and that is a self-destructive tragedy, beyond compare. In as much, the Sphinx is a powerful metaphor for ALL soulful realization, beyond our own perishing mortality.

The element which vibrates with The Wheel of Fortune turns out to be Air. The character of air is light, omnipresent and clear as mind and reason itself. As we have seen, the capacity to understand the world and its complex foundation is at the heart of this all-encompassing arcana. The point of this Tarot path is the end of The Fool's world, fully discovered and then transcended upon a higher plane of experience. The initiate has moved beyond the physical plane.

It is no coincidence that the Wheel of Fortune appears where it does in the path of the major arcana. The ancient Greeks and Hebrews both believed in the absolute divinity of the numeral 10, which explicitly vibrates in this representational figure. The Tree of Life in the Cabalistic faith, reveal the ten emanations of the Ain Soph Aur (God). In addition, the beginning of man's journey into God

Consciousness is found in the infinite, cyclical conformity of the metric constant which is the numeral 10. Finally, the ancient Greek philosopher Pythagoras, who believed in the mystical divinity of numbers, instructed his pupils about the significance of the first four numbers, which when added together in succession, could only form the perfection of being; that is, the number 10. $1+2+3+4=10$. The first four numbers represent the four elements and the four corners of ordered reality. In this, the numeral 10 becomes the underlying principle of the physical world, the axis and eternal foundation of being. In other words, the Soul within Being.

All in all, The Wheel of Fortune illustrates ALL of reality, both inside and out, seen and unseen, beyond any form of language and all of our five senses. In this path the initiate rings in tune with The Magician and his own inner magic, aware of the flash and spark of life becoming. It is at this point that the wholly ordered Magician (1) and the chaotic Fool (0) join forces and become one, the alpha and the omega. This is the enlightenment of darkness and wisdom of the unknowable. Upon the wheel itself is the word Taro, or Rota, which is the revelation of Heaven, Earth and Man; the unchanging foundation within the ever-changing eternal creation.

When this card appears in our dream, we must be prepared to look beyond the physical reality which we perceive before us. We need to gain an awareness that behind our good and bad experiences is a constant source of divinity and personal destiny which wholly transcends our present emotions and their immediate consequences. Furthermore, we are reminded that spiritual truth is reflected and manifest not only in our deepest, isolated meditations, but also in our outside, every day world. Justifiably, we must act in accordance with our ever-soulful perception of the visible world and its invisible underpinning.

JUSTICE (11) (Tarot Major Arcana) As stated in The Wheel of Fortune delineation, life out of kilter, without balance and purpose, is detrimental to the initiate on the path of spiritual truth. In the Justice figure of the Tarot, we learn to balance our paradoxical physical spectrum. In as much, we must determine a suitable equilibrium for our diverse human natures. These include: individuality and socialization, concern with the spiritual world as well as the secular world, anger and forgiveness, love and lust, greed and martyrdom and finally, perseverance and obsession. Naturally, we find an implicit connection within these opposite states of being. Formally, they exist as two sides of the same coin, separated only by the decision making process of free will. In other words, the initiate is given the opportunity to make of, and take from, the experience, whatever he or she chooses. However, there is a definitive and unavoidable balance in nature, explored in The Wheel of Fortune, which must be recognized. Hence, if the initiate chooses obsessive, unbalanced pursuits, The Justice (11) card explains why he or she must be prepared to pay the price of the harsh and extreme return to natural equilibrium. This is why the wise king pictured on the Justice card holds a sharp and threatening sword aloft, to remind The Fool, (or initiate,) of the inherent danger found in the foolish enactments of unstable and unfair deeds.

In the simultaneous awareness of diversely opposed behavioral attitudes, (otherwise known as well-rounded wisdom,) we find a dynamic cancelling out (at least on the conceptual level) of extreme and one-sided prejudices. Therefore, even when we find ourselves momentarily lost in the excesses of an emotional outpouring, we still can maintain the ability to find the flip side, or alternative point of view. In this reasoning, (given time and patience) we may justify a return into healthy emotional equilibrium. For example, if a man decides to work two jobs in order to provide a healthy income for his family, first he must consider the effect of his absence in the dynamic of a family's social unity. In order to accomplish this, he must examine in great detail the pros and cons of time spent within his family. In this, he may eventually come to realize that what is lost in the togetherness of family, cannot possibly be compensated financially. This is merely an example and may not hold true in real circumstances. The point is found in the wisdom of examining fully the opposite alternative of our contemplated decision. In this observation of both realities, an internal compromise may be reached which satisfies both fronts. In the prior example, the man may (wisely) decide to work several hours more each week to provide extra income, yet still remain in the union of a loving family.

The scales therefore, are a mental construct of the Ethereal Plane and operate prior to the visible choices made in life. In this sense, we understand why the element which vibrates in this particular path is Air. Air is synonymous with mind and reason. Justice is the concrete materialization of reason in its highest human sense. In fact, in the legal terminology, being of 'sound mind', refers to ones ability to justify ones actions and behave in a just and reasonable manner in society. In other words, the mind is itself, balance. In this logic, we fully understand the advice to stop and think, before acting. We are infusing spiritual reason into our emotional instincts, and consequently widening the viewpoint of our overall situational perceptions. Accordingly, we begin to see the entire projection of the potential of our behavior and can deliberate upon the consequences of our decisions.

Herein, we discern the connection of age, wisdom and justice. The data base of experience gained in ones life assists in the process of visualizing possible outcomes. Therefore, an older individual enjoys a greater understanding of reality's multiple faces. The elders mental framework is a veritable storehouse of memories taken directly from the context of life. In this, he or she is less likely to repeat mistakes, and conversely, more likely to engage in reasonable endeavors.

The royal path of the Tarot is well aware of this connection of age, wisdom and justice. Appropriately, the Justice (11) arcana is a combination of The Emperor (4) and The Chariot (7), which represent respectively, order and forward movement. In short, we witness what amounts to a keen insight into potential and the ensuing confidence to proceed in an irrefutable direction, undaunted. Conclusively, we learn to fully utilize the gift of an experienced mind in our elaborate choices throughout life's labyrinth. In this wisdom, we seek to obtain the fairness and equilibrium natural to creation and hence, select options we honestly deem necessary, for a healthy and relatively long existence.

The Hebrew letter for the Justice arcana is Lamed, which means ox goad. In this symbolism, we re-establish the sound and productive groundwork for life, found in carrying a steady mortal load (rational and material choices). If the goad is unbalanced, the ox will lose its load (achievement) and in all likelihood, injure itself. As we have seen, this depiction holds true for the initiate as well. (See the threatening sword held high by the Justice figure!)

We have noted a variety of associations in this figure with the natural world. Nature is inseparable from the concepts of balance and parity in existence. The relative food chain is supportive of each group of predator species which subsists upon an equal and available supply of prey species. These prey species, conversely, depend upon the availability of flora and vegetation respectively. These distinct living creatures, in turn, rely on seed carriers, microbes and favorable weather conditions. In each case, a delicate equilibrium of need and subsistence must be maintained. If any of these consistent variables change, the effected breed of living creature will not survive. History has demonstrated how nature was, (and still is,) harsh for species unable to cope with sudden changes in their environment. They find themselves extinct! Dinosaurs and Wooly mammoths are two examples of once dominant creatures which were both unable to alter their lifestyles enough to withstand the sweeping environmental changes which caused their ultimate demise. In this, we see how Justice is relative and sometimes extremely harsh. Likewise, the real life decisions we may be forced to make in life, can be inhumanly rigid. For example, murder is unacceptable to all cultures. However, the concept of 'kill or be killed', (when we are attacked by some unreasonable and violent force,) is called self-defence and found to be entirely acceptable behavior in the justice system of the United States of America and many other countries. Wisdom helps us discern necessary actions in life, such as the previous example, otherwise known as fight or flight. Being far older than the United States legal system, however, the Tarot demonstrates that FINAL JUDGEMENT of an individual is reserved for a power HIGHER than our human selves and ALL our social mechanisms. This is why Justice, as a concept and faith, is understood as a principle of our spiritual learning. It is the method we utilize PRIOR to making decisions and ultimately, taking real action.

The appearance of the Justice card in a dream may simply be a warning to be cautious in the approach of an upcoming decision. On another level, our unconscious may be reminding us about both our material and spiritual maturity and the necessary development of a sound, well-rounded and open-eyed wisdom. This may occur at a certain point in our life, when our judgement and decision making may have a new and powerful effect upon our overall social structure. For example, when we leave school and enter the work force, or when we bring a child into the world, or perhaps, when we become a political leader or head CEO in an international conglomerate. Regardless, when wisdom is needed, Justice is paramount in our perceptive organization. We must learn to trust ourselves in judgment, without ever looking back. Prudence is built upon our ongoing and broadening experiences, for better or worse, richer or poorer, til' DEATH do us part. Albeit, before we can get to the DEATH (13) ARCANA, we need to first examine the NEXT arcana upon the Tarot path, and that is, The Hanged Man (12).

THE HANGED MAN (12) (Tarot Major Arcana) There are times when ones spiritual wisdom and worldly experience offer no solution for difficult questions and predicaments encountered in life. Nevertheless, decisions need to be made in the continuation of life and forward progression. It is to this end that the initiate encounters the path of The Hanged Man who dangles from a crucifix-like tree, suspended by one leg. This is the passage where the initiate must surrender completely to his faith. Hanging perilously from the ETHEREAL world, the initiate places all his trust in the higher power of GOD (Ain Soph Aur) and the SPIRITUAL PLANE. His fear of falling is overcome by the physical sacrifice he offers to the wisdom of creation, reiterated in the symbolism of the tree of knowledge/wisdom/life, from which he now hangs. As such, The Hanged Man is fastened between two worlds, the ETHEREAL PLANE and the higher still, SPIRITUAL PLANE. In so many ways, this path echoes The Fool's first prayerful step into the great unknown and The Hermit's final release of the material self in order to enter the Ethereal Plane. It represents the plummeting descent into absolute faith in the universal blueprint, the successive falling into the outstretched hands of God.

The Hanged Man is not as pure as The Fool and must therefore, rely on his steadfast trust and belief in creation. This is in the humble wish that God will return Divine Wisdom into his (the Hanged man's) own operating world of experience. The Fool seeks all experience, conversely, The Hanged Man aspires for momentary and specific guidance. God helps those who help themselves, however, we find in this path an inability to help ourselves any longer, through material or ethereal wisdom. Instead, we (the Hanged Man) must surrender ourselves completely to the FINAL wisdom of our primal creator.

The image put forth in this arcana, of faithfully dangling over the unknown, is highly representative of immersing oneself into the unconscious. In this sense, we conceptualize falling into a deep sleep and sinking into the surreal abyss of our symbolic dream consciousness. As we have witnessed repeatedly, ancient cultures around the world have associated this dreaming with the voice of their particular deity and His or Her respective message to a waiting community. In this, we evoke Carl Gustav Jung's idea of The Collective Unconscious which links all life forms, transcends linear time, and nonchalantly accommodates all universal (and divine) knowledge. At this point, we ask ourselves, where does the Collective Unconscious end, and God (Ain Soph Aur) Consciousness, begin? Are they one in the same? The Hanged Man (12) figure, (though silent,) seems to answer loud and clear in the affirmative. As such, he is unremittingly associated with dreams, his own and those of the Tarot initiate. Accordingly, The Hanged Man must leave his Ethereal Body behind in the corpse-like state of hanging and approach the higher wisdom of his eternal self. Like Native American Shaman, he embarks on a journey, otherwise known as a Spirit Vision, where his Ethereal Body remains (more or less) earthbound, while his mind, heart and soul enter the immortal realm of spirit. In this Spiritual Plane, everything heard, felt and seen is understood in terms of eternal, archetypal symbolism. Hence, a spirit familiar, or guide, may appear as a hawk, donkey, waterfall or spider, depending on the enlightenment sought after (and received) by the Shaman. In as much, the 'mechanical' reality of the guide in the etheral world of consciousness is meaningless, only the characteristics and behavior of that representational form of Spirit needs to be understood. As such, a bald eagle is more than just a majestic bird, it is the far-seeing vision of high spiritual wisdom and the very image of tranquil spiritual peace. Its white head signals purity and purpose as it circles, high above the world of mankind's follies. Moreover, it flies alone, in the replete confidence of self in a trance-like and utterly timeless, reminder of its creator. In parallel fashion, all visionary symbolism pertains to our own unconscious and the dynamic language of dreams. The Hanged Man seeks answers in his spiritual dream world, a world, or plane, which is perfectly removed and apart from himself and all his respective experiences thus far.

One linguistic point needs to be examined in closer detail. We now disclose the fundamental difference between what is known as 'The Subconscious' as opposed to the concept (which we have been discussing in the course of this book,) which is called 'The Unconscious' The term 'subconscious' refers to our deepest seated actual memories, remembered experiences which may have been repressed, or perhaps remain suppressed, yet nevertheless, continue to exist as a part of our physical selves. They are alive in the banks of our memory and in theory and in practice, we are able to recapture, or 'recall', these bits of information, by way of hypnotism or psychoanalysis. Once these buried memories are retrieved, (a process known to psychologists as 'breakthroughs',) the individual is given a chance to face the past once more and having done so successfully, he or she may begin to overcome the effects of those traumatic past experiences upon a present reality base. In a very real sense, these memories no longer seethe at the edge of consciousness, but rather are thrown into the full light of reason and mature individuation. This form of revelation, more often than not, quells ALL of their profound effects. This catalog of our deep, personal memories comprises what is known as the Subconscious. The Unconscious, and moreover, The Collective Unconscious, (as we shall see,) is quite another matter. The root word 'sub', as in 'subconscious', means 'under'. In other words, the subconscious is 'under', or below, our ordinary consciousness. Conversely, the root word 'un', as in 'unconscious', means 'not'. Which is why when somebody is knocked out cold, we say they are unconscious, or 'not' conscious. The psychological terminology for 'The Unconscious' operates on this same linguistic tenet, only in far more complex manner of perception. The Unconscious is an allegorical plane which exists beyond our own plane of experience. It is a concept beyond even our primitive trace memories and evolutionary consciousness. Accordingly, we can never 'capture' our dream world, we can merely learn from its highly stylized revelations. The Unconscious exists apart from us, in a timeless plane of being. In our dreams and deepest revelations, we are allowed to momentarily cross the threshold into this visionary land as a perceptual observer, but never as an inhabitant. In every way, we must return to waking consciousness, of which that enigmatic reality is really 'not' a part. The dream of the mystical labyrinth of the Tarot grants us temporary and fleeting permission to move beyond our visible world and tap into an eternal realm of spiritual wisdom. Holy as it may sound, this is what we consider to be the Unconscious and more precisely, The Collective Unconscious.

In dream symbolism, the predominant representation of the Unconscious revolves around images of mighty oceans, because of their immeasurable depth, enigmatic mystery and overwhelming force. Moreover, an ocean can carry us away in its wake and current. As such, it can dramatically parallel our emotional revelry. Additionally, we may sink into its depths in order to re-engage our primordial past. In this, we return to the primal pools of our ancestral strains of DNA/RNA protein complexes. We return (in theory) to the massive living swirl, (the genetic soup) of life's molecular structuring. This is the scientist's Garden of Eden. The journey from sperm cell to ovum, which merge into blastula, zygote and eventually, fetus, does so in a liquid environment: not altogether unlike, the protein and vitamin rich pools of earliest existence. In fact, the fetus, in its nine month gestation, moves through various bodily stages of our (once) aquatic capabilities. This is known as our evolutionary memory and includes the appearance of a tail, gills and fins. Naturally, these appendages morph into arms and legs etc., but the ancestral levels of development are not lost to us. Consequently, only when the baby is delivered and fully formed, (into our oxygen breathing present adaptation,) can it surrender its sack of amniotic fluid in which it survived and gained nourishment. In the Soviet Union, infants are delivered from the liquid womb into an environment of warm water to lessen the trauma of a harsh birth into a world of direct light and air. However, regardless of technique, the new born child must eventually emerge into this present and novel world. In so many ways, the baby's first breath, is the harsh, revelatory entry into real and complete waking consciousness. Little wonder the poor little thing screams for dear life!

In another symbolic link, we examine the ritual of Baptism, where a child is submerged into holy water by a priest or minister in order to purify his mortal soul. In essence, the individual has returned to the innocence of his maker and creation itself. Once baptized, this child can live (religiously speaking) in peace, anointed into the Immaculate spirit of God. In fact, he or she is now considered to be a true child of God: a child returned into His spiritual womb.

In all cases, this symbolism was not lost on the ancients and accordingly, the Hebrew letter for the path of The Hanged Man is Mem, which naturally means water. In as much, the figure searches for spiritual rebirth in the baptismal waters of the eternal creation. The Hanged man needs to purify himself by removing his awareness from the Ethereal world. He does this through self sacrifice and the deepest faith he can fathom, leaving behind in the process, the society of man and their inevitable public opinion. Only when he has left behind his deepest material, social and ethereal awareness, may he be allowed a glimpse into the Eternal Unconscious. If he is allowed entry in this symbolic world of visions, (whose wisdom is eternal and archetypal,) he must transcend its Spiritual Meaning into his own conscious world of experience. God has given back to him his own birth and innate knowledge. Accomplishing this great, sacrificial, and humbling task, involved the Hanged Man suspending himself over the unseen and baffling Spiritual Plane. This is why the figure is pictured with a halo shining brightly around his head and facade. Through faith, The Hanged Man has begun the journey into his highest enlightenment.

In order to fully contemplate the dream interpretation of this figure, we must first turn to its connection with The Empress (3) Arcana. The Hanged Man (1+2) = The Empress (3). The feminine aspects of acceptance and maternal sacrifice, natural to this path of the Tarot, demonstrate the humility necessary to surrender ones built-in ego. There are times we simply must submit to powers greater than ourselves. To this end, we need to admit our own ignorance and intolerance and ask for spiritual guidance in complicated predicaments which often appear in our life. This is not saying, we should surrender our individual wisdom to societal pressures and opinions placed upon us. In fact, The Hanged Man demonstrates quite the opposite. His arcane presence reveals the imperfect consciousness found in the material world of man. He, in turn, surrenders this limited wisdom of man, to the eternal promise of God and the Unconscious. He invites us into the Spirit Vision of our deepest reality, far beyond the zenith of our human awareness and comprehension. We do this to gain wisdom far removed (and wholly unattainable) by the Self. In so doing, he challenges us to keep a faithful bridge between our own highest knowledge and the erudition of an immeasurable creation.

DEATH (13) (Tarot Major Arcana) There is no thing in the physical world which begins from nothing. New life can only spring forth from the death and gradual dissolution of some other entity. In physics we learn that matter can neither be created nor destroyed; it can however, be changed into another state of being. In this, we witness the inseparable union of life and death. Without the definitive and concrete end of experience known as extinction, we would not be able to progress forward into new life and fresh creation. In other words, death stands for the full readiness of change into new existence. As such, we rather dramatically learn in this arcana, to surrender our irrational fear of physical termination and ALL the OTHER absolute changes we must undergo. Consequently, as we witness physical and ethereal realities dissolving before us, we must accept their disappearance and boldly prepare ourselves for naked and pure beginnings. Therefore, the Death (13) card cannot be faced with trepidation. It must be welcomed into our field of experience with open-eyed respect and tolerance. We are given the opportunity to change, and therefore, definitively grow as individuals and human beings.

In the sense of the Tarot wisdom, we comprehend this path as an invitation into the divine scheme of existence. It demonstrates the necessity of our eventual passing from life on earth and the higher ethereal plane. In examples of this austere truth, (taken from the real world of human tradition,) we look to the recorded accounts of Near-Death Experiences. These descriptive accounts have been told all through chronicled history by individuals whose biological functions and heartbeat had ceased and whom were subsequently pronounced dead by medical professionals. In these detailed narratives of post-life experiences, we find a similarity in retained perceptive images including glowing white, angelic figures, many of whom were seen to be deceased loved ones welcoming the newly departed into the next plane of existence. These depictions of the afterlife, more often than not, encompass feelings of warmth and overall well-being. In most cases, initial fear is transformed into ecstatic emotional revelry and a feeling of humble thankfulness.

There are audible references to drumming and clapping, sometimes ethereal singing and chanting which quicken the departure of the soul from the enclosure of the physical body. This music is reminiscent of aboriginal shaman who create trance-like beats to enter Spiritual Vision in search of communal wisdom and transfigurative enlightenment. These Near-Death Experiences perpetually relate a transfigurative image of an otherworldly light which lulls the individual into a peaceful, yet unknowable porthole, the highest plane of reality. The entire scene is roughly comparable to birth from the womb. However, the process and conditions are reversed. Instead of traumatically bursting into the harsh, oxygen-filled world of earthly consciousness, this birth is closer to a return to the comfort and security of the womb, placid and forgiving, all nourishing and in touch with a waiting creator. In this way, it is a trip into the Unconscious, dreamlike in every detail, infinite and timeless in all imaginal scope. We have returned to our innate beginnings, the ancestral plateau where birth and death are one in the same: where the once all-important sense of our own individuality has undergone celestial transfiguration and a singular awakening with the oneness of being. In this discussion of Near-Death Experiences, we observe the creativity of death itself. In essence, we are recapitulating the wisdom of the ancient Tibetan Book of the Dead and other spiritual reflections from around the aboriginal world upon the ultimate passage into the afterlife. In a preponderance of these cultures we find a method of preparation for an individual's final demise. In some of these cultures, death is absolutely and proudly welcomed. For example, a good part of the Asian world celebrate funerals as sanctified passages into the celestial realm. The deceased are given letters, gifts and money to help guide them in their journey into the netherworld. Furthermore, descendants of departed loved ones, continue to respect and honor their ancestors as 'active' beings. As such, they often call (or pray) to them for advice and worldly guidance. In Tibet, children are encouraged to play with the bones and skulls of their ancestral dead. This deeply embeds the idea of death as normal and grateful in the sublime order of things. The process also erases fear of death in a mortal world which is harsh and sometimes devastatingly cruel. The lesson of gaining an awareness of being beyond the perceptive five senses, lends spiritual transfiguration to an entire culture, rather than merely a chosen devout person (Magic Man, Shaman), and his or her respective familial line. In short, every Tibetan understands that their Great, Great Grandmothers continue to share love with the family and her tribe, even though she is not there to break bread with them. Instead, through her remains, she has played with the children and enjoyed their company, as they have enjoyed hers. It has continued the ever-weaving fabric of natural life, on every level of human comprehension. This is death embraced in unconditional love. It is a replete metaphysical insight which brings a people into the very heart of an infinite creation. Another example of death wisdom is practiced by the Dakota Native Americans, or Plane Indians, who fully welcome their ultimate parting without fear or regret. To fear death is to challenge the great plan. This may cause the deceased agony and peril in his or her entrance into the netherworld. [Various 'Books of the Dead' describe this monstrous association with the afterlife, replete with mutant-beings, fierce obstacles and eternal suffering. Medieval christian teaching decided to utilize this approach to the hereafter, as a dogmatic system of reward and punishment bestowed on humanity. In other words, if you're good, you'll end up in a good eternal place, namely Heaven, but if you're bad, hell and Satan's terrible demons will await you in their eternal hot house far below both heaven and earth.]

In any case, the Native Americans had no such distinction. Instead, they followed the simple tenet of achieving a proud, direct acceptance of death. This tranquil recognition is believed to ease the ultimate dissolution into the unconscious realm of spirit. There is, however, one condition which the living can place upon the messenger of death. However, it is only available to elder warriors and shaman who have proved themselves in all matters of wisdom and bravery upon the worldly plain. Death must wait and listen patiently, while the wise old man or woman relive and relate the great tales of glory and honors bestowed them in their long, suffering life. Only after life's glories have been retold, can the elders soul depart into the fully welcomed beyond.

In a myriad of ways, this conceptualization of encountering and overcoming FEAR is the central lesson given in this path of the Tarot. Clinging on to a familiar past, due to concern and worry over an unknown future, induces and provokes these images of difficult, awkward and painful transitions into new realms of experience. When we accept our own Fear, we welcome the horrific, inhuman conceptions associated with all the harsher aspects of the Persian and Celtic afterlife and the medieval Christian elaboration of hell. These nightmarish perceptions equally demonstrate the effect of a persistent resistance to death (and change in general.) The early Christian movement and later Islamic principalities, used this representational fear to insure moral behavior within the context of culture. The societies law, or rules of conduct, once established, were to be followed without question and certainly without deviation. To disobey these cultural ethics became equivalent to a personal challenge placed up against Divine Retribution. It was, in fact, perceived as an invitation to all forms of Holy punishment. At some point, in the harsh history of western Europe, cultural leaders decided this sublime penance could and should happen a bit sooner than the afterlife. Consequently, clergy and religious participants performed various tortures upon accused sinners right here on the earthly plane. In these cases, the misunderstood fear of death became an active attack upon most 'free' existence and more specifically, independence of thought. It is well documented in the catalog of human history, the list of creative thinkers who were led into castigation, excommunication and even public execution. Ironic, how the ancient wisdom found in the Egyptian and Tibetan Books of the Dead, which instructed methods for a RELEASE of fear and a personal acceptance of death, could be turned upside down into an actual INCREASE of cultural terror. One must remark upon the various interpretations of the oral and written word and its respective effect upon the human psyche. Notwithstanding, and within the context of our further evaluations, we will see how certain ancient truths remain persistent, age in, and age out.

With this, we return to the last phase of our discussion on the Death (13) Arcana. This concerns the wisdom to surrender our past without fear and subsequently, progress into original and CREATIVE modes of future existence. This point was not lost on the mystic tradition of the Kabbalah. Accordingly, the Hebrew letter for the Death arcana is Nun, which means Creation. Appropriately, we find this symbolic associations with IMAGINATION in general and the CREATIVE PRINCIPLE, specifically. Only with a fearless break from our old ideology, can we progress into new and innovative births of ingenuity. The afterlife and an entrance into an enigmatic netherworld, reveals the rather dramatic completion of material and ethereal creation in its sum total. In this formulation, we unearth the means and courage of highest invention. Furthermore, this figure reminds us to keep faith in our innate ability to continue exploring new and better approaches to life and its ever expanding spectrum of probabilities.

Binding all these symbolic elements into a final and cohesive interpretation, involves one last look at the Death (13) card itself. In the Waite-Rider deck, an apparition dressed in the regalia of the Black Knight, rides a noble white steed and carries a black flag emblazoned with a flower-like emblematic bloom. The upright stature of the figure seems to reflect our righteous place upon the Ethereal Plane. Simultaneously, a sympathetic allusion to high humanism is offered in the visible suit of armor, worn only by men who risked and at times, sacrificed their own lives to support the cause of their beliefs. Moreover, this metal suit demonstrates man's inborn will to strive forward, as well as, his need to protect the sanctity of his own development. In short, the card tells us to live our lives to the fullest by pushing BEYOND our own potential. Herein, lies the unifying source of this arcana. Becoming in tune with ourselves, our strengths and our limitations, we are able to comprehend when a real change in our mortal course is undeniably necessary. Once realized, we seek ingenious ways to create outstanding metaphorical bridges to God's highest realm of existence. In this wisdom, we lay down the armor of our present ego structure on the Ethereal Plane and fearlessly step into new perceptions of Spiritual fulfillment. We are no longer afraid of change and we embody our innate creative future with pride and our deepest reverence to the life/death cycle of a miraculous existence.

TEMPERANCE (14) (Tarot Major Arcana) The striking journey into the Death (13) arcana, teaches the inevitable requirement of change in our life and our ability to cope with its dramatic transitions. To this end, we need to maintain flexibility in the waking choices we fashion for ourselves in the journey of the Tarot. Having mastered this transition we suddenly find ourselves flying forward into our next (and higher) stage of development. The wisdom of the Temperance (14) arcana is centered around finding restraint in the scope of this new-found and incredible spiritual awakening. (How often have we seen the devastating effect of unbalanced behavior in the face of higher spiritual development?) The first winged figure in the Tarot series is beautifully pictured in this arcana. This angelic archetype signals our complete entrance into the fourth level of the Royal Path. In short, Temperance (14) signals the initiate's emergence onto the Spiritual Plane. In finding some measure of emotional moderation and a modicum of self-restraint, we may remain pliant, and therefore compliant enough, to sustain the reality of this highest transfiguration.

However, we should never confuse this sensitive equilibrium with mediocrity and a general lack of passion. In fact, a major component of emotional maturity is built upon tempering childish behavior which operates exclusively upon instinctual impulses. The ability to stop and think, to measure our feelings and motivations and to ascertain the real consequences of our actions, deepens the capacity of our emotional commitment in ALL given situations. We may choose to withdraw from a particular experience, or spend the rest of our lives enriching its most articulate details. In any case, our decision will be steady and fervent, rather than superficial and reminiscent of the immediate gratification sought after by a child, who in reality, doesn't understand any better. The initiate on the illuminating path of the Tarot has earned his wings. He has already moved past Death and now enters the realm of his deepest self knowledge. He comprehends in this arcana, the need to sight his parameters and realistic limitations. He has come full circle from The Fool (0), who leaps without thought into the great beyond. The initiate has since learned the significance of this leap of faith and its concern with the spiritual world and ones relationship to God and creation. On the Ethereal Plane, Temperance (14) guides the wisdom of man, allowing leeway, for the ever changing nature of the sometimes severe, Spiritual Realm.

In the Temperance (14) card itself, we observe an angel-like being who pours liquid from one cup to another. The winged angel maintains a calm demeanor and an almost surreal stillness, which defies fallacy and mortal stumbling. He/She is in a state of timeless, static bliss, a kind of relevant Satori which defines the Spiritual Plane. Furthermore, behind the winged being, a path leads to an illuminated mountain which glows in the promise of high and uplifted spiritual transcendence. The angel wears the emblem of a triangle inside a square, centered upon his/her chest. This symbolizes the nature of spirit residing inside or within matter, which drives every bit of data received by the five senses. This realization of spirit-infused matter, or what the alchemists term the Operatum Modus, holds the philosophical key to enlightenment. In this sense, the blissful angel may have originated from the mountain itself (spirit from matter) and followed the descending path to where he/she now stands, or, he/she may have materialized from the netherworld, otherwise known as the Unconscious, solely to guide the initiate, (The Fool (0),) to his own highest existential plateau. In either case, the deepest faith of the Temperance Angel found in this path allows for the individual's free and weightless movement from the Ethereal to the Spiritual Plane.

On the card itself, this visible and perpetual interplay of liquid from cup to cup parallels the ebb and flow of life. Moreover, the necessity of emptying one cup to fill another, displays the ever changing focus of universal existence. In other words, we rightfully juggle the strength of our being, (in whatever form that strength may take), into the position where it is foremost required. Consequently, we find ourselves with a list of changing priorities, which must be addressed in the zenith of their relative importance. Naturally, this variable focus of priority may become a maddening, unending cycle of behavioral drudgery without an operational set of fundamental parameters. To this end, we must know when to push and when to pull, likewise, we need to be aware of ALL our energy expenditure. On every level of spiritual enlightenment we must gain the wisdom to perpetuate a fluid and flexible sense of Self, capable of adapting to multidimensional revelations. In direct response to this conceptual belief, the Waite-Rider deck displays the fluid flowing from cup to cup in the Temperance card, suspended between the cups themselves. In this sense, our ability to comprehend a wide picture of the complex reality around us, and immediately adjust to its needs, becomes preeminent in our perceptual learning. As such, the initiate must balance his strengths in a graceful, rhythmic state of eternal readiness. This is understandably superior to a chaotic state of irrational fear and uncertainty.

In another symbolic interpretation, the suspended flow of fluid found in the arcana, is roughly comparable to ones possessions and worldly gifts. This endless cycle of continual filling and emptying, prevents our metaphorical cup from being overfilled and consequently, wasted in its excess. Instead, we return our good graces into the world from whence they came and retain a dire appreciation for life's innate harmony. This way, we will not horde what we choose to continually reinstate into our surroundings. This idea is echoed in the doctrine of the Karmic wheel, which is an allegorical device signifying the ten-fold return of good deeds released from oneself into the external world of expereince. In other words, our good deeds return to us ten times over. Naturally, this truth also holds sway for bad deeds which are sent out into the world and returned to their OWN sender in ten-fold vengeance. In all cases, we find a direct cause and effect mechanism operating in the world of the Tarot, as it does in the recognized world of science. As stated earlier, the delicate ecosystem of nature maintains equilibrium via a dramatic succession of checks and balances within nature's tolerance. Darwin's theory concerning Survival of the Fittest demonstrates this abstract link in the picture of the weakest animal in a herd, (perhaps a young bison,) who becomes injured, falls and ends up as prey. On the other end of the chain, we find the strongest of predators, (a dominant female lion for example,) killing and eating this prey's carcass. Descending down the line of relative fitness, we may find a pack of hyenas, who will devour all the scraps and most of the bone structure. Next in line, scavengers such as vultures, will gnaw at the fetid corpse and suck the pulp of the marrow from the softening bones. The process is still not complete, as insects invade the oils and bacterium of the remaining strands. Eventually, only the single-celled bacterium will linger to feed on the micro-organisms of the animal. The last stage is the once living animal's complete absorption into the soil itself, as fertilizing nutrients for plant life which will in turn be ingested for nourishment, perhaps by (members of) the same herd of bison who began the entire chain. All in all, nothing is lost, or wasted, and virtually every part is utilized for the common good. The Temperance card is fully representational of this simple truth. The Angel summons the perpetual movement of life's equilibrium, held aloft betwixt her two symbolic cups of universal balance.

The idea of the 'common good' refers to the communal reality of all systems of checks and balances. We turn now to look at a few of the real social implications of Temperance, (as a working human behavior.) The initial treatment of the subject begins with an examination of interrelationships. In this thoughtful procedure we regard the connection of self-control and personal flexibility with external attachments within society. Individuals who display easy and immediate accessibility and adaptability to others, seem to universally possess three common traits. The first of these characteristics is an ability to listen attentively to others. The second trait involves gathering up a real concern for the quandary or crisis of others. Lastly, this concerned listener makes all speakers aware that this consideration and concern is not forced and given by choice. In this subtle comprehension, the speaker realizes that any particular wisdom he or she may receive in the meeting, is not offered to just anybody, without any discrimination whatsoever. It is for the listener alone and no one else in the universe. This feeling of special individual attention, serves at least two basic and fundamental purposes. The first is the accumulation of trust, which is paramount in the union of fragile and cautious human beings. A willingness to set ones own concerns and needs aside to assist others, signals civility and altruistic human kindness. This selfless behavior inspires profoundest confidence in ALL relations. The second purpose of special attention allows for the introduction of oneself. Without a solid foundation of self identity, all selfless behavior runs the risk of appearing spineless, submissive and ultimately, self-serving. This of course, defeats the entire purpose. In an example of this behavior we may think, 'I'll help you, because then, you may like me better.' as opposed to, 'I'll help you, because I CHOOSE to help You.' The difference in these two statements is as large as the human ego itself. We witness the balance of Temperance within the individual, becoming the very support mechanism in social relationships. The flexibility and balance of a secure Self, assures the strong measure of ones altruistic brace.

As in the entire Tarot Arcanum, this wisdom was not lost on the ancient Kabbalah mystics. The Hebrew letter for this path is Samech, which loosely means Tree which Supports. As we have seen repeatedly, the symbolism of the tree refers to straight and firm wisdom. To support others with our righteousness, honesty and deeply embedded roots, reflects a sonorous understanding of the Temperance (14) arcana. In a similar symbolic sense, the animal associated with this path is the Horse. In this allusion we embody the strength of individuality which when trained and focused, may acquire the skill to leap through the living experience with deft magic, self-awareness and replete self-control. With the acquisition of personal power and flexibility, (innate in most breeds of horses,) we find our own greatest adaptability. This is why man and horse have been set together in an almost mythical union since ancient times. We are in our own best regards, two beings which mutually support one another: with pride, poise and loyalty.

The presence of the Temperance card in a dream refers to gaining self-control. Understanding the parameters of Self and maintaining honest stature figures prominently in the social context of our lives. If we calmly study the spectrum of possibilities in a presented situation beforehand, we may not become cornered and paralyzed by the difficulties of that situation. This strength of wisdom gives our soul wings to rise above our own human ambition. We must note the connection between The Heirophant (5) Arcana and the Temperance (14) Arcana. In the fifth arcana, Man gained his fifth element, this we understood to be his unmitigated 'SOUL'. In the fourteenth arcana (1+4= 5), this 'SOUL' has been given wings and begins its final journey into Spiritual Consciousness.

THE DEVIL (15) (Tarot Major Arcana) Contrary to the myriad of media-related images presenting the prediction of unchangeable evil in the appearance of The Devil (15) arcana, the card itself is entirely instructive. The card reminds the initiate of his human frailty, even at this highest echelon of the Royal Path. In this sense, the card is not in and of itself wicked, but rather demonstrative of our deepest weakness. In the darkness of this arcana and this figure, we logically surmise a link to our Spiritual desires and Unconscious Emotional passions. This is actually, the arcana of instinctual human drives, which quite literally, damn all consequences. Moreover, this dramatic human potential is etched upon the background of our psyche, a naturalistic reminder of all worldly possibilities. To avoid this reality is to denounce manifested creation itself. Unfortunately, (and at the same time,) to become possessed by this hunger for experience can be, (especially on this high plane,) ultimately devastating to the initiate. In total, we see how the demonic figure in this path deems to warn us about the destructive nature of Personal indulgence. Simultaneously, The Devil figure only offers us a slight hint as to the real consequences of his real and effective influence over us in the journey through the Tarot.

Curiously enough, this ambivalence is part of the archetype of the Devil figure itself, as it appears throughout human history. He is forever the sweet tempter and irrepressible trickster. From antiquity to modern times, we see good, heroic archetypes paired off with evil, treacherous villains whose power and seductive influence is equal, if not greater, than the hero him/herself. Naturally, this is entirely logical in the theological sense, since there can be no understanding of GOOD whatsoever, without an equal and opposite EVIL, to weigh it up against. In fact, good deeds can only be internalized and appreciated after the reverse consequences of bad deeds have taken their cruel and fully comprehended toll upon our memory. This is why a cat taken home from the freezing cold of a shelterless existence, will in general terms, be more grateful of his new abode, than a similar feline, born on the living room sofa. In other words, good, or God, needs evil, or the devil, to create brutal hardships which human beings must overcome to realize the intense joy of good, or God's Holy Enlightenment.

But there is far more to the conceptual reality of the trickster than adversity and burdensome tasks given to man to prize and relish the superior world of Spiritual Existence. The real strength of this demon lies in his replete knowledge of man's full range of desires. Subsequently, the devil understands the craving of each man and woman and it is his mission to lull humanity into this entirely personalized and rather extreme world of Spiritual pleasure and Holy seduction.

Let us delve upon this point for a moment. In doing so, we must return to Antiquity, to observe early personifications of the Devil, Satan. In the book of Genesis of the Holy Bible, God is quoted, "Let there be light," and there was light. God saw that the light was good, and so He divided the light from the darkness."

In this quote, we witness darkness, or evil, already present in God's existence. As such, a monotheistic God splits Himself in half and becomes a duality. That is to say, half darkness and now, half light. (Compare the High Priestess.) Once this initial split occurs, ALL darkness is removed from Him and replaced by the remaining creation of Celestial Light. This essential detachment occurs because the miraculous God of all creation cannot have any associations with darkness, or evil. He cannot be perceived by his followers as wicked, profane and diabolical. Hence, he must 'cast off' the dark side of His own infinite nature. A rather important work of antiquity further describes this plurality of divinity. In the first Book of Enoch, we witness God as a collective. He is surrounded by his 'Sons of God', who are called the Bene ha-elohim. These sons of God become known as The Watcher Angels and fall from His good graces as they submit to earthly lust for the 'dauthers of Men'. In as much, a veritable part of God Himself has fallen (or been cast out) into darkness. In all cases, God brings His own evil into the world, and at the same time, entirely away from Himself. In this respect, He consciously delivers to Man a very real and divided aspect of Himself. This 'cast aside' dark facet of The Almighty is perceived as the Devil, or Satan. The word Satan in Hebrew is translated as an obstacle or obstruction. Logically, we begin to understand why this obstruction (or harsh learning of evil) leads us directly back into the realm of God. By bravely stepping directly into God's Dark Side and weathering (and overcoming) its grotesque and all-violent aspects, we open up a Holy Path toward the good (or Light) side of His pure Consciousness. Thus, The Devil (15) represents the perilous bridge from God to Man and more importantly, the return trip of Spiritual Man, back into his Eternal God.

In concrete terms, man must surmount his indulgent gratification as well as his grievous suffering, to return to the center of God. Undeniably, we see how the trickster (God) is playing with a full deck and exists on all sides and parameters of reality. He is the positive/negative influence which keeps the soul suspended over the incomprehensible vortex of Himself. This is why the Devil's appearance is so dramatic and captivating, in both its diametric faces of seduction and repulsion. The Devil (15) arcanum in the full representative sense, is God's complete vision of humanity's potential return into Himself. Accordingly, the initiate must pierce directly though this fervent image, in order to reach ever deeper into himself and move ultimately, beyond even the highest aspiration of his realized Self.

Little wonder, the Hebrew letter for this path is Ayin, which can mean both Eye and Foundation. To see the infrastructure of the establishment of the world is to possess that world in the elaboration of thought. To carry the image of Evil in ones mind, opens up the possibility of manipulating that conception and hence becoming part of its ongoing creation. Herein lies man's glory as well as his downfall. The concept of God's creative principle placed in the hands of human beings demonstrates the Supreme Being's faith in man and full use of his prior creation, the Devil. Here we see God giving mankind the chance to create and fulfill the wide breadth of his existence without question and with complete creative solitude. Of course, as in all endeavors of the divine consciousness, there is a catch which enables man to prove his ultimate worthiness as a manifest prodigy in the grand stratagem of his creator. A chaotic revelry of prospective reality keeps man spinning in the delirious swirl of his own unending visions. His need to experience further and deeper corporealities, can and often does, prevent him from completing any significant innovation and more importantly, thwarts him from thankfully and humbly returning unto God. The test which man must pass involves once again moving beyond his highest mortal self and his own miraculous gifts, in order to once again find God. In this sense, God's split into duality to challenge Man is synonymous with The High Priestess' division of the universe. This connection of The Devil and The High Priestess can be seen in the crown of taurean horns worn by the High Priestess and suggestive of the lunar horns of The Devil. The sexually destructive connotations of both figures determine the real force of their outward natures. When Man overcomes this split by accepting the full opposition of reality (and moving beyond it,) he becomes akin to The Empress. As we remember, it was she who rejoined the universe with her highest attainment of maternal Love. Therefore, the Tarot indicates that God in His divine wisdom depends upon Man (whom He truly loves) to carry the burden of His own infinite creation. It is, as we are apt to say, our cross to bear on this earth.

Hence, The Devil (15) arcanum and the archetypal Devil itself, is given the task to provide sight and knowledge as well as darkness and eternal chaos. No wonder Lucifer, (or the bearer of light,) was once considered to be God's highest angel. However, in what seems to be paradoxical imagery, the card is pictured black and utterly ominous: in direct polar opposition to God's light and holy transfiguration. Herein, is a clue to a rather important riddle of the ancient world known as the Riddle of the Light. It is this: "Why is the brightest of lights not seen by the sharpest of eyes?" The answer is simple for the initiate/fool who charges headlong into the unknown. The Fool knows he cannot make the mistake of confusing celestial brilliance with his normal image of earth's illuminating solar light. The radiance of God refers to the clarity and purity of truth, wisdom and faith. As such, it will never be witnessed by the naked eye. It can only burn eternally, inside our very own spiritual center, or soul. Sensed, but not seen. This leaves the OTHER conception of light, the physical conception of light, (or perceptive awareness of the world,) in the hands and direct manipulation of the devil himself. This is why the self-same evil one is called Lucifer, which once again means 'Bearer of the Light.'

This does not mean that the natural and physical light of the world is evil, or immoral. Nothing could be further from the truth. It simply implies that beyond the physical awareness of the world, their lies an underlying mechanism which maintains its very order and direction, a random quantum code, which generates the structure of the entire visible miracle. This is the SOUL of the world, the true light, unseen by the naked eye.

The outward perception of the world operates on principles of hard logic and visible memory. The Life we perceive is an enactment of principles evolved over millennia and perfected by the needs of creative survival. Even so, when we speak of this visible reality: a cat, a dead volcano, your mother-in-law, the law of gravity, or your boyfriends eyelashes, we are still not referring to Satan's Physical

Universe. The Satanic Universe only erupts its particular light when we become blinded by the excesses of our own material reality: (Ex: 'My cat is the greatest feline in the world and she loves me more than any other pet possibly could!'.) Only then, do when we begin to lose sight of the world's true meaning and underlying spiritual arrangement. We replace the true light of God with the false light of fascination. In such a state of obvious and over-indulgent materialization, The Devil has us viewing his blinding face of darkness, the superficial and highly influential contours of the world. In this way, we behold a world without a spiritual center and obliviously surrender to the domination of its unsteady emotional sway. This ensnarement of evil is hastened by a steady flow of earthly gifts (and horrors) which monopolizes the attention of our external senses, rather than our well rounded and well balanced wisdom. In this persistent light, the devil is the chaotic whirl of undisclosed potential. He is the eye opening wide, the clarity of all things seen simultaneously. He is the horrific revelation of all being: past, present and future. All things considered, he weilds time and space incarnate. In his physical kingdom of emotional intensity, we internalize the extreme parameters of both love AND hate. Eventually in this tempestuous conceptualization, anguish and fear underly our daily existence as the cruel pendulum-like swing of reality moves us (with very little warning) from absolute elation to dire suffering. Accordingly, it is our purpose as spiritual human beings, to move beyond these blinding, mesmerizing visions and regain the order of our soulful foundation. To this end, we can overcome the pain of heartless injustice and heart-breaking, grievous loss and even its antithesis, the transcendence of pleasure, in our correct comprehension of The Devil (trickster) in this particular Path of the Tarot Arcana. We have brought a life and spark back into the world into which we humbly belong. In tackling the darkness of our infinite being, we are given the opportunity to become, (as the Kabbalah Mystics,) at ONE with the forgiving universal truth. The Alchemists echo: "As above, so below, thus: as below, so above." Only at this point, can we begin a discussion of the specific figures present in The Devil (15) Arcana.

It is relatively safe to say, the union known as Love is the deepest emotional and passionate drive in the spectrum of our human capacity. It is built upon the necessity of procreation and the continuation of life as we know it. Without it, humanity disappears forever. Therefore, it is only natural for society to have written extensively and figuratively about its eloquence and the zenith of its absolute culmination, (which is of course,) marriage and family. In this sense, The Devil (15) path is linked with The Lovers (6) card: (1+5=6), in as much as the devil represents the downfall of the lovers, and hence, mankind in general. The tragedy of the lovers is depicted in their blind lust. This lust and pride supersedes their highest purpose, which is a sacred Love, beyond themselves and their egoistic perceptions. The Devil (15) card portrays the lovers chained to Satan and more importantly, to each other. This symbolism refers to our past discussion about the devil and his worldly influence. The lovers in lust only desire the sole physical reality of each other and lose their true spiritual union in the process. Their connection involves self-gratification and self-pride which is fed simultaneously, one from the other. They become satiated by the 'light' of their individual contact. In this sense, they are blinded by the light of Lucifer and lose the soul of God Consciousness, now far out of reach.

In stark contrast, Love, being selfless and altruistic, concerns itself predominantly with the needs of others. This love, in both the naturalistic and spiritualistic senses, is a divine means towards an end. The love of another, (one's mate), leads to love of still others, (their children) and eventually, ALL others, (the greater society). Modern society has demonstrated a formidable need to reconsider our attitudes about relationships in general. Yet, the same principles apply. We have gone through the sexual revolution and gained a basic understanding of man and woman as sexual beings. Today, we are mature individuals, who do not necessarily wish to mindlessly populate the world with children, just to experience a modicum of intimacy. We do not need to ask ourselves if this is an insurmountable contradiction to the ancient laws of union. The question has long been answered by humanity itself, which has demonstrated and still demonstrates a myriad of loving relationships which produce no children and most certainly does not lead to marriage. In fact, society condones this behavior and calls it 'dating'. We experience honest, open alliances, where the needs and apprehensions of our significant other is addressed and with any luck, merge with our own (in agreeable consolidation.) Nevertheless, If we fail to find our spiritual, mental and physical link in these relationships, we are given the societal permission to gracefully discontinue the union and try again elsewhere. We are not castigated by our community and sent off alone into the wild woods, or worse, damned to the perception of a promised hell for our immoral behavior. We have progressed to a new stage of development and all these charted mechanisms of modern behavior, (because of their concern with the requirements of others,) reflect the perceptual spiritual evolution of our contemporaneous interrelationships. Desire, or lust, is merely a part of the overall connection, perhaps only the catalyst in many a long term relationship. Hence, The Devil (15) arcana reveals itself through the reality of romance, and True Love. The card tells us we must find the deepest connection of ourself with another. At the same time, we must use this intensity as a springboard, or catalyst, to move beyond ourselves ultimately, into the purest Love which the Devil finally reveals to us: proclaiming God Consciousness.

In the dream therefore, the appearance of The Devil path refers to our obsession with the physical side of reality. Hence, we may need to review current situations in our life and try to decide if we have removed our own soul in our relative behavior within the context of these experiences. The realization of a greater meaning and eternal purpose beyond our physical, ethereal and spiritual selves sets us firmly upon the perilous bridge toward Purity and the end of the tarot journey. In the Devil Arcana, we have finally touched God.

THE TOWER (16) (Tarot Major Arcana) The Tower (16) arcana is a direct expansion of The Devil (15) Arcana. The path reminds the initiate about the danger of climbing too high into the dark side of his extreme potential. The lightning which strikes The Tower is reminiscent of an all-powerful divinity who can dismantle our lofty plans whenever He chooses. As such, man is ultimately and always subservient to God, regardless of his personal status in the kingdom of mankind. In fact, the card depicts two separate and distinct figures which are blown out from the heights of a once mighty tower. One is a crowned king and the other, an ordinary citizen. This split image carries a dualistic meaning. The first embodiment demonstrates the equality of man under the Supreme Being. In other words, whether a man be a king or a pauper, he still remains a man, and hence, far below his creator, who is the absolute author of the world. In his appropriate humility under the Almighty, man remains equal in his wisdom upon the Spiritual Plane. Secondly, the card examines the folly of personal ego. In this sense, both a king, or an ordinary man may become wholly enamored with his own spiritual accomplishments. In this empowerment, a man may believe himself equal to a divinity. While this may seem illogical, history has demonstrated whole societies who worshipped specific men as Gods, for example, the pharaohs in Egypt, the high emperors in Rome and countless megalomaniacs such as Alexander the Great, Genghis Khan, Napoleon, Hitler and Jim Jones in the modern world. These men all faced The Tower of their self-grandiosity blown to smithereens in an instant of grim and all too mortal realization, (whether on their death beds, or hiding underground in meticulously preplanned concrete bunkers, which doubled rather congenially as tombs.)

The logical continuation of this discussion involves the blinding lust for POWER. This includes politics, business and not too surprisingly, religion. The written record of organized religion and its terror campaigns against humanity in the name of God, fills volumes of text and continues into the present day all around the circumference of this otherwise contemporary world. Put simply, any murder in the name of a Supreme Being, past or present, places the acting individual in the judgmental role of the creator Himself. Needless to say, The Tower (16) arcana has a special message for such an individual and any so-called holy organization, which supports his or her actions. Paraphrased, its sounds something like this, 'Judgement will be His and His alone, those who would take into their own hands the Lord's judgement, will themselves in turn be judged.' (The Holy Bible: Revelations.) In other words, don't attempt to do God's job. Worry about your own mission here on earth instead! However, if you must believe yourself to be more capable than the Almighty, then God will be forced to demonstrate His own unique and unbridled capacity. He will demonstrate this force in his own way and his own time. But most assuradly, in time, he will reveal it to you, and you alone!

There is another side of this figure which parallels our fall from grace and the utter deflation of our human ego. It involves the presence of a benevolent God whose lightning bolt is representational of divine insight. This divine insight serves as a brilliant illumination of self-realization. We suddenly find the answer to our most perplexing questions and riddles in a virtual instant, a nano-second of God Consciousness. In our astonishment, we acknowledge this flash of genius comes from outside ourselves, as if from nowhere. In this approach, we find an allegorical reward from a Supreme Being who follows our perseverance and more worthy aspirations.

In both cases, the creator has demonstrated His absolute dominion over physical man. However, when man follows his spirit and sound judgement, divine intervention is always welcome and fully appreciated. Its flash represents the transition from the dark spirit of infinite reality into the absolte light of Pure Soul.

Perhaps this is what the ancient mystics had in mind when they associated the letter Peh, with the devastating path of The Tower. The letter Peh, translates to Assessing an Agreement. As such, when the mortal initiate aspires to selflessly achieve his or her goal for the greater good of mankind and in full humility and thankfulness to a Supreme Being, he or she may be aided, rather than thrown asunder. In this case, man has thought out his goal, his prerogative and his catalyst, hence, a natural concordance has been determined and all is well in the overall scheme of existence.

The purifying fire of the lightning blast, renews our course in life and returns our previous and primal balance of perceptual awareness. We have rediscovered divinity's place in our heart and in our daily lives. This is why prophets from diverse religions and globally criss-crossing cultural diversities reveal a common theme in their rhetoric involving an individual's need to be redeemed under the all-encompassing sight of God; be that prime mover: Allah, Jesus, Yahweh, Shinto, Buddha, Shiva, Krishna, Horus, or the four compass points of Waken-Tanka. We have to fall headlong before the Almighty, prior to completing the return upward cycle of spiritual awakening and final enlightenment. The Tower (16) arcana represents the blink of God's eye which returns us to our original spiritual bearing. In its humbling intensity, the bright flash of the powerful lightning bolt, is our first visible perception of the true Celestial Light.

In the dream appearance of the Lightning Struck Tower, our Unconscious may be warning us about our lofty status in the society which surrounds our daily existence. We may feel untouchable and impenetrable. As such, we may have built and fashioned walls around ourselves which are seemingly insurmountable and can withstand all efforts to break through to our rather fragile inner sanctum. The Tower arcana reminds us that this self-imposed safety net is not at all fool proof. When we least expect it, we may find disaster and a drastic alteration of our lifestyle and social position. However, this lightning bolt is also double-sided and consequently, its flash of divinity may embody a needed psychological breakthrough into the very framework of our rather elaborate beliefs and waking consciousness. In either case, we're in for a new, wide and wholly unexpected awakening!

THE STAR (17) (Tarot Major Arcana) Having travelled this far down the royal path of the Tarot, the initiate has nearly reached the goal of finding his own unique place in the order of the world. He has struggled with his own ideology, fought to maintain physical, mental and spiritual balance, transcended death and then was led into the temptations of a kaleidoscopic Devil. In reaching for his absolute apex and the zenith of his spiritual potential he has been struck down to absolute nothingness. In the process, he has been given a clear glimpse of divine enlightenment and the full culmination of his goal. In his fall from grace from The Tower (16) arcana, the initiate has regained his innocence and purity. He has been granted the insight into the real meaning of his faithful beginning as The Fool (0). Without purity, curiosity and belief in fate, the Fool would never have been granted this remarkable journey into the Royal Path of the Major Arcana. He can now gaze upon the Celestial Light which initially struck him in the intense flash of its luminosity.

The ancient Kabbalah mystics, being well aware of this final positive path in the transfigurative journey into illumination, identified this arcanum with the Hebrew letter He, which means window. The appearance of a gateway which reveals a consciousness outside our own realm of experience, gives us strength and determination on this, the last leg of our voyage into completion. In this sense, we see the connection of The Star (17) with the Strength (8) arcana, (1+7=8). However, the force we accumulate in this path slightly differs from that of the Strength path. The Star figure represents more than Strength's spirit overcoming matter. It symbolizes instead, the internal faithful wisdom of God consciousness, which transcends both matter AND spirit, revealing knowledge far beyond any ordinary sense of Self. We watch in slow motion as the stars illuminate the night sky pulling our perception out past existence and into the infinite reaches of the everlasting heavens. As we gaze through this 'window' at the limit of our own grasped reality, we feel in the core of our being, the undeniable assurance of celestial order and the incomprehensible scheme of far-reaching divinity. Herein, lies the true strength of this path, the clockwork turning and tuning of our dreams and aspirations into hope and eventually absolute faith. In a warm, welcoming swell of increasing inner light, the initiate assimilates and embodies in this cycle, the highest wisdom of Spirit and Soul. This is the Spirit/Soul as an intricate and intrinsic component of creation, beyond all conceptions of measurable time and space.

The Star (17) arcana portrays a nude and divinely pure, female figure. We recall the symbolism of the feminine aspect comprises two definite and nearly opposing principles, The High Priestess (2) and The Empress (3), respectively. The High Priestess represents the split of reality and the beginning of conceptual awareness. As such, she creates the nature of opposition and the energizing axiom of negative and positive polarity. Creating this gap in the center of existence, the High Priestess allows her counterpart, The Empress, to begin the process of healing and maternal union, the bearing of unconditional love. In short, the successive arcanas demonstrate how the feminine aspect creates and completes itself by dividing nature and then returning that austere division into finite and cyclical order. Accordingly, the female figure in The Star (17) arcana utilizes both principles of her nature to bridge the internal world of our Unconscious with the external world of our conscious awareness, the union of utmost polar opposition. This singular metaphoric enactment is depicted by the nude figure placing one foot in the water and one on dry land. Simultaneously, she pours from her two earthen and womb-like vessels, soil into the water and conversely, water onto the dry land. In placing each element into the heart of its opposite, the feminine aspect has gained the strength of divine acceptance and universal redemption.

This oneness is still further emphasized in the connection of The Star (17) with the combination of the Magician (1) and The Charioteer (7) arcanas. The path of the Magician initiates the spark of creation and embodies its underlying uniformity. The alchemist-like figure represents the balance of the four elements, or four corners of the universe, crowning him with the halo-like figure-eight symbol (1+7=8,) representing infinity and divine wisdom. The Charioteer, we remember, depicted conviction, controlled perseverance and ultimately, forward progress. Together, these respective arcana bring the erudition of an eternal persistence in the sublime order of all things to the initiate, on this his final cycle upon the Royal Path. The ongoing creation illuminates the darkness of our potential human ignorance and blesses us with the sanctity of our own soul. In this sense, we may compare The Star (17) Arcana with Temperance (14). Temperance, we recall, represented the flight of our soul which grew wings when it entered the Spiritual Plane of existence. The Star in turn, represents the final flight of that soul through the portal, or 'window', of our highest conscious into the full illumination of God's Celestial Light. This divine flight of soul is further suggested in the image of the red bird which sits atop a branch beside the female figure in the Star Arcana. The little bird, with its wings outstretched, is prepared to fly up into the weightless glimmer of divine translucence. The red color of the bird is loosely suggestive of the Phoenix, a mythical 'Bird of Fire' which is eternally reborn from its own ashes. This immortality of the Phoenix is comparable to the eternal integrity of the Soul. We also find an association in this red coloring with the God's Mercury and Thoth, as well as Hermes Trimegestus. The Mercury/Thoth/Hermes combination, the collective messenger of Gods, is comparable to the information gathering transfigurative soul and the transmutation of Alchemical metals into lighter and more powerful substances. Hence, the Hermetic principle is well documented in the Tarot Major Arcana. The initiate's soul is reflected in the immortal eternal flight through heaven, hell and earth of the trickster Mercurius Trimegestus.

The Star (17) Arcana symbolizes the telescopic aim of this Mercury/Soul/Initiate/Fool figure moving directly into the heart of The Sun (19) Arcana, which literally proclaims the Celestial Realm. The seven stars and one central star behind the naked figure in The Star Arcana represents the Gnostic Ogdoad. This Ogdoad is reached by an ascending soul which successfully passes through seven planetary archons (astrological spheres demonstrating successive levels of indoctrination.) Consequently, the Ogdoad represents the eight and highest spiritual level. As we have seen, the figure-eight refers to the absolute formula for infinite rebirth. Therefore, the Ogdoad is itself sugggestive of eternal God Consciousness (in our midst.)

The first stage of light in the path toward the Celestial Realm is found upon The Moon (18) Arcana. We are immediately reminded of the lunar crown of The High Priestess. This first light in the sky must be understood, internalyzed and transgressed before the initiate can move beyond its pull and into the divine purity of The Sun. The Queen Moon demonstrates yet another deceptive side of the trickster Mercurius, who doubles as The Magician, The Devil and The Fool and now, The Moon, in his never-ending embodiment of our soul's journey into Heaven.

To simplify the beginning journey into heaven, the appearance of The Star

(17) card in our dream, may well refer to feelings of sanctity and security surrounding a wide variety of circumstances and our responsive behavior in their behalf. The acceptance of our ultimate return into the immortal, fills us with glowing compassion and a functional ability to provide confederation with our fellow man. In our confidence and charity we can help fuction within a society with purpose, devotion and above all, grace.

THE MOON (18) (Tarot major Arcana) The last obstacle in the initiates journey through the major arcana and toward enlightenment is the unforgettable influence and elusive deception of The Moon (18) Arcana. The world of shadows, illusions, and magic, fills the realm of this rather complex level of the Tarot Path. We are faced with a warm inviting light in the night sky, which tugs at our most impassioned embrace of reality. However, this particular light is merely a reflection of The Sun. Nevertheless and without fail, the initiate craves to confuse it with the guiding light of spirit. The alluring pull of shadows and emotions, especially romantic ones, keeps the initiate bouncing from light to dark, in search of the dynamic cycle which will announce his definitive revelation. In this mad rush, the initiate mistakes The Fool for The Magician, The Devil for The Hermit and most importantly, The Moon for The Sun. Operating from this complete deception, the initiate tangles himself tighter into the inner spiritual maze and deeper into the perilous labyrinth of supernatural enlightenment. Lunacy becomes so prevalent in this arcana, that even the Tarot deck itself, becomes confused with worldly powers and unalterable future prophesy. The initiate believes his spiritual learning up to this point, has given him strength in and over the entire world. In this, he muddles matter and spirit and loses all sense of balancing their absolute opposition. He wildly dances with little faith in himself. Instead, he relies on the divine knowledge of his past journey and respective collected experiences. Unfortunately, his voyage is wholly incomplete and in this extremely self-evident void, the initiate leaves himself entirely vulnerable to the worldly pull of Self Aggrandizement. Needless to say, the initiate has returned to the most foolish behavior of The Fool (0), and worse, he has no awareness of his own folly. He has entered with exuberance, the rather visceral psychosis of personal delusion which could potentially harm him and cause him immense distress. Even if he remains rational enough to believe the reality of his own hype and establishes a foundation upon its frantic groundwork, he will eventually return, to the reality-check of The Tower (16) of destruction, given ample time. Unfortunately, this miscalculation may cost him a majority of his life time here upon the earth. Accordingly, it may have been The Moon (18) path itself, which inspired the phrase, 'So close and yet, so far!' In any case, the Tarot works in strange ways and the Moon card is the final litmus test for the ultimate realization of our own artifice.

The ancient mystics learned from experience and wisely associated this arcana with the letter Qoph, a frightening written term, which means Rear, or Back of the Head. The symbolism prevalent here is extremely remarkable, in that it examines a rather well known figure of speech. It concerns Ideas lodged in the back of ones head. We somehow have been behaviorally programmed to scratch the back of our heads when thoughts are muddled, or at least not readily available. Its as though, we plan to shake concepts loose from the rafters of our own cranium. In truth, our perception and memory is linked with our eyes, ears, nose and mouth, which are located in front of our head and facing an oncoming reality. In this paradox, we witness the metaphor of The Moon: knowledge which is ours, yet not quite, at hand. The back of the head holds wisdom, but we have yet to bring it to the forefront. Herein, we begin to discern the key to The Moon (18) arcana.

In the study of witchcraft, the student is warned about influential elementals or wandering spirits which possess a great deal of strength. The fledgling is instructed in exact procedure in casting spells and performing rituals. To misread a chant opens an initiate up to immediate and real danger. There is good reason for technical mastery. The wise old crone is quite aware of the hazards of shadows and misunderstood spirituality. It is her business to open the eyes of her students to the oneness of being, rather than the limited force of material manipulation. The source of all creation, is not to be perceived as simple magic, and should not (in any way) be taken lightly. Harmful effects and undesirable elementals represent the initiates folly into simple sorcery and material manipulation. The weakness of worldly control obscures the real journey of our Spirit Guide into the singularity of creation, known as the Ain Soph Aur. When a Zen master asks, 'What is the sound of one hand clapping?', he expects no reply other than, 'It is the center of being which allows me to speak of its singular glory.' To answer literally, would reveal the limitation of language and human awareness. Instead, the student must demonstrate his ignorance and humility under the eternal and many named creator. All in all, we find an aversion to trickery and self-deception in all forms of authentic spirituality. In wisdom, when the answer is not known, no answer should be offered. However, before we condemn The Moon (18) entirely, we must understand that the force of ritual and the elementals of the spiritual and natural world need not be ignored. In fact, they are ABSOLUTELY needed in the path of enlightenment. WE remember the crucial nature of the High Priestess who wears a wholly symbolic lunar crown. Simply put, we need to understand the force of the underside, or reflection, of spiritual enlightenment. At the same time we cannot be dragged into the alluring circus mirror of its hallucinatory and nonsensical reality. This necessary reflection of Celestial Light, gives the natural world the gift of depth and complex dimensionality. It reveals the subtle energy flow of creation and its healing and furtive principles. To follow our naturalistic drives, while mastering the balance of our internal energy swirl, offers us a significant glimpse into the overall miracle of creation.

This is why a glorious red bird launched the soul's flight from a tiny tree in the previous Star Arcana. The bird is reminisceent of the serpent in the Garden of Eden who lures Eve into decit by promising worldly wisdom and even God's own Divine knowledge. But in the end, we must not mistake the forest, for its lovely and exquisite leaves. In other words, man cannot force God Consciousness into himself; instead, man can only bring himself before God's definitive judgement. Hence, it is not for souls to judge God, but rather for God to judge souls. The bird/ snake in the Star Arcana returns to God. On this level, man has passed the test of his own pride and greed. Humility has erased Original Sin. Herein lies the elusive riddle which the interpretation of The Moon (18) arcana, cracks wide open.

The Moon (18) waxes and wanes and follows cycles which effect the rhythm of the seas, the skies and all life forms. Female Wicca tribes, dance under the moonlight in singular appreciation of this fertile and dynamic principle of swelling emotional power. Nature worshippers and nature herself, all species of life to the letter, react to the spinning, revolving moon orb and are drawn toward its intense pull. Mammals bark, yelp and howl when facing its pale facade in the night sky. This intensification of emotions leads all life forms into Spiritual Revelry. When the moon is full the police force readies itself for an increase in crime and mayhem as lunacy grips the populace of mankind. The astrological wheel and the dynamic principles of psychic awareness all focus upon the melodious pirouette of the moon beam on this intense plane of the Tarot. The initiate on this path dances in the 'Madness of the Moon'. He must be cautious of this first level of Spiritual Enlightenment. He must not mistake this level of illumination for the final God Consciousness. He cannot mistake spiritual power for the Source Spirit itself. In this, we observe the real influence of the moon in our life. It is a force which drives us, yet one which should not be followed with blind fascination. Instead, its reality needs to be integrated into our daily awareness. When we consider (for example) its all absorbing madness of desire, we immediately witness the sharpness of its double-edged sword. In one manner, the 'romantic' individual expresses his or her love under the moonlight and finds eternal bliss in the eyes of his or her soulmate. If the romantic individual's mate just happens to reciprocate this emotion, the couple may well live happily ever after, (or at least for a little while.) However, if the 'moon madness' is not mutually fulfilling, a broken heart may be the least of our very real concerns. These intense emotions could easily run the gamut from abuse, to rape, even outright murder. Courts of law recognize the outstanding number of 'crimes of passion' which occur across the globe. This brutal account of madness and mayhem is as far from our Valentines Day association of romance, as we dare to think about. Hence, we see in grim detail, how the REAL force of The Moon must be recognized, internalized and then absolutely held in boundary to run its proper course. The depth of our spiraling emotions (even on this level) must be balanced by our deepest faith in a power still greater than ourselves. It is plain to all, just how elusive this final proposal can be in the genuine intricacy of life. Little wonder this stage of the Tarot represents the last and greatest obstacle for the initiate, before he or she can cross over into final enlightenment. With incredible insight, the ancient mystics had discerned a perfect symbolic allusion for The Moon (18). They placed the Arcana's literal imagery at the 'back of ones head', where (as we shall soon see) it properly belongs. Later, we will witness why the 'Face of God' is symbolic of the true God Consciousness. This is why we are created in 'His Image, made them.' This coded message refers to our direct awareness of the Holy Work of Creation. We are in this light, (or perception,) face to face with the miracle of life, and there are NO shadows, illusions or deceptions. In sharp contrast, in the 'back of one's head,' we find intuition, sensitivity and memory. We are aware of the dazzling beams and shadows reflected from the true Light, but we have yet to bask directly in the Celestial Light itself. In every sense, we have yet to 'face the music!' We are empowered, intensified and mystical in this wizardry of The Moon. Indeed, we are magical, healing, even ghost-like, but even with all this craft-mastery, we are still not Spiritually Complete. We have yet to surrender ourselves completely to the brightest of lights, the far away white light which we first perceived way back upon the initial entry of the Ethereal Plane in this Complex Journey through the Royal Path of the Tarot.

As The Moon (18) arcana enters our dreaming mind, we must examine the complexity of its imagery in order to understand its exact statement in our waking experience. We witness the melancholy moon overhead two towers. In between the towers, (yet far off in the distance,) we witness a mountain range with a river emanating from its central apex. This great river flows directly toward our point of perception travelling a supposed great distance. At long last, this once mighty river has become a tiny stream which empties into a still pool directly before our frame of reference. Out of this pool, a crayfish crawls up toward the moon. Near the pool and ignoring the crayfish altogether, two large dogs are captivated by the countenance of the moon and bark at its morose expression. In this expansive symbolism we find a deceptive destination incurred by the potency of the moon itself. We are drawn toward the spiritual mountain beyond the towers of our own psychological development. In fact, our natural instincts seem to push us forward toward this immense pilgrimage, a representation embodied by the crayfish and dogs. The subterfuge, or full deception of the Royal Path becomes apparent when we realize the river from the mountain is flowing TOWARD us. The journey has already been taken, and we have already arrived at the pool of creation. Hence, to move toward the river's source would be the equivalent of walking backwards. We would be illogically following the force at the 'back of ones head'. Instead, we must learn to 'turn away' from The Moon and its symbolic mountain. The Sun (19) and its True Light is directly behind us. We must make a U-Turn and follow the same path as the river. We must never forget that The Moon is not The Sun, but a holy reflection of her Divine Light. The Moon in all its glory acts as our LAST symbolic compass heading. We must find and embrace The Moon and then turn around to come face to face with God Consciousness, just as The Moon herself does! The Moon is not at war with The Sun, the two are counterparts and perfect partners. In as much, the Unconscious bids us caution in following false prophets, ill-intentioned sorcerers and ANY one-sided fanatic spiritualists. The existence of the Unconscious reminds us that we must make the spiritual journey on our own. As such, we are certain to find the Divine truth within ourselves. Because, as the Royal Path demonstrates with ALL its individualistic characteristics: We are ALL the children of God Consciousness!

Returning to Earth and considering The Moon, (that is to say, in an every day sense,) the enigmatic arcana is reminding us to 'keep our heads' in romantic situations which could very easily lead us astray from our own better judgement and higher wisdom. Finally, the card tells us that we have approached sanctity in our own lives. We need not be drawn away from that illumination, by an illogical necessity to possess 'mysterious' power to overcome our world of hardships. We must learn NOT to conquer the world, but move instead with the fluctuating rhythm of its dynamic spirit.

THE SUN (19) (Tarot Major Arcana) In the full, life-giving radiance of The Sun (19) arcana, the initiate has attained the final stage in his search for enlightenment. In his calm and inner stillness, he accepts the presence of God within the totality of his being. He no longer needs to find, or chase, the truth of reality, as it symbolically shines above him and within him. This is the Spiritual Sun of God Consciousness. This is the elusive and divine 'Midnight Sun' as ancient mystics and seerers appropriately called it. This is The Sun (19) which never sets and holds us steady within its omnipotent luminescence. If we are centered within ourselves and our reality, we will surely be in tune and in line with its brilliance. The Fool (0) had to walk away from The Sun to begin the journey into himself. Nonetheless, he was completely empowered by the faith of that same radiant orb, which gave him 'hope beyond hope', that he would discover a true place and meaning in the world of experience. After his entire journey through the arcana, he finds himself under the same Sun (19) from whence he began. However, he is now deeper in knowledge, experience and everlasting faith. He always knew the surety of his innocence and belief in the wisdom of creation would eventually lead him back 'home'. This is why The Fool, being a fool, begins every far-off journey with the goal of reaching his own 'home'. It is no small coincidence that in The Sun (19) arcanum, we find a nude child with arms faithfully outstretched, joyfully riding a white horse. In this symbolism, we witness the glee of childhood innocence and its natural connection with Divine purity. The Fool is the child and he has returned 'Home'. Taking this to heart, the initiate on this path has surrendered all his Worldly, Etherel and Spiritual motives and motivations. He has returned to the purity of his utmost faith in life. At long last, he can now bask in the direct sunlight of his creator.

The true path of the Tarot is NOT complete, yet a center has been found which will remain the absolute beginning and ending of all return journeys into self discovery. Only in the wisdom of this singularity and highest purpose of existence, can the initiate complete the final two stages of the Tarot Major Arcana, Judgement (20) and The World (21), respectively remain.

The mystics of the Kabbalah, associated The Sun (19) path with the letter Resh, which means Face. This symbolism refers to the face of man and the face of God facing one another in union, one connection, in the totality of creation. As stated earlier, this is what was meant by the biblical passage, paraphrased, 'God created man, unto His own image.' The wisdom is not literal, but metaphoric, as the ancients understood the 'face' or 'image' as it referred to the human awareness of the Divine. The face of creation upon us and within us, guides our way in the world, which is gained through our direct comprehension of the one spirit, the soul of our being. Moreover, we face this reality with faith in our purpose and overall meaning in God's explicit creation. When Descartes said, 'I think, therefore I am.', his words echoed the concept of our awareness as the paramount and prime mover in reality. Naturally then, complete awareness of life's divine source replenishes us each day in our purpose in the Physical, Ethereal, Spiritual and finally Holy Universe of all existence.

To substantiate the highest symbolism of The Sun, we return to the physical sun of The Milky Way Galaxy which provides ongoing nourishment to all life forms on Earth and holds the planet itself in a constant life sustaining rotation. Before science, only faith guaranteed the return of this imperative sun after each Earth rotation. Likewise, The Sun (19) card may be viewed as the faithful magnetism beind ALL worldly behavior. It is the magnetic axis which bolsters our spiritual hope through all calamity and despair. It is The Hermit's lamp, which guides him through the darkness of worldly fear and the physical unknown. It is the lighthouse which provided each successive leap from lower to higher planes of our spiritual development. It is only through The Sun's spiritual light that our own mortality must be transcended. In this, death itself is accepted in its due time, without fear and with replete assurance of the intamacy of divine creation. We have a home to return to, even in death. We are a crucial part of God Consciousness and its infinite plan of being.

In so many ways, The Sun (19) has been the Celestial Light at the end of the tunnel, which revealed its omnipresent radiance in each stage of our otherwise blinding journey. In fact, the most perilous stage of the Major Arcana was the elusive Moon (18) path, simply because it falsely depicted the light of The Sun (19) and sent the initiate reeling backwards. However, it was only when the initiate finally realized the reflective powers of The Moon came from The Sun, (and appropriately reversed his heading,) that he was able to continue his direct journey into enlightenment. In all cases, the reality of faith is acknowledged prior to the initiate's passage into ANY and ALL Spiritual Development. As such, The Sun (19) is the first and final wisdom of faith itself. This concept of 'knowing faith', is not a contradiction in the land of the Midnight Sun, where the Unconscious guides The Fool (0) who holds all the world's wisdom in a tiny satchel cloth, suspended on a fragile branch, resting upon his narrowest of shoulders.

In The Sun Arcana we have moved beyond ALL contradictions. Spirit and Matter are no longer divided and we are far beyond any conception of the physical world as we once knew it. On this highest plane, the last phase of our long, Spritual journey, we must prepare ourselves for the final initiation into Eternity, in other words: Final Judgement. In a blink of an eye we have been spot-lighted by the lightning flash of Nirvana, Heaven and Satori! At long last the initiate's goal is at hand. We have come face to face with the Infinite Source of All Creation. The question now persists: "Are we worthy enough to remain in paradise, forever?" We will explore this question in the next full Path of the Major Arcana. That path, as we know, is called Judgement (20).

When The Sun (19) card appears in our dream, we may well be embracing the wisdom of our best decision making. In such a scenario, we demonstrate a complete confidence in our deepest inner faith. We have behaved consistent with our most integral and vital spiritual convictions. Nevertheless, chances are pretty high, we will continue to make foolish mistakes. However, as long as the source of our wisdom remains burning within us, we will maintain a fairly reasonable balance and relatively clear outlook on things. We regret to admit, there is a negative side to The Sun card's dream imagery. If the card should be turned upside down, the dreamer may need to question the absolute clarity of his or her insight. We may be offering our innocence to a worldly or deceptive force which seeks to turn us away from our deepest faiths and highest convictions. In as much, we may need to reexamine ALL powerful influences in our life and their real motivating factors.

JUDGEMENT (20) (Tarot Major Arcana) The previous arcana referred to man's unique place and purpose in the world. Conversely, the Judgement (20) figure points to God's singular intention for mankind. In short, its time for Judgement!

Is the diversity of human capacity, including: war, famine, murder, injustice, lust, hunger, greed, passion, sorcery, seduction, control, elation, devastation and mayhem, all directed for man's own amusement? The Tarot doesn't think so. Instead, these daily realities represent the replete learning process of humanity and one by one, test his ability to remain centered in spite of their overwhelming effect on his body, mind and soul. In short, the source of creation engages man to be at one with ALL universal transfigurations.

The Judgement (20) figure, calls every man, woman and child, (all pictured on the card itself,) to join in the union of creation. The archangel Michael/Gabriel blows his horn in triumphant announcement of the oneness of being. The human personifications emerge from coffins and their own figurative death. Those who cannot hear the horn, even after a life-time of learning, remain dead to the truth and suffer the consequences of an entirely disjointed and meaningless existence. This fundamental loss of truth (and ones eternal soul) is presented as an archetype throughout human history in a variety of metaphorical images of the afterlife, (and its natural counterpart,) the End of Time.

The conceptualization of Judgement (20) is a rather complex issue which involves several cross-cultural theological viewpoints with a myriad of diverse discernments. Notwithstanding, ALL these cultures possess more than a few ideologies (in common) about possible outcomes and occurances of Judgement Day itself. In all cases, the central denominator, or theme, of these arguments demonstrate the punitive aspects of The Almighty, in connection with his messenger, the human soul. Before we explore universal principles of the afterlife and immortality, we will examine cultural perceptions of The Human Soul.

Traditions such as the ancient Egyptians and Celtic Druids, linked the human soul with the living 'mouth', or breath of life. In Egypt, mummies were given the sacred rite of 'The Opening of the Mouth' to insure the five powers of sight, speech, hearing, taste and smell in the afterlife. As such, the soul was prepared (as a living functioning entity) for its final journey into the netherworld of Osiris and The Dead. In similar fashion, The Celts believed in the concept of an immortal soul which lived in ones mouth and necessitated three 'balanced' human aspects to assure its safe transition into paradise. They were crabhadh, creideamh and iris, which can be loosely translated as spirit, heart and mind. If the individual lacked any one of these characteristic traits in his behavioral existence, his or her soul may have run the risk of eternally wandering away from the body into other spheres of worldly existence. These outside spheres included animals, plants and even, inanimate matter. The best connection is made when we witness how this wandering soul moved up from the mouth of its original owner, into the mouth of another person or thing in search of a balanced nature. Hence, for both the Celts and Egyptians, the mouth was in fact, the true haven of the soul.

In this sense, we understand the interpretation of the Hebrew letter Shin and its association with the Judgement (20) path. Shin is translated as Fang or Tooth. We saw in the previous arcana of The Sun (19), how Face represented God in the archaic world. And now we see in the Celts and Egyptians how 'The Mouth' symbolized The Haven of Soul. Intuition follows that the sharp Tooth upon that Face, and within that mouth, rather graphically represents the ferocious bite (and blockade) of a singular Supreme Being. The fang illustrates to us that the time for judgement rapidly approaches the initiate'soul. Concerning this eventual judgemental bite, we analyze the controversy around specific punishments implemented upon individual human beings who refuse their souls entry into the final Spiritual Light. We say this to remind ourselves about one important fact. The choice of Spiritual Attainment has belonged to the initiate AND the individual, all along. Therefore, the choice of Satori has been His and his alone, all the way through the Tarot journey! No one else in the universe possesses power over an individual's (internal) spiritual choices.

We would like to say a few words about this choice and its compass-like targeting of either the humble light of spirit, or conversely, the proud darkness of the physical world and self-will. The decisions made in the course of a life-time sway from one extreme to the other, depending on a wide complexity of factors. The path of the Tarot examines this ongoing trial of errors and assesses the initiates wisdom and faith to 'stay the course' toward enlightenment. The Royal Path has been a maze of distinctly human possibilities, which involved several ascending stages of reason and wisdom. Each stage was justly needed in order to maintain forward progress toward the final knowledge of Self. At this moment, before the treasure of the labyrinth can at long last be attained, the seeker must ultimately face himself. Is the initiate truly worthy of eternal life? This fatal confession of Self is represented by the minotaur, symbolic of every individual's final affirmation, or denial, of Spiritual Worthiness.

To this end, the Royal Path has reached the culmination of its fourth cycle and the final aspect of its teaching. We find an allusion to the confession of self-worthiness, necessary before the human soul can voyage into eternity, in the embodiment of the Egyptian Sphinx. The mysterious half man/half lion which guards the entrance to the holy city of the great Pyramids of Giza, is regarded by many historians as the 'Great Sentinel of the Soul'.

The ancient Egyptians believed in eternal life for individuals who preserved their bodies and directly aligned (and sustained) their respective spiritual essences, Ba and Ka, (or mind and heart.) Having done so, the Pharaohs prepared themselves for the afterlife both internally and externally with their paradise-inspired miraculous pyramids. The Sphinx, which gaurds these pyramids, has faced the same sunrise for thousands and thousands of years. In its stolid nature it demonstrates the royal strength of the Pharaoh's perfectly sustained mind, heart and spirit. As such, he has remained eternally intact and has moved into the realm of the gods: Ra, Horus, Osiris and Nuit. Having reached the Holy Afterlife, the Pharaoh began a whole new existence fraught with dangers which needed to be successively overcome, simply by the balanced union of Ba and Ka. The proof of a deceased individual's worthy spirit in the afterlife was determined in a place called the Judgement Hall. In Judgement Hall, an individual demonstrated his 'declaration of innocence' in the elaborate retelling of his past (earth-bound) conduct and deportment. This moral proclamation was given to a collection, or jury, of forty-two gods. The last stage of the judgement of the fourty-two gods involved the weighing of a persons Ba, or heart, against one single feather. In Egyptian folklore, a feather represented purity, and hence, divine truth. If the man failed the test (by having too heavy of a heart, in other words, a guilty conscience,) he was devoured by another zoomorphic creature roughly half-Hippo and half-alligator. In this, we find powerful allusions to both the Soul's safe haven into the mouth of God, rather than that of the fierce Devil-like creature; AND, the critical self-examination of ones mortal Soul necessary before any entry whatsoever can be permitted into God Consciousness and the Eternity of Enlightenment.

In the image of The Minotaur we find a fierce bull/man with sharp horns who gaurds the treasure of the labyrinth. Like the Sphinx, this zoomorphic (half-man/half-bull) icon is both threatening and alluring at the same time. His strength, passion and will-power reminds us of our own perserverance in the long, spiritual journey of the Tarot maze itself. Similarly, the creature's sharp, ivory horns remind us of our own pointed honesty and the piercing of our physical body as we ritualistically scaled the successive stages of our spiritual learning. In this end of the Tarot Maze, we realize the Bull/Man is nothing more than an accurate reflection of our own final self-examination. We know this to be true because a real (and not symbolic) bull is not at all a violent animal by nature. In the world, it merely protects its herd and its territory. Furthermore, a bull charges toward a matador's red blanket ONLY because that blanket appears threatening, (like fire or blood.) Hence, the bull is not a violator, but rather a protector, even a gaurdian. Categorically, we come to understand why The Minotaur, (like the Sphinx,) must be the gaurdian of the entrance to Paradise. Accordingly, he will only attack the initiate on his way to Heaven if the initiate (who we have learned is actually a reflection of himself) has bad or harmful intentions within the bounds of Heaven. Does this mean we, the initiate, may intend to harm Paradise, or God? Of course! If our soul is not pure and our motivations are weak, we risk polluting the sanctity of God Consciousness forever. On the other hand, if our intentions are caring, moral and good, AND, we have served to protect rather than harm, we may (with great humility) be accepted into the eternal folds of the Divine Kingdom of the Royal Path. We, the initiate, have finally come head to head with our own moral conscience.

This is why The Minotaur, like The Sphinx, is the great tooth which gaurds the mouth (or Soul) of eternal transcendance. Will we chew ourselves up in our own worldly evil on our way to the final Judgement (20)? Or conversely, will the struggle of Self reveal our purity and humble acceptance of Satori. The time for decision is upon us; will we move into the mouth of Paradise?

The Egyptian is reminded of this Final Decision in the awesome sight of his Sphinx, which (as we have learned) guards the entrance to the timeless city of the netherworld. As such, both the Minotaur and the Sphinx represent the Supreme being's growling teeth, challenging man to test and approve his own worthiness in the face of eternal salvation.

The Judgement (20) arcana, in this same tradition, indicates the inevitable point in time when an initiate must ultimately face himself and choose between the internal light of truth, or the external world of selfish experience. If the wrong choice is made, the light of eternity is denied in favor of a finite material existence which ends our spiritual journey, perhaps forever.

Before we further explain this point, we should first address the cross-comparison between the Book of Revelations, found in the Holy Bible (remarkably similar to the Quran's view of Judgement Day entitled: The Great Event,) and the Tarot's Judgement (20) Arcana. We observe in both traditions a call to redemption and a rather practical 'End of Time'. In Revelations, we witness the end of the known world, with the second coming of Christ the Redeemer. Unlike his first appearance on the worldly plane, Jesus is no longer tolerant of man's sins. The time for judgement is now at hand. Jesus brings with him the unstoppable force of the seven angels of plague and wages an all out war against Satan right here in the physical world of man. Inevitably, the human race is divided into two armies, the faithful who stand alongside Jesus and the wicked, who comply with the sign of 'the beast', and follow Satan's Antichrist. In a violent upheaval of nature, (which includes the great seas changing into fiery cauldrons of peril,) good systematically conquers ALL evil. In the aftermath those human beings who sided with the Devil perish into the torturous darkness of nonbeing along with the Antichrist himself. Satan and his demons are forced into submission. They will not emerge again into the world of man for 'one thousand years'. On the good side of things, the one hundred and forty four thousand 'without sins in their mouth' (another allusion to the symbolic Soul) continue following Jesus and join Him in a new Heaven right here upon the Earth. Furthermore, those who have died throughout history with faith in God, raise out of their coffins and resume their previous forms, now unified with the Supreme Being. Those who have not died in Christ, remain in the death and darkness of Satan and await Judgement and individual punishment from God.

Now let us turn to the Judgement viewpoint of the Tarot. The symbolism of the Tarot begins with this same vivid imagery of Revelations, but varies quite a bit in its metaphoric translations; bringing it much closer to the archaic understanding of ancient Egyptians, Celts, Oglala Sioux Native Americans and a few modern Christian theologians. The end of time as it is portrayed in the Judgement (20) Arcana, pertains to an individual and his or her ultimate behavior in society, rather than the drastic end of society itself. Emerging from (symbolic) death, as pictured on the card itself, the initiate removes him or herself from the darkness of nonbeing. In welcoming the Light of Spirit, man becomes eternally revitalized in the purifying source of creation.

Likewise, modern Christian and Gnostic thought, sights the gospel of John 4:14 paraphrased, 'But whoever drinks the water I give: will never be thirsty. The water I give will become a spring of water gushing up inside that person, giving eternal life.' and John 4:5, 'I tell you the truth, unless one is born from water and the Spirit, he cannot enter God's kingdom. Human life comes from human parents, but spiritual life comes from the Spirit.' As such, the initiate flows into the infinite waters, rather like Loa-Tsu's ancient teachings concerning the circulating Way of Zen. In another sense, when we visualize the Collective pool of the Unconscious, we peer into the eternal and idealized formulation of God Consciousness. To accept evil involves a gradual degeneration of ones humanity, absorbed into a myriad of worldly forms, each with its own deceptive spirit, utterly unlike the sound human soul. In the Royal Path, the sanctity of SOUL is central to the conceptualization of eternal life. To this end, the Pharaohs of ancient Egypt sought to preserve their original human forms of flesh, in proper spiritual mortification techniques and in artistic renditions of themselves (in both sculpture and visible etchings.) All this was done to insure a soul's safe passage into the eternal realm, past Judgement Hall and into the paradise of the afterlife. For both the Pharoah and The Fool, union with God is no casual matter.

Undeniably, the Judgement (20) Arcana's imagery of fully realized man, or soulful man, does signal an ultimate death and rebirth of oneself, both internally and externally. In the numerological sense, we return to The High Priestess (2) (parallel to Judgement (2+0=2), who causes a chaotic duality which will eventually be mended by the matriarchal Empress (3) (parallel to The World (2+1=3). Judgement (20) signals the final division of all spirit and matter. This choice between spirit and matter is clearly elaborated in historic texts in the metaphorical imagery of both the Minotaur and Sphinx. However, (as we may have guessed) in the end of the Tarot labyrinth, spirit and matter are reunited as one principle, the reality of God Consciousness. This is the symbolic Heaven upon Earth mythified in most cultures belief systems. In the western tradition, Jesus Christ is the living metaphor, or archetype, of this union of spirit and matter (as Saint Peter is the metaphor for The Minotaur, the judge at the gate of Heaven.) The existence of Jesus reflects a beginning and ending, an Alpha and Omega, as Jesus himself phrased it. The statements of Jesus concerning redemption defy temporal exactness and enter a kind of Jungian Collective Unconscious. They persist omnipresent throughout the duration of existent time. For example, in John 11:25, Jesus declares, 'I am the resurrection and the life. Those who believe in me will have life even if they die. And everyone who lives and believes in me will never die.' As such, Jesus is psychologically linked with the past, present and future, simultaneously. This restates the concept of the spaceless and timeless realm of the Supreme Being. In this sense, we witness the actual fusion of both spirit and matter. Physical man becomes eternal, a being beyond body and soul. We have entered a new level of creation. It is in fact, the last golden age of existence. This is the plane which is aptly represented in the last and ultimate arcana, The World (21) Arcana.

Accordingly, Judgement (20) seems to indicate, in its similarity with Revelations and the Egyptian Book of the Dead, an individuals risk of losing the awareness of this new and fully ordained Heaven upon the Earth. Having refused to accept the divine light at the end of the Major Arcana the initiate has ultimately defeated himself. His lack of faith has caused him to be beaten by the minotaur Judgement (20) and he is justly denied entrance into the Eternal World (21) of infinite fulfillment. He must perish at the very gate of Heaven. So close, and yet so far...

At this point, we examine the symbolic resurrection of the dead at the commencement of time, when spirit and matter become one. If at the moment of death, a single human being steps into God Consciousness (into the White Light), he or she has entered the often mentioned, spaceless and timeless realm of the Supreme Wisdom. Hence, should the physical world of man (spirit and matter) come to a crashing, cataclysmic end, ten thousand years after that individual's singular death, his or her resurrection into the Heavenly plane is still gauranteed. Having moved into the Celestial Light the individual immediately appears in the End of Time. Logically, the transition would not be recognized by the individual who has been in the timeless, spaceless suspended animation of the Almighty Being. The initiate, unhampered by physical time, would move directly from his death into the perfected Heaven on Earth created at the end of time. In this Light, and in a single moment, all of mankind simultaneously joins in the fellowship of its own miraculous existence. Moreover, The Creator in this way, reunites all men and woman from all time and disparate stations of existence, into a single and equitable confederation of permanent and profound consciousness. Mankind becomes one with the singular awareness of the all-encompassing foundation of Eternal Being. This realm will be elaborated still further in our discussion of the World (21) arcana, which culminates the Royal Path and transcends The Fool (0) into the allegorical wholeness of complete self-realization.

Appropriating this conceptualization of Judgement (20), and its intricate concern with eternal life, we need to systematically reconstruct its visual appearance in our dream scenario. On the surface, the card could be warning us not to lose spirituality in our waking worldly behavior. However, on a much deeper level, the arcana symbolizes the exact moment in time when an individual must face himself in a truthful assessment of his own personal merit and virtue. The darkness, often mentioned in this section, concerns the lies within oneself, the hiding of ones soulless actions in life. The dream may inquire if we are truly prepared to face the light of honest exposure? In another sense, The Unconscious may be aware of an individual's real progress toward Personal Enlightenment and now forces the hand. In all cases, the key revolves around the knowledge of self and its honest internal verdict. Before we can be judged by The Celestial Light, (symbolic of not only God, but also, society at large,) we must first fully surmise ourselves. If we are worthy of the light of truth, we can return to our existence upon Earth and assist in the creation of a veritable Heaven upon its sacred surface.

THE WORLD (21) (Tarot Major Arcana) In the examination of The World (21) symbolism, we will address both ecclesiastical visions of paradise, as well as philosophical interpretations of a worldly Utopia. At first, the two paths toward eternal fulfillment may seem radically different. However, we will observe how and why, both conceptual tenets operate as one fully functional mechanism, both designed to guide an individual toward the context of a cohesive society.

In order to accomplish this, we must first turn to the conceptual meaning of morality and social ethics in general. In the orthodox spiritual tradition, we observe the position of 'Goodness' as a conscious effort to achieve a sociable fairness which effects the whole of the community. In this sense, we find a built-in balance of human involvement. Within this communal nurturing, the individual is subordinate to his entire people. In this light, no man strives to advance personal gain at the expense of his brother, neighbor or fellow man. In fact, great measures are taken in the form of laws, or commandments, to insure this selfless behavior.

We find in this order of tantamount existence, a structure where each man and woman cares about the entire populace more than him or herself, a link with a unifying principle, or God. In theory, God too is concerned with the whole of mankind. As such, human beings do not need to be overly concerned about their own needs, rather, in this pious observance of social equality, man pleases his creator and is each taken care of, one at a time. Since, this conceptualization of a sympathetic and benevolent God is beyond man, He is attributed to his laws, or commandments, of human justice.

Unfortunately, man lives and dies and experiences extreme and profound difficulties in his worldly existence. This causes many men to question a caring God, who seems to have abandoned their particular needs and human consolation. To this end, man begins to ignore the needs of his fellow man, in favor of accumulating his own requirements. Gaining power in the world, man loses his sense of communal unity and increases his personal force and desire. He reaches a point where he has conquered all his fear of hunger, pain and personal destitution. He feels untouchable and impenetrable. This single behavior is symbolic of man's ultimate fall from grace.

In answer to this fierce individualism, religious and political leaders, (most of whom have already surrendered to this personal temptation of gain themselves,) provide man with a two-fold vision which is meant to guide them back toward the equality of spirituality under their just creator. The first image details an angry God, who is intolerant of man and his greedy, obsessive behavior and prepares to destroy the whole sinful lot of them. The second image depicts a forgiving God, who is willing to return man to the splendor and sanctity of His own presence, if and only if, each and every man and woman willingly changes their selfish, anti-social ways upon the earth. Naturally, there is only one way to explain this vision of divine reward or punishment to a logical mankind.

Herein, we introduce the historic meditation upon eternal life. Only in the vision of life after death, may we find an instantaneous return to the Face of God. In this sense, whether The Supreme Being will be angry (or pleased) with our chosen actions upon the earth is what we literally need to question. Instantaneously, the concern of morality is returned to the earthly plane of existence. Man, in order to find eternal happiness and avoid eternal pain in the process, needs to return to his selfless behavior. He is taught to fear a divine reality (God) far greater than himself. Be good on earth, or suffer the pain of hell, forevermore. The Tarot seeks to teach The Fool, rather than threaten him. The Tarot realizes the truth of God in all things and in all worlds. Lastly, the Tarot accepts no conceptualization of Hell, other than the loss of Heaven. As such, It is an extremely personal decision to accept God Consciousness. If this freedom of choice threatens the society of man, then that society of individuals needs to fully examine themselves. Likewise, we must each answer to ourselves and our own presonal merit before God to create a better society. But we cannot be driven by our own fears. We cannot expect our fear of a promised damnation to help us to build a loving and altruistic society of man.

In the Judgement (20) Arcana, we examined some of the connections between Judgement Day and Eternity. We theorized the possibility of all life after death occurring simultaneously, a mass awakening in the context of a Judgement Day which occurs at the end of time. We are finally and definitively judged at this moment and there is no turning back. Nevertheless, we deliberately omitted a key discussion concerning the temporal occurrence of this End of Time.

Legitimately, we can never know the exact date of such a cataclysmic event; however, we CAN speculate on the ideal futuristic climate for such a phenomenon to occur. In this, we explore the connection between the secular and nonsecular Utopian visions of a paradisiacal society. The concept of an evolving community of man which gathers information and incorporates this information into a clearer understanding of its own future goals, is one which we readily agree to accept in today's world. Modern philosophy continues to gear the human race toward an inevitable communal mind which concerns itself with the whole of man as well as with each and every individual being. To this end, we seek to break down the barriers of historical prejudices and age-old fears. Slowly, but surely, the wisdom of diverse cultures are comprehended and the world grows ever smaller, falling within the visible scope of personal reason. We are now able to deal with our fellow men and women and demonstrate our actual respect for each person and his or her society. In time, we realize the common thread of our humanity and formulate a meeting of minds.

However, we soon discover the ideal sanctity of this meeting, or confrontation, involves a serious discussion concerning the absolute means necessary to provide a final social justice and individual contentment for all human beings, (who now seek to altruistically come together.) In this time, the great and final swell of individuality will rationally be felt, as each side offers its own 'wisest' solution toward world peace and reconciliation. In this increasingly heated debate about the highest wisdom, (or best Holy Laws,) the spectacle and history of man may well become re-ignited and create a towering inferno of hatred and animosity which would block the entrance into a Utopian reality, perhaps forever.

Consequently, this would be the reasonable climate for an active Judgement Day, both physically and spiritually. Man, having done everything in his power to bring about peace, would now be facing his figurative Self. This is the whole of society, (rather than just the individual;) facing its reflective Minotaur and Sphinx.

In this struggle, the battle between human love and human hate would be fully waged. In the final decision of peace over war, man would indeed reinvent himself. The aftermath of this struggle would explore the Utopian world of a Heaven upon Earth, or man's final and complete acceptance of the miracle of his own kind.

If conversely, humanity deems itself unworthy of continued existence, absolute death and extinction was always there as an option. The creation of atomic weapons and the senseless disregard of the natural environment, signal two proponents of this willful destruction. Sigmund Freud spoke about the Death Instinct within man, which seeks to utterly destroy itself out of existence. Although this behavior has been deemed fashionable and hip in a modern world whose future seems dark anyway, the truth nevertheless weighs heavily upon our human mind. We have always known the truth. Each man is his own worst enemy. No man can deny the harm he's done to himself living in a world of hatred. If, on the other hand, each man chose to follow the light of his highest self, he would soon be embodying the best of everything which life has to offer. In our darkness we attack not only the whole perceived world, but most importantly, ourselves. We can (once and for all) embody the personality which we expect to see in others. We can do this if we realize we are all reflections of the same Light. In this simple examination of self, both philosophers and theologians find the eventual Heaven on Earth, where mankind is well taken care of and mutually supportive of life itself. In this we find an ideal world of spirit. This is the fifth plane where God Consciousness fuses spirit and matter. All realities have merged and we live in a loving (and logical) harmony.

Naturally, the Kabbalists are always right on top of things. Which is why the Hebrew letter for the World (21) Arcana is (and can only be) Tau, which means cross, or balanced connection. As we have seen earlier, the archetypal image of Jesus upon the crucifix, presupposes the fusion of spirit and matter, and furthermore, marks the metaphoric resurrection beyond all life and death. In as much, we witness the final Heaven on Earth signalling the highest plane of ALL existence, bringing full circle the wisdom of The Almighty and His (once cast out) creation, called: man.

The numerological interpretation of the World (21) Arcana agrees with this logic. Accordingly, the World (21) path is linked with the High Priestess (2), or separation, and The Magician (1), or world unity, finally completing its indicative descending pathway into The Fool (0), or THE NEW POTENTIAL OF FAITHFUL ENLIGHTENMENT.

In this sense, The Fool (0) and The World (21) become one and the same, the symbolic alpha and omega of purposeful human existence. Moreover, the connection of these Major Arcanas, returns us to the allegorical Empress (3) or $(0)+(21)=(3)$, which once again indicates the acceptance of BEING in her own immaculate matriarchal fashion. We see how the cycle never ends and is Eternally reborn.

In a vivid representation of its connection with The Fool and The Empress, the World card depicts a welcoming female-like figure who is beyond all opposites, including spirit and matter as well as male and female. She is the hermaphroditic allusion to Celestial Being, the center of all reality, which transcends the four elements of creation. On the outside corners of the card itself, we find the bull, eagle, lion and man, which represent the four elements. They also represent the heart, mind, spirit and will of man. The wreath which surrounds the male/female figure and welcomes the world of man, signifies the peaceful union of everything that ever was and everything which will ever be. He/she is the completion of the Major Arcana and the beginning of everlasting wisdom. She is the past, present and future of all the World's potential.

The appearance of The World (21) card in our dreams implies all the love and faith we carry within us in the context of our waking world. It demonstrates the promise we offer to the overall existence of man. Our actions are reflected in society and have a profound impact upon our future lives. If we long for a Utopia, or eternal paradise of being, we need to actively strive toward this goal. We cannot lie back and complain about all the outside evils presented in the world around us. When confronting our own personal spirit, we must understand what we can actually do to improve the genuine quality of life on the earth. This must include the full acceptance of diverse humanity and its complex historical condition. We must view existence as a whole, fully aware of the undeniable chain-reaction of ALL our behavior. In as much, we need to treat humanity and nature as our own children, because in every way, we are the guiding light of tomorrow... And this is the message of the Tarot, the aptly titled Royal Path of Spiritual Enlightenment.

TAR PIT The conceptualization of the Tar pit revolves around the stagnation of self and all its possibilities. Due to its extreme nature, the pit may refer to repression which halts our entire living process rather than certain isolated elements within that life. As such, these limitations may be very abstract and all encompassing. For example, we may be referring to a difficult childhood or a problematic marriage. In either case, an allusion is made to permanence and this may need to be addressed by the dreamer, especially if the dream is recurring and/or occurs quite often.

TATTOO The image of a tattoo elicits deep passions concerning freedom, aggression and perhaps, anti-social behavior. As such, the dream tattoo may be reflective of our escape from social norms and/or constraints. Moreover, since a tattoo is permanent, our unconscious may be illustrating a fixed determination concerning our iconoclastic new lifestyle. Furthermore, a tattoo is symbolic of the symbol itself, embodying an image which portrays the spirit of the individual who wears it. In this sense, the tattoo can be viewed as a complex icon which elucidates the alliance of portrait to artist, artist to subject and subject to portrait.

TEA The symbolism of Tea may refer to calm repose and a temporary cessation from the difficulty of everyday life. Moreover, the drinking of tea may depict a delicate contemplation of being. As such, we need to explore where we drink the tea and why we drink the tea. Moreover, we need to examine the symbolism of hot liquid, which may involve a delicate warming of emotion, and the cup itself, which may illustrate rather complex feminine sensibilities including passion, love and childbirth. (see Water) (see Cup)

TECHNICAL   The Technical dream may imply complicated workings in our life which function in painful, yet dynamic symmetry. As such, our unconscious may be illustrating the combination of all our responsibilities and endeavors and demonstrating the effect of this conglomeration upon our psyche. In as much, we need to determine the complex process of our waking life and whether or not it needs to be simplified. Perhaps, we function well in this stressful prism of reality, in which case, our technical skill may come fluidly and with apparent naturalistic ease.

TEETH   In the dream sense, a loss of Teeth refers to our feelings about aging and death, especially in a dream involving the loss of teeth or the rotting of teeth. Moreover, the conceptualization of bad teeth may refer to our fears about poverty or inadequacy in a relationship or social situation involving status. We may be illustrating feelings of ineptitude in our occupation, social sphere interaction, or even in maintaining the responsibilities of our family life. In this sense, a sort of forward regression may be taking place where we view ourselves obsolete in our present environment. Accordingly, the image of perfectly intact teeth may imply hunger, aggression and sexuality which seeks to bite into present realities. (see Bite) (see Mouth) (see Jaws)

TELEPATHY   Examining the theoretical approach of Carl Gustav Jung's collective unconscious, (see Collective Unconscious) we find the internal and personal world of individuality, linked to the external world of an entire human species. Compounding this theoretical union, with the elaborate system of retaining unspoken details about one another in family and loving relationships, we begin to witness a seemingly mystical, yet entirely corollary understanding of the human nexus. Further clarifying, in a relationship, we begin to know the thought patterns and in fact, the very thoughts (and feelings) of our mutual partners, whom with we share life's experiences. When these individuals are no longer involved in our immediate experience, we nevertheless retain a part of their fundamental being. Accordingly, the collective unconscious and the unconscious dreaming mind, occasionally bridge together to 'see','hear' and 'feel' these individuals, especially in times of intensely high levels of stress or anxiety, and even though they are literally thousands of miles away from us. For example, Mrs. Rosalie Richardson, a respected editor in broadcasting, conveyed a dream she had experienced involving an old boyfriend from her teenage years. She had not seen or thought about this man in over fifteen years, yet one night he suddenly appeared in her dream full of life, charismatic and entirely animated. Both he, Rosalie and the entire group of 'kids' who hung out together in that particular period of her life materialized in the dream landscape. Mrs. Richardson went on to explain how her once boyfriend was not only curiously lively, but also bright and vivid in rich chromatic hues of color, while she herself and her other friends appeared drab and essentially black and white in demeanor. Several months later, she learned that her resplendent ex-boyfriend in the dream had passed away after a long period of suffering illness. After mourning the loss of a once dear friend, Mrs. Richardson's dream came flooding back in her memory. Reflecting on the strange vision, she recalled a book she had read based on channeling spirits. In this book, she recounted, a certain 'spirit' chastised the working medium for his lack of knowledge and understanding in the fundamental matters of reality. The spirit alluded to the drab darkness of the medium's ignorance and his limited use of a fantastic elemental soul. In this instance, Mrs. Richardson understood the vivid, knowing spirit nature of her friend, who at the moment of his dream arrival, no longer joined the ranks of the one-dimensional, earthbound living... (see Clairvoyance)

TELEPHONE The Telephone has become such a normal part of our existence, we barely acknowledge its ever present reality. However, in a dream landscape, its appearance is almost always symbolic of communicating with someone who is virtually unreachable. This is why we often dream of receiving telephone calls from departed loved ones, famous persons, angels or even God. In this sense, the call generally refers to a warning or communication about ourselves or our loved ones which we cannot perceive for ourselves, for whatever reason. As such, the phone voice may refer to a part of our consciousness (belief system, desires etc) which is repressed and barred access from our reality in waking life. Nevertheless, the phone metaphor reaches beyond that line of repression and rings in the news of the self, directly to our waiting finger tips and eager ears.

TELEVISION The bright screen in virtually every home and known as T.V. illuminates our existence with fragmentary images of the entire world of perception. As such, in a dream, the television screen becomes the dream within a dream. Its images reflect the concerns of our unconscious who recreates them through memory. The purpose for this image within an image centers around the need for focusing in on its intended message. Our dream may be revealing a media medium for comprehension of data. Accordingly, we need to watch the 'show' and determine its symbolic language.

TEMPTATION The conceptualization of Temptation in a dream sense, involves a symbolic desire. That is to say, what tempts us in our dream may represent deeper longings and/or wishes, than the single objects which are witnessed in the dream itself. For example, gazing hungrily at a candy bar in a chocolate shop window, may illustrate a perceived separation from the sweet, good things in life. We may feel guilt in procuring the more precious experiences offered in existence. In this sense, temptations become a sort of meeting ground between craving, physical needs and moral, judgmental, spiritual restraints per se. Akin to a scale of decision, temptation asks us which way we want to go; the way of indulgence or the way of abstinence. From a psychological point of view, the middle ground is perhaps the healthiest and obviously best balanced ethical existence, the space between the demon and the zealot. (see Demon) (see Devil)

TERMITE Since a house is representative of the self, the image of Termites may well involve forces eating away at the fabric and very foundation of self. The conceptualization of infestation involves a slow process wherein tiny pests, symbolic of obstacles and dilemmas, gradually accumulate into swarms, which eventually cause us unimaginable turmoil. Appropriately, we need to address our difficulties in waking life, one problem and solution at a time, thereby beginning the business of reducing their overall impact upon us. In this way, a step-by-step healing procedure may begin to take effect on our psychological perception of the world around us.

TERRACE The view from a Terrace symbolizes our gaze at the outside world, from a comfortable vantage point. In this sense, we may be illustrating high spirits and/or lofty results in our undertakings. In an archetypal sense, we are akin to kings and queens who address their courts with towering and commanding status; status which may in fact be unreachable to us, were it not for these convenient and relatively democratic terraces. In this sense, in a capitalistic society, the more successful one becomes, the more elevated of a terrace he or she may be privileged to enjoy.

TEST In a dream, a Test may refer directly to being challenged by some force (institution, society) greater than oneself. As such, the dreamer is asked to prove knowledge and/or ability. In waking life, these tests of merit occur quite often. However, in the psychological sense, these recurring test dreams may imply a fear of performance in quite specific terms. In as much, cases where dreamers score high results in examinations are exceedingly rare. Predominantly, we find anxiety and difficulty in the test undertaking. Naturally, many of us abhor the thought of having to certify our relative worth. In the case of the test dream, we are absolutely rebelling against the entire concept. (see Quiz)

THREE The number Three, or the triad, involves the unbreakable strength of spirit. Moreover, the first odd numeral illustrates uniqueness and the principal dialectic creation born of dualism. As such, the number three becomes a new beginning on which to build the ultimate dualism of four (see Four), or two twos. Herein, lies the strength of the number, embodying a completion and an introduction simultaneously. In the dream sense, three-sided figures represent permanence and the infinite potential of transfiguration. Note the resilience of the triangle and taken one step further, the great pyramids based on the same geometric design. (see Tarot Major Arcana: The Empress (3) arcana)

TIE The idea of being Tied up in a real sense indicates the removal of freedom. To be bound in a dream landscape reveals a forced restraint upon oneself by outside forces and/or situations. As such, our unconscious reminds us we may not be exercising our full potential freedom. Furthermore, the dream may imply that a person is tied in knots, symbolic of complication and hard misunderstanding. We may need to simplify matters, thereby unwinding their knots and otherwise cut free from the physical, mental or spiritual noose they insistently become. In another interpretation, independence requires a certain amount of courage and responsibility, therefore being tied up illustrates a way out of this accountability without remorse or regret. In this sense, being tied may refer to sexual indulgence without condemnation, guilt or liability. We cannot be blamed for actions we are forced into and cannot hope to escape (even if we ourselves purchased the rope, straps and/or handcuffs!). (see Knot)

TIGER As opposed to a lion, which exhibits nobility, the Tiger remains wild, untamed and inhumanly ferocious. However, because of these characteristic traits, the tiger is thought to represent sexuality in all its unlimited carnal release. Moreover, the strength of the tiger comes to symbolize a powerful sexual partner who assumes control of the entire experience. In the potent imagery of the leaping animal, we interpret a leap of instinctual faith in ones abilities, sexual or otherwise. In the Chinese zodiac, the tiger personality is seen as aggressive and courageous, yet also as a deep thinker who dwells within his or her own being. The connection with our deepest primal memory is rather complex in that it demonstrates our fiercest survival instincts, as well as our profoundest union with earth and her natural elements. The tiger dream may explore the tenets of our intuitive behavior and all its inherent consequences in a so-called 'civilized' world.

TIME In the dream sense, Time refers to our concern about temporal elements. For example, a dreamer may be expressing anxiety involving his or her difficulty with punctual deportment, in a dreamscape where he or she arrives late for a high-profile business meeting, wearing only polka-dot shorts. Another example of temporal dreams, revolve around the repetitive image of a clock, or symbolic 'clock-watching' behavior. Moreover, a dreamer may be depicting the reality of becoming a slave to time, when the concern of the physical hour dominates all other dream considerations. (see Clock)

TOILET The image of the Toilet may represent the lowest position of our relative humanity, that is to say, the reality of our bodies eliminatory functions. In this sense, when we become nauseous, incontinent and otherwise irregular, we almost instinctively and entirely automatically run to the proverbial toilet. Besides its obvious function (the miracle of plumbing!), the reason we escape to the john, may involve our first lesson of bodily control and proper human behavior, that is: Toilet Training. Ergo, in our time of need, we return to our roots and root understanding of a solution to our discomfort and the elimination (disappearance) of our bodily waste. The combined reality of our inescapable animal nature and a hope to effectively hide this nature, may be involved in the dream analysis of the toilet. Accordingly, the john may symbolize guilt and/or a rationalization concerning our animal needs and/or functional behavior. (see Feces)

TORCH The age-old symbol of the Torch involves victory and outright power innate in humanity's control over flame. Moreover, the image of fire held in hand invokes dominance over the natural world, including and especially, the world of darkness (night). In yet another sense, the torch represents real wisdom which blazes through the darkness of ignorance. In all cases, the hand-held flame acts as a trigger and catalyst of fortitude, both internal and external. Therefore, in a dream landscape, the actions involved around the manipulation of the torch and that which is illuminated by its fire, may reveal the potential of our personal and/or social abilities, dynamic and mighty as any metaphorical flame. (see Lantern) (see Ablaze)

TORNADO The symbolism of the Tornado may refer to the real possibility, yet not certainty, of chaotic danger in our life. As such, we need to determine which facets of our waking condition may place us in the potential path of this harrowing peril. Moreover, the image of solid structures dislodged and uprooted, may involve a threat which concerns our deeply rooted psychological fabric, including perhaps, the equilibrium of our home and family life.

TOWEL The concept of the Towel may involve wiping away the wetness of ones drenched emotions and moving into another psychological plain. Furthermore, since a towel is associated with the completion of cleansing oneself, our unconscious may be illustrating the conclusion of a purging event. In other words, we may be implying to ourself, that we have paid our dues and are prepared to begin anew. As such, we may need to evaluate conditions, relationships or situations in our waking life, which may in fact be resolved and/or readied for transition into another and entirely new stage of experience. (see Water) (see Wash)

TOY The image of the Toy carries with it the reality of our childhood. In this sense, we need to interpret our feelings about the toy. Are we almost unnaturally drawn toward it? If so, we may be exhibiting signs of regression which may in turn signal difficulty in coping with the complexity and responsibility of our present waking life. On the other hand, if the toy is discarded, we may be displaying feelings of wasted youth or intolerant youth, which may indicate mental barriers which need to be overcome. Naturally the color and type of toy is essential in the meaning of the entire dream sequence. (see Wall) (see Wagon) (see Child)

TRAFFIC The idea of Traffic is synonymous with being held back from ones goals. The reasons for this personal cessation are many and varied, however, the predominant cause involves the accumulation of many individuals with the same purpose and intent as ourselves. Consequently, a dream involving traffic may illustrate a personal psychological struggle to succeed or be left behind. Moreover, our unconscious may be revealing a feeling of personal anonymity, thereby relinquishing our individuality into the grand mix of society at large. This loss of identity, may in turn, act as the very catalyst which holds us back from our goals and subsequently, impedes all forward progress we may have enjoyed on a self-created and entirely individuated path of life.

TRAIN In the modern world, the Train harks back to an earlier age where transportation was slow, deliberate and entirely scenic. In as much, the train dream involves a survey of changing landscapes and metaphoric lives. In this, we may see a physical act of decision making, concerning our fundamental heading in life. Moreover, the image of one lover departing another by train represents a long, painful separation with much thought and lingering emotion on the part of both parties. This exaggerated parting implies a desperate hope for a last minute change of heart, perhaps directly proportional to the moving distance of the partner left behind. As such, we witness a moment by moment change of landscape, which changes our internal point of view of life in general and precisely. Accordingly, the train dream may illustrate our 'train' of thought and list of possible life options. However, if we find ourselves tied to the tracks and a locomotive train is steaming toward us, we may be implying disastrous life consequences based on erroneous decision making.

TRANSMUTATION The concept of Transmutation involves man changing into animal. In this we see a visual transition of psychological states of mind. Metaphorically, the 'animal' represents our primal, ancestral and deepest consciousness. Conversely, the 'man' which undergoes change, becomes symbolic of our modern civilized world and the moral decision making, which takes place in that world. In the act of transmutation, our unconscious may be illustrating the relative levels of movement between these two internal worlds of our experience. Moreover, in cases of dream zoomorphism, we find a direct balance and poignant interaction between our foundations of perceptual memory. (see Zoomorphism) (see Reincarnation)

TREE The complex symbolism of a Tree involves wisdom, strength and silent contemplation. As such, the mighty tree reaches toward heaven with branches extended and digs deep into mother earth with stolid and laborious roots. In the dream sense, the image of a tree may refer to our spiritual and/or well-balanced heading in life. Accordingly, a bowed tree may indicate a harmful or destructive path taken in life. Conversely, a rounded and spiralling tree may illustrate a wealth of rich experience in ones animated journey. (see Oak) (see Evergreen) (see Joshua Tree)

TRENCH The act of digging a shelter into the soil of earth may represent a return to the womb, in other words, regression back into the familiar territory of mother and childhood. In the illustrious dream scenario of a fox hole, where soldiers hide from bullets and violence, our unconscious may be illustrating a fear of being exposed and targeted by outside forces. Taken together, we witness the symbolism of the Trench as it involves insecurities and a refuge from painful realities. In yet another sense, a trench may represent a ditch which we unexpectedly fall into, most especially when we waver from our direct course of ideas, ideals and personal faith. (see Den)

TRIBE The basic tenets of social interaction and group organization can be clearly focused on in the systematic study of Tribal behavior. As such, the tribe reflects the physical, mental and spiritual connection innate in highly interactive human beings. Consequently, the tribal dream illustrates our innermost union with one another and moreover, the universal implications of this elaborate network of association. Accordingly, we witness a transfiguration toward nature's spiritual source when we embrace the family of man and deeper yet, the interconnectedness of ALL life on earth. (see Taboo) (see Ritual)

TROPHY In the dream sense, a Trophy may refer to a richly deserved reward given in life. Accordingly, our unconscious may be illustrating the merit of our time spent on a noble and perhaps difficult, project. However, a trophy lost or imparted to a competitor, may symbolize resentment involving a lack of desired recognition for our efforts. Furthermore, if the trophy is broken or damaged, we may be indicating a spurious social or interpersonal appreciation for our laborious task.

TRUNK A Trunk may be symbolic of restless behavior which entails incessant travel. Furthermore, the clothing and necessary belongings found in a trunk suggest ones possessions and acquisitions appropriated in life. Therefore, a single chest of goods may reflect a simple or meager existence, while a truckload of trunks (i.e. commodities) illustrates wealth, power and perhaps old wisdom. In an alternative dream landscape, we may find ourselves burying a chest, or conversely, searching for 'buried treasure'. In both cases we may be illustrating a poignant concern about our economic well-being and subsequently, the security of ourselves and our entire family. (see Chest)

TUNNEL The trip through dark, subterranean regions in search for light and a re-emergence into new psychological landscapes, may involve a narrow and difficult period in our life which searches culmination, redemption and a return to a freedom of movement. Furthermore, the concept of the Tunnel pertains to the peculiar restriction of claustrophobia, which roughly parallels a fear of death replete with isolated coffins and graves. In yet another variation, this tunnel image is equated with being trapped in the pre-existence of the womb, where hope for complete expression is yet to be fulfilled. Hence, we search for the light of birth and creation at the end of our long, dark tunnel of uncertainty and slow, yet consistent, development. (see Labyrinth)

TWINS The symbolism of Twins may refer to different underlying characteristics in similar appearing entities. Consequently, the dream image of twins may refer to a split personality in oneself. In other words, this characteristic twinning effect may imply an internal argument which equally explores opposing sides of a particular conjecture. (see Double)

TWO The archaic symbolism of the numeral Two involves the paradoxical nature and division of balance found in duality. Accordingly, the image of two items represents the partition of one item into two halves. Conversely, a reflection of one object may become a dual image of a single entity. In other words, two connote the double-sided nature of existence. In the dream sense, two persons or objects may refer to two sides of a single story. (see Double) (see Twin)

TYRANT   In the dream sense, a Tyrant may refer to improper and self-serving leadership. Accordingly, we need to determine the motivations of our dream tyrant, and what this symbolic person tells us about ourselves. Moreover, we need to analyze any and all representational uses of force or aggression indicated in the dream landscape. In most cases, the Tyrant is not meant to be king, and implies a confusion in the natural order of things. (see King)

U

UFO   The image of a UFO, or space crafts in general, involves a dire hope for something entirely new in the realm of experience, which hold the key to deliver us from ourselves, in other words, the limitations of our reality. The UFO perceptively travels through space, and perhaps even time, and, in the very essence of their living breathing being, transcend all earthly realities. In this, they may in fact, seem able to solve ALL our self-imposed, yet nevertheless complex, ensnarements of civilization. This factor gives them unbelievable emotional, as well as, psychological appeal. It is assumed, that these beings immediately understand the troubles facing our world and once prepared, will begin the process of healing all the unnecessary wounds. Conversely, we may find a fear of aliens, which may involve a general insecurity about our own well being. In this sense, we may feel ever-vulnerable to an invisible enemy who observes us from the heavens. Alternatively, the alien who comes to conquer mankind and is instead defeated by (mankind), may involve a complex compensation concerning individual and social strengths, as if to say, even though we seem weak, chaotic and vulnerable, when we stand together, we can conquer the stars themselves. The dream itself therefore, is as complicated as the dreamer's psychological perception of the world. Accordingly, we need to determine the hopes and fears of the dreamer. Moreover, we may need to analyze religious or spiritual tenets to uncover the dreamer's relation and thoughts about an unseen outside force. Naturally, in many ways, aliens may be (and have been) compared to deities. (see Stars) (see Extraterrestrials)

UMBILICAL CORD   The symbolism of the Umbilical Cord refers to our attachment to maternal sustenance. In other words, in the dream sense, we may be expressing anxiety about supporting ourselves and otherwise creating a self-sufficient psychological and emotional foundation. Moreover, the image of cutting ones umbilical cord, refers to the forced removal of matriarchal nurturing, for better or worse. This dream image may imply the unconscious message that proper learning involves falling and lifting oneself back up. The self which fails to symbolically stand on its own represses its distinguished potential of individual freedom.

UMBRELLA The symbolism of an Umbrella may refer to a hapless attempt to block out stormy and down-pouring emotions. However, the image of a parasol may represent well-defined social parameters in a romantic courtship. Traversing further down this line of thought, we explore the circle, or ring, of passion which circumscribe lovers embraced under an umbrella in the coursing rain. Accordingly, in the dream sense, we need to interpret the color, shape and practical use of the visually stimulating dream umbrella.

UNCLEAN In a very real sense, Unclean objects or persons have become symbolic of evil or demonic activity. The primary reason for this archetype centers around the connection with wild (life) and therefore, inhuman behavior. Another name for the devil is Beelzebub, which can loosely be translated as 'lord of the flies', consequently, we once again witness this thought construct of foul and unclean realities linked with otherworldly evil and chaos. In dreams, we find levels of uncleanliness and subsequently, at times, we behold only certain body parts unwashed. These respective body parts may illustrate differentiated aspects of our guilt or moral fear. For example, dirty hands may represent deceitful manipulations recently transpired, including perhaps, deviant sexual transgressions. (see Cleaning)

UNCONSCIOUS, THE To understand the Unconscious, it is necessary to first analyze the cognitive processes of the human brain. The mind, such as it is, provides us with instantaneous reception and transmission of an almost infinite array of information. Information, is the abstract term for the reality perceived by one or all of our five senses. Each of our sense organs is specialized to differentiate subtle distinctions in the specific reality which that organ is adapted to perceive. For example, our sense of hearing 'listens' to waves of sound within a wide spectrum of audible frequencies. Likewise, our sense of smell recognizes the most minute shades of separate fragrances found in the world. The most complex of these senses, is our sense of sight, which involves spatial relationships such as depth, height and distance, as well as, three-dimensional shapes and the entire prism of visible color. Over countless millennia, the brain evolved these sensory organs to 'reach out' and process the outside world. As such, in the action of this sensory perception, the brain receives information in all its focused complexity and is therefore able to accurately coordinate this elaborate information with all other forms of sensory input. In this sense, the mind builds information into memory and memory in turn strengthens with each correlation of experience. Therefore, if separate units of sensory input are continuously repeated in sequence our mind essentially will link them together. Over time these continuities become our worldly perception and supply the background for our individuated points of view.

When we lie down to sleep, we bring our fears, concerns and daily elations, all still fresh in our memory, into our dream consciousness. This dream consciousness is referred to as the Unconscious, because it contains all the sensory information gathered over a life-time by the human brain via the continuous operation of the sensory organs. In the process of dreaming, our unconscious reveals the furthest elaboration and deepest memory traced on the human being's mind. In this elaboration, or clarification, of memory, our brain illuminates a series of (visual, auditory, olfactory etc.) sensations to best understand the present application of reality. This series of sensations act as a language of symbols (and archetypes) and serve to create the dream landscape such as we know it.

Naturally, the complexity of memory experiences and the huge storehouse of recollected sensory perceptions associated with them, reveal an outstanding number of dream images, which taken together, appear nonsensical and perhaps even random. Appropriately, the dreamer needs to sort out the more powerful and/or poignant references found in these images and in this manner, akin to a cryptographer, decipher the message offered by the unconscious and its life-time of experience. Furthermore, examining the Collective Unconscious, we witness how the individual mind may tap into the racial memory of humankind, revealing innate tendencies and preferential aptitudes in a diversity of intelligence variants. In all these tenets, we find a phenomenal union of consciousness and an overall cohesiveness of being...(see Collective Unconscious)

UNIVERSITY All the elements and various aspects of higher education may be prevalent in this dream scenario. Moreover, our academic history (or future) directly effects our occupation and livelihood. Therefore, University dreams may reflect anxieties or relative concerns about our financial stability, present or future. In another sense, our unconscious may be illustrating facets of our social interactions or simply reminding us about crucial lessons or beliefs (theories) once held. Naturally, any significant or traumatic experiences which occurred in college figure prominently in the overall dream interpretation. (see School) (see Academy)

UPHILL In the dream sense, an Uphill journey refers to a difficult path taken to reach an emotional or psychological summit. As such, our unconscious may be illustrating the persistent courage and fortitude necessary to achieve worthwhile goals. However, an uphill battle, may also imply the very real possibility of failure. Accordingly, we may need to access our abilities and our relative fears. Are we able to scale the mountain of our own apprehensions, anxieties and perceived limitations? The dream may hold the answer we desperately need to discover and utilize in our waking experience. (see Wall) (see Path)

URBAN DREAM The complex conceptualization of the urban environment, replete with droves of people, loud noise, confusion and hyperactive energy in general, may refer to a specific psychological drive. This drive or desire, may involve fully embracing the sheer exuberance of crowded and diversified city life, or conversely, running from its chaotic madness. Naturally, this distinction is based upon our relative perceptions about urban life. In either case, it may need to be said, that bright lights can be entirely illuminating AS WELL AS utterly blinding. In this sense, we see that reality, unlike a sometimes prejudiced perception, is always a two sided coin.

URINE   In the dream sense, the expulsion of Urine, may refer to a release of pressure. Moreover, since urine is primarily water, we may be expressing the removal of an internalized and impassioned relationship. However, since urine also removes potential toxins, our unconscious may be informing us that this purging may in fact be healthy and cleansing. Consequently, we are now able to drink in new and fresh waters of experience. (see Baptism) (see Water)

URN   The complex symbolism of an Urn refers to a personal shrine or sanctuary for memories of deep and eternal love. In this sense, the memorial vase which contains ashes of a loved one, or simply flowers, conveys a physical space embodying the immaterial emotions of love, devotion and respect. As such, an urn may be compared to an icon, in that it symbolizes far more than the sum of itself. Appropriately, in the dream sense, an urn may refer to the embrace and unabridged acceptance of our abstract feelings which we sometimes lose sight of in the physical world. (see Ashes)

V

VALLEY   The image of the Valley carries with it the promise of fertile lands, exaggerated activity and a safe haven for human life. Furthermore, this sanctified geographical womb implies an invitation into sexuality, love and ultimately, family. All in all, we seem to be witnessing a desirable and secure plain of existence. However, the reality of the valley is divided by the mountain dwellers who were perhaps removed from the fertile plain or simply denied unmolested entry, due to a lack of force or social standing. In this sense, we find the archetype of the valley of shadows and the biblical terminology of the valley of death (into which 600 men rode and alas, never returned). In the dream interpretation, we may need to determine whether or not the valley is in fact desirable and/or safe for our entry. In turn, we find the complexity of this dualistic dream image narrowing down to its minute individual components. As such, every tree, fruit and resource in general obtained in the dale, glen or vale, may be beneficial and fulfilling to our well being, or conversely, poisonous, rotten or barren of any prospect of vitality, whatsoever. Hence the term, 'How green is your valley?'

VAMPIRE   The complex symbolism of the Vampire involves seduction, sensuality and death. In this diversity of meaning we find unique elements of contrasting images. The first and most obvious paradox is that of hot-blooded lust and cold-bodied death embodying the same individual via the drive and hunger for rich and animating life-blood. The second contradiction is the vampire's civilized nobility paired off with his animal (vampire bat) ferocity and aggression. Lastly, in the inconsistencies of this creature, is its attractive lure and fairly converse, horrendous, long-fanged and generally monstrous behavior. Accordingly, in the dream sense, our unconscious may be utilizing this complex dream figure to demonstrate extreme and diverse feelings involving a situation or individual (if not oneself), whose charm may be ultimately harmful. In this sense, a vampire may represent an addiction to drugs or alcohol, or conversely, a romantic obsession involving a partner with little or no emotional concern for the relationship itself. (see Impale) (see Bleed) (see Shark)

VAULT The complex image of a Vault involves a powerful arched structure which supports a heavy roof. In the symbolic sense, we may be referring to the psychological support of our abstract conceptualizations. In medieval times, artists such as Michelangelo, were encouraged to paint enormous cathedral ceilings supported by vaulted architecture (ex: Sistine Chapel). This representation of God's work was presented in a symbolic sky buttressed by a powerful and upright faith. Accordingly, in the dream sense, we may be illustrating a stolid conviction in some person, or idea. Moreover, since vaulted architecture is sometimes used in mausoleums, our faith and belief may concern unshakable wisdom imparted by deceased loved ones.

VENTRILOQUISM In the dream sense, Ventriloquism may involve deception and otherwise, speaking out of the corner of ones mouth. Moreover, the image of a puppet which blurts out words which are not its own, may refer to politicians and political figure heads, who read speeches created not by themselves, but spin-doctors, trained in the art of propaganda. Taken together, we see the symbolism of hollow, and therefore, untrustworthy, individuals appearing in the context of our waking life. Furthermore, we may be referring to our own parroting behavior which emulates some other person's language, behavior and original ideas.

VICTIM To be Victimized involves power and the desperate lack of it in ones own life. A natural and beneficial human trait involves a keen awareness of vulnerability in a particular situation. Normally, we strive to remove ourselves from these vulnerable situations and locations as quickly as possible. However, in waking life, we often find ourselves forced to remain in physically, mentally and spiritually hostile environments simply to make a living (occupation) and otherwise exist in a modern aggressive society. When we repress these feelings of victimization, they loom large in our unconscious and we may find ourselves submerged in nightmares where we are relentlessly pursued and/or tortured. Psychologists almost universally recommend facing and challenging ones tormentors in a dream landscape. In theory, when the dream abusers have vanished, we may gain courage to face those who seek domination over us in waking life, whether they be bosses, criminals or even (and sometimes especially) loved ones. (see Attack)

VIKING The symbol of the Viking involves relentless aggressive behavior in the acquiring of goals. However, although these vikings did in fact, plunder for gold and valuable goods, they nevertheless should not be confused with pirates and other outlaws. The reason for this justification is centered around the cultural acceptance of their practices and the subsequent social, rather than individual, motivation which prompted their ventures. Accordingly, the viking is not anti-social, but rather ultra-social, in the minds of his people. Hence, the appearance of a viking in a dream landscape, may refer to an aggressive exertion toward some valuable and gregarious goal. For example, an Olympic swimmer, may illustrate a dream image of a viking ship which rows relentlessly toward shore and the gold (medal) it offers.

VILLAGE The dream Village may be symbolic of simplicity and childhood reassurance. Naturally, these two factors of our psyche are indeed intricate and entirely complex in their own right. Accordingly, we need to closely analyze all the features of the village landscape. The internal social interactions combined with the accesibility into the communities inner sanctum (bar, general store, festival, church etc.), especially by a stranger (the dreamer and dream cohorts), may illustrate the psychological layout of social stability, status and ultimately, adaptability. Therefore, a harsh, alienating village, may represent an unconscious learning ground (or stage) for unstable or ill-advised waking behavior. On the other hand, an idealic wonderland may involve fantasy and wish-fulfillment revealing various and perhaps pernicious, forms of regression; which is of course, an example of a dream being far more problematic than a nightmare. Another facet of this dream landscape involves the Village Idiot, who may represent ourselves, and as such, may be yet another tool utilyzed by the unconscious to demonstrate elements of our personal folly. However, it must be remembered that the archetype of the fool (or Idiot), carries much wisdom in its ability to perceive the world with an empty (open) mind which sees and learns with earnest integrity and spiritual faith in the ability of self.

VINE The image of the winding Vine which covers our home (or castle?) with its lush growth and long reaching artery-like network of stems, may symbolize our ancestry, family, or the roots we've planted in the community of our upbringing. In this sense, the conceptualization of ever-reaching tendrils, may be positive in their skeletal support of oneself and ones rich history. However, these same vines may represent a trap or prison imposed by the moral structure of ones family, town or entire nation. Furthermore, a restrictive image of vines may involve ethical fears concerning sex and other naturalistic impulses which may bind us in blind emotional passion. In yet another interpretation, our dream may be alluding to the intellectual institutions known as the 'ivy league' schools, famous for their old coveted buildings (and edifices) covered in rich vines of ivy. In this case, we may be expressing a concern about our education, learning or knowledge in general. Accordingly, our occupation or the occupational aspirations once held (or still hold) may be intimately involved with these ivy league dream visions.

VIRGIN The complex symbolism of the Virgin, refers both to purity AND potential. As opposed to the eunuch who is rendered sexually incapable, a virgin is the embodiment of unblemished coitus and therefore, sanctified motherhood. In this sense, a pharaoh gave birth to noble children, from the bodies of his cluster of virgins. Taken one step further, we see the image of the virgin mary, who remains intact, even after the birth of baby Jesus, who becomes a sort of symbolic super-nobility, or 'king of kings'. Along these lines, we see the dream image of the virgin pertaining to spiritual harmony and the potential for higher love and ideal motherhood. However, the virgin reflection may involve a repressed fear of sexuality or the difficulties of child-bearing, or relationships in general. As such, we need to determine the behavior and demeanor of the dream virgin for apparent similarities with, or radical differences from, our own waking experience.

VOICE In our dreams, a Voice primarily represents an internal and very personal part of our understanding, which we somehow distance from the self we wish to personify in waking life. As such, the dream voice becomes our own knowledge disembodied and therefore acceptable to our belief system and ongoing personal agendas and/or philosophies. Naturally then, the voice is primarily a balancing force in our overall psyche. For example, a timid person may find a powerful narrator in his or her dream landscape, who eggs them on to perilous and inspiring adventures, while a reckless daredevil, may hear a voice of calm reason and various warnings about the merits and outright intelligence of caution. Additionally, the unconscious may utilize voice dreams to work as reminders of role models who exercised influence over our life, and who's 'words' remain with us.

VOLCANO The image of the Volcano is extremely symbolic of the disruption of stability and good firm ground in general. The red, hot lava, which flows from this mountainous eruption seems to indicate emotional disruption. Suitably, since earth is associated with womanhood, we may gather that this gusher involves extraordinary feminine characteristics. These features may include evaluations of relationships, child-rearing and occupational difficulties due to sexist bias. In any case, we find the rumbling volcano to be a fine descriptive metaphor for increasing stress levels which eventually reach the boiling point and explode figuratively over the entire landscape in a torrid and inescapable flood of emotion.

VOMIT The purging of toxins from within is graphically symbolic of throwing away harmful persons or situations. Interestingly enough, that which is regurgitated is often initially perceived as grand, sweet and entirely desired. In this sense, we witness a physical metaphoric reversing of intake or acceptance. The violence of Vomiting seems to reveal the real danger involved in the reality of that which is only symbolically discharged. Consequently, our dream may be indicating that our actions are rapidly dragging us into peril and we must reverse our drastic behavior, thereby releasing the poison which has internalized itself into our waking reality. (see Stomach) (see Regurgitate)

VOODOO In the dream sense, the practice of Voodoo may involve a complex fear of castigation and death caused by our own immorality. Comparable to many religions, Voudon stresses humility and worship offered to a God or Gods. However, as opposed to many creeds who threaten punishment to the immoral in the realm of the afterlife, voodoo promises immediate retribution in the form of priests, who are extremely capable of providing a 'hell on earth', here and now. Accordingly, the dreamer may be experiencing a very real anxiety about his or her sinful behavior and the immediacy of its harsh retribution.

VOYEUR The symbolism of the Voyeur may involve a physical alienation from life's activities, which are instead experienced vicariously. Accordingly, in the dream sense, a voyeur may refer to a person who watches or imitates our own behavior, or conversely, our own jealous observation of a some other person's actions or life-style. We may need to determine the exact nature of this dream estrangement and compare the physical scenes observed by the voyeur, with our own imaginative explorations. Along these lines, the invasion of privacy committed by this Peeping Tom, may reflect a direct probe by our conscious awareness into the unconscious ocean of our repressed memory.

VULTURE The dual symbolism of the Vulture involves both a struggle for survival and a wish for death. In the dream vision, flying vultures embody a forewarning of our own psychological or emotional death. In this particular case, our demise should be evaded by every method at our disposal. This is perhaps why the vultures reveal themselves in the representational sense. This revelation gives the dying victim something to think about before giving up the struggle. Conversely, a dream vision involving the birds eating carrion, may be reflective of our own parasitic behavior which may take advantage of the destruction, or loss, of another. Appropriately, we need to analyze all other elements of the vulture dream landscape, including flight, heat, the desert, absence of water, and the full connotation of death itself.

W

WAGON The little red Wagon, which carried our toys and goods reflected the beginnings of our intimate association with tools and technology. In this sense, our dream may be alluding to simpler times and simpler tools necessary for successful endeavors. In an age of space satellites and mainframe computers, virtually incomprehensible in design and repair maintenance, even to the very persons who operate and rely on them day in and day out, wagon, shovel and pail dreams have become far more commonplace.

WAIF Although sensationalized in our current media and modeling industry, perhaps because of its natural allusion to fragile and certainly reckless youth, a Waif has nevertheless primarily symbolized poverty and a lack of basic needs. As such, we need to examine the reasons, if any, for this inadequacy and metaphoric malnutrition. Moreover, we need to determine if repressive behavior forbids the intake of these needed requirements. Therefore in a dream, we may need to analyze the fears, repulsions and conversely needs and realistic desires of the waif figure.

WAKE UP To Wake Up in ones dream implies the rousing of a crucial realization, which may have been overlooked by a sleeping (lazy, wandering, delusionary) mind. Moreover, since waking involves opening ones eyes, we may be alluding to clarity of vision in understanding an object or person who has always (or at least previously) been present in our field of experience. In another interpretation, our waking up, may signal a spiritual, mental or physical form of calling, or enlightenment, to 'wake up' others around us who are sleeping through the fulfillment of their own lives. This sort of zealot dream scenario, occurs quite often, and therefore may provide a desired psychological quiet. This may be accomplished by building relevant status in the perception of self. Moreover, ancient Persians believed in reverse dream interpretation. In which case, the dream of waking up implies a necessity to dream, or live out ones dreams, in waking life. It is interesting to note that all these dream interpretations carry a common thread of undeniable spiritual transcendence.

WALK In the dream sense, Walking may refer to our perception of the world and the society around us. Accordingly, as we walk through a dream landscape, we may need to interpret every facet of the series of images which we come across. Moreover, any changes of direction, or relative obstacles, should be noted and analyzed. However, the natural and casual ease of walking, usually implies a slow, contemplative sense of well-being. (see Journey) (see Path)

WALL The powerful symbol of the Wall represents personal barriers which seem impossible to cross, penetrate and overcome in general. Unlike a gate or fence, which implies security with controlled accessibility, the thick, ponderous wall neither receives entry nor allows escape. It is both a physical, as well as mental, stronghold. In the psychological sense, the wall is built up by the self, brick by brick and cinderblock by cinderblock. Each segment of this wall represents a disillusionment found in life's experience, for example, a bad relationship or childhood trauma. Most people overcome these stumbling blocks of social and personal reality and attempt to move on after each occurrence, remaining as intact as possible; depending of course, on their relative severity. However, when these blocks seem to appear continuously and with an exaggerated frequency, we begin to fundamentally link their causal relationship. As such, we focus on our own personal characteristics and their limitations which we realize trigger the cause and effect machination of these stumbling blocks. Naturally, if this complex socialization occurs at an early age (which it usually does), we have a tendency to accept full blame or at least full responsibility, for all these aberrations from normal behavioral interaction. When this self-depreciation occurs, we unconsciously stack the stumbling blocks, brick by brick and cinderblock by cinderblock. Over time, we find ourselves trapped within the insurmountable wall of our own creation. In waking life, this barrier figures prominently into all our decision making, weighing as heavily as it does on our perception of self-worth. The dreamer may need to slowly disassemble this wall, brick by brick. Conversely, if the dreamer finds him or herself building a wall, an active and acute unconscious may be signalling that their is still time to reverse our course in life, enabling free access to separate realities. As such, we may begin to learn to accept our limitations and moreover, the limitations of others who are unable to perceive inconsistencies in their overall picture of reality, causing them discomfort, fear and personal uncertainty in their own life.

WALTZ The art of the Waltz involves coordination and sensuality, yet with a ritual adherence to accepted social themes. In this, the waltz is roughly comparable to tribal dances with rules of communal organization and status. The free-spirited dance of peasantry has little in common with the terse, gallant pageantry of the courtly waltz. In the well known fairy tale where Cinderella arrives at the king's royal ball with her glass slippers, we witness far more than a festive dance. We see instead a rite of passage into power and wealth, where shoes are not meant to be sturdy and flexible (usually ideal for dance), but rather fine, delicate, smooth and yes, sexual glass slippers, on which to magically transport a would-be princess in her courtly waltz. As such, our dream may represent an aspiration for social order and recognized status. Furthermore, it may involve a fantasy concerning our overlooked grandiloquence in the world of our waking life. Moreover, our unconscious may be reminding us about the level of dedication and knowledge (remember the glass slipper!) needed to achieve our lofty goals in life, including love and the creation of family. (see Dance)

WAND The image of the magic Wand symbolizes the force of pointed will which bends and in some cases, creates unimaginable potential. The elements of sexuality related to this phallic object date back to ancient times where it was recorded that the phallus routinely transformed into a writhing serpent possessing a semi-divine pleasure principle. However, the wand as staff is most prevalent in written history; the sturdy axis toward heaven and God which equates balanced leadership the measure of its lowest focal point, under which, all men and women serve a common cause. Accordingly, we need to determine the full intention of the magic wand in our dream landscape and who (if not ourself) wields the stalwart staff.

WANT The expression of ones desires or wishes may stem from a lack of fulfillment which cannot be satiated by these or any other material agents. A Want, or overbearing craving for people, things or sensations in general, may illustrate an open void into which these realities free-fall without leaving anything permanent, or at very least, substantial, in their wake. Conversely, a spiritual desire or journey may involve the surrender of ego and the subsequent gratification achieved by material greed. In a dream, we may need to analyze the real worth and significance of what is coveted, to discover its symbolic draw into the waking experience of our unique psyche.

WAR In life, a human being is constantly confronting battles of one sort or another. When these battles seem to wage on incessantly without any hope of peace, we may find ourselves experiencing recurring dreams involving War. In such cases, we need to determine who is our enemy and why this person or persons seeks our destruction. Often, the enemy revealed is ourselves, more exactly, mental limitations imposed upon our acceptance of self. We may be revealing paranoia about our social relationships. Trust is often a necessary ingredient in positive alliances, therefore, when this trust is broken, we may feel an act of war has been instituted upon our psyche and prepare for the ultimate battle of our liberation and personal honor. Naturally, it should be remembered that peace involves sacrifice and equal points of submission on both sides. Psychological mercenaries achieve very little in life other than the booty of other mercenaries. (see Explosion) (see Imbrue) (see Impale)

WAREHOUSE A Warehouse is a place for storage and set aside valuables. In this context, it is roughly comparable to the human unconscious, which stores information into memory and is therefore readily prepared to transport this wealth of knowledge into our waking consciousness. Consequently, our dream may represent an act of manipulating the fluctuating inventory of our personal cognizance. In an interpretive sense, we are retaining the items of memory which we desire and may wish to use and returning all other superfluous and somewhat metaphorical memorabilia.

WARMTH In general, feelings of Warmth are comforting, reassuring and nurturing. Maintaining a balance of hot and cold, a warm environment is perfectly suited for warm-blooded human beings. As such, we may be referring to overall feelings of well being, good health and secure calm. These conditions lead to eloquent and well thought out survival skills, both personal and professional. However, in a dream, we may need to determine exactly which elements in nature provide us with this warmth. For example, if we are warmed by a pool of blood, we may be expressing conflicts in our sacrificial or martyrdom behavior. Conversely, a warm fireplace, hot tea and a loved one all in close proximity may illustrate a general contentment. Naturally, as in all dream analysis, we must compare the dream reality to our waking reality. If the two are polar opposites, we may be experiencing wish-fulfillment, which may or may not be recommended, dependent on the waking world view of the dreamer. For example, a soldier stationed in an igloo in Gnome, Alaska may do well to dream about flirting with and romancing beautiful hula girls on a warm beach in Hawaii. On the other hand, a 'happily married' father of three, living in Teaneck, New Jersey, may be expressing personal anxiety or sexual repression if he revels in this same dream. As in other theoretical sciences, everything is relative.

WARNING Everyday life is inundated with Warning devices, from alarm clocks and red lights, to sophisticated weather-scanning orbital satellites. In each case, a signal is registered to inform the human mind of sudden change and the subsequent and necessary behavioral changes needed to successfully adapt to each reality transition. A warning signal witnessed in a dream may symbolically express similar behavioral responses to allegorical situations. For example, if a voice yells stop, we may need to freeze our actions and assess the wisdom of certain waking realities we are about to become immersed into. Conversely, a bell (as in a boxing ring), may signal a new beginning and the stealth, caution and strength necessary to perform productively in this arena. Warning signs employ age-old archetypal stimuli, such as loud noises, bright lights and annoying repetitious wailing. In most cases, we human beings are well aware of the down-side of our actions, due to our internal warning mechanism (in a dream, or otherwise), however, overpowering motivations including ego, desire and youthful exuberance, often may cause us to ignore the flashing light, blowing whistle and shouts from the crowd to stop, until its too late! This is usually when the legal system takes over...

WARRIOR The symbolism of the Warrior involves a struggle within oneself to find the strength necessary to survive in a harsh and violent environment. The superior motivation in this process is the reality of being destroyed by a stronger and better prepared fighter. In this sense, the representative notion of 'kill or be killed' is still entirely relevant in today's competitive society. Accordingly, the unconscious of a dreamer may be illustrating a necessity to dig down deep inside oneself for the courage, fortitude and determination needed to stand up and fight for worthwhile goals.

WART A Wart may symbolize a feeling of appearing grotesque to the society of people encompassing ones life. Moreover, because of its association with a witch's nose and witchcraft in general, a dreamer possessing this defacement may feel as though they have been cursed, or cast aside from social interaction, by a malicious person or a peculiar situation beyond their immediate control. The dream image may indicate a serious and ongoing concern, given that a wart is difficult to remove and may last a long time. In an interpretive sense, we must ascertain the exact location of the wart and analyze the symbolic implications of this particular body part and its relative disruption.

WASH The active image of Washing involves the removal of unclean, harmful realities. In the action of cleaning oneself (or ones goods) with soap and water, we withdraw what is perceived as 'base' elements of our physical environment. These elements have become symbolic of a 'devil's playground' of flesh, dirt (soot, grime etc.) and dust (germs, viruses). Therefore in cleaning, we regain the emotional purity of self, roughly emulating the spotless spirit and image of 'God's work'. Naturally, if one continues this action of absolution, dry, wrinkled and raw skin may shriek in consummate denial, the supposed wonder of any godhead whatsoever. In another interpretive sense, we find the conceptualization of relinquishing responsibility for unethical or unsound judgements. Hence, the phrase, 'I wash my hands of the whole matter', initially uttered in text by Pontius Pilot, but almost certainly used earlier by a number of great men and women who needed to step away from sticky predicaments with uncertain popular results. Stickiness, naturally being another physical rudiment of evil design, in need of being washed away. (see Water) (see Unclean) (see Basin) (see Baptism)

WATCHING In dreams, Watching represents personal suspicion as well as various levels of paranoia. This sort of investigative imagery may result as an unconscious compensation for elusive and perhaps distrustful behavior enacted by the dreamer. However, the distinction must be made whether or not this suspicion is well founded. For example, if in a dream, a mother continually watches her three year old playing in the yard, she may harbor concerns about the child's real safety in and around her dwelling. In this case, the watching is merely cautious. On the other hand, if in a dream, an ordinary working man suddenly feels as though ALL his work mates and friends are mysteriously scrutinizing his actions and eavesdropping on his personal conversations, this man may be exhibiting a strong form of paranoid psychosis. In another interpretive sense, we may need to consider relative objects observed in dreams and determine their symbolic significance to the dreamer. For example, watching a clock and observing the ballet-like dance of a Bottle-Nose Dolphin as it spins above the surface of a crystal clear pool, elicits two quite different meanings. Unless of course, you happen to be a marine biologist/dolphin trainer, who happens to be late for a lecture and demonstration at the Public Aquarium and Waterworld.

WATER In the symbolic sense, Water refers to the diverse states of our entire emotional capacity. Accordingly, every time water appears in a dream landscape, we represent the fluid, ever-changing and insubstantial characteristics of our own sensitivity. Moreover, clear, untainted water intimates spiritual purity and cleansing. (see Baptism) (see Boat) (see Drown) (see Rain)

WAX, DRIPPING The image of Dripping Wax may involve the potential for passionate emotions which leave a decided effect upon our psyche. (see Ablaze) (see Fire) (see Melt) (see Candle)

WAX DOLL As a society, we have long experienced a fascination with Wax Dolls and wax museums. Soulless, yet vulnerable duplications of ourselves, intimately associated with flame in the heated detail of their creation, these wax figures have ceaselessly amazed us. Furthermore, in the historic and ritualistic sense, wax dolls have archetypally represented a sorcerers tool, a sort of magic mirror, which may well be manipulated to affect and inflict a depicted personage. Taken together, this golem-like formation of a human likeness, may illustrate a complex metaphorical insecurity about either our physical or spiritual body. As such, the pliable nature of a wax doll may be fully indicative of manipulative behavior enacted upon us by outside individuals or forces, or conversely, our own shaping and molding deeds enacted upon our families or close associates. Since heat and flame is involved in the melting of wax, we may need to address our anger and otherwise intense emotional responses in the entirety of these examples.

WEATHER In most cases, Weather is compared to our emotional states of mind. Consequently, we may feel gloomy and gray, bright and sunny, cold and distant, or enigmatic and moody (rapid weather shifts). There is more to this particular archetype than simply psychological behavior responses. In a biological sense, it has been discovered that weather and location, which produces a variety of disparate levels of ionization (a form of electrical activity in the immediate atmosphere), effects us directly by changing the intricate relations of our neurological operation. As such, certain southwesterly winds and low incoming storm fronts, have been known to drive people mad, while high altitudes and conversely low altitudes (at 0 sea level) with crisp weather patterns, seem to elicit ideal and socially accommodating internal pleasure. The only major difference in these two atmospheric environments is high and low levels of ionization in the surrounding air. Taking all this into account, we need to fully examine the weather conditions in our dream and all responses relative to it. This way, we may be able to determine the level of 'symbolic' as opposed to 'actual' reality of the message obtained from the elaborate, weather-inspired dream imagery.

WEB The intricate pattern which creates the dual reality of beautiful lure and deadly trap demonstrates a stunning archetype of human experience. As such, we find ourselves at times drawn toward realities which appeal to us, even though we are fully cognizant of their danger. In fact, as Sigmund Freud argued with his theory on a human death instinct, an internal predisposition which craves self-destruction, the danger itself, may invite us further into the very situation. The spider Web dream may offer some insight into this odd behavior in our own waking life. Heeded as a symbolic warning, we may need to analyze particular situations or relationships which seem beautiful in their intricacy, detail and all-encompassing invitation, but which may in fact wait to ensnare us in their complicated and preconceived net of involvement. (see Knot) (see Rope) (see Zig-Zag)

WEEDS Although Weeds are generally perceived as unwanted realities which spring up into our lives, they can also be viewed as strong, simple and honest forces of nature which refuse to be denied. In this sense, a child who grows quickly and sturdily is often referred to as a weed. We may need to determine if the weed grows in our yard, a neighbors, or out in the wild. Moreover, we may need to analyze our dream reaction to the weed. In this line of thought, we may come to learn to accept the weed as an undeniable and inescapable example of nature's supreme rule. (see Garden)

WEIGHT The implication of Weight in a dream scenario may involve a heavy burden or a significant and extremely serious decision encountered in ones life. Linked with the idea of weight, is support and naturally, the lack of it. When we talk of 'Holding the weight of the world upon our shoulders', we are saying that we are over-burdened and cannot easily support the gravity of our intentions. In this sense, we examine the quality of support, which is a crucial archetype in the psychological analysis of self. Accordingly, if a person is well grounded, well balanced and effectively creates a sound support base, he or she may be able to carry more 'weight' and responsibility than someone who is shaky all over. In fact, in the not too distant past, an overweight boss was considered well-proportioned for the importance of his position and looked every bit the role model of leader. Similarly, women who would be considered overweight by today's standards, were regarded as ideal maidens and objects of desire, able to bear children, satisfy a husband and raise an entire family. As the culture changes, so does its ideas of role models. Unfortunately, the pendulum of social mores often swings too far in an alternate direction. This being the case, obese people are chastised and made to feel inferior because of their weight. They may become despondent, depressed and shrink away from normal social interactions and activities found in day to day life. As such, the weight dream carries certain implications for overweight persons which are exclusive to their experience. In as much, the reality of support becomes superseded by the need to be supported and this support network becomes more and more difficult to find as depression increases the cycle of food and fulfillment.

WHITE The dual symbolism of the color White involves both purity as well as frigid detachment. In the sense of its stark, light-reflective brilliance, white embodies components of clarity, simplicity and intelligibility. On the other side of the coin, we find cold isolation and alienation in this severe, glaring and pallid landscape. (see Antarctica) (see Winter)

WIDOW In the dream sense, a Widow may refer to a sense of personal loss. Of course, this deprivation may involve the parting of a loved one, but may also concern a dissipation of a part of oneself. For example, when an individual in a relationship feels a loss of passion for their once desired partner, a dream landscape may characterize this feeling in the form of a widow or widower.

WILD Although man seems to have conquered the so-called Wild world with the elaborate efforts of his iron and mortar civilization, the fact is, he has only hidden himself from the natural tenants of its universal existence. Accordingly, the wild nature which is ever-present within himself, still burns vividly and displays hunger, passion and freedom, the latter supremely ironic, since freedom is billed as the major strong point of this stainless-steel man-made environment. Nevertheless, the wild impulses of man remain, and the theoretically tame society of man has found difficulty in dealing with this unfortunate internal paradox. Dreams serve as the mediators in this internal battle of metaphysical belief systems. The dream is not afraid to hunt, run, scream, act with total abandonment, and one more thing, the exercise of freedom. This way, in waking life, we can return to our safe existence without hurting ourselves or others around us. As a message from our unconscious however, we may need to heed the reflection of the dream and act (with caution, and within the limits of the recognized law) on the impulses of our wild instincts. (see Jungle)

WIND The rush of air which serves to push and pull us in ominous directions may entertain the visual equivalent of being led around by outside influences. Moreover, the Wind, which is naked to the human eye, may imply that these forces are not revealed to us, or deliberately deceptive, or simply misleading in their interaction with ourselves. From another interpretive view, we should analyze not only the force of the wind, but also its relative temperature. Is it cold, painful and numbing, or is it warm, intoxicating and inviting? Moreover, does the wind blow any object away from us? If so, what is that object (or person), and what is our exact relationship to it? Lastly, are we able to retrieve that item, or does it appear to be lost forever? (see Ice) (see Zephyr) (see Boat) (see Antarctica)

WINDOW The symbolism of a Window involves the appearance and acknowledgement of an outside world of vast possibilities. In this sense, the window may represent a focal point of the dreaming mind itself. Accordingly, the transparent glass directs our immediate attention on the dream landscape found within its frame. Moreover, the sunlight allowed into a home, is representative of reason and wisdom. Accordingly, we need to pay special attention to all objects and persons seen through our cordial pane of glass. (see Glass) (see Drapes) (see Light)

WITCHCRAFT The complex symbolism of Witchcraft refers to a unifying force which underlies nature and the archaic earth magic used to tap into this well of power. Consequently, any irresistible spells cast over a dreamer, may be represented in dreams as a form of sorcery, or wicca. Moreover, the naturalistic aspects of this earth magic contain feminine precepts of spirituality, including heightened sensual awareness and a matriarchal similitude. Hence, female wisdom may be implied in the overall dream meaning. (see Aboriginal) (see Hex)

WOLF In the dream sense, a Wolf represents beauty, solitude and pride. As such, its wild nature is elevated to a status of high passion. In this sense, a wolf is not a killer, but rather, a seducer. Consequently, when a wolf appears in a dream landscape, its symbolism is that of the noble loner who asks for nothing yet deserves the world of our respect. The interpretation of this dream may involve a dreamer's self-confidence and composure in a variety of social situations, which he or she can move in and out of with relative ease and grace.

WOMB The conceptualization of the Womb involves complete security and sanctity. The chamber of birth exhibits life entirely provided for, without worry of harm, survival responsibility, or the isolation of solitude. The image of mother and child as one, represents a sacred union of love, creation and selfless sacrifice in the image of the pregnant woman. In a real sense, this dream is quite different dependent on whether or not the dreamer is male or female. The primary reason for this is found in the example of the male, who has no concept of a having a womb, only the regressive warmth and protection which it archetypally offers him. In the case of the female dreamer, we find a complex analysis of the womb concerning fears about the sacrifice and responsibility of childbirth, mingled perhaps with the quandary of sexual pleasure versus obvious social expectations involving procreation. (see Bottle) (see Child) (see Childbirth) (see Fetal Position) (see Umbilical Cord)

WOOD The symbolism of Wood involves the complex connection of nature and man. In one sense, a wood structure or house built rather than a steel, brick or plastic one, may imply naturalistic ideals in the psychological framework of an individual. On the other hand, an ancient oak tree chopped down to obtain wood to make a house, may imply an unhealthy domination of nature. Accordingly, we need to understand our respectful association with wood in the dream landscape, and in a very real sense, our symbolic affiliation with forests and wilderness in general. (see House) (see Tree)

WORM The symbolism of a Worm in a dream, may imply an introverted behavior which attains much intelligence, but very little wisdom, gained from experience. In this sense, the worm represents a frail innocence which is entirely vulnerable. Moreover, the exposed defenseless nature of the creature implies weakness and a general lack of courage. Accordingly, a worm appearing in a dream landscape, may illustrate wallflower behavior and a general fear of social confrontation or interaction.

WREATH In the dream sense, the symbolism of a circle of flowers, or Wreath, refers to eternal love, respect and admiration. Moreover, since a circle, or ring, implies infinity and order, an encircling of flowers may indicate a natural and spiritual eternity of life. In this sense, a wreath may be representative of the concept of an immortal soul. (see Circle) (see Flower) (see Ring)

WRITING The communication of complex ideas through an organized redistribution of letters or symbols, creating words, is singular to mankind as a species. With the introduction of Writing, language as we know it, blossomed into a pool of knowledge and information which could be passed not only to our neighbors, but also, carried on to successive generations. This well thought process outlined the foundation and upward cohesive structure of society and civilization itself. As such, it is no accident that writing figures prominently in the psyche of the human population. Our dreams resort to primal archetypal images to covey messages from the unconscious into the waking conscious. Therefore, to communicate the very art of communication itself, our dreaming mind will present the image, or gesture, of writing. Moreover, this communiqué may involve a direct continuity of thought which would be absurd and unreasonable to explain in metaphor. In other words, the dream is spelling it out for us in plain English, if we choose to read and understand. If written progressively, the countless examples of authors and poets who received entire passages of their famous verse in dreams, would far exceed the length of this humble manuscript. Accordingly, we need to analyze all the particulars of the writing dream, the penmanship style, the parchment used, the writer's inspiration, and especially, the words themselves.   (see Letter) (see Book)

X

X-RAY   The symbolism of X-Rays naturally involves looking through things. In other words, in the dream sense, we may be expressing a desire to see inside a person (if not ourselves), both physically AND mentally. This internal inspection may involve finding good qualities inside a person, as well as exposing bad characteristics, or ill health, within that self.

XYLOPHONE   (see Accordion)

Y

YACHT   The Yacht dream concerns a luxurious and relaxed social happening or overall atmosphere of good feeling. Whether fantasized or not, the fanciful ship carries with it a notion of emotional ease and a lack of worry. It is very rare that we should dream about a yacht caught in a stormy sea, unless the dreamer fears being way in over his (or her) head, in a financial deal, investment or style of life, which may sink... (see Boat)

YAK   The long-haired Asian ox known as a Yak, is a paradoxical dream figure because it simultaneously represents the sturdiness and reliability of a four-legged, domestic vegetarian (akin to a cow), and an exotic and arguably rare beast, admired by easterners and westerners alike, the world over. Therefore, our dream may be expressing a double-meaning and otherwise split feeling about a certain person or situation in our lives. By and large, the qualities of uniqueness and dependability, taken together, add up to a formidable and perhaps precious person, entity or happening.

YAMMER   Loud confusion, especially verbal confusion, may indicate frustration concerning an inability to communicate ones ideas or the converse and exasperating experience of confronting an avalanche of ideas and opinions from others, none of which are useful or applicable to our own neural experience. Alternatively, the hostile nature of an animal's yammering, may be indicative of a warning against danger, or an otherwise threatening event. It may be necessary to piece together decipherable bits of information in the confused chatter to reveal single examples of what may in fact be troubling us in waking life.

YANK The action of pulling at someone or something with violent passion in ones dream, may demonstrate a desperate need to free that person or object away from its present position. Perhaps the subject is in a station or posture of symbolic paralysis. However, it should be remembered and noted, this freeing of an object, may carry with it a need to possess or 'recapture' said object, or individual, into ones own (the dreamer's), psychological ensnarement.

YARD The symbolic conceptualization of a Yard which maintains larger than life tools of human civilization (pumps,trains,ships etc.), may be indicative of our day to day machinations which propels us through a complex world. Conversely, the Yard which outlines our house or apartment building may be reflective of our synthesis or communication with the land itself. As such, we may need to examine the naturalistic condition of our physical property. Is the grass green? Are the trees tall and thriving? Are the flowers in bloom? Additionally, childhood games played in yards, reflected in bright toys, playground rides and sand-boxes, may illustrate regressive behavior or an age-old drive which our unconscious clearly displays. In this sense, we need to examine the condition of the childhood items. Are the toys broken? Are the swings rusted? Or conversely, is everything shiny and new, as though time has not passed since our animated youth. It should be remembered, that our concept of waking time is irrelevant to the unconscious, which utilizes time as a symbolic communication of a psychological state of mind.

YARDMASTER The Yardmaster is the feared and revered embodiment of our external machinations. In this sense, this dream figure is akin to a foreman who oversees our physical actions and moreover, our ability to usefully perform in all levels of society: private, public and professional. As such, the yardmaster may represent our insecurities and fears concerning our direct abilities and the harsh realities of their possible outcomes. However, if we ourselves are depicted in the body of the yardmaster, we may be illustrating a complex control over our environment. This blunt characteristic may elapse in our waking experience in the complicated network of our elaborate social interrelationships.

YARN The concept of a Yarn, refers to a fanciful story which is not meant to be taken seriously, but which may contain certain elements of wisdom. In the alternate usage of the word, Yarn, used for weaving, is often thought of in the sense of a playful kitten's ball of yarn. Once again, and perhaps not as coincidentally as one might expect, yarn contains an element of play and tomfoolery. As single strands of material which are interwoven to create imaginative knits, the individual strand of yarn is comparable to the single element of truth, the cohesive reality, found in the tall tale called a 'yarn'. Taken together, the image of yarn in our dream landscape may refer to a playful person or situation, which nevertheless, reveals to our waking selves, a necessary truth or decisive wisdom.

YAWN The immediate association of a yawn may be that of boredom, weariness, or outright exhaustion concerning some aspect of our waking behavior. However, there may be certain oral and/or sexual allusions involved in the gaping image of the long, relaxed yawn. Furthermore, its catchy, mimicking quality may illustrate an imitative interaction enacted ourselves, or by others, in our immediate sphere of experience. We need to analyze who in fact yawns in the dream, and what precedes (or causes) the automatic response, if anything at all.

YEAR The conceptualization of the Year may involve a concern about aging and the passage of time. Alternatively, the importance of significant events which may have occurred, or will occur, and cause profound changes in our day to day life, may be alluded to in our complex dream vocabulary. In this sense, we may be illustrating our more elaborate concerns, fears and desires involving time, which is in some sense our analytical, scientific perception of life and human physical reality, such as it may actually exist. On the other hand and metaphysically speaking, metaphorical comparisons can be made with the notion of the horoscope, in essence, the predicted future, which may need to be psychologically wished for, in the shape of some semblance of hope.

YEARBOOK The image of our Yearbook carries with it the people we once were and alternatively, the persons we were meant, or promised, to become. We may be expressing a concern about our relative station in life and how we managed to end up as the people we are today. The friendships and loves once maintained in our early youth certainly formed and manipulated attitudes which we carried later in life. Our unconscious may be referring to these early stages in life in the embodiment of the yearbook. Moreover, this preserved, fragile moment in our personal history may reflect a seemingly insurmountable mental block or delicate neurosis which may need to be addressed. Along these lines, elements of repressive behavior may be singularly indicated in this dream context.

YEAST The idea of potential, symbolized in the raising of bread, may be illustrated in the dream motion of yeast. Any and all depictions of growth refer to maturation and significant transitions. Bread itself is symbolic of flesh and nourishment, as such, yeast may refer to inner and crucial growth in our personal life. the combined fulfillment of our mind, body and spirit completes the story of our adulthood, and furthermore, our humanity. Therefore, we need to analyze and interpret this dream image thoroughly, as it may concern significant transformations and transfigurations in our immediate experience.

YELL The action of forcefully pushing out internal agony, which may be otherwise suppressed is purposefully actualized in the dream Yell. In our dream consciousness, we are able to express feelings which are difficult to accept or even cope with in our waking experience. The yell, in and of itself, is not at all a negative behavior trait. In fact, in the animal kingdom, the scream is used instinctively as a warning, challenge or general release of intense emotion. Moreover, loud yelling prepares the endocrine and adrenaline systems for physical confrontations and critical battles, including territorial and mating. The dream scream therefore, reflects a necessary physical response to stressful stimuli which may need to be emulated in waking life.

YELLOW The complex symbolism of the color yellow may involve light and warmth, as well as, sickness and/or cowardice. Accordingly, we need to determine if the yellow entity in the dream landscape is displaying its normal ocher color, or if it has become this color due to some cowardly or pusillanimous behavior.

YESTERDAY The conceptualization of Yesterday may refer to remorse concerning unchangeable events. As such, we understand that yesterday is gone and cannot be recaptured or replayed. The suddenness and completeness of the passing days of our life relate the reality of conclusions and resolutions to the direct machinations and decisions of our conduct, function and belief system. In other words, yesterday illustrates consequences which we must accept. A crucial part of the maturation process involves standing behind our choices and decisions, even if they have failed or been proven unacceptable. As such, we learn to admit our own errors in judgement and at times, entirely human ignorance. The replaying of yesterday in our dream, may serve to reveal our mistakes, or conversely, our triumphs, in order to learn from our unique and personal actions. Often in life, we are faced with permanent loss, allusions to firm conclusions and completions in our psychological development, may aid us in coping with these difficult irreversible realities.

YIN/YANG The balance of our masculine and feminine aspects, may be alluded to in the dream image of the yin/yang symbol proper. In ordinary life, we are often asked to behave quite differently, dependent on certain situations. For example, our sensitive, or feminine side, may be required in certain difficult scenarios, such as dealing with the personal needs of our loved ones, or handling a profound bereavement and mourning suffered by a close and personal friend. Conversely, our strong, or masculine side, may need to be called upon to address situations where we need to stand up for ourselves, our beliefs or simply our motivations. Habitually in life, we choose to favor only one of our internal gender traits. The yin/yang dream may indicate a need to find equilibrium in our complex emotional spectrum in order to become ever more complete in our humanity and human potential.

YOGA/YOGI In the dream sense, a Yogi refers to our inner meditations and the conviction of our spiritual path. The stillness and quiet of the yogi represents the archaic wisdom of fusing body and spirit. In theory, when the body and spirit become one, all physical and spiritual limitations are absolutely erased, allowing the master fakir to come and go as he pleases, guided by vision, sense and insight. (see Journey) (see Path)

YOKE The symbolism of a Yoke refers to the burden we must carry in waking life. Accordingly, if the burden is too heavy, our unconscious may be revealing the excess tasks and responsibilities which hold us down, or basically enslave us.

Conversely, if the yoke is light and well-balanced, we may be illustrating the worthwhile nature of our supportive efforts concerning work, family or social commitment.

YOUTH, FOUNTAIN OF In the dream sense, a vision of The Fountain of Youth, may represent a wish-fulfillment to regain the strength, vitality or even beauty of our youth. This escapist dream confronts the profound tribulation of aging and exposes a society which is insensitive to the very real needs and desires of the elderly. On the other side of the coin, if an individual ignores the dream fountain entirely, he or she may be displaying a sublime acceptance of self and the divine order of nature's unfolding.

Z

ZEAL Enthusiasm and excitement in a dream, may well represent a foreshadowing of some joyous event or sudden good news; for example, the arrival of a child. Conversely, Zealous behavior may be a reactionary reflection of a lack of emotion to good fortune, or performance approval, which occurs in ones own waking life. In either case, the exact nature of the dream zeal should be analyzed and interpreted comprehensively for a deeper and perhaps, complete understanding, of the unconscious message revealed.

ZEBRA The symbolism of the Zebra refers to the perfect
symmetry and unity of opposites. Moreover, this visual balance found in nature demonstrates the unanimity of life itself. Furthermore, since the zebra, unlike a horse, is a wild animal who lives in a naturalistic landscape, we may surmise that freedom and latitude, play a major role in this dream imagery. Accordingly, we see the inherent liberation found in the instinctive and fluid coexistence of opposites in our remarkable world.

ZEITGEIST When a certain historical fashion (or mood) is reinstated in a dream, we may be fantasizing about that particular way of life. Naturally, we may be indicating a dissatisfaction with our own period of time and the life it has offered us. However, it should be understood that the human mind and spirit transcends social norms of any period. As such, in the USA, we are very fortunate to be able to create our own appropriate sensibilities in todays date in time, in other words, the present. Therefore, an old-fashioned person can live alongside a modern person in this rare world of a theoretical freedom of choice.

ZEN The Zen dream involves mysticism that transcends language and behavior in all its forms. Accordingly, we may be expressing in the Zen scene, a life-style free of rigid spiritual rules created by, for and toward God, or, an otherwise complete system of personal enlightenment. In this way, the dream may be illustrating a belief in self and an acute faith in the infallible direction, administration and course, of that self. Moreover, we may need to interpret the theatrical behavior performed in the self-same Zen dream imagery, as the movements may reveal hidden truths which may need to be explored extensively. In this sense, we need to analyze particular body parts and the reflex actions they display through the overall spatial environment.

ZENITH In the dream sense, an absolute Zenith may illustrate potential and/or formidable goals. It may be essential to interpret the dreamer's reaction to the vision of the zenith atop the horizon line. Is the dream character striving to push the absolute limit of his or her being, or is he or she thrown into chaos at the prospect of tackling or associating with such a seemingly insurmountable apex of human or worldly existence?

ZEPHYR The warm caressing breeze called a Zephyr, may be a fairly accurate representation of stoic contentment, that is to say, a gentle, natural calming of internal emotions. In most cases, this sort of ease and tranquility occurs after turmoil and a difficult period in ones life. The zephyr may be the affirmation of a moral life and otherwise confident soul. However, a normal element of dream language finds sudden changes in environmental forces. Therefore, the dreamer should be aware if the warm breeze grows harsher and gradually more difficult to bear, until he or she finds him or herself in a deadly sandstorm, the unconscious may be signalling a warning. The warning reminds us to be cautious of the seeming ease which certain aspects of our lives may now display.

ZEPPELIN Apart from the well-publicized Hindenburg disaster, the usual image of a giant blimp-like craft which flies with effortless majesty over the horizon, illustrates a grand promise and the singular and eloquent overcoming of a seemingly impossible feat. In an entirely separate interpretation of this ship, we find the shape and formidable presence of the Zeppelin may imply a phallic symbol of bold and dignified proportions. In any case, the huge craft is an example of human possibility and the emotional effectiveness of human grace. It combines quiet beauty, simple elegance and gargantuan size and strength. Taken together, this symbolism may refer to large accomplishments which should, can and will be made by the dreamer in waking life.

ZERO The appearance of a Zero account figure, or the visual representation of the center of the mathematical line, both refer to a fresh beginning and an otherwise restructuring of self. The absence of finances may naturally illustrate a fear of economic devastation. however, more than likely, the bankrupt figure carries with it the conceptualization of 'creating ones fortune', both physically and metaphorically. Moreover, the absence of money may imply spiritual wholeness absent of perhaps burdening material possessions. All this conjecture is influenced by the dreamer's perception of the value of the 'almighty' dollar.

ZIG-ZAG In a dream, Zig-Zagging behavior may be symbolic of indecision and wavering sensibilities. However, analogous to the insect world (ex: moth), a chaotic pattern of movement may conversely illustrate a defensive strategy taken or planned in the near future. The dream conceptualization of a moving target implies that a person or group of persons, may be aiming negative attacks in our direction, (either real or imaginary). In a rather complex analysis and interpretation of this dreamscape, the zig-zag motion may be recreated on paper, or on video, in our waking life, to determine the intricate weave or pattern formed by the repetition of our movement. The subsequent significance of the web-like creation in space and its revealing body language, may be indicative of our unique behavior patterns in day to day life.

ZIPPER The combination of metal and the alternate covering and exposing of flesh may be illustrative of a harsh sexuality, or a sexual relation with dire consequences. The article of clothing which is zipped or unzipped may refer to a fascination with that particular body part which is revealed (boot, jacket, pants = foot, chest, groin). Furthermore, if the Zipper should become ensnared in flesh, we may be illustrating a material and perhaps unnatural approach to our own sexuality and/or overall physiology.

ZODIAC The twelve aspects of the astrological wheel, symbolic of birth and behavior, also maintain one of the four elements of fire, water, air and earth. In this sense, we need to analyze which sign is alluded to in the dream, especially if the sign is different from the birthsign of the dreamer. If all the signs of the Zodiac are present, the dreamer may be referring to the art of astrology itself. Naturally, a concern about ones future, in essence, ones horoscope, may be implied in this straight-forward dream scenario. (see Astrology)

ZOMBIE The undead in dreams generally refer to persons, or more appropriately, situations which refuse to go away. The unnatural and grotesque appearance of the Zombies may refer to the monstrous reality of a human problem which grows in significance with time and the inability to vanquish its perplexing nature. In the archaic sense, a zombie, akin to a golem, is a soulless creature, made entirely of earth and flesh and therefore, bears no relation to a deceased loved one. This ghoul is rather an archetype of our own long-standing fears and perceived short-comings, returning night after night to haunt and torment us with the simple human frailty of our own selves.

ZOO The complex symbolism of a Zoo revolves around the separate animals characterized in the dream itself and their relative condition and/or behavior. However, the sheer number of diverse animals in the dream landscape may also play a part in the overall interpretation. In this sense, we may be expressing a series of conflicting emotions and desires which reveal themselves in the specific animal which we observe. Moreover, the fact that the animals are locked in cages may refer to the long standing repression of our passions and drives, which would explain their possible sickly and otherwise strange appearance.

ZOOMORPHISM The complex symbolism of Zoomorphism refers to the connection of human and animal characteristics. Consequently, the image of a being with half-human and half-animal parts alludes to the dual expression of both of their respective physical natures. That is to say, wild, untamed and instinctive versus civilized, restrained and moral behavior in general. Appropriately, we need to examine the paired representation of the zoomorphic form and place it into the significant psychological make-up of the dreamer who conceives this unique entity in the context of his or her physical world of experience. In this, we may need to determine if the dreamer's 'animal' sense increases or decreases relative to ones 'human' sensibility. The wild or civilized bearing in the physical manifestation of our dream, may be illustrating an extreme course of action in our waking life, which may have rather distressing and perhaps unexpected, consequences in our social relationships. However, if our opposing natures are equally balanced and the dreamer feels a fluid ease and control of experiential behavior, the unconscious may be revealing an ideal symmetry in our physical, psychological, and spiritual self. This healthy, well-balanced personality is known in psychological terms as a Self-Actualized individual.

Quick and Easy Reference Guide

ABANDON: Fear of isolation, fear of individual decision making. We may feel the pressure of standing alone.

ABBEY: Represents gulit. For women, the abbey figure may denote a form of spiritual cleansing, a regaining of virtues.

ABBESS: Woman who views herself (or another) as spiritual leader. Feeling a certain matriarchal responsibility, such as nurturing.

ABBOTT: May indicate repressed fears about ones immoral behavior. The figure looms over us in sharp-eyed judgement. A spiritual leader who challenges us.

ABDOMEN: May involve sexual anxiety or other emotional longings which persist in our psyche. The sickness of emotional suppression.

ABHOR: Experiencing a feeling of alienation. May imply a sense of worthlessness. Anxiety over 'fitting' into our peer group.

ABJECT: A feeling of wretchedness or unworthiness, especially in relationships. Questioning oneself sexually.

ABODE: Our abode represents our normal state of mind. Our sense of personal grounding. Is the abode violated in some way?

ABORIGINAL: The measure of our own 'primal nature'. We must determine whether our wild nature is enpowering or threatening.

ABORTION: Something near and dear to us is suddenly 'cut-off'. This may involve a relationship or friendship. Insecurity about our own level of maturity and ability to 'care' for another.

ABOVE: Something which SEEMS TO BE entirely unreahable. This may include a distant desire, or difficult goal. The dream itself may relate clues about achieveing the goal, if it is at all possible.

ABROAD: A longing, or desire, to escape waking life. We may feel a need to regain a lost way of life. May involve regression into our youth and a simpler time of life.

ABSENCE: Guilt about an unintentional wrong-doing. We may need to find a personal and make ammends for the damage we believe to have caused this individual.

ACORN

ABSORB: Some aspect of ourselves may be changing, we are uncertain about our own individuality. We are being absorbed into an influence which is beyond our control, as such we are losing a sense of Self.

ABUNDANCE: May involve EITHER a feeling of reward for personal accomplishments, or conversely, a feeling of guilt about the unscrupulous acquisition of our goods. Involves our own sense of greed. What will we do with our abundance. How do we feel about it.

ABUSE: If we are being physically abused, we may be crying out for help. If we are the abuser, we amy be experiencing guilt about our own abusive behavior. In both cases, we are seeking an end to ALL unjust punishment.

ABYSS: May imply a suddden loss of control in ones own personal life. In certain instances, may represent spiritual humility.

ACADEMY: Represents an obstacle which must be endured and finally, overcome. Rationalizes strict and determinate behavior. Symbolic of any form of mental anxiety.

ACCEPTED: May imply a form of wish-fulfillment, especially concerning our 'position' with a group. Concern about popularity.

ACCIDENT: Expresses a momentary loss of control, or loss of reason. We may be experiencing a form of repressed aggression.

ACCORDION: Involves our own breathing and hence, involves our physical health. Mirth and contentment add a dynamic dimension to this psychological representation

ACCOUNTANT: In this, we address our own 'self-worth'. Have we been involved in unscrupulous behavior? Have we earned our own merit.

ACE OF SPADES: We are involved in 'high stakes' and we fear a great loss. We are examining levels of personal risk in our life. Do our exploits endanger others, especially, our families?

ACHAEMENDES: The historic Greek postulate which interprets dreams and the specific calender dates upon which they occur.

ACID: Implies a form of suppressed hatred and anger. We may feel threatened, or intruded upon. Slow-burning envy may be involved.

ACORN: Represents the seed our unlimited potential. Signifies the courage to change and build anew.

ACROBAT: May involve distrust in ones own ability, or, the stressful, yet well-balanced order of our own decision making. Naturally, the appropriate interpretation is dependent on the relative skill of the juggler figure itself.

ACTIVE IMAGINATION: Jungian technique which involves recreating our dreams in waking life, with characters and full dialogue. This technique is believed to dredge up our repressed, or entirely forgotten, dream symbols.

ACTOR: May involve feelings about our levels of personal deception. Are our lies replacing our truths? May also involve our concerns about 'public opinion' and our relative popularity.

ADAM AND EVE: May involve feelings or moral or sexual guilt. Have we betrayed a certain trust?

ADDICT: Unconscious warning against escapism. We must face up to our demons before we lose our sense of Self.

ADVENTURE: Concern about personal danger, or an oncoming perilous situation. Perhaps we desire conflict and horror in our otherwise, ordinary lives.

AESCULAPIUS: Ancient Greek doctor who inspired a form of dream interpretation to heal the sick.

AFRICA: May symbolize a return to our native and primal self. How do we fair in the wild? Are we 'at one' with the environment?

AGE: Involves a feeling of irrational worthlessness. May also involve the 'lessons' learned in life.

ALBATROSS: Represents tranquility which is somehow threatened. This figure depicts freedom paired with vulnerability.

ALBINO: Resisting the 'purity' of a natural event or situation. Confronting the virginal aspects of ones own sexuality.

ALCHEMIST: Represents a blending of disparate parts. Witnessing a dramatic, and nearly miraculous, change in ones own life.

ALLEY: This figure represents an extremely difficult decision with very few real options. We are forced to make a choice.

ALLIGATOR: This figure represents an emotional threat just below the level of our perception, or understanding. Danger felt, but not seen.

ALPHA WAVES: These are the measured brain wave patterns of an individual in deep sleep.

AMAZON: This figure involves a gender related imagery, concerning power or submissiveness, dependent upon our dreaming relationship with the powerful female figure.

AMPUTATE: Each body part represents a unique psychological (and spiritual) state of comprehension. We need to determine which aspect of ourselves has disappeared, or been taken away.

ANALYST: This involves the dreamer analyzing him or herself. It also involves a confession of repressed feelings.

ANCIENT ARCHITECTURE: This figure may involve spiritual longing, or conversely, a fear of aging and 'slow' death.

ANGEL: The figure involves feelings of morality, or guilt. It is also an indication of emotional euphoria, a winged 'trip' through the clouds. What does the angel demonstrate in ourselves?

ANIMA/ANIMUS Jungian conceptualization wherein men dream of the women within themselves and women dream of the men within THEMSELVES.

ANT: This figure concerns our feelings about hard work and the real obstacles which stand in the way of our ultimate success.

ANTARCTICA: This archetype represents an alienated or 'isolated' state of emotional being. Whay are we alone. Have we left someone, or something, cold?

APE: In this imagery, we refer to our unmanageable, or otherwise 'wild', huamn nature. The experience of the ape mirrors our natural instincts. Is it caged? Is it threatening to others?

APPLE: This archetype may represent health, wisdom, sexual revelation or some other form of 'worldly' knowledge.

ARCHETYPE: The terminology used for the visible symbols of the Unconscious. These symbols have existed throughout the ages, consistant in the memory of man.

ARROW: Represents a 'target', or aim, which involves some form of tension and eventual release. A direct cause and effect relationship.

ARTEMIDORUS: The ancient Roman who wrote the famous ONEIROCRITICA.

This was the first 'modern' book concerning dream interpretation.

ARTIST: This figure may refer to our untapped creative potential. In another sense, we may be concerned with our own destructive forces and anti-social behavior.

ASHES: The aftermath of a burning emotion. This is the feeling we are left with after a storm relationship. In some sense, it is a return to our 'truest' self.

ASTROLOGY: In the dream sense, we are interpreting our own psychological character via the code of the Zodiac.

ASYLUM: This dramatic figure represents a form of emotional distress which must be faced up to. We cannot 'scramble' reality to escape from its real effects. We must surrender our chaotic waking deception.

ATHLETIC: This figure refers to overcoming our own inner obstacles. Can we surpass ourselves and move into new, successful realities?

ATTACK: This imagery involves our own self-guilt. As such, we must confront our attacker and learn its real motivations. Why do we persecute ourselves? Is some outside force damaging us?

ATTORNEY: This powerful figure represents our inability to defend our own actions. Why is someone speaking for us? Are we experiencing submissiveness before an authority figure?

AURA: Represents an accumulation of 'glowing' attributes attached to an individual. Dealing with an 'out-of-reach' personage.

AUTHORITY FIGURE: This figure may involve a lapse in our personal responsibility and real direction in life. Do we experience guilt fom being OURSELVES: bad, or tyrannical, leaders?

AWAKE: This imagery may involve a concern about our dreams in our waking life. We may be confusing the message of the Unconscious with the reality of our physical perceptions.

AXIS: This figure refers to a far removed source, or force, which has a very real effect upon our waking reality. The axis refers to an unseen power which brings either balance or chaos into our lives.

BABY: May involve some form of personal regression, or, a return to innocence. Since a child's needs are fulfilled, we may be experiencing the real pressures of our own responsibility toward others.

BACKGROUND: Every element in a dream is crucial towards its absolute interpretation. The background of a dream represents our 'fixed' psychological state of mind. In another sense, background scenery represents where (or who) we want to be in the very near future. We must determine our function within that place.

BACON: In a strictly metaphorical sense, bacon represents our livlihood. Are we generous, or greedy, with our accumulated resources. Has our hunger misguided our own humanity?

BAG/BAGGAGE: A bag symbolizes the load we carry in life. Where do we bring these elaborate living emotional experiences. Is the bag heavy or light. Are we held back by our painful memories?

BALD: May represent purity and the unmasking of our own cloak of deception. We are revealing our truth to the world. We feel a need to be accepted on our own merit. We may be exibiting some form of overcompensation in our new-found radical method of exposure.

BALANCE: This concept may involve our own personal test to remain a well-balanced individual, in an otherwise shakey and chaotic world. Do any particular objects help us maintain our balance? What should happen if we fall? Is the world solid, while we teeter close to the edge?

BALLERINA: May represent a sudden loss of personal obstacles. At the same time, vulnerability remains. As such, we must determine why our Unconscious chooses the metaphors of strength and beauty. Is there a struggle between the two concepts? What is the emotional feeling of the music which moves the ballerina to dance?

BALLOON: Complex figure involving vulnerability, regression and the wayward freedom of innocence. Has a child lost his balloon? Are we somehow trapped in balloon, with no sand bags, to land us firmly back upon the ground? Why do we find ourselves aimlessly floating through life?

BAMBOO: This is a strong and resiliant plant. Therefore, it may represent native fairness. It may also represent an 'easy' life-style, in the form of wish-fulfillment.

BAPTISM: This image involves a drastic return to innocence. We may feel the need to purify ourselves, perhaps from a very adult act of sexuality, or violence. We are returning into the waters of the womb. We need a second chance.

BAR: This figure represents a 'right of passage', a sort of social and sexual testing ground upon which to measure ones level of relative maturity and communal approval.

BARREN: This image seems to suggest an impotent life-style. We may feel a need to renew ourselves in life. We may want to dirty our hands a bit with life's real experiences. As things stand now, we feel lifeless and isolated. The dream suggests a desired change.

BASEMENT: May be symbolic of the Unconscious itself. We need to face this hidden shelter which reveals our own fear and anxieties.

BASIN: Involves the relative fullness, or emptiness. of our emotional state of mind in waking life. Is the water draining? Is it dirty?

BAT: A baseball bat represents a happening with deep personal, or social, impact. How will we perform? A vampire bat may involve our owm erratic behavior and an accumulation of tiny fears which paralyzes our forward movement into new realities.

BATHROOM: May involve an honest attempt to face ourselves and purge ourselves of sin. A need to re-invent ourselves in society.

BEACH: If we face the ocean, we may be facing our Unconscious desires. If we face land, we may be returning to a 'normal' lifestyle.

BEAM: Represents our psychological framework. Are we sturdy in our emotions, or crumbling?

BEARD: This figure may represent strength and vigor, or rather conversely, a need to hide. In female, a reflection of the animus may be observed.

BED: This figure represents something close to oneself, something very personal. Who has discovered our personal secrets? Who has been sleeping in YOUR bed?

BEGGAR: A stark reflection of social alienation. This archetype may also involve feelings of unworthiness.

BELL: An Unconscious warning to be prepared for something which may be (or just seems to be,) threatening. Facing up to a difficult reality. Preperation for an idea which changes our outlook on life.

BETWEEN: This figure represents forced choices and reflects upon the absurdity of close-minded individuals. Is everything black and white in our lives? Can we find a grey area?

BIKINI: This form of pre-pubescant eroticism, may reflect a regression into our adolescence. Simple and harmless escapism, which may have very little to do with actual sexuality. Visual candy meant to disguise the bitter realities of life.

BIRDS: Complex figure which may involve spiritual longing. May also involve concerns about child-rearing, or 'nesting'.

BINOCULARS; We may be expressing concern, or guilt, about an acquired knowledge which was not meant for us to know. Conversely, we may be searching for the hidden realities of life. Is our search valid, or does it intrude upon the real privacy of others?

BISEXUAL: This image may involve compensation or wish-fulfillment due to a lack of sexual experience. May involve sexual confusion.

BITE: Involves devouring another person's attributes. It may also involve muzzling our own aggession. In the ancient and archetypal sense, it reflects a self-examination of our own moral worthiness.

BITTER: Any reality which is 'hard to swallow'. Guilt and shame about some aspect of our recent behavior.

BLACK: Involves the 'unknown' and perhaps, its frightening potential. May involve represses aspects of our own desires.

BLANKET: May represent a fear of isolation and lonliness. Expressing a need for protection. May involve chastity.

BLAZE: May involve creative, or destructive powers, or influences. An attempt to hold passion in check.

BLOOD: Represents our life force. Are we harming, or mutilating, some crucial aspect of ourself? Loss of spiritual hope.

BLIND: Closing our eyes to something we cannot cope with, especially our own behavior.

BLUE: Involves potential and our limitless mental resources. The lighter the shade of blue, the easier the psychological event.

BOAT: Represents our conscious equilibrium. How do we fair in the figurative ocean of our own emotional framework?

BONE: Involves aspects of our own fixed reasoning. Are our thoughts, or beliefs, threatened? Have we broken our own rules?

BOOK: Repesents old wisdom which rings eternally true. Is our behavior in accord with our own knowledge?

BOTTLE: May involve sexuality and a pouring of emotions. Represents celebration of physical self and human potential. Broken for luck.

BOX: A box may refer to our perception of a four-sided universe. May be a reference to our beliefs. Are we trapped in our own world?

BRAINWAVES: Variable pulse produced by the brain in MOST states of consciousness.

BREAD: May refer to our own sacrifices. Involves feelings about our peers and society in general. Do we break bread?

BREATH: Breathing is symbolic of our own health. Has it been disrupted, or accelerated into 'anxious' tension? WHY?

BRICK: May involve some obstacle, or stumbling block in our development. Do we build a home, or its opposite, a wall?

BRIDGE: Involves serious emotional ties. We pay a price for emotional commitment. To heal, we may 'burn bridges'.

BROKEN: May involve a release of tension, or responsibility. Represents change and a restructured beginning.

BROTHER: Desired traits reflected in sibling. Represents some unspoken completion of Self, either positive, or negative.

BUDDHA: May involve contemplation of life's meaning. Loosely reflective of DREAM itself. Inner calm coveted.

BUG: May indicate an inescapable annoyance. Involves psychological anxiety expressed physiologically.

BULL: May represent repressed sexual, or aggressive, emotions; perhaps the conflict of both. Self-examination necessary. Are we capable of accepting our own emotions? Can we transcend them?

BUTTERFLY: Fragile hope, the expression of ones own soul. Are we able to give up control, and 'unbind' our feelings of love?

CABIN: May indicate a psychological escape into a 'simpler' way of life. A return to ones 'comfortable' roots. Escapism and wish-fulfillment may be indicated, but not in a definite manner.

CACTUS: May concern our own defence mechanisms. Do we keep someone, something, or some knowledge, away from us. Conversely, are we kept at a distance from another?

CADET: Involves the concept of innocence versus adulthood. Self-examination of maturity and morality.

CAGE: May involve a repression of individuality, or conversely, an expression of guilt.

CAKE: Indicates acceptance in society. Is the Self, celebrated? The cake is reflective or our perceived quality of life.

CALENDER: May involve an elaborate concern about aging, or a perceived uneventful passage of time. Anxiety about our personal accomplishments, or the lack, thereof.

CAMEL: Indicative of feelings of sexuality and/or fertility. May also involve emotional maturity and trustworthiness.

CANDLE: The imagery indicates a fleeting, yet miraculous, moment of hope and/or love. Faith in significant spiritual matter.

CANNIBAL: Involves release, or the sacrifice of oneself. May involve sexual submissiveness, or confessions of corrupt behavior.

CANYON: May involve a feeling of helplessness in a vast and unreachable universe. May be reflective of personal reverence.

CAR: Modern archetype representing self-image and status. May indicate wish-fulfillment concerning freedom and sexual confidence.

CARAVAN: Indicative of a social 'connection' created to withstand harsh outside elements encountered in life. Determination found in any interactive union, including marriage.

CASTLE: Represents an incarnation of power and a form of protective isolational. Why must we feel 'above' and 'apart' from the world? Is our power protective, or, destructive? Are we guilty of our own tyranny?

CASTRATION: May involve a form of psychological impotence, or a sacrifice to a sexual partner. Are we cheated emotionally?

CAT: This figure may be linked with the Unconscious itself. The half wild/half domestic nature of the cat indicates a complex balance of these natures within ourself. Seduction planned.

CAVE: Involves a seeking of safety and protection. Some outside force causes us to feel vulnerable.

CELEBRATION: May involve new psychological development, or, a renewed sense of self. May involve form of social recognition.

CENOTAPH: May refer to a feeling of disassociation. We must determine how to re-enter a once familiar world.

CENTAUR: The archetype for being carried away by our own passionate desires. What behavior of the horse does the half/man illustrate?

CENTER: Refers to the most important aspect of any event. Seeking the 'truth' about our waking concerns. Illustrates best approach.

CEREMONY: Indicates an awareness of our own necessary self-sacrifice. Are we ready to take on responsibilities?

CHALICE: Our capacity for emotional love. Are we able to help those less fortunate than ourselves?

CHARGE: May involve a passionate release of repressed emotions. What force awakens these passions? Have we lost self-control?

CHASED: Fear of facing oneself and ones own problems. An attempt to evade the truth. May also indicate a fear of change.

CHERUB: Represents the balance of mental and emotional processes. Warns against the danger of innocent and naive behavior.

CHEST: Represents submerged memories of our past. May involve emotional commitment, if filled with new clothing, or toys.

CHILD: Regression into simpler times when ALL needs were fulfilled. May conversely, involve some form of spiritual transcendence.

CHILDBIRTH: Involves a form or revelation, or new discovery. Represents the pain of new beginnings.

CHIMNEY: May involve family and hearth, but also may indicate mischief and deception among relatives, or a common group.

CHORUS: Represents our 'performance' within a group setting. Are we disgraced, or do we stand out? Do we blend in, entirely unnoticed?

CHRIST: Complex image ranging from personal guilt to personal redemption. Christ embodies 'catalog' of biblical symbolism.

CHURCH: Reflects our feelings about morality and dogma. Is there a concealed motive behind our acts of goodness?

CIGARETTE: Refers to social ritual, sexual control, and on (yet) another level, our own self-destuctive behavior. Apprehension.

CIRCLE: This figure represents infinite potential, no stopping points, no walls. Personal transfiguration, higher consciousness.

CLAIRVOYANCE: Theorists refute it, but history and the infinite nature of the Unconscious, hint otherwise.

CLAW: Represents an attack on our sensibility or perception. May involve our own mistreatment of another person.

CLEANING: Symbolizes an attempt to erase our own guilt. We wish to 'purify' ourselves.

CLOCK: Involves a concern about time and the pressures of modern life. May also represent 'fixed' attitudes of the dreamer.

CLOWN: Paradoxical emotions, the hidden truth behind a charade. Roundabout revelations.

COCK: Represents resiliency and a determination to achieve all our goals. May represent protection of family.

COFFIN: Indicates an acceptance of the full parameters of change. Open-eyed awareness of (and preparation for) the future.

COLLECTIVE UNCONSCIOUS: Unlimited pool of knowledge into which each and every human being is connected.

COLOR: Each color has its own relevant associations. (see Red, Green, Blue, White, Yellow, Purple)

CONTRACT: Concern about keeping our 'word'. May involve the price we have to pay for choices taken in life.

CORN: A field of corn represents a feeling of inadequacy and confusion in the direction we must take in life. A single ear of corn represents a 'good feeling' about the future.

COSTUME: Represents identity of self to the public. Do we conform to society, or distance ourselves from its normal practices.

COUNCIL: Represents an appraisal by a force higher than ourselves. Who must we 'answer to' in this life?

COW: The combination of our emotions and our spirituality. Involves maternal simplicity and trust.

CRASH: Involves separate and colliding forces in our experience. A decision must be made in order to avoid incapacitating stress.

CROSS: May involve personal sacrifice and moral decision making. Reflection upon paths previously chosen.

CROW: Symbolizes a thirst for knowledge and worldly gain. Indicative of a restless spirit.

CRYSTAL: Refers to an acceptance of our own insight. Do we believe in our own gifts?

CUT: Disconnecting some reality which is far too difficult to absorb. Freeing oneself from emotional pain.

DAISY: Represents a new beginning after complete and absolute change. Life renewed after death. Symbolic of finding enlightenment through innocence.

DANCING: Involves our working interrelationships with others. Alone, we expose self-confidence and inner release.

DEATH: Refers to a deep sense of loss, however, this loss allows for a profound transcendence in our overall point of view.

DECEPTION: May involve concern about misleading loved ones. Fear of confronting (or revealing) desires.

DEEP: A vivid imagery expressing repressed emotions. Are we hiding some truth, or preparing to reveal (or expose) that truth?

DEER: Combining innocence, frailty and beauty. The stag image may involve independence and elusiveness.

DELICATE: Represents psychological vulnerability. May conversely represent a fear of our own destructive power. Lack of sensitivity.

DELTA WAVES: (Measured) low-frequency brainwaves which occur during deep sleep.

DEMAGOGUE: An attempt to control society in order to erase (or at least limit,) our own personal fear of that society.

DEMON: May refer to the struggle of moral decision making. Involves facing personal demons in order to overcome their luring influence.

DEN: Complex form of regression caused by a fear of our (perceived) mature responsibilities.

DEPOT: Involves feelngs of confusion and isolation, perhaps caused by unexpected and unavoidable adjustments in our experience.

DEVIL: May question our own deepest feelings about being seduced by someone or something.

DESERT: May refer to a cessation in our personal growth. A loss of direction. Are we mesmerized by our unfulfilled wishes and desires?

DIARRHEA: An attempt to purge oneself of a reality which was once accepted. Any 'forced' release of 'incriminating' information.

DIG: May involve a search for something in our past. A slow unraveling of Unconscious memories.

DINNER: Complex dream image involving our deepest associations with family and society. What is amiss, or erroneous, in the scene?

DIRT: May refer to feelings of impurity. Conversely, may be indicative of maternal behavior, (dependent on where the dirt, or earth, is visualized.)

DISAPPEAR: May involve feelings of insignificance. May also imply a feeling of growing distant from a loved one.

DISTANCE: Signifies our separation from important goals. Does our goal move closer, or do we fall further and further away from it?

DIVA: May involve wish-fulfillment and overcompensation due to feelings of insecurity, or inadequacy. Concern about public opinion.

DIVER: Explores the relationship between the conscious and the Unconscious. Have we regained control over our own emotions?

DOCK: Represents transitional states of consciousness. Preparing ourselves for a new emotional situation in our life.

DOG: May involve a sense of deep trust and loyalty. Has this trust been broken? Have we caused someone to turn on us?

DOLL: Refers to a perception of an ideal self. Wish-fulfillment concerning our relative appearance and life-style.

DOLPHIN: Strong representation of emotional trust combined with psychological freedom. Well-balanced outlook on life.

DOOR: Dependent on the position of the door, we are either denied entry into into a new awareness, or expressing the transition.

DOUBLE: May refer to contradictory points of view. A definitive choice may need to be made in llfe. Self image explored.

DOUBLE-JOINTED: This figure alludes to the highest potential of our being. An opportunity presents itself which will surpass the norm.

DRAGON: Refers to the limitless nature of the Unconscious. Archetypal imagery of love's uncontrollable powers.

DRAIN: The need to purge ourselves of unwanted emotions which hamper our growth and development.

DRAPES: May involve a complexity of emotions which cloud our reason and perceptual awareness of 'hard' truths.

DRIP: Indicative of a self-inflicted torture of self. An avoidance of flooding emotions which cannot be denied.

DROWN: Refers to the fear and paralysis involved in difficult emotional situations. Polar opposite of the Dolphin figure.

DRUM: Indicative of our heartbeat and our sensitivity to the true rhythm of life. A 'gut' feeling.

DRUG: A concern about social or individual limitations. May involve a desperate need to re-invent reality. Invokes dependency.

DRY: Archetypal image of mental or emotional exhaustion. Desperate isolation. In need of love's healing powers.

DUMB: Indicates a lack of understanding or lack of connection. Social unraveling. In this sense, alienation may be implied.

DYBBUK: Involves being drained of vital resources. Does our own success depend on the sacrifice and despair of others?

EAGLE: Powerful representation of freedom and inner strength. Wisdom which is gained from contemplative experience.

EARTH: This figure is symbolic of humanity itself. The acceptance of the human condition; vulnerable, yet poised and resilient.

ECLIPSE: Refers to the higher nature of ALL unions and the absolute necessity for acquiring an appreciation for true altruism.

ECZEMA: May involve a corruption or disruption in how we sense the world around us, but especially refers to how we perceive ourselves.

EDEN: A complex image involving God, love and beauty. An unnecessary need to 'possess' these miracles which are 'offered' to us freely.

EGG: Involves the nurturing of new ideas and creative potential. The birth of a new self-awareness.

EGO: In Freud's view, this image involves our highest sense of self. May simply refer to a need for personal recognition.

EIGHT: Represents strength in its symmetry, completeness and balance. In ancient times and still today, the number reflects an 'ideal' state of being.

ELECTRICITY: Represents the full 'energy' of our human (or inhuman) potential. Startling new ideas and/or spiritual revelations.

ELEMENT: This figure represents the 'spiritual' understanding of our 'physical' world. Creation seen as fully reflective of a true divinity.

ELEPHANT: Primarily refers to positive strength, determination and maintaining a grand stature in society. As the old adage states, 'Luck comes to those who stand tall and courageous in life.'

ELEVATOR: May refer to an unsteady emotional framwork. Experiencing continuous ups and downs in ones waking life. We must stop the elevator and begin a comfortable new level of self-awareness.

EMACIATE: Involves a feeling of lacking some 'true' nourishment in life. May involve feelings of social insignificance. Do people refuse to take us seriously? What are we lacking in life? How can we acquire these things?

EMBROIDERY: This figure may involve the necessity of social cohesion. We may need to organize to obtain our 'real' results.

EMPTY: Complex figure which may involve some aspect of arrested development. We must analyze the real catalyst for our negative outlook upon waking reality.

ENGRAVE: This figure addresses our feelings about permanance. Are we insecure about our 'firm' accomplishments and relative social standing? Have we built a lasting relationship?

EPILEPSY: Refers to confusion and a loss of direction. Are we fluctuating between our decision making and our actual behavior?

EQUATION: Indicates questions in need of answers, or conversely, solutions in need of inquiry. Are we deceiving ourselves?

EQUESTRIAN: In this figure, how we ride our steed represents how we perceive our own sexuality and purposeful self-confidence.

ERECT: This figure represents our own psychological and emotional 'stance' in the world. Are we lofty and strong in character, or are we unsure of ourselves? Do we feel like we're falling apart?

ERUPTION: Represents the point of zero tolerance. Refers to the consequences of emotions 'forced' to the surface of our awareness.

ESCAPE: Freeing ourelves from problems without suffering any consequences. But, to clear our conscious, we must accept guilt.

ESP: Involves an intimate connection with another human being. In some sense, civilization strives for this metaphysical connection.

ETERNITY: Refers to an honest evaluation of Self. Are we worthy of spiritual enlightenment? Do we serve our humanity well?

ETHEREAL: This figure represents our 'highest gifts', such as love, faith and all the other intangible benefactions which make us truly human. Represents the first step of spiritual transfiguration.

EUCHARIST: Personal sacrifice to purify ourselves and gain redemption. A wholehearted return to inocence.

EUNUCH: This figure represents a lack of drive, sexual or otherwise. Have we grown lazy? Are we submissive before some repressive force?

EVERGREEN: Strength, moral character and eternal life are all suggested in this powerful dream metaphor. A Christmas tree embodies our figurative spiritual journey, or return to God.

EXCAVATE: Facing a once repressed, or hidden, truth. Preparing to expose ourselves to the world: including friends, family and peers.

EXCREMENT: May involve an emotional repulsion. Perhaps we are disgusted by our own actions in the past. Accepting the absolute necessity for some form of personal change in our life.

EXPLOSION: This figure may involve a complex form of paranoia. Primarily refers to anxiety about a shocking revelation.

EXTRATERRESTRIAL: Represents help and hope from an outside force. Expressing a wish to be heard and understood.

EXTROVERT: In oneself, this behavior represents a fluid release of personal expression. In others, the behavior seems to suggest a complete loss of sanity and reason! Talk about double-standards!

EYES: This archetype represents a fear of being discovered, or 'caught', in some treacherous act. A sudden loss of privacy.

FABLE: The fable within the dream represents a decisive turn in our personal outlook on life. A personal search for fundamental truths.

FABRIC: Dream fabrics represent our moods and our ability to fold, or remove, these emotions from our immediate experience.

FACTORY: Involves a feeling of dehumanization due to mind-numbing tasks. May involve bad health or an unhealthy environment.

FAN: Replaying a difficult emotional situation over and over in our mind. Achieveing no results. Confusion as to our course of action.

FAITH: Exploring the psychological causes and consequences of our belief system. Is our faith denying our trust in Self?

FALLING: Since we have yet to fall, our Unconscious may be offering us a support beam. Will we regain our balance, or fall flat on our face? What causes us to fall in the first place?

FAMILY: Represents our safety net and our sense of sanity. Only when we establish our sense of Self will we AID those around us.

FARM: This figure represents our own health, harvest and honest ability to work for these things. Is the farm thriving, or barren?

FAT: This figure may involve excessive behavior. May be indicative of a complex fear of intimacy and ones own sexuality.

FATHER: Represents our own authoritative force. Do we act as a guide, or do we misuse our relative power over others?

FATIGUE: Indicative of emotional exhaustion. We must stand back and look at the 'big picture' in order to establish our next best move.

FEAST: Involves complex aspects of our acceptance of life's bounty. Comments on our relationship with the greater society.

FEATHER: Represents wisdom, frailty and peace. In ancient Egypt, the feather represented a divine love which was weighed against an individual's heart in the afterlife. Are our own hearts heavy?

FECES: Purging of feelings, especially those concerned with someone once desired, or greatly admired. Rejecting what was once accepted.

FERRY BOAT: In an ancient interpretation, this dream involved a deep spiritual transition. Today, our Unconscious may be illustrating a 'rut' which we are stuck within. Both are valid.

FETAL POSITION: This figure may involve a complex form of regression. Returning to a 'safe haven' to escape responsibility and the otherwise 'cold' condition of reality.

FETISH: Involves faith in ones own 'personal' magic. May involve a belief in luck and good fortune based on ones moral character.

FEVER: This figure involves either our passion, aggresssion, or fear. Why is the body sick? What influences are we fighting off?

FILM: This figure involves a 'capturing' of life. We are attempting to remember an individual, or situation, and our attachment there.

FINGERS: This image involves our potential humanity, in other words, what WE ALONE can do. Do we point a finger of blame?

FIRE: Involves intense emotions or creative potential. This figure may also involve a form of spiritual awakening, or revelation.

FISH: This figure represents how we 'adapt' to an emotional affair. May also involve ideas and memories flowing in the Unconscious.

FIST: A fist represents fighting for a cause. Are we prepared to take responsibility for our violence? Are we able to negotiate?

FIT: May involve a comfortable reality. May involve desiring someone else's comfortable reality. Looks can be deceiving.

FIT: This figure represents a split between our mind and our body. Are our needs outweighing our reason?

FIVE: This number represents man and more specifically, a human body which is fully equipped with a Soul. Ancient wisdom teaches us that the human Soul is the elusive fifth element (quintessence.)

FLAG: This figure involves a social 'movement'. Is this movement designed for the good of all, or is it self-serving and repressive?

FLOAT: This figure indicates emotional peace. May also involve our receptive attitudes in various levels of consciousness.

FLOWER: Represents the most fragile aspects of ourself: our love and our deepest faith. What color are our flowers? Are they fresh? Are they wild?

FLYING: If we are experiencing controlled flight, we may be indicating a well-balanced psychological outlook on a situation. Conversely, if we find ourselves out of control, we must prepare ourselves for some form of rude awakening.

FLY (INSECT): This figure seems to suggest demonic or immoral behavior which we cannot escape. Caught in an unhealthy reality.

FOG: Indicates a fear of the unknown. We must carefully analyze ANY object which appears in our field of vision, despite the fog.

FOREIGNER: Represents some form of social alienation. May also involve a form of disorientation. Why do we feel out of place?

FOREST: Involves a return to our primal, spontaneous and naturalistic self. Are we able to momentarily drop our human fears and act on our own instincts?

FORESIGHT: Involves metaphysical discussions about time. Is time linear, circular, or infinite? What does YOUR dream suggest?

FORGE: Involves intense emotions and our ability to give them a psychological purpose in our life. For example: Do we forge armour to protect ourselves from some form of emotional heartache?

FORM: Forms, or shapes, have diverse meanings. Primarily, we must analyze the interrelationship between lines and empty space.

FORM, PAPER: Represents the dehumanization placed upon individuals by society at large. Are we victims, or victimizers, of this inhuman behavior?

FOUNDATION: Indicative of our emotional background. We are able to grow, if we are 'solid' in the foundation of our past development.

FOUNTAIN: Represents an 'outpouring' of emotion. Signifies some sudden elation which gladdens our heart. The joys of life.

FOUR: Represents perfection, order and truth. North, south, east and west. Earth, air, fire and water. The completion of reality.

FOWL: Refers to reproduction and laying eggs, but more importantly, refers to being 'weighed down' in the physical world. Dense.

FRATERNITY: Designed to create life-long social orders, but sometimes propogate sadistic, anti-social and cult-like behavior.

FREEZE: The representation of freezing involves alienation, isolaion and a stagnation of self. Will we allow ourselves to 'heal' from our devastation, in order to 'feel' once again?

FREUD, SIGMUND: Called the father of modern psychiatry. Developed the concept of a many layered consciousness. Strict scientific approach gave him the theory of Id, Ego and Superego.

FROG: May represent a riddle, elusive truth, or hidden beauty. Does the frog indicate a strength of character we have overlooked?

FRY: May involve an internalization of home through a poignant memory. May involve being 'captured' and receiving punishment.

FUMES: This figure involves instinctual fears. We need to determine whether they are sound, or entirely prejudiced and irrational.

FUNERAL: Indicates a time for personal renewal. This figure addresses a need to stand alone in life. Building character by removing our support systems.

FUNGUS: Unconscious ideas, or emotions, which are just below the surface of our awareness. Will they aid in our development?

FUR: May symbolize our need for protection in a cold, harsh and inhuman world. Does 'status' lend us security?

FUTURISTIC: Involves a projection of reality based upon our concurrent perception of reality. What does the future tell us about our own past and present?

GADGET: Involves our skill, or ability, to realize certain goals. Is our dream gadget useless? Are we barking up the wrong tree?

GALLERY: This figure involves psychological revelations of self. Which characteristics do we wish to expose to the outside world?

GAME: This figure involves our feelings about winning and losing. What is our relationship with our competitor? Do we lose on purpose, in an effort to gain our competitors love?

GARDEN: Indicative of how we perceive ourselves and the fruits of our labor. Do we reap what we sow?

GARGOYLE: Projecting some aspect of our primal aggression in order to protect ourselves from emotional, or psychological, damage. Similar to the flashing of teeth, or a bark without a bite.

GARLIC: A potent purifying agent against harmful, or unhealthy, environments. Exposing guilt about our own 'poisonous' behavior.

GATE: Involves a self-examination of our own worthiness to pass into another state of consciousness. Are we confident in our desire?

GELATIN: May involve an elaborate form of wish-fulfillment, including an insatiable, or obsessive, form of sexual desire.

GENITALIA: Indicative of our complex feelings about procreation. May involve fears about our sexual behavior, or social conduct.

GEOGRAPHY: A dream's geography reflects the emotional and psychological state of mind of the dreamer.

GESTALT THERAPY: Frederick Perls' dream technique involving dream re-enactment. A search for the 'central' meaning of the dream, discovered from the 'fully realized' sum of its parts.

GHOST: This complex imagery indicates a direct message from our own Unconscious. Our relationship with the deceased is pertinent. What does this person wish to tell us about ourselves and our fears?

GIBBERISH: Represents personal frustration due to a lack of self-expression. Are we able to communicate with our loved ones?

GIFT: Represents our feelings of self-worth. Is the gift expected? Pregnancy may be indicated. Preparation for an unexpected, yet necessary, personal metamorphosis.

GLASS: Indicative of something, or someone, seen and desired, yet entirely out of reach. What causes this delicate separation?

GLUE: May involve our fear of social, or personal, entanglement. May indicate a need to initiate our 'peer groups' unification.

GNARLED: This powerful imagery involves our feelings about facing the truth. The truth can be ugly, but beneath its twisted mask stands dignity and moral strength.

GOAT: Indicative of our own excessive behavior, especially our sexual desire which highlights disturbed, or irrational, behavior.

GOD/GODDESS: This figure refers to the separation of man from God. Indicative of the goals we 'ultimately' strive for.

GODZILLA: Represents technical advances which threaten a mankind unable to 'accept' their absolute responsibility.

GRAB: Involves the sudden realization of being 'caught' in a fastidious situation. We need to analyze which body part is seized.

GRASS: The lawn surrounds our house and refers to a healthy, or unhealthy, living condition. Concerns about social appearance.

GREEN: Involves delayed potential in conceptualizations such as ripening, envy and immaturity. Examining a gradual process.

GRIFFEN: Combining the symbolic meanings of the Lion and the Eagle. Indicative of the strength involved in attaining moral character.

GROW: Represents the blueprint, or potential, of highest achievement. Does our environment encourage this growth?

GUARD: Represents self-imposed personal barriers. Do our past experiences interfere with our future goals? Do we fear the future?

GUMBO SOUP: Combining separate aspects of our own personality. May involve some form of social cohesion. Explores human tolerance.

GUT: Questions the 'price' of our own success. Do we destroy, or damage, others in our own insatiable quest to succeed?

GYMNASTICS: Represents our relative psychological and emotional balance. Is our performance dangerous? Are we about to fall?

GYPSY: This figure represents movement, freedom and magic. A need to move. Fear of establishing roots. Explores a restless spirit.

HADES: May involve a stagnation of self and the subsequent loss of hope. Caught up in personal despair. A need to forgive oneself.

HAIL: Indicative of a slow, yet penetrating, emotional pain. Exploring a difficult transition in ones personal life.

HAIR: Implies virility, strength and sexual ease. Is our hair long, thick and healthy, or limp, receding and patchy?

HALLOWEEN: Indicative of a need for absolute release. Becoming the embodiment of our own free spirit. Removing the 'shackles' of life's daily burdens.

HALO: Indicative of an individual's moral value. This dream may be giving us clues about an individual's 'real', (yet unseen,) worth.

HAMMER: Refers to a sense of psychological, or emotional, closure. If the pounding is incessant, we may be (needlessly) battling ourselves. A need to resolve a precise internal conflict.

HANDS: Refers to our relative 'handling' and 'manipulation' of life. What do our 'dream' hands tell us about our own behavior?

HANG: Represents accepting personal resonsibility and atonement. Disregarding public opinion. Staying true to oneself.

HARBOR: A safe haven for our social and personal relationships. Are the harbor's waters calm? Are the boats well maintained?

HARVEST: Indicative of our ability to grow as individuals. Represents an ability to withstand necessary changes.

HAUNT: Facing our own fears. What aspect of our reality are we least able to confront? Why do we needlessly torture ourselves?

HAWK: This figure represents clear vision and a keen instinctual ability to judge fairly. Looking at the 'big picture'.

HEAD: This figure represents our psychological assessment of reality. Does our image of self, clash with our image of society?

HEADDRESS: Refers to our psychological acceptance of spiritual forces. Refers to a 'rational' approach to our own inner faith.

HEALTH: This figure acknowledges our strengths and limitations. What part of our body seems to appear, or 'feels', unhealthy?

HEARTH: This archetype refers to all social unions which display peaceful wisdom and absolute tranquility. Erasing ones fears.

HEAVEN: May invoke wish-fulfillment or an actual expression of personal enlightenment. Defining the joys of life.

HEEL: May be indicative of the relationship between power and subservience. A pain which refuses to go away. Exploring healing.

HELL: This figure involves an expression of personal torture, especially one involving personal guilt. Are we being punished?

HEMP: May involve an escape from reality. May indicate a preparation for deeper wisdom. Accepting realities potential.

HERMAPHRODITE: Indicative of the well-balanced blending of our masculine and feminine natures. Exploring ones desires.

HERO: Replacing psychological fears with our primal survival instinct. Conversely, does our need to be saved prevent us from saving ourselves?

HEX: This figure represents a fear of our own power and the 'price' we have to pay for our 'manipulation' of others.

HIDE, ANIMAL: Taking on the properties and characteristics of the animal itself. Conscious entry into our primal self.

HIEROGLYPHICS: A search for ancient wisdom. Perhaps revealing some aspect of the prehistoric Unconscious itself.

HIGHWAY TRAVEL: This figure represents a need for psychological changes in ones landscape. Potential unleashed.

HOAX: Explores a form of social deception. Are we misled in our beliefs or our actions? Who have we chosen to follow? Why?

HOLE: This figure involves a dearth of space which allows for an infinite amount of potential and growth. Do we fear new prospects?

HOLSTEIN: (see Cow)

HOME: Refers to our emotional center. A house is in the head, a home is in the heart. Addressing how we truly feel about ourselves.

HOOD: This figure involves a conscious removal of our crucial individuality. Becoming annonymous. Disappearing into a group.

HORIZON: Represents the absolute beginning (or end) of our projected belief system. The end which instigates the means.

HORNS: This figure refers to a straight-forward and honest approach to life. May refer to our feelings about long-term relationships.

HORSE: This figure represents fierce individuality. Indicative of the advanced SOCIAL structure of open-minded INDIVIDUALS.

HOUSE: Represents our psychological assessment of self. Each room illustrates diverse attitudes about our relative place in society.

HUNCHBACK: Exploring the relationship between loyalty and subservience. A need to free ourselves from social 'codes'.

HUNT: May indicate our working 'relationship' within a group, especially a group which correlates its strengths toward a goal.

HYBRID: Hybrids reflect internal struggles which either strengthen us, or weaken us. We need to determine the nature of our conflict.

HYGIENE: Involves an attempt to purify oneself from a guilty conscious. In males, relates to the 'discovering of sexuality'.

HYPNOSIS: Indicative of gaining control, or power, over our peers; unless, some outside force POSSESSES OUR BEHAVIOR!

ICE: Alienation, isolation and emotional stagnation. (Difficult) ENTRY into a new relationship, or EXIT out of an old relationship.

ICEBERG: This figure may refer to an underestimation of life's 'natural' forces. Denying the reality of our deepest emotions.

ICON: Refers to the relationship between physical reality and spiritual awakening. Do we know the length and breadth of our own soul?

IGUANA: This figure refers to our 'reptilian brain' and its lurking potential. Are we poised and prepared for some form of danger?

ILLNESS: Illustrates an unhealthy situation in our life. We must determine which parts of our body experience distress, and why.

IMAGE: Involving the relationship between our 'understood' self and our 'perceived' self. Do we recognize the face in the mirror?

IMBRUE: A 'physical' attempt to capture 'spiritual' strength. A ritual which 'challenges' and attempts to 'charm' spirit forces.

IMITATION: This figure may represent a difficulty in accepting oneself, or ones worth. An urgent need to fit into society.

IMMERSION: Whole-hearted acknowledgment of an absolute change. Preparing to brave a new state of consciousness.

IMPALE: Refers to a violent, or passionate, release of our repressed emotions. What force has propelled us to the surface?

INCENSE: Embodies a radiating source of spiritual love, sanctity and inner peace. Exploring the source of our personal faith.

INCEST: This figure often involves a fear of the outside world and all its 'new' and 'strange' experiences. Narcissistic relationship.

INCONTINENT: This imagery involves a loss of self-control and a separation of body and mind. Why exactly do we feel 'deranged'?

INCUBUS: This archetype reveals a repressed sexuality which demands immediate attention. Challenges the restriction of natural urges.

INDIANS, NATIVE AMERICAN: Indicative of personal power and a union with nature. Refers to a deep acceptance of our 'highest' naturalistic self.

INDUSTRIAL: Represents the sheer explosion of our social and 'civilized' potential which sometimes ignores our individuality and true humanity. Suppressed emotional development.

INFANT: Indicative of regression. Fully examines the connection between irrational fear and protective instincts. Maturity.

INFESTATION: A conflict against individuals who attempt to invade our autonomy with therir powerful influence.

INFINITE: Explores our maximum potential. Indicative of our goals and desires. Spiritual acceptance of our own mortality.

INFLATE: Indicative of pent-up energy. We must 'release' the tension which we have built up within ourselves.

INK: Explores the value of our personal 'mark'. Are we trustworthy? Are our own judgements prejudiced by our own lack of trust?

INSECT: Indicative of a certain 'flustered' state of mind. May involve a slow, yet steady, increase in our anxiety levels.

INSTRUMENT: Unique instruments parallel unique emotional states of mind. Repressed memories lulled into consciousness.

ISLAND: Involves a deep examination of individuality. May also indicate a psychological 'trap'. Have we been abandoned?

ITCH: Indicates the error of inconclusivity. Sometimes a decision MUST be made!

IVORY TOWER: Indicative of our virtue and high standards. Explores our spiritual humility.

JACKAL: This figure questions the merits of a too strong sense of self. Explores our opportunistic behavior.

JACKHAMMER: Involved a 'fracturing' of our perceived reality. What force causes this elaborate destruction?

JACOB'S LADDER: May involve a form of escapism. Examines a self-assessment of our own spiritual worthiness.

JAGGED EDGE: Refers to our ability to enact a 'clean break'. Explores deep and very harsh emotional transitions.

JAR: Refers to emotions which are repressed, yet remain 'fixed' in our awareness. Aware of our own limitations. Helplessness.

JAW: Involves an attack on our character. A complex loss of trust. An attempt to vindicate oneself.

JAZZ: Refers to our individuality and our unique expression. Explores our 'improvisational' skills.

JELLYFISH: Examines the correlation between individual fear and social cowardice. Extreme danger in following the herd.

JESUS: When facing a figure associated with innate 'goodness', we examine our own righteous behavior, or lack of it.

JOB: Involves our relations within social groups. Explores our goals and the methods we use to achieve those goals.

JOKER: May be indicative of a sudden change of luck, either good or bad. A surprise encounter.

JOSHUA TREE: Represents the spiritual hope which motivates our upstanding faith and high virtue.

JOURNAL: Involves encoding our deepest memories. Are our recollections synonymous with the actual truth of these events?

JOURNEY: May involve escaping a harsh reality. Represents the spiritual journey into self-discovery. Growth involved.

JUGGLER: Involves the accumulation of responsibilities which we 'accept' in life. Are we able to balance these obligations?

JUNCTION: Refers to a choice which must be made in life. However, no judgement should be absolute.

JUNG, C.G.: Protege of Sigmund Freud, Jung went on to explore spiritual dimensions of the human Unconscious. Developed the concept of Archetypes.

JUNGLE: Indicative of our primitive, or reptilian, brain. Instinctual sense. A return to the wild and a momentary loss of our so-called 'rational' behavior.

KANGAROO: Examines a healthy combination of masculine and feminine natures. Explores an archetype of Jung's Anima/Animus.

KAYAK: Indicative of our individual 'tackling' of emotions. Explores personal redemption.

KEY, SKELETON: Symbolic of potential, freedom, and a new-found accessibility to previously unreachable goals. Explores the development of self-confidence.

KILL: Refers to significant changes in our life. Acceptance, or rejection, of new states of consciousness. Releasing ones pain.

KINDLING: Involves the psychological 'breaking down' of a complex reality. Establishing priorities in our life.

KING: Refers to our moral responsibility to our friends, family and peers. Are we 'just', or 'tyrannical', to these individuals?

KITCHEN: Indicative of psychological, or emotional, nourishment. May be an expression of our own regressive behavior.

KNEECAP: Indicative of our ability to land straight (and true,) in our psychological, emotional, (and especially,) spiritual, leaps of faith.

KNIFE: Refers to an intense psychological, or emotional, separation. Indicative of a deep personal 'release' or 'revelation'.

KNIGHT: Represents the strength of our spirit and moral character. Higher causes and chastity are explored.

KNOCK: Refers to our expectations, either welcomed, or feared. Only we can allow the 'entry' of these realities. Warning of change.

KNOT: Represents psychological, or emotional, entanglement. The harder we fight, the tighter the knot becomes!

KNOWLEDGE: Indicative of a desire to express our ideas and opinions. A need to be heard (and respected,) in society.

LABORER: Addressing our feelings about our own labor and the relative goals we have reached due to this labor. Exploring helplessness. Can we make our (own) labor more effective?

LABYRINTH: Refers to the changing course of our highest goal in life. Before we can reach our final goal, we must ultimately face ourselves.

LACE: Involves our repressed sexuality due to our vulnerable emotions. Does someone have an influence over our emotional well-being?

LADDER: Indicative of our ability to ascend and descend into separate states of consciousness. In order to steadily rise, we must sometimes move cautiously!

LADYBUG: Refers to unexpected pleasure. Indicative of a need for spontaneity in ones life.

LAGOON: Accepting the 'raw' purity of our deepest yearnings. Becoming true to ourselves. Physical awakening.

LAMB: Represents our spiritual, or moral, self-sacrifice. Also explores the dangers of our innocence. Beware false prophets!

LAME: Insecurity about our ability to stand up for ourselves. A feeling of helplessness. This figure examines personal faith.

LANCE: Involves the ultimate promise and potential of our sexuality and social skills. We are asserting ourselves into society.

LANDSCAPE: Represents our current perception of reality. A symbolic dream depiction of our concurrent level of consciousness.

LANTERN: Refers to the light of our hope and our ultimate faith. Guides us through our darkest times.

LATE: Refers to our relative respect, or disregard, for the group in general. May imply social fears which become self-fulfilling prophesies.

LAUGHTER: An examination of reality. An attempt to 'expose', or 'explode', the sometimes 'absurd' truths found in reality.

LAVA: Refers to a sudden outburst and passionate flood of emotions. Eliminating our cold emotional armor.

LEAF: Involves cyclical existence and eternal rebirth. Illustrates the stages of life and our humble acceptance of natural changes.

LEAK: May represent the slow loss of ones reason and better judgement. Warning about an 'explosive' and perhaps psychotic, episode. Slow torture.

LEATHER: May indicate individuality or a tough psychological resiliency. Exploring anti-social behavior in a socially acceptable manner. Marking ones personal territory.

LEMONADE STAND: Represents our developing maturity. Planning for tomorrow. In Freudian terms: Superego over Id.

LETTER: Expression of hope and the anticipation of some good news. Sharing ideas and emotions with loved ones.

LIE: Experiencing fear about the coonsequences of truth. Hiding from ourselves. Unable to face reality. Personal limitations.

LIGHT: Involves the positive and negative associations of illumination. Stare directly into the light and become blinded, conversely, follow the light's ray and witness the truth of being.

LIGHTHOUSE: May represent the misuse of 'logic' in 'emotional' situations and vica-versa. Repesents improbable directions.

LIGHTNING: May refer to a recent and devastating lesson about humility. New ideas. A higher force making itself known.

LION: Refers to a straight-forward strength of character. Indicative of bravery and nobility. Self-confidence.

LIZARD: Exploring the external physical senses. Utilizing instinct over dry and calculating reason.

LOCK: Explores a limitation in our waking reality. Who, or what, keeps us locked out of our personal fulfillment?

LOCUST: Locust remind humanity of their rightful place in the scheme of things, not on top, but somewhere in the middle! Finding humility through natural changes.

LOTUS: Involves a balance of emotional, psychological and spiritual development. If the lotus sinks, we may be experiencing a momentary loss of our personal direction.

LUCID DREAMING: The ability to modify ones dreams via imagination. Exploring the connection between memory and perception.

LUMBER: Refers to our psychological groundwork and rational development. Are we sturdy as individuals?

MADONNA: Involves our feelings about forgiveness, tolerance and unconditional love. Is the figure a contradiction, or complement, of our own behavior?

MAGIC: Represents a comprehension of our infinite reality and our own involvement in the creation of that reality. Potential.

MAILBOX: Refers to our dissatisfaction with society. Hope for freedom. However, freedom is formed from within.

MARBLE: Involves the erroneous behavior of an 'overblown' ego. Attempting to immortalize perishing realities.

MARCH: Explores the pros and cons of social unity. Are we united by moral strength, or vengeful hatred?

MARIJUANA: An attempt to broaden our perception and awareness. This shortcut creates in own limitations because of today's intolerant society.

MARIONETTE: Explores a loss of control in ones life. Are we controlling others in such an absolute fashion?

MASK: Represents how we face the spiritual world and spirituality in general. Exploring the worthiness of self.

MASON: Constructing a sturdy psychological framework. The building of spiritual strength.

MAZE: The age-old symbolism of the maze involves the blocked pathways and open doors we traverse and transgress in order to find ourselves.

MEAT: Refers to our external strength and phyical well-being. Does our physicality mirror our tenacity and inner convictions?

MELODY: Refers to the eternal mmemory of emotions. May involve some form of repession, or a fear of repeating history.

MEMORY: May involve an aspect of self which has been deeply repressed in our own Unconscious. What 'triggers' this reality's re-entry into our consciousness?

MERMAID: Represents a desire to enter new levels of emotional awareness. A deep exploration of our own sensitivity.

MERRY GO ROUND: Symbolic of adult life, replete with its ups and downs and endless repetition. Examining the childish naivete of true maturation.

METAL: Replacing difficult emotions with hard logic and innovative reasoning. The combination of metal and flesh is indicative of our psychological adaptation to technology. Accepting radical changes.

METAMORPHOSIS: In a dream, the image of metamorphosis involves our feelings about forthcoming personal changes and our ability to tansform accordingly. Attempting to keep in touch with culture.

MILK: Involves a deep desire to nuture loved ones. Are we choking on the milk of our own overprotectiveness?

MIRROR: Reveals the 'image' of who we perceive ourselves to be, rather than the 'reflection' of who we really are. Exploring the sometimes 'distorted' nature of perception.

MISSILE: Direct emotional aggression. An attempt to drop a symbolic bomb upon individuals who have 'effected' or 'disrupted' our sense of well-being.

MIST: Represents the isolation of our deepest fears. Walking through the unknown. What are we prepared to learn about ourselves?

MOAT: Symbolic of emotional barriers placed around oneself. Who seems to be 'intruding' upon our heart?

MONEY: Reveals something harsh about our social standing and perceieved accomplishments. Are we exploring our moral consciousness? Was our money obtained to 'good old-fashioned way'?

MONGREL: Two possible meanings: one: social alienation and low self-esteem, and two: the stealth involved in good and sound survival instincts. Explores the 'glory' of the underdog.

MONKEY: A connection of intelligence and sensitivity. Knowing our own feelings. Cleverness.

MOON: This figure represents various levels of our emotional potential and our ability to 'transcend' the highest passions of our vital causes. Final lesson of humility.

MOTHER: Explores the opposite poles of our own tolerance, both negative and positive, dependent on the behavior of the mother figure found in the dream itself.

MOUNTAIN: Symbolizes the hope of our highest goals. Do we climb the mountain of our highest aspirations with skill and determination, or, do we rush headlong into our own peril? Will we fall?

MUMMY: May refer to our feelings about permanance and the afterlife. Are we able to 'preserve' and 'maintain' our best qualities?

NAIL: Involves a purposeful 'binding' of opposite states of consciousness. Union of God and man, spirit and body.

NAKED: Depending upon our feelings about our own exposure, the nudist dream may reveal a fear of social ridicule, or a personal 'hunger' for 'raw' potential.

NATURE: Explores the true value of our primal awareness. Examines the gift of our instinct and intuition.

NAZI: The figure represents a complex fusion of reason without emotion, as well as, emotion without reason. Why are we torn apart?

NEEDLE: Refers to a restoration of self. Healing by bringing together. May refer to a hardship which is difficult to focus upon.

NEST: Represents our family responsibilities and our relative ability to live up to them.

NIGHT: May refer to the darker, or anti-social, aspects of our own nature which fear being 'exposed'. A safe haven for our passions.

NINE: Refers to a culmination of knowledge and a preparation for higher spiritual learning. Refers to mortal humility.

NOCTURNAL ANIMALS: Concealing our true nature in order to gain 'the element of surprise'. Increasing the effectiveness of our performance through stealth.

NOISE: May refer to a warning about an unpleasant, upcoming event. Paranoia. May conversely involve a personal 'break-through'.

NOMAD: May represent an endless search for meaning. Restlessness. A fear of commitment and personal responsibility.

NUMB: May be caused by the motionless nature of sleep itself. Symbolically linked with helplessness and personal isolation.

NUMBER: Numbers one through nine have separate and diverse meanings. Each number is closely examined in this text.

NUN: Complex figure which combines devotional femininity and spiritual masculinity. Hence, the figure is both repressive and forgiving. Do we display this same paradoxical behavior?

NURSE: Refers to a form of wish-fulfillment. May imply a desire for social contact to heal our emotional wounds. Examining control.

OAK: Refers to determination and a secure blueprint for the future. The enactment of spiritual devotion.

OASIS: May refer to a revitalized emotional involvement, or the bitter reality of false hope.

OBELISK: Implies moral direction and spiritual strength. If the obelisk is crumbling, or destroyed, we may be examining a personal loss of faith.

OCTOPUS: Its eight legs may refer to balance and 'organizational' strength. However, its simultaneous use of all arms in separate endeavors, may indicate confusion and an overextension of self.

ODOR: Refers to a memory in our distant past. Indicative of hidden feelings which have suddenly surfaced. A 'loathsome' return.

OGRE: May represent unintentional, yet still 'cruel', behavior. Refers to a general lack of awareness which may be harmful to others.

ONION: Indicative of our chaste behavior. The difficulty involved in the virtuous path

ORACLE: Refers to crucial decision making. Approaching imminent realities in our life. Are we ready?

ORCHID: Wild abandonment, free will, and sexual autonomy are equally explored in this stark dream image.

OUIJA BOARD: Yearning for the insight of a loved one who is beyond our (immediate) field of reach.

OUTLAW: Involves overcompensation, or retribution, for wrongs we feel have been commited against us (by society.) Striking back.

OVERFLOW: May refer to an excess of emotion. May refer to a celebration of life's abundance. Are we thankful, or do we lust for more?

OVERSEAS: Indicative of our sense of adventure. A desire for new experiences. Are we comfortable overseas?

OWL: Refers to the sapient reflection of our own insight. The spiritual side of our hidden self. Watching and waiting.

OX: Indicative of a hard-working individual, who nevertheless, may have difficulty in 'adjusting' to society. Social clumsiness.

OYSTER: May involve the potential, or desire, to give love (and passion,) in waking life. A need to expose ones emotions.

PAPER: Anxiety over the inhuman 'red-tape' involved in modern civilization. A desire to simplify.

PALM: Indicative of our outlook, or concerns, about the future. In accepting our 'timeless' spirit, we accept the preordained destiny of our ultimate existence.

PARADISE: Refers to the reward of our perserverance. Reveals the colorful and child-like delight involved in personal enlightenment.

PARALYSIS: An attempt to stop, or silence, our fast-moving and often difficult reality. Emotional detachment. Becoming invisible.

PARASITE: Refers to a loss of control. To become obsessed with another person, or thing. Total dependency and the subsequent loss of individuality.

PARK: Indicative of slow and sober transitions. Have our serious responsibilities removed the fun from our lives. Are we able to mix responsibility and pleasure?

PARROT: May involve duplication and emulation, or conversely, mockery. Are we overly concerned with someone else's behavior?

PARTY: Represents our 'comfort' level in the midst of society. May be indicative of our 'addictive' behavior.

PATH: Refers to our questions in life and our own skillful decision-making. Is our direction in life rewarding? Do we posses faith in ourselves and our potential future?

PEARL: Refers to a wisdom of self which is rare and polished. Has this pearl been 'honed down' by the harshest lessons of life?

PENDULUM: Involves indecision which may prove counter-productive to the necessary process of healing. Overt concern about the future.

PENETRATE: This figure involves a forced union into a new state of consciousness. Are we forcing our own emotions upon another? A surrender of self, perhaps for a higher purpose.

PENIS: Indicative of a potential for union between man and woman, yin and yang and finally, sky and earth. Recreating the life cycle.

PERPETUAL MOTION: Desiring a change in the repetitive, or predictable, behavior found in occupations, relationships, or the entire spectrum of post-industrial existence.

PHOENIX: The archetypal phoenix destroys itself with fire and miraculously becomes reborn through the 'reorganization' of its own ashes. The creature symbolizes emotional rebirth and the reincarnative path of an infinite consciousness.

PIG: Indicative of a straight-forward honesty which provides us with the tenacity to reveal our deepest desires and wholly ignore public opinion. Unfortunately, also represents a lack of restraint!

PINETREE: Indicative of a high moral character which remains undaunted by physical changes such as sickness and old age. Expresses the eternal nature of spirit.

PIRATE: A desire to take on new and dangerous risks. Exploring uninhibited sexuality. A calculated desire to 'cut loose' from social restraints.

PLAY: Explores the fundamental beginnings of our social skills. Examining our relative 'place' within the group.

POISON: May refer to suicidal tendencies which signal a cry for help. Indicative of giving up on oneself. Fighting off a harmful and very influential force.

POLICE: May represent our moral conscientiousness. May indicate our own abuse of power and consequent loss of social trust. Exploring the expectations of our moral character.

PORT: May involve desired opportunities for self-discovery. Indicative of our acceptance of society. Are outsiders welcome?

PREACHER: May involve feelings of guilt and self-admonishment. May be indicative of our own extremist, yet highly hypocritical, behavior. Do we practice what we preach?

PRIEST: Exploring our chastity and abstinence. Do our primal urges effect the reality of our spiritual enlightenment? Do symbolic rituals replace our physiological desires?

PRIZE: May involve a warning about our own material greed. Involves doing good things for the wrong reasons. Exposes self-indulgent behavior.

PROPHESY: Refers to the limitless potential of the Unconscious. All the higher aspects of humanity: soul, spirit, faith, thought, etc, are all invisible and utterly 'timeless'.

PROSTITUTE: May involve a form of overcompensation caused by emotional pain. When we remove emotions from love-making, we reveal a stagnation of our social being.

PUPPET: Refers to control and manipulation. Are we influenced by beliefs which are entirely inconsistant with our own beliefs? Why?

PURPLE: May involve a deep and honest form of eroticism. In the spiritual sense, refers to a deep, insightful and entirely soulful character. Noble motivations.

PYRAMID: Illustrates our eternal spirit and our righteous place witnin an infinite creation. Effectively bridges mind, body and spirit. Exploring eternal life and the preciousness of existence.

PYTHON: Refers tp a slowly absorbing seduction enacted by a poweful influence, or individual. Must be succumb to this power?

QUARANTINE: Invokes personal isolation. Feeling unworthy. A need to escape and 'reorganize' oneself. Renewing ones beliefs.

QUARRY: A slow and steady examination of ones own belief system. Deliberating upon serious questiions. What are we searching for?

QUARTZ: Refers to our own insight. Approaches our ability to 'sense' the subtle 'forces' of this world. Enlightenment.

QUAY: Preparing for emotional transitions in life. Indicative of a journey into self-discovery. A return to the familiar.

QUEEN: Refers to matriarchal wisdom, strength and stature. Clearly suggests our ability to forgive. The 'intuition' factor involved in some forms of judgement.

QUESTION: Questioning our outlook, or perception, of the world. Indicative of a growing sense of confusion and loss of direction.

QUICKSAND: Represents the struggle against inevitable changes in our life. Examines how fear digs us deeper into complication.

QUIET: May refer to a form of inner peace, but generally points to 'the calm before the storm'. Period before, or after, a violent upheaval. A chance to prepare oneself. Caught offguard.

QUIZ: Examines our responsible behavior. Indicative of being 'tested' by an outside force. A need to prove oneself.

RABBIT: Symbolic of new and wondrous events. Indicative of the luck, talent and intelligence needed to create. Ingenuity.

RABID DOG: Involves a feeling of betrayal and a loss of control. Scorning our own 'unjustifiable' behavior.

RACCOON: Involves a restless search for some form of fulfillment in life. Indicative of our initiative within a group. Hunger.

RACE: Invokes our own competitive behavior. Do we compete because we lack self-esteem? Do we challenge, or are we challenged? Examining the effects of 'winning' versus 'losing'. Intolerance.

RAGS: Refers to feelings of hardship, self abasement and personal estrangement. Feeling 'exposed' in society. Insecurity about social position. Wish-fulfillment concerning 'rags to riches'.

RAIN: Indicative of emotional purification and an acceptance of life's harsher realities. Transition into maturity.

RAINBOW: The revelation of ones own personal aspirations. A ray of hope. The maturity involved in embracing the full spectrum of our emotions. Associations with temperance and empathy.

RANCID: Refers to our intolerance of so-called 'evil' outside forces. Ridding ourselves of bad influences. Maintaining standards.

RAT: Refers to morality overlooked in the quest for survival. Indicative of our own 'inhuman' strive for success.

RATTLESNAKE: A warning of emotional, or psychological, danger. May refer to our own personal poison.

RAW: May involve a form of scrutiny. Indicative of our 'truest' Self, either unjustly 'exposed' or handsomly 'revealed'.

RED: Refers to the intensity of our emotions. Experiencing higher states of passion than we are normally accustomed to. Hostility.

REFLECTION: Refers to our perception of self. Do we feel that society perceives us, as we perceive ourselves. Concern with social image.

REGURGITATE: May refer to our ability to accept, or swallow, a difficult truth, or harsh reality. Have we changed our mind?

REINCARNATION: Refers to our moral behavior and its apparent consequences. The ramifications of our actions. Pay-back.

RELIGION: Refers to feelings of guilt concerning our 'straying' from a moral path. May involve the hypocrisy of placing rituals over faith. Involves the psychological aspect of faith. Rules.

REMEMBER: Refers to past experiences and their effect upon our concurrent behavior. Held back by the memory of our past fears.

RESTRICTION: Refers to any form of perceived limitaion which holds back our emotional, or psychological, development.

RICE: Refers to a well thought-out plan. Strong foundation. A firm sense of resolve and thorough self-confidence. Commitment.

RING: Represents the equality of universal truth. Refers to the infinite nature of thought and contemplative faith.

RITUAL: Refers to the physical and physiological enactment of spiritual faith. Expanding our primal desires to decry our mortal humility before a higher power.

RIVER: Refers to the emotional 'continuity' of our actions. Exploring our perseverance. Fighting for what we believe in. Swimming against the tide of 'social norms'. Self-expression.

ROAD: Refers to the aftermath of our decision-making. Indicative of our social behavior and its effect upon our future aspirations.

ROCKS: May be stacked high as a form of 'emotional' protection. The breaking of rocks may symbolize the personal sacrifice necessary to 'shape' moral character.

ROPE: May refer to the struggle involved in maintaining relationships which are dissolving. 'Tied' to a difficult and psychologically limiting situation.

ROSE: Refers to a passionate desire. A monogamist relationship. An expression of 'true' love. Love's connection of soul and body.

ROUND TABLE: Refers to the spiritual equality of ALL men. The circle of man infinite under God. Humble democracy.

RUN: Avioding confrontation. The inability to face ones fears. An attempt to step away from our own realities. Explores our personal courage and our personal faith.

SACRIFICE: Appeasement of a higher power. A giving of self in order to demonstrate our ultimate worth. Proving oneself worthy.

SADISM: Unleashing the emotional and psychological pain which is pent-up in oneself. Wish-fulfillment involving our suppressed anger and aggression.

SAINT: Represents a bridge from ordinary human frailty to profound inner strength. A faithful image meant to inspire a difficult spiritual direction.

SALT: Refers to truth, dedication and loyalty. Represents the fulfillment of an 'honest' existence. Natural rewards.

SAND: Refers to the microcosm and macrocosm. Indicative of the transient impermanence of being. Fleeting happiness.

SANDBOX: Indicative of our developmental behavior in society. Do we create with our peers, or conversely, do we destroy the goals of others?

SATAN: This figure refers to our own temptations and weaknesses. Do we give in to life's pleasures and hence, forfeit our personal virtue and merit? Overindulgence. Lust for life.

SAVAGE: Represents the awareness and acceptance of our primal consciousness. Striking out at our enemies. Lustful abandonment.

SCAR: Refers to a memory which embodies our personal struggle of self-discovery. Harsh past which dictates our future.

SCHOOL: Represents the beginning stages of our social development. Examining differences in behavior, then and now. Examining status within the group. Anxiety about social, or public, failure.

SEA: Indicative of the Unconscious and its deepest emotional pools. Are the waters calm and forgiving, or rough and unsympathetic.

SEASONS, THE FOUR: This figure reflects stages of life from innocence to maturity. Examining the human cycle of personal changes. Accepting the natural course of things.

SEED: In order to know ourselves, we must learn from the past. Employing the knowledge of experience in our future deliberations.

SEVEN: Refers to the 'random' nature of God. A miraculous force which helps us maintain our 'humble' faith, AND our strong 'ego', simultaneously. Combining faith in God and faith in Self.

SHADE: Indicative of our own mischievous, under-handed and (ever so slightly,) deceptive, behavior. A form of internal paradox. Indecision, or uncertainty.

SHADOW: Indicative of a repressed behavior which rises to the surface of our conscious awareness. Exploring primal desires.

SHAMAN: Acts as an active guide within our dream. This figure literally 'points out' the symbolic truths significant to our waking apprehensions. The embodiment of the Unconscious.

SHARK: Indicative of insensitive, or boorish, behavior. Witnessing another person's ruthless manner. Heartless decision-making.

SHEEP: Reflects innocence and purity. May refer to a form of 'blind faith' which steals our individuality. Naive behavior. Follower.

SHELL: Refers to the hidden and valuable truths lying silently beyond visible and tangible realities.

SHELTER: A form of 'temporary' refuge which helps us 'get through' a difficult period in life. Implies a need to get back on our feet as soon as we possibly can. Exploring a 'rebound'.

SIX: The number six refers to divine, or true, love. Maternal forgiveness and tolerance. A powerful union of opposites.

SKY: Refers to clear wisdom and infinite potential. Indicative of masculine expressions of freedom. In control of ones emotions.

SLAVE: Indicative of a sudden (and perhaps unjust,) loss of individual, or social, freedom. A loss of personal control. Outside Restrictions placed upon us.

SLEEP CYCLES: Refers to variable brain waves. The variable cycles of these waves are dependent upon separate levels of consciousness.

SLOW MOTION: Revealing minute peculiarities and subtleties of our behavior under a spotlight. A slow, point by point revelation of our own active decisions. Replaying a painful memory.

SMOKE: Seems to imply a rugged emotional 'skin'. An attempt to smoothly and confidently blend into a crowd of peers. Ritual of social bonding. Nervous reaction.

SNAKE: Refers to 'blind' determination which leaves little leeway for compromises. Indicative of 'stealthy' sexuality. Influential.

SNOW: Involves purity and the innocent pleasure of emotional peace. A blizzard on the other hand, may warn us about a drastic change in an otherwise 'stable' relationship.

SPIDER: Refers to a 'powerful' force which seems to guard our own self-destructive behavior. An authority figure who 'cares'.

SPOTLIGHT: Concentrating a bit too hard on some personal aspect of self. Exaggerated self-perception. Intense concern about social performance. Proving oneself to the crowd.

SQUARE: Involves fairness and proper judgement. May also refer to being 'boxed-in'. A so-called 'normal' behavior, which we find to be stifling.

STAGE: Refers to our social performance. Are we timid, or outgoing. Concern about public failure. Proving oneself.

STAIN: May refer to a minor and entirely reversible 'misunderstanding' enacted in waking life. Overlooking things. Social embarrassment.

STARS: Repesents the limitless reality of our own potential. Inner peace. Serenity. The expression of our deepest faith in existence.

STOMACH: This figure says a great deal about our social tolerance and personal acceptance of others. May involve personal 'intuition'.

STORM: Involves paying for ones sins. Learning to 'weather' the more difficult circumstances of reality. Gaining humility and hence, strengthening character.

STRANGULATION: Refers to any severe restriction, or limitation, of our personal expression. Surrendering all reason to 'passion'.

SUCCUBUS: Represents a 'release' of once 'repressed' sexuality. Exposing the 'hunger' of a 'reptilian brain'.

SUGAR: May involve 'compensation' for a general lack of love in ones life. A sweet demeanor may disguise a bitter reality.

SUN: Involves the undeniable light of truth. May involve some form of personal exposure. Coming clean. Confession of sins.

SURGERY: Represents a drastic release of passion and the consequent transition of our sensibilities. Manipulation. Helplessness.

SUSPENDED ANIMATION: Explores the transition from a physical plane to a higher 'ethereal' plane. Do are irrational fears trap us between two states of consciousness? Meditation. Prayer.

SWAMP: May represent an unstable 'emotional' foundation in a new relationship. Unhealthy affiliation. Personal Stagnation.

TABLE: Entails a meeting of opposites. Confronting diverse attitudes. Social tolerance explored, face to face.

TABOO: The restrictions of a dream/tribe may be loosely suggestive of our own restrictions. Rational versus superstitious behavior.

TAIL: May invoke happiness, fear, or sexual arousal, dependent, of course, on the placement and movement of the tail itself.

TANGO: May represent a sexual, or libidinous, equal. The expression of a mutual passion. Combining social performance and individual affection. Demonstrating our love to the world.

TAPESTRY: Involves a weaving together of society. Exploring the merging points of diverse individuals.

TARGET: Concerns about the future, dependent upon whether we are the intended victims of an archer's arrows, or the archer himself.
Aiming for ones goals.

TAROT: Concerns about the future. Exploring our spiritual journey through life. Does spiritual enlightenment guide our way?

TAR PIT: Refers to a deep emotional stagnation which effects our psychological 'handle' upon life. Examining a loss of love and/or a loss of faith.

TATTOO: Illicits deep feelings concerning our free, aggressive and perhaps, anti-social behavior. The tattoo's symbol itself must be interpreted. What are we saying about ourselves? Is it true?

TEA: Involves deep calm and emotional repose. Meditating upon the feminine side of life, including childbirth and family plans.

TECHNICAL: Refers to our 'mastered' skills. Have they benefitted, or restricted, our goals in life. Keeping in touch with progress.

TEETH: Invokes feelings of inadequecy. Indicative of a self-examination of ones true worth. Blocking ones 'right of passage'. Heaven denied.

TELEPATHY: Refers to our Unconscious connection with ALL other living beings. Refers to our awareness of the Collective Unconscious. Exploring a consciousness which exists far beyond the concept of linear time and space.

TELEPHONE: Refers to a repressed, or supressed, wisdom which 'rings-in' with a revelatory voice. An important message from the outside world. Are we afraid of the news?

TELEVISION: May invoke the insincerity of our 'good-intentions'. Explores the 'performance' of our good deeds. Ulterior motives.

TEMPTATION: Refers to the battle between our desires and our sacrifices. Can there be a middle-ground?

TERMITE: Involves insignificant problems which accumulate and then begin to threaten the basis of our psychological well-being.

TERRACE: Viewing the world, (life,) from a comfortable vantage point. Beware, because we are mortal, we are likely to fall. Examines ones ego and relative humility.

TEST: Anxiety over how we are perceived by society. Concerns about social failure. Anxiety over proving oneself.

THREE: This number refers to maternal love, forgiveness and our highest state of tolerance. Mending a world torn apart. Examination of creation and continual 'rebirth'.

TIED: Refers to an ever-tightening trap imposed by our own foolhardy behavior. To free ourselves, we must stop, calm down and reason our way out. A losing battle. Negotiations.

TIGER: Instinctual faith. The aggressive drive of a fearless passion. Bold leaps of faith.

TIME: Concern about an upcoming event. Fear and anxiety over aging. Indicative of time lost, or wasted, on some worthless endeavor.

TOILET: Refers to removal of unwanted realities. Indicative of a psychological escape from a harsh physical life. Loss of a burden.

TORCH: Involves the light of wisdom and the determination of will. Overcoming our own fears. Bravely facing the unknown.

TORNADO: Symbolizes a very real 'possibility' of danger. Exploring helplessness. Examines faith. Can we avoid this random destruction?

TOWEL: Preparation for a new state of consciousness. Removing our emotional shackles. A utilization of calm, cool reason.

TOY: May refer to a regression into our own childhood. Represents a far simpler time. What does the toy itself symbolize? Is our business interfering with our pleasure?

TRAFFIC: May refer to a loss of individuality. Also refers to a cessation in our forward progress. Are we 'stuck in a rut'? Why?

TRAIN: Symbolic of a thoughtful transition in life. Indicative of a slow and difficult separation. A gradual upheaval of ones roots.

TRANSMUTATION: Involves an awareness of our deepest changes. Are we better for this transition? What have we become? Duplicity.

TREE: Refers to the joining of earth and sky. Refers to the direction of our spiritual development. Do we stand tall and proud?

TRENCH: Involves our insecurities and a refuge, or shelter, from painful realities. Eventually, we must face reality. A frightened return to the womb.

TRIBE: Involves the true spiritual interconnectedness of our social unions. Do we experience support from others? In our particular group, which phrase fits best: 'one for all, and all for one, or, 'every man for himself'?

TROPHY: May be indicative of a lack of social support. Wish-fufillment involving social acknowledgement of our unique skills.

TRUNK: May refer to a sense of financial insecurity. Examining the concept of quality over quantity. Exploring true prosperity.

TUNNEL: Involves the narrow and difficult path toward certain realities. Examines dedication and a search for personal truth.

TWINS: Regarding both sides of an argument. Internal turmoil or confusion. Reflecting upon ones 3rd person behavior.

TWO: Refers to the evenly balanced sides of polar oppositions. Setting up the reality of infinite motion. Involves division. Only division can allow for subsequent unification. Splitting the world.

TYRANT: This figure refers to an abuse of power, bad judgement and a general lack of self-confidence. Unjust leadership. Corruption.

U.F.O.: Refers to our social fear and personal instability. Searching for answers outide of our own realm of experience.

UMBILICAL CORD: Indicative of a 'direct line' of nourishment. Dependent upon others for support. Learning to stand alone.

UMBRELLA: May refer to 'closeness' found in relationships. Keeping both members of a couple away from emotional harm. Reflections upon our emotions.

UNCLEAN: May involve feelings of guilt pertaining to our so-called 'unnatural' behavioral tendencies. Have we removed the handcuffs?

UNCONSCIOUS, THE: The pool of our 'collective memories'. The consciousness of an infinite existence. Exposing ones deepest desires.

UNIVERSITY: Refers to concerns about the future based upon our vital performances in the past. Social testing. Reliving our youth.

UPHILL: Refers to the struggle involved in reaching our highest aspirations. Indicative of the moral character necessary to achieve these goals.

URBAN DREAM: Indicative of psychological confusion and a high state of nervous energy. Exploring common sense. Looking for action.

URINE: Refers to a purging of emotions. Preparation for a new state of reality. Lightening ones burden. Marking the territory of ones own home.

URN: Indicative of our deepest memories. Remorse. Cherished toughts involving some person, (who was once,) quite close to us.

VALLEY: Dual meaning involving a social move away from the valley and into the mountain, or conversely, a transition from the mountain into the fruitful valley. Examining transitions.

VAMPIRE: Paradoxical imagery of hot passion and cold emotion. Heartless creature. Insatiable hunger. Emotional alienation.

VAULT: The psychological support of our abstract conceptualizations. A strong cerebral buttress of faith.

VEGETABLE: This figure involves concerns about our overall health and aging. We may need to examine the relative 'freshness' and 'color' of the vegetables on our plate. Pass the salt!

VENTRILOQUISM: Involves some form of behind-the-scenes control. A form of social decption. Why do we speak out of the corners of our mouths?

VICTIM: A warning from the Unconscious to face up to our fears. Examining a loss of power. The slow process of empowerment.

VIKING: Aggressive exertion toward some valuable and worthy goal. Social bonding. Overcoming our own emotions. Strength of faith.

VILLAGE: Indicative of social stability. May also refer to feelings of strangeness in a new place, situaton, or state of consciousness.

VINE: Refers to an individual's rich history. May indicate some form of higher learning. Explores our self-development.

VIRGIN: In an archaic sense, the figure refers to higher love and ideal motherhood. Today, the figure stands for innocence and a simple lack of experience.

VOICE: Refers to an internal voice which questions our external behavior. A hidden part of our consciousness which attempts to maintain our balanced well-being.

VOLCANO: Refers to the termination of ones future plans. Indicative of an intense emotional release. Reaching the boiling point.

VOMIT: Purging evil, or harmful, realities which were once 'accepted' and perhaps even, invited.

VOODOO: This figure represents a fear of immediate 'retribution' due to one's immoral behavior. Fear of consequences.

VOYEUR: May involve an inability, (or insecurity,) to experience life first hand. An attempt to steal another individual's freedom.

VULTURE: A distraught feeling of helplessness due to our own emotional alienation. Surrendering to our emotional pain.

WAGON: Refers to a simpler time. Examines a 'grasp' of reality which seems to be slipping away. Concern about our personal effectiveness.

WAIF: Indicative of self-denial. Why do we deprive ourselves of life's fulfilling experiences? Examining social expectations.

WAKE-UP: Refers to Unconscious revelations which profoundly effect our being. Opening ones eyes to the truth. Radical insight.

WALK: A well-adjusted and faithful acceptance of reality. Observing our world. Slowly 'taking it all in'.

WALL: Involves personal barriers increased over time. Poor developmental skills. A need to break the chain.

WALTZ: Refers to a desire to achieve social status. Exploring our social image. Reflecting on society's rules of courtship.

WAND: Involves the 'effective' balance of Spiritual concerns and Worldly concerns. Involves faith in oneself and ones ability.

WANT: Invokes the 'true' desires hidden beneath our surface and readily expressed desires. Explores our deviant fetishes.

WAR: Involves a set of seemingly endless confrontations and personal battles. Can we meet others half-way?

WAREHOUSE: May involve our storehoue of memories. Is the warehouse overstuffed with our 'psychological baggage'.

WARM: May indicate a sense of well-being. May involve wish-fulfillment, dependent upon the pressures of a 'cold' reality.

WARNING: Indicative of our need to reorganize. Finding a new and superior plan of action. Preparing for the worse.

WARRIOR: Refers to the step by step development of our 'highest' and most honorable 'characteristics'. Combining our natural and spiritual instincts. In tune with nature's ebbing flow.

WART: Indicative of a self-imposed social isolation. Disgrace. Feelings of unworthiness. Feeling cursed. Low self-esteem.

WASH: Involves the absolvement of personal sins. An attempt to wash our hands of a problem. A way out. Overcompensation for lack of purity.

WATCHING: Addressing our immediate fears. Exercising extreme caution. Obsessive behavior. Mesmerized by a wholly seductive force.

WATER: Represents the sensitivity of our emotional resources. How we behave in and around water reflects our present temperament.

WAX, DRIPPING: A building internal passion. The 'potential' of our growing emotions. Creating something from nothing. Seduction.

WAX DOLL: Refers to being manipulated by influential outside forces. Fear of being exposed. Feeling threatened by vulnerable.

WEATHER: Reflects diverse states of consciousness and our ability to absorb, or transgress, their effects. Lesson learned.

WEB: Involves the complex lure associated with danger. Drawn toward dangerous, or threatening, situations. Mesmerized by an antagonist. Victim of reverse psychology.

WEEDS: Refers to an acceptance of nature on her own terms. Giving up on all control. Letting things slip away. Introversion.

WEIGHT: Indicative of the burdens we must carry in life and our relative ability to actually 'carry' those burdens. Bending from pressures and responsibilities. A need to stop and rest. Fatigue.

WHITE: This figure involves purity. However, it may also involve a cold sense of detachment. 'Stark' realities. Emotionless behavior.

WIDOW: May involve a deep personal loss, or a sudden and traumatic disruption or our normal behavior. Confronting oneself, ones needs.

WILD: Refers to any aspect of our primal self. The instinctual 'purpose' of the self. Bodily awareness. Loss of 'reason'.

WIND: Indicative of outside forces, or influences, who mislead us, or attempt to change our 'purposeful' direction. Obstacles.

WINDOW: Indicative of an outside world full of infinite possibilities. Taking a good, hard look at the future. Alternatives. Feeling slightly removed from the outside world.

WITCHCRAFT: Fusing our own personal power with the formidable powers of nature. Comfortable in a natural setting. In tune with all the elements of nature. Manipulation of ordinary perceptions.

WOLF: Involves a dreamer's self-confidence and overall composure in a variety of social situations. Self assurance of the loner.

WOMB: Refers to security and sanctity. This figure may involve conflict with our social responsibility and our personal sense of pleasure. Dependency. All needs fulfilled. Addictive behavior.

WOOD: Explores the psychological connection between man and nature. Using reason to better understand our instinctual drives. Adapting.

WORM: Indicative of our 'blind' lack of experience. Digging oneself into the very heart of a situation without knowing the full parameters of the situation itself. Being exposed and vulnerable.

WREATH: Combining the concepts of 'love' and 'infinity'. Exploring the forgiving human soul. Charity, good deeds and blessings.

WRITING: This figure may be indicative of a direct message from the Unconscious. A letter addressed to oneself. Personal revelation.

X-RAY: This figure refers to looking through people. Dishonest behavior which is readily recognized. Exposing ulterior motives.

YACHT: Emotional and psychological well-being. Hedonism. Loving life's material side. Feeling desired and admired. Comfortable in a new waking reality. Will the yacht eventually sink?

YAK: Involves a complex combination of domesticity and 'wild' behavior. Examining 'exotic' aspects of mundane realities.

YAMMER: Involves a failure of communication. However, may also refer to a warning of danger. A cessation of personal control.

YANK: Involves freeing someone, or something, from someone, or something which is wholly threatening. Saving oneself. Reflexes.

YARD: Represents our perception of the outside world, replete with love, magic, violence and a myriad of other entirely human traits. Are we afraid to step outside? Getting ones feet wet. Caution.

YARDMASTER: This figure refers to an outright abuse of power. An attempt to control, or manipulate, ones surrounding environment. Exposing unjust and wholly anti-social behavior.

YARN: A tiny element of 'divine' truth hidden within the context of a tongue-in-cheek tale. Expressing oneself in a roundabout manner.

YAWN: Suggestive of complete mental exhaustion. Indicative of a restless sleep. Resonant anxiety. A need to thoroughly unwind.

YEAR: Concerns about the passage of time and aging. Reflections on our Astrological sign and its symbolic connection with our working and current personality. Who are we, and where are we going?

YEARBOOK: Concern about our present condition enbodied in our reflections of the past. Have we achieved our goals?

YEAST: Refers to growth and maturation. Reflects upon our overall psychological and emotional development. Strong mental health.

YELL: A powerful expression of a once repressed emotion. A preparation for crucial changes. Emotional release. Purging.

YELLOW: May refer to physical warmth, or conversely, psychological cowardice. In the latter example, the dream figure's color is entirely different from his normal waking color. Sudden dread.

YESTERDAY: Replaying yesterdays mistakes and erroneous decisions. Learning from mistakes and accepting personal responsibility.

YIN/YANG: Involves the balance of our masculine and feminine natures. Explores the entire spectrum of human awareness. Focus.

YOGA/YOGI: Refers to our deepest convictions and spiritual meditations. Indicative of a well-centered outlook on life.

YOKE: Refers to the functional balance of our chores, burdens and responsibilities. Are we able to carry the load? Is one difficult reality 'effecting' our otherwise dependable behavior?

YOUTH, FOUNTAIN OF: May involve wish-fulfillment concerning the strength, vitality and beauty of youth. If the fountain is ignored, sublime aceptance of self is wholly indicated.

ZEAL: Overcompensating expression of emotions due to a lack of social acknowledgement. Exhilarating experience far beyond words.

ZEBRA: Refers to the liberating emotions found in joining opposites. The real power of union. Healing a divided reality.

ZEITGEIST: May invoke a slight feeling of alienation. Feeling out of place. Freedom allows for individualistic behavior.

ZEN: Involves the ever-renewing faith of our own purposeful existence. Living in the moment. Spiritual freedom.

ZENITH: Approaching and accepting the apex of ones personal goals. Realizing the cyclical quality of a spiritual journey.

ZEPHYR: Intense contentment which 'immediately', can be taken away from us. Fleeting pleasure. A slightly unnerving impulse.

ZOOMORPHISM

ZEPPELIN: Indicative of the emotional self-confidence involved in proper graces and personal dignity. refinement.

ZERO: May refer to new beginnings. Creating ones own fortune. A release of material limitations.

ZIG-ZAG: Exploring our own 'defensive' behavior. Becoming a moving target. A fear of being 'captured', or 'influenced', by any and all outside forces. Resilience.

ZIPPER: May involve the harsh realities of our own desires. Exploring the connection between our mental and instinctual drives.

ZODIAC: Concerns about the future. Indicative of ones 'accepted' personality traits. Enbodying a philosophy.

ZOMBIE: Refers to a loss of soul, or other entirely 'humane' attributes. Fear of emotionless confrontations. Any inhumanity.

ZOO: Refers to a harsh repression of our own desires. Psychological and emotional stagnation. Ignoring our own instincts.

ZOOMORPHISM: Involves the complex connection of both our 'civilized' and 'primal' natures. Expanding ones sense of reality. Exploring the synthesized potential of mind, body and soul.

Final word:

The world we view within ourselves is the resonant memory of our deepest and most furtive experiences. Each night we journey further and further into this realm of self. What we learned in memory, yesterday, has become a part of the very fabric of ourselves, here today. Hence, each night we become further enmeshed in creation and we will continue to grow in that infinite spectrum of 'comprehensive' being. In an unmistakable fashion, our dreams mirror, echo and scrutinize our most subtle of positions in life's revolving kaleidoscope. When we finally do open our eyes, our dreams will still be there within us, gracefully woven into the infinite tapestry of being. Pleasant dreams.

ABOUT THE AUTHOR

R. M. Soccolich studied Psychology, Theater and Literature at Glassboro University and Hunter at CUNY. After graduating, he continued several years of intense study upon the human mind and its collective historical development. He has followed humanity's progressions and digressions over a period of fifteen years. In the process, he has focused upon the source of our universal beliefs and our deepest fears. In his relentless search and research, he has travelled the labyrinth path of thousands of generations of mankind and witnessed first-hand the subtle variations of our highest and deeply held perceptions of "The Truth".

Naturally, R. M. Soccolich's first book entitled THE 100 STEPS NECESSARY FOR SURVIVAL ON THE EARTH reaches a culmination of his studies and as such, details an elaborate human history and its wholly apparent and critical initiative. He went on to co-sponsor a series of these titles called THE SURVIVAL SERIES which included THE 100 STEPS NECESSARY FOR SURVIVAL IN THE GLOBAL VILLAGE which unravelled a dramatic view of society's most intimate series of upcoming adaptations. The series included several other thought provoking Survival Titles.

This encyclopedia of archetypal symbols and their universal interpretations showcased the authors deep commitment to research and the ultimate psychological imperative of the world's people. His latest project, along with Sam Chekwas, is entitled MISCHIEVOUS ACTS & REPERCUSSIONS, a book which addresses KARMA and its elaborate, bizarre and far-reaching impact.